T0396809

Honest Errors? Combat Decision-Making 75 Years After the *Hostage* Case

Nobuo Hayashi · Carola Lingaas
Editors

Honest Errors? Combat Decision-Making 75 Years After the *Hostage* Case

Editors
Nobuo Hayashi
Centre for International and
Operational Law
Swedish Defence University
Stockholm, Sweden

Carola Lingaas
Faculty of Social Studies
VID Specialized University
Oslo, Norway

ISBN 978-94-6265-610-9 ISBN 978-94-6265-611-6 (eBook)
https://doi.org/10.1007/978-94-6265-611-6

Published by T.M.C. ASSER PRESS, The Hague, The Netherlands www.asserpress.nl
Produced and distributed for T.M.C. ASSER PRESS by Springer-Verlag Berlin Heidelberg

This T.M.C. ASSER PRESS imprint is published by the registered company Springer-Verlag GmbH, DE, part of Springer Nature
The registered company address is: Heidelberger Platz 3, 14197 Berlin, Germany

To Our Fathers

Acknowledgements

"Ah, this is how we used to do research!"—one of the present volume's contributing authors once said of our endeavour. In today's relentlessly accelerating environment where we live and work as scholars, quick turnarounds and fast publications have become the new norm. This publication, which embodies careful research, attention to detail and the time invested, has long been in the making.

It all started in 2006 when Nobuo Hayashi came to Oslo. He had already been conducting research on military necessity for some time. Unsurprisingly, he found himself more and more curious about Northern Norway's devastation during World War II and the 1948 *Hostage* trial held at Nuremberg where Lothar Rendulic, the German Commander who had made the decision, successfully argued military necessity in his defence. The idea of a multi-disciplinary anthology marking the 75th anniversary of Rendulic's acquittal was born.

With this entirely self-funded undertaking, we aimed to ensure several things. First, we wanted to take it slow. We felt that this project should be an opportunity for participating authors to pause and enjoy reflecting on their discoveries. Second, we wanted to facilitate in-depth collaboration among historians, lawyers, and ethicists. We believe sharpening our understanding of Rendulic's actions using contemporaneous sources has enabled us to offer truly original insights into modern law and raise timeless ethical questions. Third, we wanted our volume to read more like a cohesive book written by a team of authors than a loosely stitched together bundle of meandering chapters. This meant, among other things, bringing our contributors from around the globe to an online conference in June 2021 and a hybrid workshop in September 2022. No doubt they will also remember our somewhat laborious editorial process.

We are proud that *Honest Errors? Combat Decision-Making 75 Years After the* Hostage *Case* becomes available to readers just in time for the anniversary. For this we thank our contributing authors who have placed so much of their expertise, dedication and patience at our disposal. We gratefully acknowledge Sven G. Holtsmark's tireless efforts to help us with all the historical details, as well as original files, photographs and charts. This project has also enjoyed the backing of our employers. The Swedish Defence University in Stockholm and VID Specialized University in

Oslo co-organised our June 2021 conference, alongside the Lieber Institute for the Law of Land Warfare at West Point and the DILEMA project at the Asser Institute in The Hague. Bård Mæland, VID's rector, graced one of our conference panels as moderator. The same goes for all the other presenters, chairs and participants. We also express our gratitude to Frank Bakker and his team at T.M.C. Asser Press for seeing potential in our thoughts and for agreeing to commit them to print.

This anthology would have been impossible without the support and indulgence of our respective families. Sadly, two of them are no longer with us to share this moment. We dedicate our book to their loving memory.

Stockholm, Sweden
Oslo, Norway
April 2023

Nobuo Hayashi
Carola Lingaas

Contents

Part I Introduction

1 **Honest Errors in Combat Decision-Making: State of Our Knowledge 75 Years after the *Hostage* Case** 3
Nobuo Hayashi and Carola Lingaas

Part II Devastating Northern Norway and Forcibly Evacuating Its Inhabitants

2 **Occupied Norway 1940–1945: A Brief Background to *Hostage*** 25
Sven G. Holtsmark and Gunnar Åselius

3 **Rendulic and the Military Necessity Defence in *Hostage*: Did He Speak the Truth?** 47
Sven G. Holtsmark

4 **Devastation and Forced Evacuation: The Actors and Their Motives** 81
Stian Bones and Gunnar D. Hatlehol

Part III Trying Rendulic and Developing the No Second-Guessing Rule

5 **The Inclusion of Finnmark's Devastation and Forced Evacuation Charge in *Hostage*** 111
Stian Bones and Gunnar D. Hatlehol

6 **The Adjudication and Findings of Finnmark's Devastation Charge in *Hostage*** 127
Emily Crawford

7 **The Genesis and Significance of the Law of War "Rendulic Rule"** 155
Sean Watts

8 The Limits of Honest Judgment: The Reasonable Commander Test and Mistake of Fact 177
Yasmin Naqvi

Part IV Assessing an Error's Reasonableness

9 The ICT Revolution, 21st Century Warfare, and Honest Errors ... 217
Tae Hoon Kim

10 Empathy at War: The Distinction Between Reasonableness and the Reasonable Military Commander Standard 233
Valentin Jeutner

11 Drone Warfare, Civilian Deaths, and the Narrative of Honest Mistakes 261
Matthew Talbert and Jessica Wolfendale

Part V Conclusion

12 Conclusion: The *Hostage* Case, Present Day Knowledge, and Future Implications 289
Carola Lingaas and Nobuo Hayashi

Annex 301

Editors and Contributors

About the Editors

Nobuo Hayashi Associate Senior Lecturer in International Law, Swedish Defence University, Stockholm, Sweden. Visiting Professor, University for Peace, San José, Costa Rica, and the UN Interregional Crime and Justice Research Institute, Turin, Italy.

Carola Lingaas Associate Professor of Law, VID Specialized University, Oslo, Norway.

Contributors

Gunnar Åselius Swedish Defence University, Stockholm, Sweden

Stian Bones UiT The Arctic University of Norway, Tromsø, Norway;
Narvik War and Peace Centre, Tromsø, Norway

Emily Crawford The University of Sydney Law School, The University of Sydney, Camperdown, NSW, Australia

Gunnar D. Hatlehol Narvik War and Peace Centre, Tromsø, Norway

Sven G. Holtsmark Norwegian Institute for Defence Studies, Norwegian Defence University College, Oslo, Akershus Fortress, Norway

Valentin Jeutner Faculty of Law, Lund University, Lund, Sweden

Tae Hoon Kim Swedish Defence University, Stockholm, Sweden

Yasmin Naqvi Office of International Law, Attorney-General's Department, Canberra, Australia;
Graduate Institute of International and Development Studies, Geneva, Switzerland

Matthew Talbert West Virginia University, Morgantown, WV, USA; Lund-Gothenburg Responsibility Project, Lund, Sweden

Sean Watts United States Military Academy, West Point, NY, USA; Lieber Institute for Law and Warfare, West Point, NY, USA

Jessica Wolfendale Case Western Reserve University, Cleveland, OH, USA

Abbreviations

AI	Artificial intelligence
AOK	*Armeeoberkommando*
API	Additional Protocol I
C4I	Command, control, communications, computes, and intelligence processing
CIA	Central Intelligence Agency
CROWCASS	Central Registry of War Criminals and Security Suspects
DBK	Dominant battlefield knowledge
DPR	Donetsk People's Republic
ECtHR	European Court of Human Rights
FDSP	Federal Directorate for Supply and Procurement
GPS	Global positioning system
HUMINT	Human intelligence
ICAO	International Civil Aviation Organization
ICC	International Criminal Court
ICL	International criminal law
ICRC	International Committee of the Red Cross
ICT	Information communications technology
ICTR	International Criminal Tribunal for Rwanda
ICTY	International Criminal Tribunal for the Former Yugoslavia
IDF	Israel Defense Forces
IHL	International humanitarian law
ILC	International Law Commission
IMINT	Imagery intelligence
IMT	International Military Tribunal
IRGC	Islamic Revolution Guards Corps
ISIS	Islamic State of Iraq and Syria
ISR	Intelligence, surveillance, and reconnaissance
JAG	Judge Advocate General
JSTARS	Joint surveillance and targeted acquisition radar system
KTB des OKW	*Kriegstagebuch des Oberkommandos der Wehrmacht*

MOK	*Marineoberkommando*
MSF	*Médecins Sans Frontières*
NATO	North Atlantic Treaty Organization
NCW	Network-centric warfare
NGO	Non-governmental organization
NS	*Nasjonal Samling*
NSDAP	*Nationalsozialistische Deutsche Arbeiterpartei*
ODS	Operation Desert Storm
OEF	Operation Enduring Freedom
OIF	Operation Iraqi Freedom
OKW	*Oberkommando der Wehrmacht*
OSCE	Organization for Security and Co-operation in Europe
OTP	Office of the Prosecutor
PGM	Precision guided munitions
POCIMO	Protection of Civilians in Military Operations Act
RMA	Revolution in military affairs
Sipo-SD	*Sicherheitspolizei-Sicherheitsdienst*
SS	*Schutzstaffel*
TOC	Tactical operations centre
UK	United Kingdom
UN	United Nations
UNTS	United Nations Treaty Series
UNWCC	United Nations War Crimes Commission
US	United States
USAF	United States Air Force
WBH	*Wehrmachtsbefehlhaber*
WFStab	*Wehrmachtführungsstab*
WWII	World War II

List of Figures

Fig. 1.1 Lothar Rendulic's order, 29 October 1944 7
Fig. 1.2 Defendants and their counsels at the *Hostage* Trial, 1947/ 1948 12
Fig. 2.1 German occupation regime in Norway, October 1944 35
Fig. 2.2 20th Mountain Army front lines, 6 September 1944, and subsequent withdrawals 38
Fig. 4.1 "*Führer*'s Order" (*Führerbefehl*), 28 October 1944 94
Fig. 4.2 Josef Terboven and Rendulic's posters, 31 October 1944 100

Part I
Introduction

Chapter 1
Honest Errors in Combat Decision-Making: State of Our Knowledge 75 Years after the *Hostage* Case

Nobuo Hayashi and Carola Lingaas

Contents

1.1 Introduction 4
1.2 Devastating Northern Norway and Forcibly Evacuating Its Inhabitants (Chaps. 2–4) 5
1.3 Trying Rendulic and Developing the No Second-Guessing Rule (Chaps. 5–8) 11
1.4 Assessing an Error's Reasonableness (Chaps. 9–11) 17
1.5 Conclusion 20
References 21

Abstract Seventy-five years have passed since *Hostage*, a post-World War II case in which Lothar Rendulic was acquitted of Northern Norway's devastation and forcible evacuation on account of his faulty yet honest judgment. This introductory chapter surveys the current state of our knowledge about honest errors in modern combat decision-making by synthesising the findings of the anthology's contributing authors. First, contemporaneous sources suggest that Rendulic did not consider it militarily necessary to devastate the region in its entirety or to evacuate all of its residents by force. Second, even though Rendulic's acquittal was factually contentious, it was arguably on firmer legal ground. His case has led to the emergence of an eponymous rule against second-guessing difficult combat decisions, the reasonable commander test in international humanitarian law and the mistake of fact defence in international criminal law. Third, assessing the reasonableness of battlefield errors remains challenging because of the limitations of modern information technology, the diminishing room for empathy in the soldierly profession, and the salience of institutional bias.

N. Hayashi (✉)
Centre for International and Operational Law, Swedish Defence University, Drottning Kristinas väg 37, 114 28 Stockholm, Sweden
e-mail: nobuo.hayashi@fhs.se

C. Lingaas
Faculty of Social Studies, VID Specialized University, PO Box 184, 0319 Vinderen, Oslo, Norway
e-mail: carola.lingaas@vid.no

N. Hayashi and C. Lingaas (eds.), *Honest Errors? Combat Decision-Making 75 Years After the* Hostage *Case*, https://doi.org/10.1007/978-94-6265-611-6_1

Keywords Northern Norway · devastation · forcible evacuation · Lothar Rendulic · Josef Terboven · military necessity · honest judgment · Rendulic Rule · reasonable commander · mistake of fact · revolution in military affairs · empathy in war · moral equality of civilians · drone warfare

1.1 Introduction

> The Germans, upon discovering the Russian halt at Tana, made the most of their new opportunity. With more time to evacuate the population and take hostages throughout Finnmark, they rounded up people along the coast, in the hills, in caves and even turf houses, forcing them to join the German retreat.
>
> Tulloch 2011

"'When the war is over,' said Mother, 'we shall always have birthday parties.' She had omitted to say, 'If we survive the war'"[1]—this is how Bjarnhild Tulloch recalls 14 October 1944, the day when she turned ten, as she and her family fled burning Kirkenes to the countryside. They eventually reached a shed near Jarfjord, some 20 km southeast of Kirkenes, where they were liberated by Soviet forces and did indeed survive the war.

Not all local residents of Northern Norway were so lucky. From late October 1944 until February 1945, tens of thousands of them were forcibly evacuated by retreating German forces, scores of them perishing in the process. German troops also systematically destroyed the region's public and private property, moving from one settlement to the next as they withdrew.

Two years later, Colonel General Lothar Rendulic, commander of the German 20th Mountain Army which implemented his scorched-earth policy in the Norwegian counties of Finnmark and Troms, stood accused of war crimes before a US military tribunal in Nuremberg. In the case commonly known as *Hostage*,[2] Rendulic argued that military necessity imperatively demanded the area's devastation if feared Soviet advances were to be successfully impeded—although, in the event, no such advances materialised. In 1948, the tribunal acquitted him of the devastation committed in Northern Norway. In so doing, Rendulic's judges found it inappropriate to question his decision with hindsight. Rather, they based their ruling on the situation "as it appeared to the defendant at the time"[3] and held that Rendulic's conclusion might have been faulty but was not criminal.[4]

Today, the notion that one should not second-guess military decisions made in good faith amid difficult circumstances with limited and often inconsistent information available finds widespread support. Indeed, modern international humanitarian

[1] Tulloch 2011, p 163.

[2] US Military Tribunal V, *The Hostage Case (United States of America v Wilhelm List et al.)*, 1948, 11 Trials of War Criminals Before the Nuernberg Military Tribunals 757 (*Hostage*).

[3] Ibid., p 1296.

[4] Ibid.

law (IHL) contains various iterations of a "Rendulic Rule" against second-guessing that is named after the general himself. Finding an IHL breach in combat situations frequently involves the application of a "reasonable commander test", and international criminal law (ICL) entitles a war crimes suspect to plead a mistake of fact.

Three-quarters of a century have now passed since Rendulic's acquittal in *Hostage*. This anthology takes *Hostage*'s 75th anniversary as an opportunity to consider the following questions:

- From late 1944 until early 1945, what military threats did Rendulic perceive as his 20th Mountain Army retreated through Northern Norway? To what extent did the timing, manner and scale of the property destruction and forced evacuation carried out in Northern Norway match his perceptions?
- How diligently did the tribunal in *Hostage* examine whether the military threats Rendulic actually perceived justified the timing, manner, and scale of the measures taken? On what grounds do IHL's Rendulic Rule and ICL's mistake of fact defence really stand? What requirements do these concepts contain?
- By what frame of reference should we construe the "reasonable commander" when assessing the reasonableness of his or her errors? What role, if any, does the intelligence-gathering and organisational environment of modern armed forces play in such assessment?

The passages below weave the main findings of this anthology's contributors into a tapestry depicting the current state of our knowledge about honest errors in combat decision-making.

1.2 Devastating Northern Norway and Forcibly Evacuating Its Inhabitants (Chaps. 2–4)

Germany occupied Norway from 1940 until 1945. Between June 1940 when the Battle of Narvik ended and October 1944 when Soviet forces crossed the border to Eastern Finnmark, no major military operations took place on Norwegian territory. Germany nevertheless attached significant value to controlling Norway, given its strategic North Atlantic coast and metallurgical industry, as well as its proximity to *Barbarossa*'s northern front and mineral resources in the north of Finland allied with Germany at the time.

In June 1944, the Soviet Union's Leningrad and Karelian Fronts attacked Finland. The ensuing months saw heavy losses among Finnish forces, resulting in a Soviet-Finnish ceasefire on 4–5 September and a formal armistice on 19 September. It now fell upon Finland to expel or intern all German forces present on its northern territory. Finland's early hesitation to fight changed when its former ally attacked a Finnish garrison, and direct confrontations between Finnish and German forces escalated from mid-October until late November.

Meanwhile, following the Soviet-Finnish ceasefire struck in early September, Rendulic was ordered to extract his 20th Mountain Army from Northern Finland to positions behind fortifications in Northern Norway known as the "Lyngen Line". During their withdrawal through Finnish territory, Rendulic's troops scorched large areas and displaced approximately 100,000 inhabitants. Infrastructure was destroyed not only to deny facility to Finnish pursuers but also in retaliation for their attacks on retreating German forces.

The XIX Mountain Corps, one element of the 20th Mountain Army, initially remained on Soviet and Finnish territories to ensure supplies of nickel ore and matte from the Kolosjoki production site for the German war effort. On 7 October 1944, the XIX Mountain Corps came under attack by the Karelian Front. Advancing Soviet troops entered Norway on 18 October and reached Kirkenes on 25 October. The Soviets continued some 150 km westwards to the Tana River, where they engaged German forces for the last time and took defensive positions in early November.[5]

It is during this end-phase of Red Army advances that, on 28 October, Adolf Hitler ordered Rendulic to devastate Northern Norway to the east of the Lyngen Line. Rendulic followed this up the next day by issuing an order of his own, instructing subordinate units to destroy or burn down all houses and forcibly evacuate local inhabitants, ostensibly on account of imperative military necessity. See Fig. 1.1. These measures culminated in the decimation of Hammerfest, a major town in Western Finnmark, in February 1945.

There is solid evidence that, from late 1944 until early 1945, Rendulic perceived military threats to his 20th Mountain Army retreating through Northern Norway that were diverse, uncertain and variable.[6] First, Rendulic contemplated at least three major possibilities:

(a) A Soviet land invasion from the Tanafjord area in the east, in pursuit of the retreating 20th Mountain Army westwards across the length of Finnmark;
(b) A Soviet offensive from Finnish and/or Swedish territory in the south towards the Lyngen-Skibotn area in Troms, where Northern Norway's territory significantly narrows, in an attempt to cut off the German retreat; and
(c) Combined Soviet-UK landing operations at Hammerfest, Narvik, or elsewhere.

Two further threats, namely a Soviet entry into central Finnmark along the Ivalo-Lakselv axis and land advances towards Narvik, were also perceived.

Second, Rendulic's perceptions were highly uncertain. Any combination of the aforementioned eventualities could materialise at different moments. This prospect was exacerbated not only by the limited capacity Rendulic had to gather good intelligence but also—though unbeknown to him at the time—by the absence of evidence indicating a clear Soviet disengagement and the lack of coordination among Allied leaders.

Third, not all of these perceived threats remained constant. From late November 1944, it became increasingly clear to Rendulic that a Soviet invasion from the

[5] See Chap. 2.

[6] See Chap. 3.

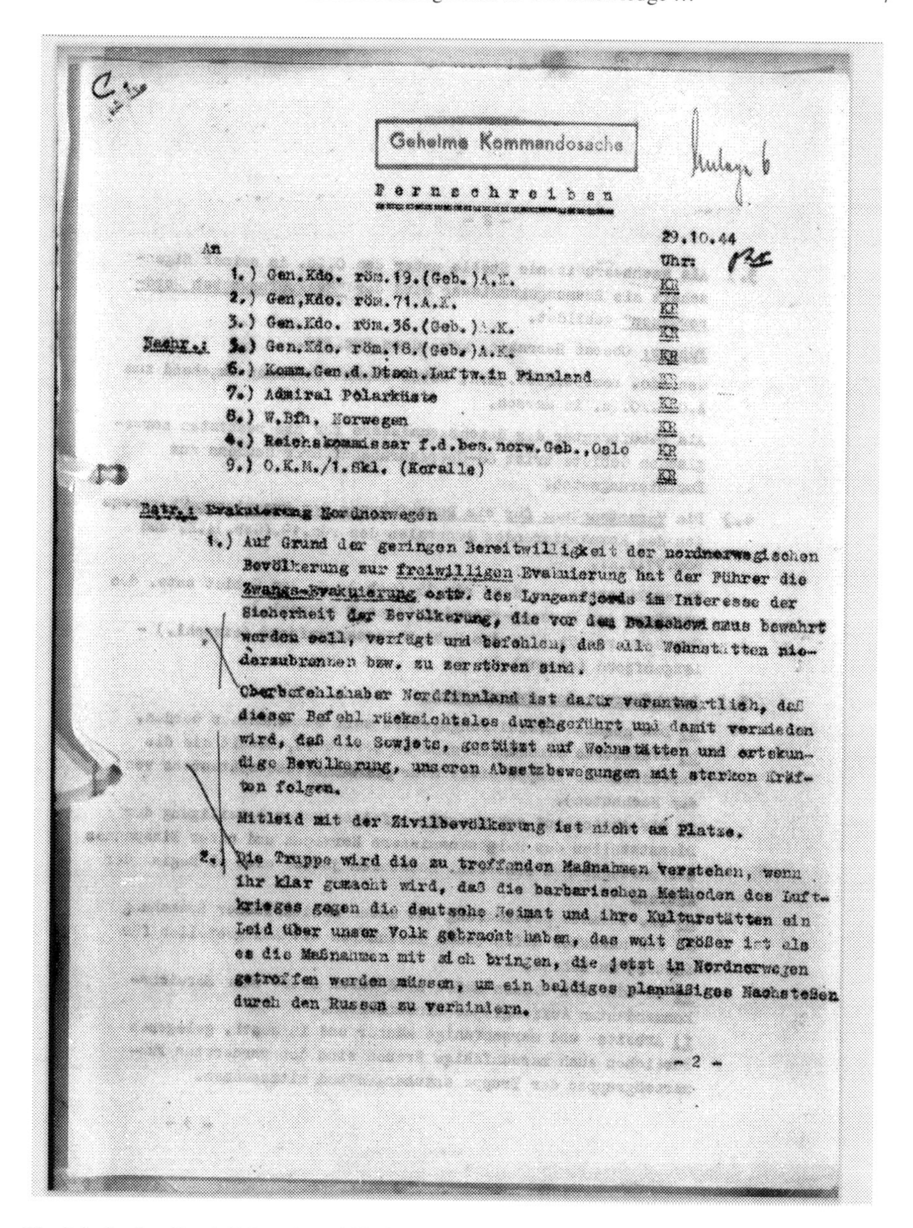

Geheime Kommandosache

Fernschreiben

29.10.44

Uhr:

An

1.) Gen.Kdo. röm.19.(Geb.)A.K. KR
2.) Gen,Kdo. röm.71.A.K. KR
3.) Gen.Kdo. röm.36.(Geb.)A.K. KR
Nachr.: 5.) Gen.Kdo. röm.18.(Geb.)A.K. KR
6.) Komm.Gen.d.Dtsch.Luftw.in Finnland KR
7.) Admiral Polarküste KR
8.) W.Bfh. Norwegen KR
4.) Reichskommissar f.d.bes.norw.Geb.,Oslo KR
9.) O.K.M./1.Skl. (Koralle) KR

Betr.: Evakuierung Nordnorwegen

1.) Auf Grund der geringen Bereitwilligkeit der nordnorwegischen Bevölkerung zur freiwilligen Evakuierung hat der Führer die Zwangs-Evakuierung ostw. des Lyngenfjords im Interesse der Sicherheit der Bevölkerung, die vor dem Bolschewismus bewahrt werden soll, verfügt und befohlen, daß alle Wohnstätten niederzubrennen bzw. zu zerstören sind.

Oberbefehlshaber Nordfinnland ist dafür verantwortlich, daß dieser Befehl rücksichtslos durchgeführt und damit vermieden wird, daß die Sowjets, gestützt auf Wohnstätten und ortskundige Bevölkerung, unseren Absetzbewegungen mit starken Kräften folgen.

Mitleid mit der Zivilbevölkerung ist nicht am Platze.

2.) Die Truppe wird die zu treffenden Maßnahmen verstehen, wenn ihr klar gemacht wird, daß die barbarischen Methoden des Luftkrieges gegen die deutsche Heimat und ihre Kulturstätten ein Leid über unser Volk gebracht haben, das weit größer ist als es die Maßnahmen mit sich bringen, die jetzt in Nordnorwegen getroffen werden müssen, um ein baldiges planmäßiges Nachstoßen durch den Russen zu verhindern.

– 2 –

Fig. 1.1 Lothar Rendulic's order of 29 October 1944 reflected the *Führerbefehl* of the previous day (see Chap. 4, Fig. 4.1), with detailed instructions added. The order was addressed to the four corps then under his command (XVIII, XIX, XXXVI, LXXI), designated as *Generalkommandos* (Gen.Kdo.), another term for the army corps level in the *Wehrmacht* structure. Here, the standard use of Roman numerals to identify individual corps (in contrast to Arabic for armies) is substituted by Arabic numerals and the abbreviation "röm." before the numbers. *Source* NARA, PG 65635/8, microfilm T 312-1063, pp 340–342

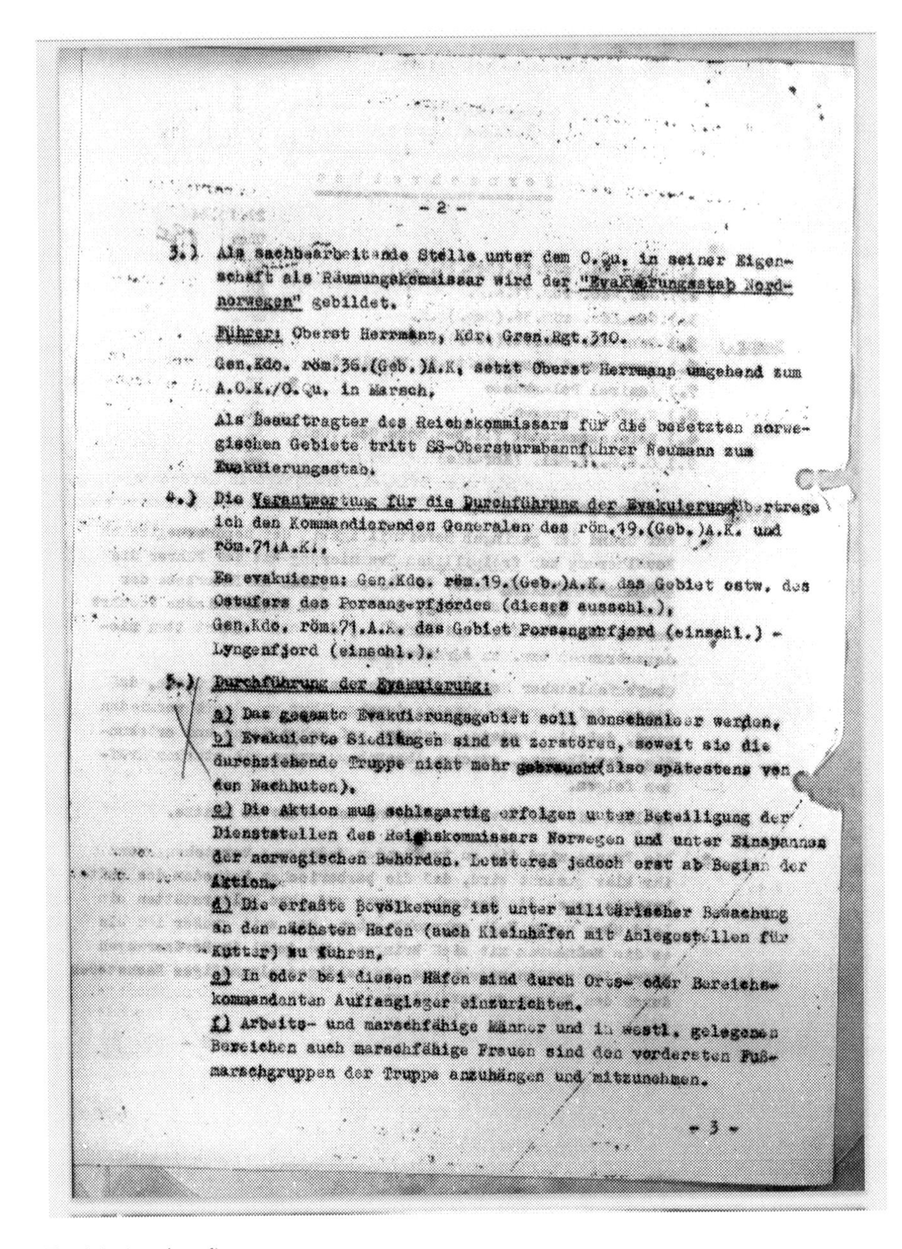

\- 2 -

3.) Als sachbearbeitende Stelle unter dem O.Qu. in seiner Eigenschaft als Räumungskommissar wird der "Evakuierungsstab Nordnorwegen" gebildet.

Führer: Oberst Herrmann, Kdr. Gren.Rgt.310.

Gen.Kdo. röm.36.(Geb.)A.K. setzt Oberst Herrmann umgehend zum A.O.K./O.Qu. in Marsch.

Als Beauftragter des Reichskommissars für die besetzten norwegischen Gebiete tritt SS-Obersturmbannführer Neumann zum Evakuierungsstab.

4.) Die Verantwortung für die Durchführung der Evakuierung übertrage ich den Kommandierenden Generalen des röm.19.(Geb.)A.K. und röm.71.A.K..

Es evakuieren: Gen.Kdo. röm.19.(Geb.)A.K. das Gebiet ostw. des Ostufers des Porsangerfjordes (dieses ausschl.),
Gen.Kdo. röm.71.A.K. das Gebiet Porsangerfjord (einschl.) - Lyngenfjord (einschl.).

5.) Durchführung der Evakuierung:

a) Das gesamte Evakuierungsgebiet soll menschenleer werden.
b) Evakuierte Siedlungen sind zu zerstören, soweit sie die durchziehende Truppe nicht mehr gebraucht (also spätestens von den Nachhuten).
c) Die Aktion muß schlagartig erfolgen unter Beteiligung der Dienststellen des Reichskommissars Norwegen und unter Einspannen der norwegischen Behörden. Letzteres jedoch erst ab Beginn der Aktion.
d) Die erfaßte Bevölkerung ist unter militärischer Bewachung an den nächsten Hafen (auch Kleinhäfen mit Anlegestellen für Kutter) zu führen.
e) In oder bei diesen Häfen sind durch Orts- oder Bereichskommandanten Auffanglager einzurichten.
f) Arbeits- und marschfähige Männer und in westl. gelegenen Bereichen auch marschfähige Frauen sind den vordersten Fußmarschgruppen der Truppe anzuhängen und mitzunehmen.

\- 3 -

Fig. 1.1 (continued)

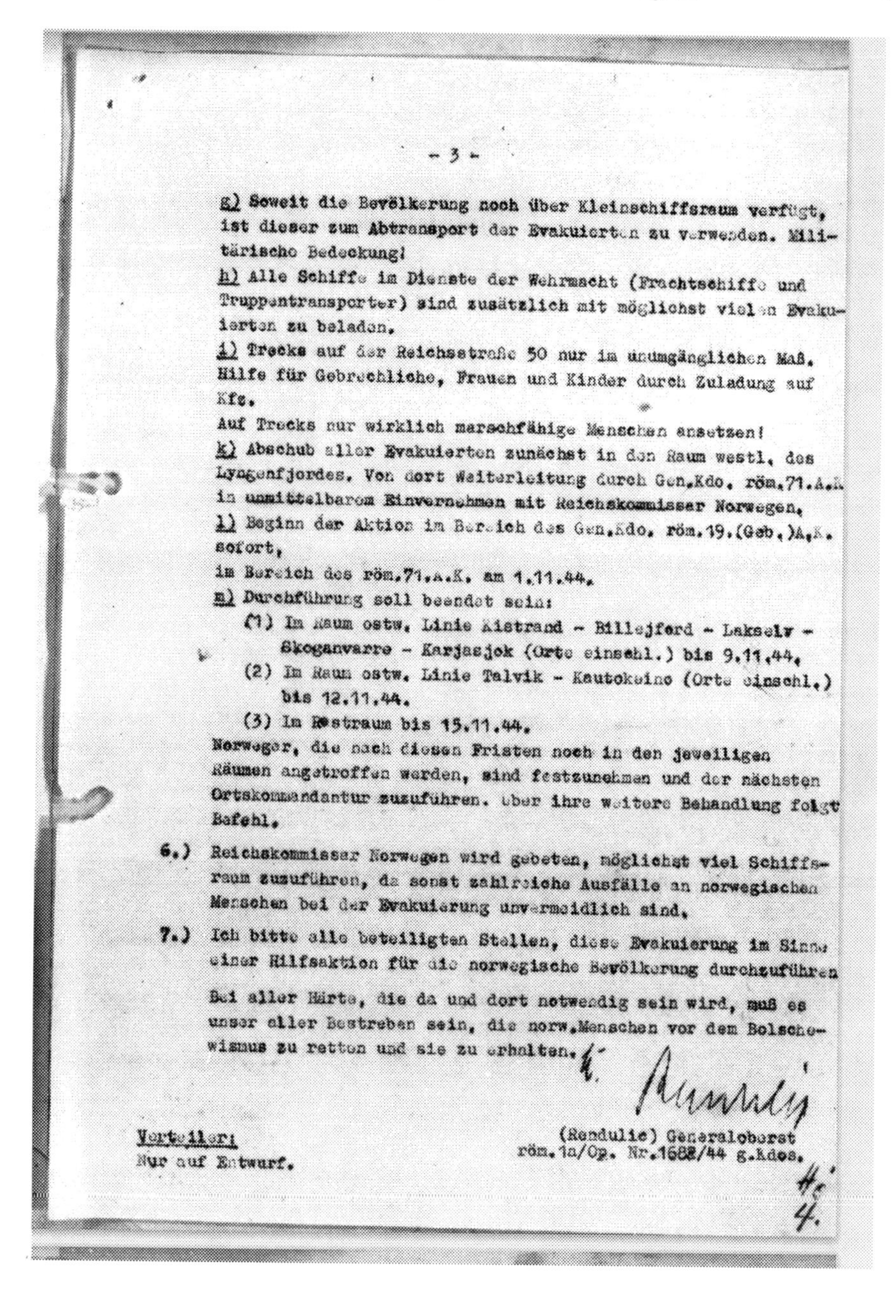

\- 3 -

g) Soweit die Bevölkerung noch über Kleinschiffsraum verfügt, ist dieser zum Abtransport der Evakuierten zu verwenden. Militärische Bedeckung!

h) Alle Schiffe im Dienste der Wehrmacht (Frachtschiffe und Truppentransporter) sind zusätzlich mit möglichst vielen Evakuierten zu beladen.

i) Trecks auf der Reichsstraße 50 nur im unumgänglichen Maß. Hilfe für Gebrechliche, Frauen und Kinder durch Zuladung auf Kfz.

Auf Trecks nur wirklich marschfähige Menschen ansetzen!

k) Abschub aller Evakuierten zunächst in den Raum westl. des Lyngenfjordes. Von dort Weiterleitung durch Gen.Kdo. röm.71.A.K. in unmittelbarem Einvernehmen mit Reichskommissar Norwegen.

l) Beginn der Aktion im Bereich des Gen.Kdo. röm.19.(Geb.)A.K. sofort,

im Bereich des röm.71.A.K. am 1.11.44.

m) Durchführung soll beendet sein:

(1) Im Raum ostw. Linie Kistrand - Billefjord - Lakselv - Skoganvarre - Karasjok (Orte einschl.) bis 9.11.44.

(2) Im Raum ostw. Linie Talvik - Kautokeino (Orte einschl.) bis 12.11.44.

(3) Im Restraum bis 15.11.44.

Norweger, die nach diesen Fristen noch in den jeweiligen Räumen angetroffen werden, sind festzunehmen und der nächsten Ortskommandantur zuzuführen. Über ihre weitere Behandlung folgt Befehl.

6.) Reichskommissar Norwegen wird gebeten, möglichst viel Schiffsraum zuzuführen, da sonst zahlreiche Ausfälle an norwegischen Menschen bei der Evakuierung unvermeidlich sind.

7.) Ich bitte alle beteiligten Stellen, diese Evakuierung im Sinne einer Hilfsaktion für die norwegische Bevölkerung durchzuführen.

Bei aller Härte, die da und dort notwendig sein wird, muß es unser aller Bestreben sein, die norw. Menschen vor dem Bolschewismus zu retten und sie zu erhalten.

Verteiler:
Nur auf Entwurf.

(Rendulic) Generaloberst
röm.1a/Op. Nr.1682/44 g.Kdos.

Fig. 1.1 (continued)

Tanafjord area was unlikely. This remained so, although the distant possibility of a spring 1945 offensive, at least in theory, existed. The situation was arguably different with some of the other threats, however. Contemporaneous material suggests that, from the autumn of 1944 until early 1945, Rendulic continued to take seriously the dangers of a cross-border attack from Finnish and/or Swedish territory towards the Lyngen-Skibotn area, and of combined Soviet-UK landing operations along the coasts of Northern Norway.

Countering such threats might as well have necessitated some degree of pre-emptive property destruction in areas that could prove useful to the invading forces. The key question, then, is whether Rendulic kept the timing, manner, and scale of such pre-emptive measures in proportion to that need.

This anthology's findings give us reason to be sceptical here.[7] The material available at the time portrays a man convinced that some destruction of property was necessary. There is no indication, however, that Rendulic's conviction encompassed the wholesale devastation of Northern Norway and the evacuation of all of its residents by force.

Records suggest that the idea of Northern Norway's total devastation and evacuation originated elsewhere.[8] Finland's exit from the war in September 1944 prompted existential angst among key members of Norway's occupation apparatus. The prospect of at least parts of Northern Norway coming under Allied control, now increasingly likely, would mean the London-based Norwegian government-in-exile staging a comeback and gaining a foothold there. This would, in turn, bring about the demise of Vidkun Quisling's collaborator government and Joseph Terboven's *Reichskommissariat* for Norway. Lessening the impact of a liberated Northern Norway by removing its local population therefore became a priority.

By early October, destruction of military installations in the north, as well as evacuation of armed and labour-capable locals, had already been underway as part of the 20th Mountain Army's withdrawal to the Lyngen Line. Nevertheless, Terboven initially failed to secure Rendulic's support he needed to implement what was nominally a voluntary evacuation of the region's wider population. In mid-October, when German forces began cooperating, they faced widespread resistance from deeply reluctant residents. On 26 October, while addressing high-ranking German officers in Tromsø, Terboven opined that Soviet forces would invade Northern Norway and that the area should be completely destroyed. Terboven then set in motion a proposed devastation of Northern Norway that would reach Hitler and receive his approval on 28 October.

Rendulic and his senior officers in the 20th Mountain Army had different priorities. They were mainly concerned with its successful retreat to the Lyngen Line and looked upon Northern Norway's total devastation and forcible evacuation as a distraction. Even some of Terboven's own subordinates were opposed. There was also an element of competition—a power struggle in which Terboven ultimately prevailed over Rendulic—for control of the *Wehrmacht*, the SS, and the police in

[7] See Chaps. 3 and 4.

[8] See Chap. 4.

Norway. Once in receipt of Hitler's order, however, they all fell in line and largely followed its instructions.

Careful examination of contemporaneous sources leaves us with a distinct impression. Hitler's 28 October order rendered the implementation of Terboven's political manoeuvre a foregone conclusion. It is unlikely that devastating all of Northern Norway and forcibly evacuating all of its residents was a military solution to which Rendulic's own assessment of the danger imperilling the retreating 20th Mountain Army had led him.

1.3 Trying Rendulic and Developing the No Second-Guessing Rule (Chaps. 5–8)

At Nuremberg, Rendulic was charged with four counts of war crimes and crimes against humanity. See Fig. 1.2. Count Two details "plundering and looting of public and private property, the wanton destruction of cities, towns, and villages, frequently together with the murder of inhabitants thereof, and the commission of other acts of devastation not justified by military necessity, in the occupied territories of Norway, Greece, Yugoslavia, and Albania …"[9] Rendulic allegedly

> ordered troops under [his] command and jurisdiction to burn, destroy, and level to the ground entire villages and towns, and, on numerous occasions, to execute the inhabitants of such villages and towns. Such arbitrary, inhumane, and disproportionately harsh measures of reprisal dislocated hundreds of families, made thousands of peaceful non-combatants homeless and destitute, and brought untold suffering, humiliation, misery, and death to vast numbers of innocent civilians.[10]

More specifically for Northern Norway:

> On or about 10 October 1944, the Commander in Chief of the 20th Mountain Army, the defendant Rendulic, issued an order, to troops under his command and jurisdiction, for the complete destruction of all shelter and means of existence in, and the total evacuation of the entire civilian population of, the Northern Norwegian province of Finmark [*sic*]. During the months of October and November 1944, this order was effectively and ruthlessly carried out. For no compelling military reasons, and in literal execution of instructions to show no sympathy to the civilian population, the evacuated residents were made to witness the burning of their homes and possessions and the destruction of churches, public buildings, food supplies, barns, livestock, bridges, transport facilities, and natural resources of an area in which they and their families had lived for generations. Relatives and friends were separated, many of the evacuees became ill from cold and disease, hundreds died from exposure or perished at sea in the small boats and fishing smacks used in the evacuation, while still others were summarily shot for refusing to leave their homeland – in all, the thoroughness and brutality of this evacuation left some 61,000 men, women, and children homeless, starving, and destitute.[11]

---

[9] *Hostage* Indictment, above n. 2, p 764, para 7.

[10] Ibid.

[11] Ibid., para 9(a).

Fig. 1.2 This photograph shows the defendants in the dock and their lawyers following the proceedings of the *Hostage* case. The US Military Government for Germany created Military Tribunal V on 28 June 1947 to try the *Hostage* case. Lothar Rendulic was one of the twelve defendants indicted on 10 May 1947. The trial against Rendulic opened on 15 July 1947 and dealt, among other things, with the participation in the plundering and looting of public and private property, the destruction of cities, towns, and villages, and other acts of devastation in Norway, Greece, Yugoslavia, and Albania by troops of the German armed forces. The trial closed on 9 February 1948, with only ten defendants. On 19 February 1948, the tribunal returned its judgment, finding eight of the defendants guilty of at least one count, and acquitting the other two. *Source* US Holocaust Memorial Museum, courtesy of John W. Mosenthal. Photograph number: 16806

The indictment does not articulate the legal provisions underlying Count Two in detail. Rather, it alleges:

> This program of wholesale devastation was carried out not only as part of a cruel, senseless pacification-through-terror scheme, wholly unwarranted and unjustified by military necessity and in flagrant violation of the laws and customs of war, but also in furtherance of a long-range plan to despoil and retard for decades the economic and industrial potential of the occupied territories[12]

and

> [t]he acts and conduct of the defendant[...] set forth in this count were committed unlawfully, willfully, and knowingly, and constitute violations of international Conventions, of the Hague Regulations of 1907, of the laws and customs of war, of the general principles of criminal law as derived from the criminal laws of all civilized nations, of the internal penal law of the

[12] Ibid., para 8.

countries in which such crimes were committed, and were declared, recognized, and defined as crimes by Article II of Control Council Law No. 10.[13]

Article 23(g) of the 1907 Hague Regulations forbids destruction and seizure of enemy property unless "imperatively demanded by military necessity."[14] Though not specified in the indictment, this article became the focal point of Rendulic's devastation charges. What prohibition undergirded his forcible evacuation charges is less clear. When the alleged events occurred, none of the sources listed in the indictment arguably prohibited forcible evacuation of residents from one part of occupied territory to another part of the same occupied territory.[15] Nor does the judgment address this matter.

In the event, the entire case against Rendulic over Northern Norway collapsed on a particular take of military necessity. The judges held that Rendulic had honestly, albeit erroneously, considered the region's devastation militarily necessary in view of feared Soviet advances. The judgment summarises Rendulic's threat perceptions thus:

> The evidence shows that the Russians had very excellent troops in pursuit of the Germans. Two or three land routes were open to them as well as landing by sea behind the German lines. The defendant knew that ships were available to the Russians to make these landings and that the land routes were available to them. The information obtained concerning the intentions of the Russians was limited. The extreme cold and the short days made air reconnaissance almost impossible. It was with this situation confronting him that he carried out the "scorched earth" policy in the Norwegian province of Finmark [*sic*] which provided the basis for this charge of the indictment.[16]

The judgment goes on to describe how the Germans "removed the population from Finmark [*sic*]"[17] and left property destruction in their wake that was "as complete as an efficient army could do it."[18] When concluding that the Germans did anticipate a Soviet attack, the judges found "mute evidences"[19] in the form of "gun emplacements, fox holes, and other defence installations … in the territory."[20]

These are the only factual findings the judgment contains regarding Northern Norway. Two observations are in order here. First, the judgment does not account for

[13] Ibid., para 10.

[14] Regulations concerning the Laws and Customs of War on Land, annexed to Convention (IV) respecting the Laws and Customs of War on Land, opened for signature 18 October 1907, International Peace Conference, The Hague, Official Record 631 (entered into force 26 January 1910), Article 23(g).

[15] Unlike deportation, forcible transfer not involving the crossing of a boundary out of occupied territory first became prohibited under Article 49 of Geneva Convention IV and criminalised as a grave breach, effectively a war crime, under Article 147 of the same convention. See Geneva Convention (IV) relative to the Protection of Civilian Persons in Time of War, opened for signature on 12 August 1949, 75 UNTS 287 (entered into force 21 October 1950), Articles 49, 147.

[16] *Hostage* Judgment, above n. 2, pp 1295–1296.

[17] Ibid., p 1296.

[18] Ibid.

[19] Ibid.

[20] Ibid.

the geographical and temporal variability of Rendulic's evolving threat perceptions. This omission is particularly noticeable given the diminishing prospect of a Soviet invasion from the Tanafjord area over the course of November and December 1944. Second, the judgment does not examine whether the property destruction and forcible evacuation carried out in different areas of Northern Norway geographically and temporally matched how Rendulic perceived military threats.

Part of the explanation may be that the prosecution did a poor job of preparing and presenting its case.[21] Dissimilar approaches and haphazard interactions among Norway's local authorities, its government-in-exile in London and the Nuremberg-based US prosecutors meant that neither the indictment filed against Rendulic nor the evidence adduced at trial fully reflected the material Norway had gathered.[22] Court transcripts also show how significant testimonial inconsistencies between key witnesses, including Rendulic himself, went unchallenged.[23] The prosecutors did not ask why Rendulic had left the severity of property destruction and forcible evacuation in various parts of Northern Norway unadjusted to the threats he had perceived; it appears that the prosecution actually chose to exclude various degrees of military necessity from its core assertions.[24] Nor did the prosecutors vigorously argue the existence of multiple motives, some plainly political rather than military, that had shaped Rendulic's decisions. There is no indication that the prosecution effectively pre-empted or countered assertions of an honest error and accusations of second-guessing, either.

It is also apparent that the defence skilfully exploited the prosecution case's weaknesses.[25] For instance, the defence attorneys highlighted how no evidence revealed the absence of military necessity for property destruction and how the testimony of prosecution witnesses was either inexpert or in fact favourable to Rendulic. His lawyers also utilised arguments likely to resonate with the panel, such as Allied practices and opinions, the longstanding martial tradition and worldview to which the defendant had dutifully dedicated his professional life, and the importance of judging the situation contemporaneously, to good effect.

The tribunal itself did not scrutinise Rendulic's factual claims with any vigour.[26] On the contrary, the bench appears to have accepted his stated interpretations of the military situation—some arguably in contradiction to one another—more or less at face value. While the judgment notes the "uncertainties" with which "the course of a military operation by the enemy is loaded,"[27] it does not delineate the contours of such uncertainties *vis-à-vis* Rendulic by assessing what was and was not known or reasonably knowable to him in relation to different locations and moments. Instead, the judges cursorily ruled that "the conditions, as they appeared to the defendant at

[21] See Chaps. 5, 6 and 7.

[22] See Chap. 5.

[23] See Chap. 6.

[24] See Chap. 5.

[25] See Chaps. 6 and 7.

[26] See Chap. 6.

[27] *Hostage* Judgment, above n. 2, p 1297.

the time were sufficient upon which he could honestly conclude that urgent military necessity warranted the decision made."[28] At no point did the judges articulate what made these conditions "sufficient"—although, in fairness, war's objective uncertainty and Rendulic's subjective uncertainty at the relevant time might have well combined to bring his conditions over that threshold.

Rendulic's acquittal is perhaps on firmer ground in law.[29] We can discern two closely related yet distinct legal bases for this. One is the admonition against second-guessing battlefield decisions made in good faith with limited information, while the other points to a reasonable mistake of fact.

Where the judges located the former admonition in international law is unclear.[30] The judgment does not go through the usual list of sources found in Article 38 of the Statute of the Permanent Court of International Justice[31] or in Article 38 of the Statute of the International Court of Justice.[32] Rather, having noted "customs and practices accepted by civilized nations generally"[33]—possibly a mixture of custom and general principles of law—the judges cautioned against "adding rigidity where resiliency is essential" and against "plac[ing] the principles of international law in a formalistic strait-jacket."[34] The judgment's plea for flexibility, while understandable to some extent, still does not explain its omission to discuss the origin of a no second-guessing rule at all.

If the rule's provenance was obscure, however, its desirability and subsequent acceptance seem well-settled. Nowadays, treaty provisions governing the methods and means of warfare as well as individual criminal responsibility often make implicit allowances for honest errors. Domestic enactments, declarations accompanying instruments of treaty ratification and influential law of armed conflict manuals also exhibit states' belief that only contemporaneously available information should be used to assess battlefield decisions. It may be said that, though born of a contentious factual setting and with meagre legal reasoning, the Rendulic Rule is now firmly entrenched in the fabric of IHL and ICL.

Hostage is also a precursor to the so-called reasonable commander test in modern IHL and the mistake of fact defence under contemporary ICL.[35] One may synopsise today's law as follows. Where a commander acts reasonably in light of the information available at the time, an IHL violation cannot be established even if the commander errs in his or her assessment of the situation. Nor, where acting

---

[28] Ibid.

[29] See Chaps. 7 and 8.

[30] See Chap. 7.

[31] Statute of the Permanent Court of International Justice, opened for signature 16 December 1920, 6 LNTS 379 (entered into force 1 September 1921), Article 38.

[32] Statute of the International Court of Justice, opened for signature 26 June 1945, USTS 993 (entered into force 24 October 1945), Article 38.

[33] *Hostage* Judgment, above n. 2, p 1235.

[34] Ibid.

[35] See Chaps. 7 and 8.

reasonably in the sense just described negates culpability or the mental element of an offence, can individual criminal responsibility be established.

The tribunal in *Hostage* took the truth of Rendulic's allegedly honest factual misapprehension for granted. This does not mean, however, that no trier of fact may revisit combat decisions made in difficult circumstances. On the contrary, IHL's post-*Hostage* development shows that both the honesty and reasonableness of a factually erroneous battlefield decision are amenable to judicial review and objective assessment afterwards.

The reasonable commander test becomes important in areas where IHL grants commanders a degree of decision-making discretion. Examples include military necessity—such was the case in *Hostage*—as well as precaution and proportionality in attacks. Implicit here is the notion that actively seeking and verifying information about the status of a target and about the prospect of incidental civilian harm forms an integral part of precautionary measures codified in Article 57 of Additional Protocol I.[36] If attackers err in their decision because of a failure to check the accuracy of available information, they act unreasonably and in bad faith.[37]

Key passages of the *Hostage* judgment reveal clues that Rendulic's acquittal had partly to do with the absence of culpability and guilty mind.[38] We can find similar signs in several other post-World War II trials, too. It appears that most of these cases assessed both the subjective genuineness of the defendants' beliefs and their objective reasonableness.

Article 32(1) of the Rome Statute of the International Criminal Court (ICC)[39] specifically provides for a mistake of fact. When interpreting this defence plea, the ICC should require any alleged mistake to be objectively reasonable by applying the reasonable commander test.[40] Imposing such a requirement would enable the court to exclude wilful blindness from Article 32(1). This would also help deter reckless use of faulty information in battlefield decisions and strengthen civilian protection as a result.

---

[36] Protocol Additional to the Geneva Conventions of 12 August 1949, and relating to the Protection of Victims of International Armed Conflicts (Protocol I), opened for signature 8 June 1977, 1125 UNTS 3 (entered into force 7 December 1978), Article 57.

[37] See also Chap. 11.

[38] See *Hostage* Judgment, above n. 2, pp 1296 ("If the facts were such as would justify the action by the exercise of judgment, after giving consideration to all the factors and existing possibilities, even though the conclusion reached may have been faulty, it cannot be said to be criminal"), 1797 ("We are concerned with the question whether the defendant at the time of its occurrence acted within the limits of honest judgment on the basis of the conditions prevailing at the time") and 1297 ("It is our considered opinion that the conditions, as they appeared to the defendant at the time were sufficient upon which he could honestly conclude that urgent military necessity warranted the decision made. This being true, the defendant may have erred in the exercise of his judgment but he was guilty of no criminal act").

[39] Rome Statute of the International Criminal Court, opened for signature 17 July 1998, 2187 UNTS 3 (entered into force 1 July 2002), Article 32(1).

[40] See also Chap. 11.

1.4 Assessing an Error's Reasonableness (Chaps. 9–11)

Hostage's significance goes beyond the no second-guessing rule, the reasonable commander test and the mistake of fact defence to which it has given rise. Far from being a footnote in IHL and ICL development, the trial raises questions about battlefield errors that continue to preoccupy us today. This anthology explores three themes—i.e., revolution in information technology,[41] diminishing space for empathy,[42] and institutional bias[43]—that may affect an error's reasonableness in modern warfare.

Rendulic's judges found the "limits of his honest judgment on the basis of the conditions prevailing at the time"[44] shaped by two things. First, war itself was "loaded with uncertainties, such as the numerical strength of the enemy, the quality of his equipment, his fighting spirit, the efficiency and daring of his commanders, and the uncertainty of his intentions."[45] Second, Rendulic's ability to collect intelligence was limited due to "the extreme cold and the short days."[46]

Rendulic would have been less limited in the exercise of his honest judgment had he had a clearer picture of the battlefield. US proponents of the so-called revolution in military affairs argue that this is precisely what today's extraordinary advances in information communications technology (ICT) bring.[47] Improvements in intelligence-gathering and processing, coupled with modern capabilities to execute missions more accurately and precisely, equip soldiers with dominant battlefield knowledge. As the fog of war and friction dissipate, technologically superior forces create information dominance over their opponents and usher in a change in the very nature of warfare. Russia also practices its own variation on the idea of information dominance, although it stresses network-centric and non-contact warfare carried out through long-range precision-guided munitions rather than battlefield clarity *per se*.

Recent wars in Afghanistan, Iraq, and Ukraine present a mixed picture. Initial overall successes of ICT-driven US forces in the conventional battlefield soon gave way to close-quarter combat with insurgents using urban and rugged terrains proficiently for concealment, dispersal, and cover. More importantly, abundant and accurate intelligence alone did little to mitigate elementary mistakes arising from negligence, poor judgment and fatigue. Nor did such intelligence clear away the soldier's pervasive sense of uncertainty and insecurity. Russia's invasion of Ukraine has exposed crippling deficiencies in situational awareness, communications security, imagery intelligence and army-air force coordination.

Unassisted with advanced technology, warfighting invariably reverts to its uncertain and error-prone ways. ICT advantage is, contrary to what its advocates argue,

---

[41] See Chap. 9.

[42] See Chap. 10.

[43] See Chap. 11.

[44] *Hostage* Judgment, above n. 2, p 1297.

[45] Ibid.

[46] Ibid., p 1295.

[47] See Chap. 9.

perhaps not the panacea to war's human element, that is, the psychological, physical and cognitive strain to which soldiers remain vulnerable.

Rendulic's case was ultimately about whether he had "acted within the limits of honest judgment."[48] His judges answered this question in the affirmative. It is unclear, however, whether they did so by comparing Rendulic's action to what a hypothetical reasonable commander would have done in his situation.

The reasonable commander test in IHL closely echoes the reasonable person test in common law.[49] A product of sentimental enlightenment, the latter test engages the actor's imagination about his or her own conduct from the standpoint of another, hypothetical person—i.e., the proverbial "man on the Clapham omnibus". This test also engages the actor's empathy as to what kind of concrete sentiments that hypothetical person would deem appropriate for members of society to have. So understood, the reasonable person test is essentially an exercise in the taking of external and social perspective.

Portraying the reasonable commander test as an empathy-based perspective-taking technique invites tricky questions. One issue involves the reasonable commander's identity. Is it an ordinary person concerned with saving lives who happens to find him- or herself in the position of a commander (the "human rights lawyer"[50])? Or is it a military person accustomed to making life-and-death decisions in the battlefield (the "experienced combat commander"[51])? Opinions on this matter vary,[52] but a test that accounts for the experience of all persons affected by war and the need for democratic oversight in military affairs broadens the reservoir of relevant perspective-holders and arguably offers more relatable and predictable decision-making guidance.

Another issue concerns the perspective's societal reach. Is the reasonable commander to emphasise with members of his or her national community, or with all human beings? Acting as a state representative might justify prioritising the welfare of that state's civilians. In contrast, acting as an agent of humanity would entail treating all civilians equally and construing proportionality accordingly.[53]

Empathy itself poses a formidable challenge, too. The reasonable commander test is predicated on the actor's perspective-taking and empathetic capacity. According to

---

[48] *Hostage* Judgment, above n. 2, p 1297.

[49] See Chap. 10.

[50] ICTY 2000, para 50.

[51] Ibid.

[52] It is arguable that *Hostage* employed the latter standpoint when it held (*Hostage* Judgment, above n. 2, pp 1245–1246): "In determining the guilt or innocence of an army commander when charged with a failure or refusal to accord a belligerent status to captured members of the resistance forces, the situation as it appeared to him must be given the first consideration. Such commander will not be permitted to ignore obvious facts in arriving at a conclusion. One trained in military science will ordinarily have no difficulty in arriving at a correct decision and, if he willfully refrains from so doing for any reason, he will be held criminally responsible for wrongs committed against those entitled to the rights of a belligerent. When room exists for an honest error in judgment, such army commander is entitled to the benefit thereof by virtue of the presumption of innocence."

[53] See also Chap. 11.

studies,[54] the more power a person possesses, the less able he or she is to empathise. This raises the possibility that the reasonable military commander—who may be assumed to hold great power to alter the state of those subjected to it—is already hampered in his or her ability to empathise with other persons and to take their perspectives into account when making decisions. The fact that commanders who lack empathy often accomplish their military missions, especially those involving killings, more efficiently, only makes the matter worse.

Modern militaries expand physical and psychological distances from their adversaries and actively promote de-empathetic modes of fighting. This might make one wonder whether the reasonable commander test is really fit for purpose when assessing today's battlefield decisions. It would arguably be, if for nothing else, should the test help reduce the lethality of combat on all sides.

Whether Rendulic honestly found imperative military necessity in Northern Norway's property destruction and forcible evacuation is one matter. Whether he grasped the magnitude of harm these measures would inflict on the region's residents is quite another. Rendulic's case was that forcible evacuation had saved them from the hardship of devastation in the end and, had the Soviets invaded, it would also have saved them from Bolshevism.[55] This reveals Rendulic's self-serving and ideologically coloured view of his own actions and their consequences.

Views like these resemble portrayals of civilian harm caused by US drone strikes as "tragic mistakes" and "awful but lawful".[56] Such reportage perpetuates and amplifies assumptions about the US military's moral superiority as an organisation dedicated to protecting civilians with precision weapons and about the blameless inevitability of civilian deaths in modern combat. These accounts also help mask individual and institutionally embedded forms of blameworthy indifference to the lives and well-being of those killed in drone strikes.

Key here is the idea that a harmful act's blameworthiness depends on its moral impropriety seen from the victim's point of view, rather than the actor's belief about his or her conduct. In particular, it is the lack of moral regard the actors owe their victims that makes blame appropriate. Applied to drones, one may ask, for instance, whether strike crews display a morally sufficient level of concern by verifying their targets and mitigating risks of civilian harm.[57] Where such risks increase because of the policies, practices, and attitudes of the organisation through which the crews execute their tasks, these policies, practices, and attitudes themselves become morally suspect, too.

Knowledge also plays an important role here. As is the case with other complex and hierarchical organisations, a military distributes, suppresses, and withholds knowledge amongst its personnel. Drone operators would be hard-pressed to go out of their way and authority to check all accessible as well as hidden target data. The Rendulic

[54] See Chap. 10.

[55] See Chap. 6.

[56] See Chap. 11.

[57] See also Chap. 8.

Rule would therefore protect resulting errors in their attack decisions against second-guessing. The fact remains, however, that the objective reasonableness of their belief might depend on how judgments about legitimate and illegitimate targets had been formed higher up in their chain of command. There are worrying signs that the US military denies its soldiers true knowledge about the impact of drone strikes on civilians and, consequently, true belief about the sincerity of its stated commitment to minimising incidental harm.

The US military would do well to make good on its professed concern for civilians by treating all civilians, American or non-American, as morally equal.[58] This would go some way to injecting empathy into US drone operations and to redressing culpable indifference to civilian harm as a result.

1.5 Conclusion

This anthology lays bare some crucial situational nuances that are missing from the Rendulic ruling. It also shows how, without articulating any basis in law, Rendulic's judges felt justified to accept the honesty of his error. These factual and legal shortcomings may make *Hostage* "a shaky pillar to lean on," as one commentator put it.[59]

The judgment's "shakiness" need not—indeed, it does not—invalidate no second-guessing as an idea. If not from Rendulic's acquittal, his eponymous IHL rule would in some form have eventually emerged from elsewhere. Most of its normative development would have followed broadly similar lines as well. That is so because, at the end of the day, all battlefield decisions are to some degree limited in their honesty and reasonableness, and law demands their meaningful assessment in one way or another.

Our findings also offer food for thought. For example, should second-guessing be permitted where it benefits the defendant? We have reason to suspect that Rendulic invoked military necessity less as his honest and reasonable belief of the situation prevailing at the time than as a *post factum* rationalisation for Terboven's political project. Had the Red Army invaded, however, the total devastation of Northern Norway and forcible evacuation of all of its inhabitants would have slowed its advance. As long as these measures generated the right results, few might protest afterwards that they had been conceived for the wrong purpose.

Can a sound legal rule come out of a factually unsound case? The *Hostage* tribunal could have chosen to uphold the idea of no second-guessing in principle and reject the alleged honesty of Rendulic's errors on its merits, but it did not. The prosecution's lackadaisical work and the tribunal's apparent readiness to take Rendulic at face value lend support to the notion that those involved in *Hostage* at Nuremberg deemed the atrocities committed in Northern Norway *de minimis* compared to those committed

[58] See also Chap. 9.

[59] Best 1994, p 330.

in the Balkans. This may explain why, despite its central importance to IHL and ICL, the Rendulic Rule has remained relatively obscure and its precise content difficult to articulate.

Will tomorrow's warfare compel us to re-imagine the reasonable commander test under IHL and the mistake of fact defence under ICL? Full combat decision autonomy will not eliminate room for error. When an error occurs, questions such as what it means for relevant information to have been available to the decision-maker (human or otherwise), what counts as its honest and reasonable assessment, and when accountability is engaged, will need raising and answering.

References

Best G (1994) War and Law Since 1945. Clarendon Press, New York

ICTY (2000) Final Report to the Prosecutor by the Committee Established to Review the NATO Bombing Campaign Against the Federal Republic of Yugoslavia. https://www.icty.org/x/file/Press/nato061300.pdf

Tulloch B (2011) Terror in the Arctic. Matador, Leicestershire

Nobuo Hayashi Associate Senior Lecturer, Swedish Defence University; Visiting Professor, University for Peace, UN Interregional Crime and Justice Research Institute. Address: Drottning Kristinas väg 37, 114 28 Stockholm, Sweden, e-mail: nobuo.hayashi@fhs.se

Carola Lingaas Associate Professor of Law, VID Specialized University. Address: PO Box 184 Vinderen, 0319 Oslo, Norway, e-mail: carola.lingaas@vid.no

Part II
Devastating Northern Norway and Forcibly Evacuating Its Inhabitants

Chapter 2
Occupied Norway 1940–1945: A Brief Background to *Hostage*

Sven G. Holtsmark and Gunnar Åselius

Contents

2.1 Introduction 26
2.2 1940: Norway Attacked and Occupied 29
2.3 The German Occupation Regime in Norway 31
2.4 *Barbarossa*, Finland, and the Northern Front 32
2.5 The Commanders and Their Troops 33
2.6 Preparing for the Offensive in the North—June–October 1944 35
2.7 October–November 1944: The Petsamo-Kirkenes Operation 39
2.8 Brief Note on Historiography 40
References 44

Abstract This chapter gives background and context to the events that provide the material for this anthology—the systematic devastation of Finnmark and parts of Troms and the concomitant forced evacuation of the civilian population from October 1944 to February 1945. Although Rendulic issued the 29 October 1944 order in his capacity as Commander of German forces in Northern Norway, he was not alone responsible for that fateful order. The chapter therefore includes but also goes beyond the 29 October order's immediate military background. It discusses the dramatic developments in the 20th Mountain Army's area of operation in Northern Norway, Finland, and the Soviet Union in the summer and autumn of 1944. The chapter starts with an outline of the occupation regime in Norway and the role of key decision-makers behind the events that led to Rendulic's indictment at the US military tribunal. Afterwards follow some remarks on Norway's—and Northern Norway's in particular—role in the war, as well as a presentation of the political and military events that preceded the return of the 20th Mountain Army to Norway and Rendulic's order of 29 October 1944. The chapter ends with a brief note on German and English language literature about this fragment of Germany's Second World

S. G. Holtsmark
Norwegian Institute for Defence Studies, Norwegian Defence University College, 0150 Oslo, Akershus Fortress, Norway
e-mail: sholtsmark@mil.no

G. Åselius (✉)
Swedish Defence University, Stockholm, Sweden
e-mail: gunnar.aselius@fhs.se

N. Hayashi and C. Lingaas (eds.), *Honest Errors? Combat Decision-Making 75 Years After the* Hostage *Case*, https://doi.org/10.1007/978-94-6265-611-6_2

War military history and Norwegian occupation experience, as well as references to selected Norwegian and Russian-language texts.

Keywords Operation *Weserübung* · Operation *Barbarossa* · Operation *Silberfuchs* · Operation *Birke* · Operation *Nordlicht* · Karelian Front · 14th Army · 20th Mountain Army · Petsamo-Kirkenes Operation · destruction of Finnmark 1944 · *Hostage* Case · Lothar Rendulic · Kirill A. Meretskov · Vladimir I. Shcherbakov · Lapland War 1944

2.1 Introduction

On 29 October 1944, Colonel General Lothar Rendulic, Commander of the German *Wehrmacht*'s *20. Gebirgs-Armee* (20th Mountain Army) issued an order to subordinate units. Rendulic's Army had until then conducted operations in Northern Finland and on occupied Soviet territory along the Finnish-Soviet border. At this time, he was in the midst of a huge operation to retreat to positions behind the fortifications of the Lyngen Line in Northern Norway. The order opened as follows:

> Subject: Evacuation North Norway
>
> 1.) Due to the low level of willingness of the northern Norwegian population to evacuate voluntarily, der Führer has ordered the forced evacuation [of the population] east of the Lyngenfjord in the interest of the security of the population, which is to be protected from Bolshevism, and ordered that all dwelling places will be burned down or destroyed.
>
> Commander-in-Chief northern Finland [i.e., Rendulic] is responsible for ensuring that this order is carried out ruthlessly, thereby preventing the Soviets, supported by dwelling places and a population who knows the country, from following our retreats with strong forces.
>
> Pity for the civilian population is out of place.
>
> 2.) The troops will understand the measures to be taken when it is made clear to them that the barbaric methods of air warfare against the German homeland and its cultural sites have brought suffering to our people surpassing by far that which will follow from the measures that now must be taken in northern Norway in order to prevent an early pursuit by the Russians according to plan.[1]

[1] Emphasis in the original. The author's translation from the German original in National Archives and Records Administration, Washington D.C. (hereafter NARA), PG65635/8, microfilm T312/1063, pp 340–342. Elements of the translation of the 29 October 1944 order are taken from the translation used in the Tribunal, available at The Harvard Law School Library's Nuremberg Trials Project, NMT 7: The Hostage Case, Ferdinand Jodl's testimony 22 August 1947, pp 2554–2557, https://nbg-02.lil.tools/transcripts/4-transcript-for-nmt-7-hostage-case [accessed 1 April 2023]:

> 1. Because of the lack of willingness of the north Norwegian population to evacuate the country voluntarily the Fuehrer has ordered the compulsory evacuation of the population East of the Lyngenfjords [*sic*] in the interest of the security of the population, which is to be preserved from Bolshevism and that all houses be burned down or be destroyed. It is the responsibility of the Commander-in-Chief of Northern Finland that this order is carried out

With this order, Rendulic set in motion a process that culminated in February 1945 with the destruction of Hammerfest, a major town in Western Finnmark. It also led to the near-complete devastation of Finnmark county and parts of the neighbouring county, Troms, in Northern Norway. The decision was immediately made known to the Norwegian population by posters[2] that bore the signature of Rendulic as well as that of Josef Terboven, Adolf Hitler's *Reichskommissar* in occupied Norway, followed by instructions to local communities about where and when to assemble for further transport.[3] The systematic destruction that followed included civilian dwellings, other private and public buildings, harbours, bridges and other infrastructure in towns, villages and even isolated settlements on distant islands. Parts of the population avoided evacuation by hiding in the wilderness, in cottages, caves and other improvised dwellings. These events—the destruction and the forced evacuation—remain some of the most extensive acts of Nazi Germany's destructiveness in Norwegians' memory of war and occupation from 1940 to 1945.

---

ruthlessly so that the Soviets supported by dwelling places and a population which knows the country will be prevented from following our withdrawal with strong forces. Pity with the civilian population is out of place.

2. The men will understand the measures to be taken if it is explained that the barbarian methods of the air war against the German homeland and its cultural places have brought a misery on our people surpassing by far that which will follow in the wake of the measures which must be taken now in North Norway in order to prevent an early thrust by the Russians, according to plan.

German original:

Betr.: Evakuierung Nordnorwegen

1.) Auf Grund der geringen Bereitwilligkeit der nordnorwegischen Bevölkerung zur freiwilligen Evakuierung hat der Führer die Zwangs-Evakuierung ostw. des Lyngenfjords im Interesse der Sicherheit der Bevölkerung, die vor dem Bolschewismus bewahrt werden soll, verfügt und befehlen, dass alle Wohnstätten niederzubrennen bzw. zu zerstören sind.

Oberbefehlshaber Nordfinnland ist dafür verantwortlich, dass dieser Befehl rücksichtslos durchgeführt und damit vermieden wird, dass die Sowjets, gestützt auf Wohnstätten und ortskundige Bevölkerung, unseren Absetzbewegungen mit starken Kräften folgen.

Mitleid mit der Zivilbevölkerung ist nicht am Platze.

2.) Die Truppe wird die zu treffenden Massnahmen verstehen, wenn ihr klar gemacht wird, dass die barbarischen Methoden des Luftkrieges gegen die deutsche Heimat und ihre Kulturstätten ein Leid über unser Volk gebracht haben, das weit grössser ist[,] als es die Massnahmen mit sich bringen, die jetzt in Nordnorwegen getroffen werden müssen, um ein baldiges planmässiges Nachstossen durch den [*sic*] Russen zu verhindern.

[2] Reproduced in Bones 2022, p 86.

[3] An example from Hammerfest in ibid., p 170.

At the behest of the Norwegian government, charges stemming from the destruction of Finnmark and Northern Troms and the forced evacuation of the population were included in the indictment against Rendulic in the so-called *Hostage* case of 1947–1948.[4] This was one of a series of trials heard by US military tribunals that followed the case brought before the International Military Tribunal (IMT) of 1945–1946 against the 21 most prominent political and military leaders of Nazi Germany who had not committed suicide or otherwise avoided being brought to justice. *Hostage* is named after one of the major issues in the prosecution's case against the defendants, Rendulic included, who had all held commands in Southern Europe and the Balkans: the widespread practice in German-occupied areas of taking and executing civilian hostages as retribution for what the occupiers deemed "illegal" acts by resistance fighters. The judges concluded that taking and even executing hostages was not necessarily illegal under the reigning laws of war. Therefore, none of the defendants received the death penalty.

Terboven avoided trial and a likely death sentence in a Norwegian or international court by taking his own life on 8 May 1945, the day of Germany's capitulation, at his residence Skaugum outside Oslo. Although Rendulic was sentenced to 20 years' imprisonment, he was acquitted on the charges related to Northern Norway. Soon Rendulic's sentence was halved, and in 1951 he was released. He spent the rest of his life writing a series of apologetic memoirs, presenting himself, like so many of his colleagues, as a principled officer, *ein Soldat wie andere auch*,[5] who just did his honourable duty, never transgressing against the rules of lawful warfare or crossing any ethical boundaries.

Hostage was set in a framework that limited the selection of events to be considered in the indictment against Rendulic. For example, it did not include his decisions during the 20th Mountain Army's retreat though Northern Finland from September 1944, where his troops from mid-October practiced a scorched earth policy comparable to what they later did in Northern Norway. Nor did the tribunal address the issue of the approximately 100,000 inhabitants of Northern Finland who were forced to leave their homes.[6]

The difference in the tribunal's approach to events in Norway and Finland is easily explained: at the time of the US military tribunal, Finland was perceived as a defeated country, which until September 1944 had been at war not only with the Soviet Union but also with the United Kingdom. Therefore, there was never a discussion of requesting the Finnish government to provide material to widen the charges against Rendulic to include the destruction of large areas of Northern Finland. It can be argued that including Rendulic's actions in Finland from September to November 1944 could have strengthened the prosecution's case: there is, for instance, clear

---

[4] For a brief discussion, see Best 1994, pp 328–330. More in Bill 2012, pp 119–155. Also, see Chap. 5.

[5] The expression is taken from the title of former SS General Paul Hausser's 1966 book (Hausser 1966), a shamelessly apologetic work that was part of Hausser's campaign to create an image of the Waffen-SS as a perfectly normal military organisation.

[6] Nehlin 2017, p 145 and Frieser et al. 2007, pp 999–1000.

evidence that the destruction of Rovaniemi, Northern Finland's regional centre, was at least partly motivated by factors other than military necessity.[7]

2.2 1940: Norway Attacked and Occupied

In the early morning of 9 April 1940, German naval, land, and air forces attacked Denmark and Norway during a well-concealed joint operation code-named *Unternehmen Weserübung*. Denmark capitulated almost immediately: the small size of the country and its location as Germany's direct neighbour, as well as the country's topography that provided few natural defences, made continued resistance seem futile. In Norway, Allied (British, French, and Polish) and Norwegian forces continued the fight until 10 June 1940 when the last Norwegian troops in Northern Norway finally capitulated. At that point, the Allied troops that had fought in the Narvik area had already been withdrawn to strengthen the defence against the expected German attack on the United Kingdom.[8]

On 7 June 1940, King Haakon, Prime Minister Johan Nygaardsvold and most members of the Norwegian government, as well as some prominent politicians and officials, boarded the Royal Navy cruiser HMS *Devonshire* in Tromsø to join the rising number of governments-in-exile from continental Europe that had taken up residence in London. For the remainder of the war, Norway's military contribution to the Allied war effort remained, by necessity, limited, although a reorganised Navy and Air Force continued the fight under mostly British operational command. A brigade-size army was organised in Scotland for the purpose of taking part in the future liberation of Norway, while Norwegian special forces operated as part of the British Special Operations Executive. Back in Norway, clandestine structures for civilian and military resistance were gradually developed, the latter primarily preparing for the same task as the Norwegian brigade in Scotland—to take part in the liberation of the country from German occupation. Communist resistance groups operated largely independently of the government-controlled *Milorg*, the military wing of the Norwegian resistance movement. In Finnmark county, the Soviets organised their own network of Norwegian intelligence agents to report on German activity, mainly on German shipping. The existence of UK-based Norwegian military forces and of resistance groups that would support Allied attacks on the German forces in Northern Norway, were part of the German threat evaluation of Allied operations in Northern Norway.[9]

From the end of the fighting in the Narvik area in June 1940 until Soviet troops crossed the border to Eastern Finnmark in October 1944, no large-scale military

[7] Frieser et al. 2007, p 999.

[8] See Haarr 2010, 2011 for an updated and fundamental work on the German attack of 9 April 1940 and the campaign in Norway that followed. For brief introductions, see Mann 2012, pp 1–11, and Riste 2001, pp 138–153. See also relevant parts of Andenæs et al. 1996.

[9] These issues are covered in Andenæs et al. 1996.

operations took place in Norway. Nevertheless, Norwegian territory continued to play a prominent role in the German conduct of the war. The number of German military personnel stationed in Norway reflected the significance that Hitler and his generals attached to controlling the country, i.e., to stop any Allied attempt to retake it after the defeat in 1940. Hitler personally assigned great importance to Norway and correspondingly directed huge resources to the construction of defences along the entire Norwegian coast.[10] After June 1941, when tens of thousands of German soldiers were transferred from occupation duties to take part in the invasion of the Soviet Union, approximately 170,000 German personnel were stationed in Norway. In November 1944, the 20th Mountain Army's withdrawal to Norway increased the number to around 280,000.[11]

German armament was dependant on aluminium and other products of Norway's metallurgical industry (which was significantly expanded during the war using prisoners of war as slave labourers). In the north, much of Germany's import of iron ore from Sweden was transported by rail to Narvik and from there by ship to Germany. However, the Norwegian territory's role in Germany's war strategy was manifold. First, Norway provided basing areas along its Atlantic coast for the German Navy and Air Force. With its fjords, inlets, and thousands of large and small islands and archipelagos, Norway's Atlantic coast provided harbours and anchorages for both merchant ships and naval vessels, as well as natural protection for shipping routes. From bases in Norway, the German Navy and Air Force presented a significant threat to the sea lanes between Great Britain and the Soviet Union, including the transport of weapons and other supplies for the Soviet war effort. The sheer presence in Norway of major German vessels such as the battleship *Tirpitz* (from January 1942 until it was finally sunk in November 1944) bound up significant Allied naval forces. The *Tirpitz* was not alone: from early 1942, most major German naval vessels were stationed in Norway, at bases from Trondheim in the south to Kirkenes in the north-east.

Second, Northern Norway was a staging, supply and resting area for the 20th Mountain Army, in particular the XIX Mountain Corps fighting in the Litsa sector. Supplies and troops to Kirkenes in Eastern Finnmark arrived almost exclusively by ship, as there were no rail or road connections covering the entire distance from Southern Norway to Eastern Finnmark.

Third, there was an economic side to the German military presence in the north: the import of nickel matte from the nickel ore smelting works at Finnish Kolosjoki (today Nikel' in Murmansk *oblast'* in Russia), just across the border from Eastern Finnmark. Nickel ore and matte from Kolosjoki, shipped from Kirkenes, in 1943–1944 made up four-fifths of Germany's total nickel supplies. On several occasions, Hitler himself emphasised the need to protect Petsamo and the nickel resources at any cost.[12]

---

[10] On the Allied planning (or non-planning) related to Norway, see Chap. 3.

[11] Stipulations kindly supplied by Gunnar D. Hatlehol.

[12] Rowe 2021, pp 56–57 and 172–173, n. 36.

2.3 The German Occupation Regime in Norway

The German occupation regime in Norway was formally divided between a civilian and a military arm. The civilian structure was headed by Terboven, a German Nazi Party (*Nationalsozialistische Deutsche Arbeiterpartei*, NSDAP) *apparatchik* who carried the title *Reichskommissar für die besetzten norwegischen Gebiete*, or Reich Commissioner for the Occupied Norwegian Territories. At the head of the military structure, from 25 July 1940 to 18 December 1944, was Colonel General Nikolaus von Falkenhorst. As *Wehrmachtsbefehlshaber Norwegen* (*Wehrmacht* Commander Norway, *WBH Norwegen*), von Falkenhorst established his military staff as *Armeeoberkommando Norwegen* (Army Command Norway—*AOK Norwegen*).

In practice, however, this seemingly straightforward structure was less clear-cut. As in other occupied countries and in Germany proper, Heinrich Himmler's *Schutzstaffel*, or SS, played a semi-independent role, despite the SS as well as police structures (such as the *Sicherheitspolizei*, i.e., the security police) being formally subordinated to the *Reichskommissar*. The duality of the German occupation regime, with its civilian branch under Terboven and its military branch under von Falkenhorst, are central to the historic events that are at the core of this anthology. In addition to Rendulic and some of his subordinates, these two men played important roles in the process leading up to the orders in October–November 1944, for which Rendulic had to answer before US Military Tribunal V in Nuremberg.

In addition to these German structures, the Germans also put in place collaborating Norwegian governmental structures, with Vidkun Quisling as the key person. Quisling was founder and *Fører* (Leader, as in German *Führer*) of the *Nasjonal samling* (National Unity, NS),[13] a fascist and self-declared Nazi party that cooperated closely with the Germans. The NS was the only political party that was allowed to operate legally during the occupation. On 25 September 1940, a governing body of Norwegians, largely consisting of NS members, was set up as a council of "commissary ministers"[14] (*kommissarische Staatsräte*), each directly subordinated to Terboven. These "ministers" worked for the larger part through pre-war ministerial and other administrative structures that were themselves nazified by putting Quisling loyalists in key positions.[15]

The nazification of central governance structures was repeated on the regional and local levels: persons loyal to the occupation regime took the place of pre-war elected or appointed officials. On 1 February 1942, Quisling was formally proclaimed *Ministerpresident* as the head of an allegedly fully constitutional Norwegian government. He remained in this position until the end of the war, when he was taken into custody, tried, sentenced to death, and executed. Quisling's "government" remained subordinated to *Reichskommissar* Terboven, both in theory and practice. In reality, Quisling's room for manoeuvre was restricted by the German occupation authorities as they saw fit. In the process leading up to the order of 29 October 1944

[13] Here translated as in ibid., p 37. An alternative translation could be "National Rally".

[14] Here we use the translation of "*kommissarische Staatsräte*" in Hetland et al. 2021, p 86.

[15] About Quisling and his party, see Dahl 1999.

and its subsequent implementation, the Quisling government appeared alongside the German military and civilian authorities as an actor and as an interested party.[16]

2.4 *Barbarossa*, Finland, and the Northern Front

When Germany launched operation *Weserübung* in April 1940 and took control over the entire country in June, Germany and the Soviet Union were still in a state of semi-alliance following the Hitler-Stalin pact of 23 August 1939, supplementary agreements, and complex German-Soviet trade arrangements. A few months later, the relationship gradually soured. In December 1941, the German *Wehrmacht* High Command, *Oberkommando der Wehrmacht* (*OKW*), received the decisive order to prepare for the next major step in the war—namely, an attack on the Soviet Union code-named *Fall* (later *Unternehmen*) *Barbarossa*.[17] Hence, German forces and supplies were concentrated in Northern Norway in preparation for an offensive from Eastern Finnmark, across the "Finnish Corridor" and into the Soviet Union towards Murmansk. The town and harbour of Kirkenes near the border became a major supply hub for the invasion forces.[18]

The invasion of the Soviet Union was envisioned as much more than a fight to remove a threat or to gain new territories for Germany. It was, in Hitler's own words, to be a *Vernichtungskrieg*, a War of Annihilation.[19] And so it did indeed become one, but with the partial exception of the 20th Mountain Army's northern theatre of war. This was not because the attitudes among German commanders about annihilation in various theatres differed, but rather because fighting predominately took place in the Arctic wilderness with no or only scarce population.

The Finnish Corridor was a narrow strip of land stretching some 130 km along the Norwegian border from Nautsi in the south to today's Pechenga in Murmansk *oblast'* in the north. The final stretch of the 550-km *Eismeerstrasse* (Arctic Ocean Road) went through the corridor from Rovaniemi, the administrative and communication centre of northern Finland. Created by the 1920 Peace Treaty between the newly

---

[16] See Chap. 4 for the detailed story.

[17] *Weissung Nr. 21*, or *Barbarossabefehl* of 18 December 1940, overtook and incorporated earlier staff studies of a war against the Soviet Union.

[18] For details, see Ziemke 1959.

[19] For an overview of the implications of this term, see for example Müller 2012, the chapter "*Totaler Krieg und Vernichtungskrieg*". Hitler himself used similar expressions, as in his speech to *Wehrmacht* officers on 30 March 1941: "We must depart from the standpoint of soldierly comradeship. The Communist is not a comrade before and no Comrade afterwards. It is a matter of a battle of annihilation". (Wir müssen von dem Standpunkt des soldatischen Kameradentums abrücken. Der Kommunist ist vorher kein Kamerad und nacher kein Kamerad. Es handelt sich um einen Vernichtungskampf). Here quoted after Streit 1997, p 34.

independent Finland and Soviet Russia,[20] this corridor gave Finland access to the ice-free coast of the Barents Sea and the Atlantic Ocean.

According to the Stalin-Hitler pact of 23 August 1939, Finland belonged to the Soviet "sphere of influence". Yet, starting in 1940, Finland and Germany developed increasingly close relations, including German contributions to Finland's rearmament after the Soviet-Finnish Winter War of 1939–1940. Moreover, the Finnish leadership was informed of Germany's intention to invade the Soviet Union and prepared to join in the fight. Ostensibly aiming at regaining territory that was lost to the Soviet Union in the Peace Treaty of March 1940, the Finnish plans evolved into something more ambitious, namely to continue the offensive beyond the 1939 borders into Soviet Karelia in order to create a "Greater Finland". In earlier Finnish and Western historiography, the ensuing Finnish-Soviet war of 1941–1944 used to be called the "Continuation War". Newer Finnish historiography has dismissed this term, however, since it conceals Finland's expansionist ambitions that came to light when, in the summer and autumn of 1941, Finnish forces continued the initially successful offensive beyond Finland's 1939 borders.[21]

Further to the north, the more than 1,200 km-long front line partly crossed Soviet territory and partly followed the Soviet-Finnish border. Finnish forces operated in Southern and Central Finland, while German forces operated in the north.[22] In the northernmost sector, the German forces' advance towards Murmansk ground to a halt in late 1941. They established their forward line defences along the river Zapadnaya Litsa[23]—often simply called Litsa in Soviet and German sources—some 60 km to the west of Murmansk city and harbour, the offensive's main aim. Despite mutual attacks and counterattacks, including a major Soviet effort in the winter of 1942, the situation along the front line of the 20th Mountain Army and the Finnish Army to the south largely remained unchanged until June 1944 in Southern Karelia and until October 1944 in the Litsa sector.

2.5 The Commanders and Their Troops

As *Wehrmacht* Commander in Norway and Commander of *AOK Norwegen*, von Falkenhorst oversaw *Unternehmen Silberfuchs* (Operation Silver Fox), the invasion of the Soviet Union from occupied Finnmark over the Finnish corridor. (He had previously overseen *Unternehmen Weserübung*, the attack on Denmark and Norway.) *Gebirgskorps Norwegen* (Mountain Corps Norway), commanded by Lieutenant General Eduard Dietl, would lead the attack from Norwegian territory. In

[20] That is one of the two Tartu agreements of 1920, the other being the peace treaty between the Soviet government and Estonia.

[21] See Meinander 2023 and Jonas 2012. For an updated and broad introduction to Finland during the Second World War, see Kinnunen and Kivimäki 2012.

[22] Some German units were under Finnish command and vice versa.

[23] Meaning Western Litsa—there is an Eastern Litsa River further to the east on the Kola Peninsula.

November 1942, the Corps was renamed *XIX Gebirgs-Armeekorps* (XIX Mountain Army Corps, hereafter XIX Mountain Corps).

In January 1942, parts of *AOK Norwegen* formed the core of a new Army-level formation, *Armeeoberkommando Lappland* (*AOK Lappland*). In June of the same year, *AOK Lappland* was renamed *20. Gebirgs-Armee*, i.e., the 20th Mountain Army mentioned above. Dietl, at this point *General der Gebirgstruppe*, was appointed Commander of the new Army. In addition to incorporating the XIX Mountain Corps, large Finnish formations and various specialised units, the 20th Mountain Army was made up of the XXXVI Mountain Corps and (from May 1942) the XVIII Mountain Corps, both stationed to the south of the XIX Mountain Corps along the front line between Northern Finland and the Soviet Union. At the time of the events that form the topic of this anthology, the 20th Mountain Army comprised around 200,000 men.[24] Besides Northern Finland and occupied Soviet territory, the 20th Mountain Army's area of responsibility comprised parts of Finnmark county. Thus, since early 1942, Norwegian territory was divided between two *Armeeoberkommandos*, the north-eastern part under the 20th Mountain Army and the rest of the country under von Falkenhorst's *Armeeoberkommando Norwegen*. Both were subordinated directly under the *Oberkommando der Wehrmacht* (*OKW*) with its staff element being the *Wehrmachtsführungsstab* (*WFStab*).

In June 1944, Dietl was killed in an air crash. Rendulic, who at that time was Commander of a *Panzerarmee* in Yugoslavia, was appointed the 20th Mountain Army's new Commander. Rendulic remained in this position until 18 December 1944. At that time the German military command structure in Norway was again reorganised and unified, now brought under Rendulic in his role as *Wehrmachtsbefehlshaber*, von Falkenhorst's successor, in Norway. The Commander of the XIX Mountain Corps, from May 1944 until the end of the war, was General (*General der Gebirgstruppe*) Ferdinand Jodl. Alfred Jodl, his elder brother, was the head of the *WFStab*, i.e., Chief of Staff of the *Wehrmacht* High Command.[25] See Fig. 2.1.

The Red Army's Karelian Front (*Karel'skii front*), commanded by General Kirill A. Meretskov (who in late October 1944 was promoted to Marshall of the Soviet Union), confronted the German 20th Mountain Army on the Soviet side. In the Red Army, a *Front* was the highest-order unit and comprised a number of Armies. The closest German equivalent to a *Front* was called *Heeresgruppe* (Group of Armies). Thus, opposing Jodl's XIX Mountain Corps in the Litsa sector was not an equivalent Soviet unit, a corps, but an entire Army, namely the 14th Army under Lieutenant General Vladimir I. Shcherbakov. The Karelian Front's other Armies manned positions along the front line opposite first German and then, further to the south, Finnish forces , all the way to the southernmost positions along the Svir' River between the

[24] Ziemke 1959, p 302.

[25] For additional information about both Finnish and German operations and organisational details, see Ziemke 1959.

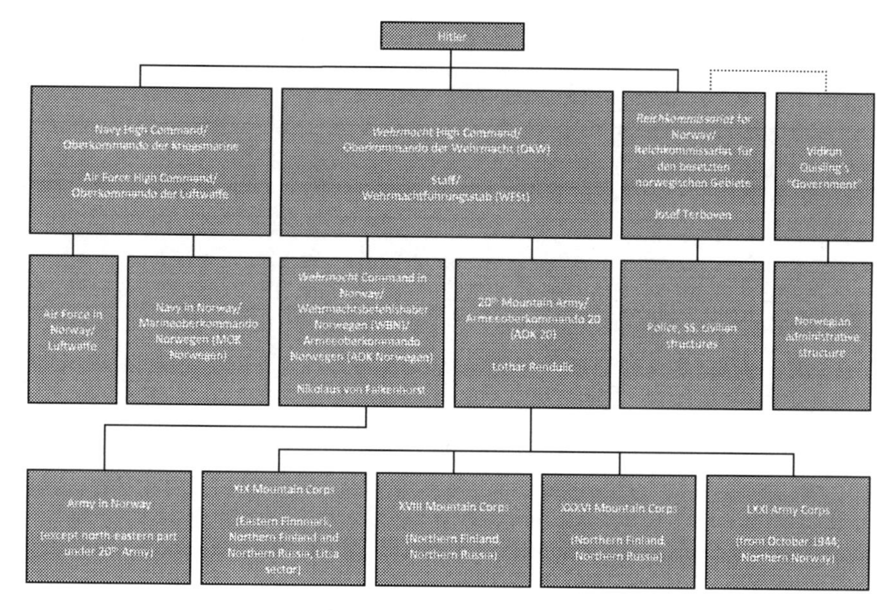

Fig. 2.1 This chart gives a simplified overview of the occupation regime in Norway as of October 1944, after the LXXI Army Corps, based in Northern Norway, was transferred to the 20th Army. The *Oberkommando des Heeres*, the Army High Command, is not included in the chart, since both *Wehrmachtsbefehlshaber Norwegen* (*WBH Norwegen*) and the 20th Army (*AOK 20*) were subordinated to the *Wehrmacht* High Command (*OKW*), not to the Army High Command. In contrast, both the Navy and Air Force Commands in Norway were subordinated to their respective High Commands. On 18 December 1944, the *AOK Norwegen* was dissolved, and Rendulic appointed the new *Wehrmachtsbefehlshaber Norwegen* (*Wehrmacht* Commander Norway) with responsibility for all remaining Army units in Norway. He was succeeded by General Franz Böhme on 21 January 1945. Böhme remained in this position until Germany's capitulation. *Source* Sven G. Holtsmark 2023

lakes Ladoga and Onega in Southern Karelia. The Karelian Front's neighbour to the south was the Leningrad Front (*Leningradskii front*). Once the siege of Leningrad was broken in January 1944, the Leningrad Front built up strong forces opposite the Finnish positions on the Karelian Isthmus, the decisive sector of the Soviet-Finnish war.

2.6 Preparing for the Offensive in the North—June–October 1944

On 9 June 1944, the Leningrad Front launched an overwhelming attack on the Isthmus, followed on 21 June with the Karelian Front's offensive over the Svir' River. The Finns were forced into the defensive on both the Isthmus and in Southern Karelia. The Finnish Army sustained heavy losses during the retreat, but nevertheless thwarted the Soviet aim of breaking the Finnish resistance and continuing the offensive into Finland's interior. The Soviets, who after the end of the siege of Leningrad saw the war against Finland as secondary to the sequence of huge offensives that followed in the theatres in the Baltics, Belarus and Ukraine, on 29 August declared to the Finnish government their conditions for negotiating a ceasefire. The Finns accepted the Soviet terms with some additional stipulations, and on 4 September the Finnish Army stopped firing, followed by the opposing Soviet forces at 8 a.m. the next day. A formal armistice was signed on 19 September.[26]

According to the Soviet terms declared on 29 August, Finland was to break off relations with Germany and to expel or intern German forces in Northern Finland, i.e., units of the 20th Mountain Army. This last point may have served a double purpose: to Finland, it was of crucial importance to avoid a Soviet military presence on Finnish territory (in this regard, the clause accommodated Finnish considerations); to the Soviets, it was a guarantee that, once Finnish troops started fighting their former ally, the split between Finland and Germany would be irreversible.

Ceding the Petsamo area and the adjacent Finnish corridor to the Soviet Union was not among the Soviet government's conditions of 29 August 1944. Nevertheless, it came as no surprise to the Finns when this clause appeared in the armistice agreement of 19 September 1944. Since the early days of the war, it had been clear that Stalin would demand Petsamo as part of any peace deal with Finland.[27] This meant that Finland lost its only access to the Barents Sea (and its only ice-free port). Norway and the Soviet Union became neighbours with a common border nearly 200 km in length. It was the same border that had separated Northern Norway from imperial Russia from 1826 to 1917 when Finland became independent following Russia's October Revolution. Finnish *Petsamo* became Soviet *Pechenga.*

With Finland out of the war, Meretskov and his Karelian Front could focus on the remaining enemy: the German 20th Mountain Army. Meretskov envisioned an offensive against the two southern German Mountain Corps (XVIII and XXXVI) that would continue deep into Finnish territory, effectively cutting off the two corps' retreat to the Gulf of Bothnia or to Norway.[28] Such an offensive would have run counter to the 19 September armistice, however, since it was Finland's responsibility to expel the Germans from its territory. Stalin kept his word and rejected

---

[26] Linna 1954 tells the story of a Finnish machine gun company in Southern Karelia from the optimism of the successful offensive in 1944 to the terrible losses during the retreat in the summer of 1944. The book's characters are convincingly portrayed in Aku Louhimies' movie and television series of 2017, the third film version of this Finnish post-war classic.

[27] In Soviet terminology and Soviet and Russian historiography, Petsamo was in 1944 "returned" to the Soviet Union. This usage is based on the fact that the area was not part of the Grand Duchy of Finland in Czarist Russia before the revolutions of 1917 and the ensuring Finnish civil war of 1918 and intertwined war with Soviet Russia. Thus, when Petsamo and the corridor became part of Finland via the Tartu peace treaty of 1920, this was subsequently described in Soviet parlance as a "gift" to Finland from the Soviet Union. Interestingly, the Soviets did not demand the transfer of the area to the Soviet Union as part of the March 1940 peace treaty that ended the Winter War of 1939–40—a result of their limited interest in the military-strategic value of the area throughout the interwar years. See the introduction in Holtsmark and Petrov 2020.

[28] See Chap. 3.

Meretskov's suggestions. Initially, Finnish and German forces in Northern Finland did their best to avoid direct confrontations. Their relations hardened after a failed German attack on the Finnish garrison on the island of Hogland in the Gulf of Finland. The ensuing fighting between them, in which the Finns sought to force the Germans out of Northern Finland, is remembered in Finnish history as the "Lapland War" of 1944–1945.[29]

This effort was to some degree futile: after the Soviet-Finnish ceasefire of 4–5 September 1944, Rendulic was ordered to implement the prepared plans for withdrawing the two southern corps (Mountain Corps XVIII and XXXVI) to positions in the Lyngen-Skibotn area, i.e., behind the so-called "Lyngen Line" of fortifications, in Northern Norway. On the northernmost sector along the Zapadnaya Litsa, the XIX Mountain Corps should remain in place to secure continued control over the Kolosjoki nickel ore smelting works and the continued deliveries of nickel matte to Germany. This first plan for the 20th Mountain Army's retreat to Norway was given the code name *Birke*—Birch. From mid-October 1944, as German-Finnish fighting intensified, Rendulic gradually extended the scorched earth policy to which he had resorted in Northern Finland to include all infrastructure that could be considered useful to the pursuing Finnish Army. The regional centre of Rovaniemi was almost completely destroyed, due in part to the fighting and the explosion of a German munitions train but also to the German troops' systematic demolition, building by building, on Rendulic's orders as an act of revenge for the Finnish Army's attacks on the retreating Germans.

With the possibility of a retreat to the Gulf of Bothnia blocked by advancing Finnish troops, three escape routes remained open to the Germans. First, they might withdraw from Rovaniemi to Muonio in north-western Finland and further up the Torne Valley along the Swedish border directly to the Lyngen Line in Norway. Second, the Germans might pull back from Rovaniemi in a north-easterly direction to Ivalo and from there across the Norwegian border to Lakselv and the *Reichsstrasse 50*. Third, they might continue northeast from Ivalo along the *Eismeerstrasse* towards Kirkenes or into the positions of the XIX Mountain Corps. In the event, parts of the XVIII Mountain Corps followed the Rovaniemi-Munio-Lyngen passage, while the XXXVI Mountain Corps retreated partly along the highway from Ivalo to Lakselv and partly along the final stretch of the *Eismeeerstrasse* towards the Kirkenes-Petsamo area. By late November, most of the German forces had withdrawn to Norway, and the fighting between the former brothers-in-arms subsided. See Fig. 2.2.

[29] For an in-depth analysis of the planning process that culminated in the Karelian Front's offensive against the German XIX Mountain Corps on 7 October 1944, including Meretskov's repeated proposals for operations that contravened the 4–5 September 1944 ceasefire conditions, see Holtsmark 2021a, b.

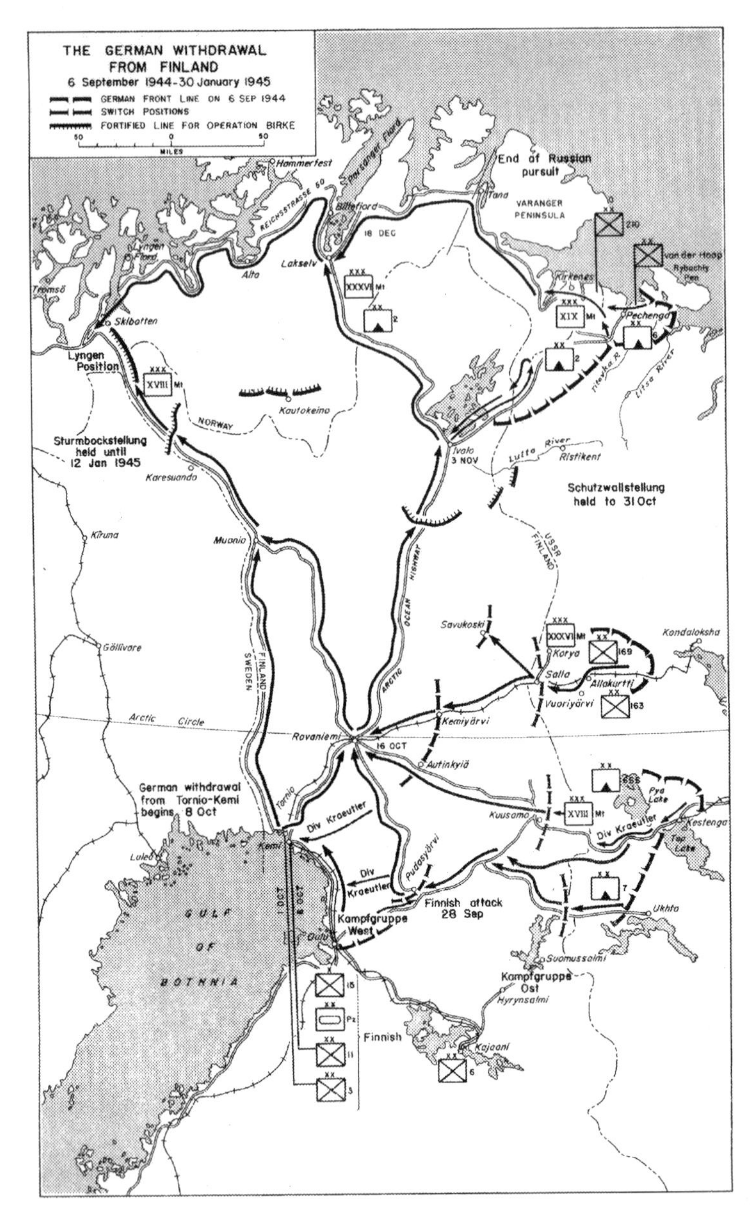

Fig. 2.2 This map shows the approximate front lines of 20th Mountain Army units as of 6 September 1944, and their retreat routes to the Lyngen position in Northern Norway. It also depicts intermediary defensive lines, as well as fortified positions that German forces prepared and then abandoned successively during their withdrawal: *Schutzwallstellung* on both sides of the Arctic Ocean Road to the south and southeast of Ivalo, fortifications in the area of Kautokeino, the *Sturmbockstellung* on Finnish territory in front of the Lyngen Line (abandoned in January 1945), and finally the Lyngen position itself. Included are corps (XXX) and divisions (XX). *Source* Ziemke 1959

2.7 October–November 1944: The Petsamo-Kirkenes Operation

Birke stipulated that the XIX Mountain Corps should remain in its position on Soviet territory and included setting up defensive positions on Finnish territory further to the south. *Birke* was not least predicated on the continued role of supplies of nickel ore and matte from the Kolosjoki production site for the German war effort. In late September, however, Albert Speer, Germany's minister of armaments, reported to Hitler that Germany had accumulated supplies of nickel large enough to make deliveries from the Petsamo complex redundant. Consequently, *Birke* was changed to *Nordlicht*: the entire 20th Mountain Army, i.e., including the XIX Mountain Corps, was ordered to withdraw to positions behind the Lyngen Line.[30] In other words, and contrary to Soviet presumption, not only the Petsamo-Kirkenes area but all of Northern Norway east of the Lyngen fjord was also to be abandoned.

These developments were unbeknown to Stalin, his *Stavka*,[31] and Meretskov, Commander of the Karelian Front: they based their planning on the presumption that the Germans would make every effort to remain in control over Petsamo and the Kolosjoki nickel production site, and therefore also over Kirkenes and the rest of Northern Norway. Indeed, it was on this basis that Meretskov planned an operation by the numerically superior forces of Shcherbakov's 14th Army to attack, encircle, and then destroy or capture major parts of the XIX Mountain Corps while it was still on Soviet territory.[32]

The Soviet offensive on the Murmansk sector can be quickly summarised: on 7 October 1944, the 14th Army launched its long-awaited offensive against the XIX Mountain Corps. On 15 October, Soviet soldiers seized control over Petsamo, by then Soviet Pechenga, which was the declared aim of the first part of the offensive. On 18 October, a Soviet battalion crossed the Norwegian border and, on 25 October, Soviet soldiers moved into the abandoned ruins of Kirkenes. Soviet detachments continued westwards to the Tana River some 150 km to the west from Kirkenes, where they took up defensive positions.

The Karelian Front was then disbanded, with its units transferred to other Fronts. There was one exception in this regard. Now partly stationed in Norway, the 14th Army was made "independent"—i.e., directly subordinated to the General Staff and Stalin's *Stavka*—reflecting its detachment from the continued fighting on other sectors of the vast Eastern Front. In the remaining months of the war, the Soviet military presence in Norway was reduced from 45,600 immediately after the end of the fighting in early November 1944 to approximately 35,000 by the end of the year, and to 6,000 at the time of Germany's capitulation in May 1945.[33]

---

[30] About the change from *Birke* to *Nordlicht*, see Ziemke 1959, pp 300ff.

[31] About *Stavka*, see Chap. 3, Sect. 3.2, n. 20.

[32] See Holtsmark 2021b. As a result of the 19 September 1944 Soviet-Finnish ceasefire agreement, the area between Murmansk and the Norwegian border belonged to the Soviet Union.

[33] Thanks to Rune Rautio who has calculated and provided us with these numbers based on his detailed study of Red Army archival sources.

Rendulic's order for the forced evacuation was dated 29 October 1944—four days after the Red Army had taken control over Kirkenes yet more than one week before the Soviet and German troops fought for the last time as the last German soldiers crossed the Tana River. Soviet planning and the Germans' evaluation of Soviet intentions (and those of the Western Allies) as the events developed will be analysed in Chap. 3.[34] Suffice it to note here that, in late October, the Germans had no reliable information about Soviet plans. Would the 14th Army remain behind Tana River, or would Shcherbakov regroup, resupply, and rest his troops before continuing the offensive in pursuit of the retreating Germans? Would the Soviets or their Western Allies launch landing operations or otherwise obstruct the withdrawal of German troops along the only road connecting eastern Finnmark to Lyngen-Skibotn and Narvik?

With no conclusive knowledge about Soviet intentions, Rendulic and his superiors had no choice but to take into account the possibility of new Western Allied or Soviet attacks in Norway. This, however, does not necessarily provide a reasonable justification for the *scale* of what followed in the wake of the 29 October order—namely, the total destruction of parts of Northern Norway and the attempted forced evacuation of the entire population in the same areas. Did factors other than purely military consideration fuel such extreme measures? How might German perceptions of Allied options and plans have changed as weeks passed and no Soviet offensive or Western naval landing materialised? These issues are discussed in Chaps. 3 and 4.[35]

2.8 Brief Note on Historiography

The first scholarly discussion in English of the military operations that provided the immediate background for Rendulic's order of 29 October 1944 is Ziemke 1959, published as part of the (then) US Army Historical Division's series of works on German operational history during the Second World War. The book's chapter 14 ("The undefeated army") contains a valuable overview of operations in Northern Scandinavia in 1944–1945, including a concise presentation of operation *Nordlicht* and its predecessor *Birke*.[36] In 1989, James F. Gebhardt of the US Army Command and General Staff College published a monograph entitled *The Petsamo Kirkenes*

[34] See Chap. 3.

[35] See Chaps. 3 and 4.

[36] Ziemke 1959, pp 292–314. Earl F. Ziemke was a historian born in the United States. He had fought in the Pacific during the Second World War and received his PhD from the University of Wisconsin. He had been employed by the US Historical Division only in 1955 and had no links to former German Army Chief of Staff General Franz Halder or the former *Wehrmacht* establishment that strongly influenced the post-war writing of German campaign histories within the US Army Historical Division (today's US Army Center for Military History). As part of this, Halder contributed to the creation of the myth of the "clean" *Wehrmacht* that was widespread in historical narratives until the 1990s.

Operation: Soviet Breakthrough and Pursuit in the Arctic, October 1944[37]—a work that tells the story of the Soviet offensive from 7 October 1944 that forced the 20th Mountain Army's XIX Mountain Corps from its positions on Soviet territory back into Norway. Gebhard based his work mainly on Soviet memoirs and military-historical publications. Ziemke's and Gebhardt's works remain valuable as operational histories, although Gebhardt's work has been supplemented by more recent studies that make use of Red Army archival sources that became progressively available in Russian document collections after the demise of the Soviet Union and have since 2015 been extensively and easily available on the Russian Ministry of Defence-affiliated website *Pamyat naroda.*[38]

Neither of these two works, however, discusses the 20th Mountain Army's scorched earth policy in Norway (and Finland). The same is true for other English-language books on the Second World War in Norway and Scandinavia.[39] However, Lund 1947 provides an excellent overview of socio-economic conditions in the area and basic data on the repercussions of the Germans' actions, backed up by some moving photos, among them of sites in Finnmark and Troms before and after the destruction.[40] Hunt 2014 brings vivid stories of eyewitnesses and contains some valuable illustrations.[41]

There is a voluminous Russian-language literature on the war in the north, including the final offensive in October–November 1944—the *Petsamo-Kirkenesskaya nastupatel'naya operatsiya*, the "Petsamo-Kirkenes Offensive Operation". Meretskov and Shcherbakov both presented their versions in memoirs,[42] and numerous monographs and anthologies deal with aspects of the military operations in the area of operation of Shcherbakov's 14th Army. These and other Soviet and Russian works are crucial for the understanding of Soviet perceptions and the background of Soviet decisions that became decisive for the Germans' conduct of the war and occupation policy in Northern Norway. They do not, however, discuss German decision-making or otherwise contribute to our understanding of the Germans' implementation of the scorched earth policy and forced evacuation of the civilian population that followed Rendulic's order of 29 October 1944.[43]

Additional relevant literature is available in German, starting with the memoirs of participants such as Rendulic himself,[44] his Chief of Staff Hermann Hölter[45] and the

---

[37] Gebhardt 1989.

[38] http://www.pamyat-naroda.ru/ [accessed 1 April 2023]. As the Putin regime continues to tighten its authoritarian grip on Russia, it remains to be seen whether this will continue to be the case.

[39] Mentioned briefly in Nissen 1983, pp 306–309 and Andenæs et al. 1996, pp 115–116.

[40] Lund 1947. See also Knudsen 1995.

[41] Hunt 1947. The book is less reliable when it comes to details of the political and military background.

[42] Meretskov 1968, Shcherbakov 1994.

[43] For references to Soviet and Russian sources and literature, see Holtsmark 2021a, b.

[44] Rendulic 1952, 1953.

[45] Hölter 1977.

German liaison officer to the Finnish headquarters, Waldemar Erfurth.[46] These and some other related works are discussed in Chap. 3.[47] They are all unconditionally apologetic about the German conduct of war, including the destruction of Northern Finland and parts of Northern Norway, while at the same time presenting pieces of useful information about tactical and operational issues. Roland Kaltenegger[48] and F. W. Thorban[49] have written operational histories, from the German perspective, that are useful supplements to Ziemke's more overarching narrative.

Among scholarly works in German, the place to start is Frieser et al. 2007, which covers the Eastern Front and the *Nebenfronten*—the side theatres—1943–1944. Bernd Wegner's chapter (Wegner 2007) starts with an overview of the political and military events that culminated in the Finnish-Soviet ceasefire of 4–5 September 1944. It tells the story of the fighting between German and Finnish troops in Northern Finland, including the German destruction of Finnish civilian infrastructure, not least in Rovaniemi, and the evacuation of a large part of the population to Sweden. In the author's evaluation, the Germans' scorched earth policy "clearly" (*ganz offenkundig*) went beyond military necessity.[50] The discussion of similar events in Norway, including the forced evacuation of the civilian population, covers key events and statistics. Unlike his discussion of the preceding events in Northern Finland, however, the author does not evaluate the German policy's rationality or reasonableness as measures of alleged military necessity.[51]

Two texts from the 1990s introduced key issues and sources that remain relevant: the first is Bohn 1995, a chapter in an anthology about the year 1944 in the war in Europe. It focuses on political developments that are comprehensively covered in Bernd Wegner's book chapter discussed above.[52] The second text is the still eminently readable book chapter by Lang 1995.[53] It covers many of the issues that remain prominent in public and academic debates about the events in Northern Norway of 1944–1945 up to this day. Among these are the different views and evaluations of Allied options and intentions not only between civilian and military German authorities in Norway, but also between the *Wehrmachtsbefehlshaber Norwegen* in Oslo, von Falkenhorst, and Rendulic, as well as between Rendulic and the Commander of the XIX Mountain Corps, Ferdinand Jodl. These differences notwithstanding, all involved agreed, according to Lang, on one thing: "the desire to avert the feared

[46] Erfurth 1977. The book contains numerous factual mistakes, among them the surprising statement that Soviet forces did not cross the Norwegian border (pp 311–312, 323).

[47] See Chap. 3.

[48] Kaltenegger 2003.

[49] Thorban 1989.

[50] Frieser et al. 2007, pp 998–1000.

[51] Ibid., pp 1001–1003.

[52] Bohn 1995. At the end of Bohn's text are some plainly wrong statements about Soviet annexationist ambitions in Norway.

[53] Lang 1995.

events by appropriate military measures which prevented the Soviet forces from moving into the territory of northern Norway".[54]

This may have been so at least at the time of the Soviet offensive from 7 October and the move into Norway that followed on 18 October. The question remains, however, of how Rendulic's evaluation of the situation evolved as weeks passed without the feared Soviet or Western Allied offensives or landings materialising. Moreover, even if the German authorities in Norway agreed about the need to prepare for possible Allied attacks, this does not mean that there was a reasonable proportionality between, on the one hand, the nature and scope of possible enemy moves as the Germans perceived them and, on the other hand, the comprehensiveness and geographic extent of the systematic destruction of an entire region as a consequence of Rendulic's order to his subordinate troops on 29 October 1944.[55] Nor is there a necessary link between the existence of such scenarios of enemy threats and the order to evacuate by force the entire population of the region.[56] These are some of the issues that will appear as key elements in discussions in this anthology of the US military tribunal's "not guilty" verdict in *Hostage*.[57]

Unsurprisingly, there is a rich and varied literature in Norwegian about the dramatic events in Northern Norway. It is much too voluminous to be adequately summarised here. However, the task was made easier by the appearance in 2022 of the first comprehensive history of the Second World War in Northern Norway, the three-volume publication by Fagertun 2022a. One of the volumes, Fagertun 2022b, focuses on the last stages of the war, including the start of the liberation in Eastern Finnmark in October 1944 and the devastation and forced evacuation in Finnmark and Troms counties that followed.[58] The volume incorporates and summarises discussions and knowledge from previous works. Moreover, Elstad 2020 covers the forced evacuation comprehensively in range and depth, including detailed treatment of issues that were absent or scarcely covered in earlier literature.[59] These two major works should be supplemented by a two-volume collection of participants' reminiscences that appeared as early as 1949–1950.[60] The two volumes contain highly illustrative and often moving photos of localities, the victims, and the perpetrators, making it worthwhile to look at even for those without knowledge of Norwegian.

[54] Lang 1995, p 29: "Die unterschiedlichen Motivlagen aller genannten Beteiligten—deutsche zivile (Reichskommissar Terboven) und deutsche militärische Seite [...] sowie die norwegische 'nationale Regierung'—trafen sich in einem Punkt: dem Wunsch, die befürchteten Ereignisse durch geeignete militärische Massnahmen abzuwenden, die verhinderte, dass die sowjetischen Kräfte auf das nordnorwegische Gebiet nachfolgten".

[55] See Chap. 3.

[56] See Chap. 4.

[57] See Chap. 5.

[58] Bones 2022.

[59] Elstad 2020.

[60] Hellesnes 1949, 1950.

References

Andenæs J, Riste O, Skodvin M (1996) Norway and the Second World War, 5th edn. Aschehoug, Oslo
Best G (1994) War and Law Since 1945. Clarendon Press, New York
Bill BJ (2012) The Rendulic "Rule": military necessity, commander's knowledge, and methods of warfare. Yearbook of International Humanitarian Law 12:119–155
Bohn R (1995) Der Rückzug am Eismeer und die Zerstörung der Norkalotte. In: Salewski M, Schulze-Wegener G (eds) Kriegsjahr 1944. Im Grossen und im Kleinen. Franz Steiner Verlag, Stuttgart, pp 105–124
Bones S (ed) (2022) Kampen for frihet [Fighting for freedom]. Volume 3 of Fagertun F (ed) Andre verdenskrig i nord [The Second World War in the North]. Orkana Akademisk, Stamsund
Dahl HF (1999) Quisling. A Study in Treachery. Cambridge University Press, Cambridge
Elstad I (2020) Tvangsevakueringa [The Forced Evacuation]. Orkana Akademisk, Stamsund
Erfurth W (1977) Der finnische Krieg. Limes Verlag, Wiesbaden
Fagertun F (ed) (2022a) Andre verdenskrig i nord [The Second World War in the North]. 3 volumes. Orkana Akademisk, Stamsund
Fagertun F (ed) (2022b) Kampen for frihet [The Struggle for Freedom], Volume 1 of Andre verdenskrig i nord [The Second World War in the North]. Orkana Akademisk, Stamsund
Frieser K-H et al (2007) Das Deutsche Reich und der Zweite Weltkrieg. Band 8: Die Ostfront 1943/44. Der Krieg im Osten und an den Nebenfronten. Deutsche Verlags-Anstalt (DVA), Munich
Gebhardt JF (1989) The Petsamo Kirkenes Operation: Soviet Breakthrough and Pursuit in the Arctic, October 1944. US Army Command and General Staff College, Fort Leavenworth
Haarr GH (2010) The Battle for Norway, April–June 1940. Seaforth Publishing, Barnsley
Haarr GH (2011) The German Invasion of Norway, April 1940. Seaforth Publishing, Barnsley
Hausser P (1966) Soldaten wie andere auch: Der Weg der Waffen-SS. Munin-Verlag, Osnabrück
Hellesnes BR (ed) (1949) Finnmark i flammer. Fortalt av den brente jords egne kvinner og menn. Vol 1. Bruns bokhandels forlag, Trondheim
Hellesnes BR (ed) (1950) Finnmark i flammer. Fortalt av den brente jords egne kvinner og menn. Vol 2. Eget forlag, Kragerø
Hetland Ø, Karcher N, Simonsen KB (2021) Navigating troubled waters: collaboration and resistance in state institutions in Nazi-occupied Norway. Scandinavian Journal of History, 46:84–104. DOI: https://doi.org/10.1080/03468755.2020.1846075
Holtsmark SG (2021a) Improvised Liberation, October 1944: The Petsamo-Kirkenes Operation and the Red Army in Norway. Part I. The Journal of Slavic Military Studies 34:271–302. DOI: https://doi.org/10.1080/13518046.2021.1990554
Holtsmark SG (2021b) Improvised Liberation, October 1944: The Petsamo-Kirkenes Operation and the Red Army in Norway. Part II. The Journal of Slavic Military Studies 34:426–458. DOI: https://doi.org/10.1080/13518046.2021.1992707
Holtsmark SG, Petrov PD (2020) Den sovjetiske Nordflåtens operasjonsplaner (1939–1940). In: Septentrio Reports, No. 6. UiT The Arctic University of Norway, Tromsø. DOI: https://doi.org/10.7557/7.5617
Hölter H (1977) Armee in der Arktis. Die Operationen der deutschen Lappland-Armee. Schild Verlag, Munich
Hunt V (2014) Fire and Ice. The Nazi's Scorched Earth Campaign in Norway. The History Press, Stroud
Jonas M (2012) The politics of an alliance. Finland in Nazi foreign policy and war strategy. In: Kinnunen T, Kivimäki V (eds) Finland in World War II: History, Memory, Interpretations. Brill, Leiden
Kaltenegger R (2003) Krieg in der Arktis. Die Operationen der Lappland-Armee 1942–1945. Graz–Leopold Stocker Verlag, Stuttgart
Kinnunen T, Kivimäki V (eds) (2012) Finland in World War II: History, Memory, Interpretations. Brill, Leiden

Knudsen AM (1995) Refugees in Their Own Country. Alta Museum, Alta
Lang A (1995) "Operation Nordlicht". Die Zerstörung Nordnorwegens durch deutsche Truppen beim Rückzug aus Finnland im Spätjahr 1944. In: Bohn R, Elvert J (eds) Kriegsende im Norden. Franz Steiner Verlag, Stuttgart
Linna V (1954) Tuntematon sotilas (Unknown soldier). WSOY, Helsinki
Lund DH (1947) The Revival of Northern Norway. The Geographical Journal 109:185–197
Mann C (2012) British Policy and Strategy towards Norway, 1941–45. Palgrave Macmillan, Basingstoke
Meinander H (2023) Mannerheim, Marshal of Finland: A Life in Geopolitics. C Hurst & Co Publishers Ltd, London
Meretskov KA (1968) Na sluzhbe narodu. Stranitsy vospominanii. Politizdat, Moscow
Müller R-D (2012) Hitlers Wehrmacht 1935 bis 1945. Oldenbourg Verlag, Munich
Nehlin A (2017) Building Bridges of Trust: Child Transports from Finland to Sweden during the Second World War. War & Society 36:133–153
Nissen HS (1983) Scandinavia in the Second World War. Universitetsforlaget, Oslo/Bergen/Tromsø
Rendulic L (1952) Gekämpft, gesiegt, geschlagen. Welsermühl, Heidelberg
Rendulic L (1953) Glasenbach-Nürnberg-Landsberg. Ein Soldatenschicksal nach dem Krieg. Leopold Stocker Verlag, Graz/Göttingen
Riste O (2001) Norway's Foreign Policy: A History. Universitetsforlaget, Oslo
Rowe L (2021) Industry, War and Stalin's Battle for Resources. I.B. Tauris, London
Shcherbakov VI (1994) Zapolar'ye – sud'ba moya. Knizhnoe izdatel'stvo, Murmansk
Streit C (1997) Keine Kameraden, new edn. Verlag J.H.W. Dietz Nachf., Bonn
Thorban FW (1989) Der Abwehrkampf um Petsamo und Kirkenes 1944. Operationen "Birke" und "Nordlicht": Die letzte Schlacht an der Eismeerfront im Oktober 1944 – Die Absetzbewegungen nach Nordnorwegen und das Kriegsende im Raum Lyngen-Narvik. Podzun Pallas Verlag, Friedberg
Wegner B (2007) Das Kriegsende in Skandinavien. In: Frieser K-H et al (authors) Das Deutsche Reich und der Zweite Weltkrieg. Band 8: Die Ostfront 1943/44. Der Krieg im Osten und an den Nebenfronten. Deutsche Verlags-Anstalt (DVA), Munich
Ziemke EF (1959) The German Northern Theater of Operations 1940–1945. Department of the Army, Washington D.C.

Sven G. Holtsmark Professor of History, Norwegian Institute for Defence Studies, Norwegian Defence University College. Address: Oslo 0150, Akershus Fortress, Norway, e-mail: sholtsmark@mil.no

Gunnar Åselius Professor of Military History, Swedish Defence University. He is a member of the Swedish Royal Society of Naval Sciences and the Royal Academy of War Science, e-mail: gunnar.aselius@fhs.se

Chapter 3
Rendulic and the Military Necessity Defence in *Hostage*: Did He Speak the Truth?

Sven G. Holtsmark

Contents

3.1 Introduction 48
3.2 Rendulic's *Post Factum* Narratives 51
3.3 View from the *Oberkommando der Wehrmacht* and the *Wehrmachtführungsstab* 54
3.4 The 20th Mountain Army and the *Wehrmachtsbefehlshaber Norwegen* 57
3.5 Allied Planning and Options—Naval Landings? 67
3.6 Allied Planning and Options—The Red Army 69
3.6.1 A Soviet Offensive from the Tana Positions? 70
3.6.2 A Soviet Offensive Over Finnish or Swedish Territory Towards Troms County? 72
3.7 Concluding Remarks 76
References 78

Abstract This chapter starts with General Lothar Rendulic's contemporaneous view of possible Western Allied and Soviet operations against the 20th Mountain Army during its retreat from positions in the Litsa sector and others in Northern Russia and those in Northern Finland and, from November 1944, Eastern Finnmark. The chapter compares the German threat perceptions about their enemies' intentions to Soviet and Western Allied planning as it actually developed. When Rendulic claimed before the tribunal that he saw Soviet and/or Western attacks in Northern Norway at the time as not only possible or even likely, but also as a major threat to his Army, was he telling the truth? As regards the Allies, the chapter focusses on the planning and operations of the Red Army's Karelian Front that culminated in the 14th Army offensive on the Murmansk sector in October-November. What were the Soviet intentions after the offensive came to a halt in early November? The chapter also summarises the Western Allies' thinking about landing operations in Norway during the same period. The chapter's main conclusion is that Rendulic's courtroom version of his thinking from autumn 1944 to early 1945 about possible Western Allied or Soviet operations in Northern Norway largely corresponds to his

---

S. G. Holtsmark (✉)
Norwegian Institute for Defence Studies, Norwegian Defence University College, 0150 Oslo, Akershus Fortress, Norway
e-mail: sholtsmark@mil.no

N. Hayashi and C. Lingaas (eds.), *Honest Errors? Combat Decision-Making 75 Years After the* Hostage *Case*, https://doi.org/10.1007/978-94-6265-611-6_3

contemporaneous thinking as it can be reconstructed from German archival sources. We know in hindsight that his evaluation of Western Allied and Soviet thinking was wrong, but there was nothing unreasonable in his expectation that the Western Allies or the Soviets would launch operations against his retreating Army.

Keywords Lothar Rendulic · *Hostage* Case · Northern Norway 1944 · scorched earth policy in Northern Norway · Petsamo-Kirkenes Operation · Kirill A. Meretskov · 20th Mountain Army (*Wehrmacht*) · 14th Army (Red Army) · Karelian Front (Red Army)

3.1 Introduction

General Lothar Rendulic's successful defence in *Hostage* against the charges related to Northern Norway was based on the premise that the orders for the destruction of infrastructure in Finnmark and part of Troms county, and to evacuate the civilian population by force, were grounded in military necessity—the need to create obstacles to possible Allied moves to attack or cut off the retreat of the 20th Mountain Army and, after the retreat was completed, to launch offensives against the remaining German positions in Northern Norway. Among the options he described before the US military tribunal were a range of Soviet land-based offensives and Soviet or other Allied naval landing operations. The tribunal took him at his word and concluded that the orders he issued were based on credible scenarios that made military sense. Thus, they were within the remit of military necessity as that term was understood at the time in international law.[1] Rendulic was wrong in his evaluation of Allied plans, but it was an *honest error*, and his judgments were reasonable.[2] He was acquitted of the charges in the indictment related to Northern Norway.

Thus, for the verdict it was irrelevant what Soviet or Western Allied plans actually did exist at the time: Rendulic's retelling of his subjective perception in 1944 and early 1945 of Allied options and the ensuing danger to his Army was accepted by the judges as credible and true. The tribunal accepted Rendulic's account of his state of mind when he issued the crucial orders. It applied the same logic to both elements of the charges related to Northern Norway—Rendulic's orders to destroy all infrastructure and his orders to evacuate the population by force.

This chapter's aim is twofold. First, it endeavours to establish Rendulic's contemporaneous view from October 1944 to early 1945 of Soviet and Western Allied options and intentions in Northern Norway; more precisely the possibility and likelihood of both land-based offensives and naval landing operations in the areas under his command.

---

[1] See Chap. 6 for a discussion of the tribunal's adjudications and findings.

[2] For an in-depth discussion of the term "reasonable" in the case of a military commander's decisions and the need for a mistaken decision to be *both* honest and reasonable in order to excuse the commander of its consequences, see Chap. 8 and, from a slightly different perspective, Chap. 10.

When Rendulic claimed before the tribunal that he did at the time see Soviet and/or Western attacks in Northern Norway as not only possible or even likely, but also as a major threat to his Army, was he telling the truth? If it can be proven that the opposite was the case, i.e., that at the time he saw no real threat to the territories under his command, there would be no *military* necessity for a scorched earth policy or to evacuate the population by force. Such a finding would soundly undermine the basis for Rendulic's acquittal in 1948. From a German perspective, there could have been solid *political* grounds for scorching Northern Norway,[3] but these would certainly not have served Rendulic's defence at trial.

Second, this chapter discusses Soviet and Western Allied plans or intentions, or the absence of such as the case may be, for land and naval operations against German-held territory in Northern Norway from October 1944 onwards when the region's destruction and forced evacuation was ordered and then carried out.[4] One major focus is on aspects of the planning and operations of the Red Army's Karelian Front that culminated in the 14th Army offensive on the Murmansk sector in October–November. Also, what were the Soviets' intentions after the offensive came to a halt in early November? This discussion follows a brief summary of the Western Allies' thinking about landing operations in Norway during the same period.

Knowledge of Soviet and Western Allied thinking and planning as they actually developed may indicate something about the accuracy of German perceptions of the same issues. Such a comparison is, in itself, of historical interest.

The chapter begins by summarising key points in Rendulic's version of his perception of Allied intentions, as he presented them before the tribunal in Nuremberg and subsequently in his various memoirs. Next, this chapter reconstructs German thinking, starting in October 1944, about possible Soviet and Western Allied moves against Northern Norway and the 20th Mountain Army.

Of relevance here are events and evaluations as recorded during the war in the relevant volume of the *Kriegstagebuch des Oberkommandos der Wehrmacht* (War Diary of the Wehrmacht High Command, hereafter *KTB des OKW*), i.e., events as recorded at the highest German command level. The *KTB des OKW* presents a narrative of major military developments based on contemporaneous documents, including, to some degree, oral information from key decision makers. Organised according to theatres of war or major operations, the *Kriegstagebuch* includes a section on the "northern theatre of war (Finland, Norway, Denmark)".[5] As was often the case with war diaries and battle journals at lower levels in both German and Soviet military formations, the text was compiled at intervals after the events described, which may have affected how it represented these events.[6]

---

[3] See Chap. 4.

[4] This part is based on existing literature, including the recently published two-part study of Soviet decision-making prior to the entry into Norway on 18 October 1944. See Holtsmark 2021b, c.

[5] "Der nördliche Kriegsschauplatz (Finnland, Norwegen, Dänemark)". The translation of this phrase and, unless otherwise stated, all following translations from German and Russian are my own.

[6] Schramm 1961. In the first part of the volume there is an explanation of how the *Kriegstagebuch* was compiled, rescued from destruction and finally prepared for publication. It is not a diary in the

The most extensive part of the chapter brings German archival sources into the discussion. These materials speak directly about the views and information that there is reason to believe were brought to the attention of Rendulic himself, or at least were available to him, as he made his decisions and issued the crucial orders that formed the basis for the prosecution's case at the tribunal.

This chapter does not discuss the German rationale for the *scale* of the destruction or the forced evacuation, or *how* these measures were carried out. It is rather concerned with what formed the basis of Rendulic's defence strategy. As will be seen below, in the crucial weeks when the destruction and forced evacuation were ordered and then implemented, it was reasonable to assume that the Soviets could launch offensive land operations against the 20th Mountain Army during its retreat to the Lyngen positions. There was also the possibility that the Soviets could attack the Lyngen positions themselves from Finnish or Swedish territory. The Germans also imagined that the Western Allies (possibly including Norwegian forces), independently or in cooperation with the Soviets, could launch landing operations to obstruct the 20th Mountain Army's retreat or possibly even to take and hold Norwegian territory.

Nor does this chapter attempt to give a definite answer as to who was actually behind, and what was the rational for, Hitler's crucial order of 28 October 1944, which led to Rendulic's own order the following day[7] (and to subsequent decisions and orders).[8] Suffice it to mention here that Hitler's order was the direct result of an appeal from *Reichskommissar* Josef Terboven to Martin Bormann, leader of the German Nazi Party (*Nationalsozialistische Deutsche Arbeiterpartei*, NSDAP) secretariat and effectively Hitler's private secretary, bypassing the military chain of command. In other words, it was not *Wehrmachtsbefehlshaber Norwegen* (*WBH Norwegen*) Nikolaus von Falkenhorst or Rendulic himself who at that crucial moment argued the need for this extreme version of destruction and evacuation, as one would expect if the rationale behind Hitler's order was strictly military.

Moreover, although the *Oberkommando der Wehrmacht* (*OKW*) with its core staff element *Wehrmachtführungsstab* (*WFStab*) used arguments of military necessity when instructing Rendulic and the order's other recipients, Hitler's 28 October order linked the forced evacuation to a very different alleged concern. Evacuation was supposedly "in the interest of the safety of the population" ("*im Interesse der Sicherheit der Bevölkerung*") that had proved "unwilling" to follow appeals to evacuate voluntarily.[9]

literal sense of that word, but a compilation of thematic chapters each composed after the events described on the basis of available documents.

[7] Rendulic's order of 29 October 1944, National Archives and Records Administration, Washington D.C. (hereafter NARA), PG 65635/8, microfilm T 312-1063, pp 340–342. I am indebted to Kjetil Korsnes who generously put at my disposal his extensive and systematic digitalized collection of German military sources related to the occupation of Norway 1940–1945.

[8] This is discussed in detail in Chap. 4.

[9] OKW (*Fernschreiben*) of 28 October to AOK 20 as main recipient. Translated from tribunal document 754-PS, prosecution's Exhibit 503, kindly provided to the author by the Harvard Law School Library. My translation differs slightly from the translation used at the tribunal.

In a message to Borman dated 16 November 1944, Alfred Jodl, chief of the *WFStab*, emphasised that the *WFStab*'s original recommendation had been a *partial* destruction and evacuation, which had then been changed into *total* as the result of Terboven's intervention. This notwithstanding, Jodl insisted that the measures as previously ordered should be fully carried out, now allegedly for military reasons:

> Through the evacuation of the population and the destruction of all man-made constructions in North Norway, the enemy will for a longer time be deprived of the preconditions for a rapid advance in the Polar regions and of attacks on our still unfinished final positions. For these military reasons is it necessary to stick to the ordered measures in North Norway.[10]

Such inconsistencies in the German decision-makers' alleged motives may reflect a deeper issue. It may be misguided to look for a clear divide between "military necessity" and other reasons behind the forced evacuation and the destruction of Finnmark and parts of Troms county in 1944–1945. German warfare in World War II cannot be understood in strictly military terms. Rather, it was permeated to the core by ideology. This is most clearly seen on the Eastern Front and in the Balkans, where the *Wehrmacht* and SS formations fought against "racially inferior" peoples. Rendulic, an ardent Nazi, had in his previous commands fully demonstrated the gruesome nature of Nazi Germany's understanding of "military necessity"—as was richly documented during the tribunal procedures in Nuremberg. Thus, we may presume that two sets of motives coexisted—a "rational" one based on military necessity in a traditional sense that could be related to the rules of war in international law, and the other grounded in a mixture of political, ideological, and emotive impulses.

3.2 Rendulic's *Post Factum* Narratives

At the US military tribunal in Nuremberg, Rendulic emphasised two factors that allegedly influenced his decision-making after the start of the Soviet 14th Army's offensive on the Murmansk sector on 7 October 1944. One was the Soviets' ability to make full use of their numerical superiority despite "the barely negotiable terrain". The other was the order he received to transfer four of his "best" divisions to the continent—more than half of his army, meaning a significant reduction of the 20th Mountain Army's fighting strength.[11] In other words, he evaluated the Red Army to be able to conduct offensive operations against the 20th Mountain Army.

[10] "Durch die Evakuierung der Bevölkerung und Zerstörung aller Kunstbauten in Nordnorwegen werden dem Gegner für längere Zeit die Voraussetzungen für ein schnelles Nachfolgen im Polargebiet und Angriffe gegen unsere noch unfertigen Endstellungen genommen. Aus diesen militärischen Gründen muss an den befehlenen Massnahmen in Nordnorwegen festgehalten werden". Here quoted from the facsimile in Korsnes 2021, with reference to NARA, OKW 138/1, microfilm T 77-1419.

[11] "The four best Mountain Divisions were to be sent to the Continent, which meant more than half of the strength of the Army", as stated by Rendulic to the tribunal on 30 October 1947. When not otherwise stated, quotes, and references to the tribunal are retrieved online from the Harvard Law School Nuremberg Trials Project (hereafter HLSNTP undated), p 5335.

Rendulic made no attempt to distance himself from the order to destroy. Destruction was a necessary measure that he allegedly would have taken even without Hitler's order of 28 October:

> the quarters that would have become available [after the inhabitants had been evacuated], the highways which existed, all bridges and harbour installations, and everything else – would have been destroyed. The necessity of these measures was never doubted for a single instant by anybody.[12]

As regards the locals, however, his intention prior to the 28 October order had been to "concentrate" them in a "tolerable area of living space" with "necessary sanitary installations".[13] His statements were somewhat ambiguous: while suggesting that he did not think that "it was absolutely necessary to transfer the population to other areas", he could not "close his eyes" to "Hitler's reasons of military necessity". Having added some allegedly humanitarian considerations, he concluded that "in the final analysis it was the best thing for the population that they were removed".[14] Nevertheless, Rendulic's statement at the tribunal gave the impression that the forced evacuation, as it was ordered and carried out, was *not* grounded in his considerations of military necessity. He also reverted to the "I had to follow orders" argument: despite identifying himself with the alleged 'military necessity' of the total destruction and forced evacuation, he repeatedly emphasised that he was not in a position to refuse to sign orders that came from Hitler or Terboven and that there was "nothing illegal" in these orders.[15]

As for the Soviet options after the end of the Petsamo-Kirkenes Offensive, Rendulic at trial highlighted the possibility of naval operations with landings along the 20th Mountain Army's retreat (along *Reichsstrasse 50* in Finnmark). This would have saved the Red Army the "strenuous effort" of marching through Finnmark during winter. Such operations "had to be anticipated". The *OKW*, he told the tribunal, also expected landings, "even from the British". According to Rendulic, the Allies had ships available in Murmansk that were needed to transport the troops for such landing operations.

Rendulic "assumed" that it was "towards the latter part of November" that he became convinced that the Red Army would not continue the offensive from their positions at the Tana River. Until then, it had been considered possible that the 14th Army was consolidating and preparing the troops for a new offensive.[16] According to Rendulic, he had weak knowledge about when and how many troops the Soviets removed from the northern areas. However, this was not a decisive factor: "the restricted area in Finnmark" could only accommodate limited forces and "[t]he withdrawal of forces from the Lappland area could not give us any information concerning the real interests of the Russians in Finnmark".[17]

---

[12] Ibid., pp 4335–5336, 30 October 1947.

[13] Ibid., p 5335, 30 October 1947.

[14] Ibid., p 5346, 31 October 1947.

[15] Ibid., p 5357, 31 October 1947.

[16] Ibid., pp 5341–5342, 31 October 1947.

[17] Ibid., p 5343, 31 October 1947.

At trial, Rendulic stated that the evacuation had "for all practical purposes" been carried out by the time when it became clear that the Soviet forces would not launch an offensive from "Northern Finnmark"—presumably from their Tana positions. However, this was only something he "assumed" based on the date of "the report concerning the evacuation", namely 25 November 1944. Moreover, the destruction of southern parts of Finnmark "had to be continued" because "[t]he even more likely operations as of November would have been a landing in Southern Finnmark".[18] He considered a landing at Hammerfest, a "good starting point" of further operations as well as "the best point for supply for troops which had already landed", likely.[19]

In his war memoir (Rendulic 1952), Rendulic unsurprisingly repeated key points of his explanation to the tribunal, including his unambiguous defence of the scorched earth policy and his agreement with Hitler's order to evacuate the entire population by force. From early on, a Soviet attack on the retreating 20th Mountain Army's right flank, including the use of Finnish territory, emerged as a possible, and threatening, scenario in case of a Finnish-Soviet ceasefire. This was just the kind of operation that General Kirill A. Meretskov, Commander of the Karelian Front, proposed to *Stavka* for the first time in early August 1944, and started implementing in early September before *Stavka* ordered him to halt the operation.[20] Regarding the forced evacuation, Rendulic in his memoir underscores his fundamental agreement with Hitler's order ("I considered this order to be absolutely justified"), although he had originally planned for a more limited evacuation.[21]

As in his statements to the tribunal, in his memoir Rendulic emphasised the danger of Soviet landings and possible landing operations by the Western Allies: "There is no doubt that a landing would have been the most effective and dangerous means to obstruct the movement of the Mountain Army. In these areas it would have been very difficult to prevent a landing of stronger forces".[22] The Hammerfest area was seen as particularly suited for Allied landing operations. Hitler, allegedly with this in mind, in mid-October "brought together a large number of submarines at the Norwegian coast".[23] Rendulic further pointed to King Haakon's declaration of 26 October 1944, when the Soviets had taken control of Kirkenes, that allegedly stated "in the near future Norwegian forces will intervene in cooperation with" the Red Army.[24] In truth,

[18] Ibid.

[19] Ibid.

[20] See Sect. 3.6.2 below. *Stavka Verkhovnogo Glavnokomandovaniya* (VGK), i.e., the Supreme Command's Stavka–*Stavka* being an established word for Commands and Head Quarters, used variously in different periods. The Stavka was Stalin's key organ for strategic planning and command during the war.

[21] "Ich habe diesen Befehl für absolut gerechtfertigt gehalten". Rendulic 1952, p 299.

[22] "Eine Landung wäre zweifellos das wirksamste und gefährlichste Mittel gewesen, den Marsch der Gebirgsarmee zu unterbinden. Wir hätten in diesen Gegenden eine Landung stärkerer Kräfte nur schwer verhindern können". Rendulic 1952, p 299.

[23] Hitler "liess eine grössere Zahl von U-Booten an der Küste Norwegens zusammenziehen". Rendulic 1952, p 299.

[24] "dass in Kürze norwegische Kräfte im Zusammenwirken mit russischen eingreifen würden". Rendulic 1952, p 298.

the King did make the point that "Norwegian forces will take part in the operations together with Russian troops" on Norwegian soil, but he made no reference to "in the near future" or additional details; the Norwegian government made a declaration similar to that of the King.[25]

Recapitulating his thinking at the time about why the Soviets never launched a land offensive, Rendulic suggested as possible explanations the difficulties of operating in winter, as well as the destruction of communications and lodgings by his forces. In addition, he had allegedly speculated at the time that Norway might have been considered a British sphere of interest. Harder to explain was the non-materialisation of Soviet or Western Allied landing operations, "as such undertakings would have constituted an extremely great danger to the Mountain Army".[26] A British report from December 1944, relayed by radio and apparently somehow captured by the Germans, allegedly reached the same conclusion—German transfers of troops from Norway to the continent could have been obstructed more effectively by intervening in the north than by attacking German transports further south.[27] The memoir of Lieutenant General Hermann Hölter, Rendulic's Chief of Staff, adds little substance. Hölter was as strongly apologetic about the entire German war enterprise. Hölter presents the region's destruction as a matter of military necessity and its forced evacuation largely as a humanitarian enterprise, which the German troops carried out selflessly and with a deep concern for the wellbeing of the civilian evacuees.[28]

3.3 View from the *Oberkommando der Wehrmacht* and the *Wehrmachtführungsstab*

How does Rendulic's version of his thinking about Soviet and Western options, as presented at the tribunal and in his memoir books, correspond to contemporaneous German sources and, no less importantly, to German preparations on the ground for possible Allied moves?

Starting with the last part of the question, the essence of these preparations is easily summarised: after the change from operation *Birke* to *Nordlicht* in early October 1944, and right up to the final weeks of the war, the Germans prepared to halt a Soviet offensive at the fortifications that were hurriedly being constructed on Finnish and Norwegian territory to block the passage from the east to the Lyngen Fjord area. The *WBH Norwegen*'s orders for the large-scale construction of what has since been

---

[25] Kjære landsmenn 1955, p 153; Holtsmark 1995, document no. 264 (Russian version Komarov et al. 1997).

[26] "als solche Unternehmungen für die Masse der Gebirgsarmee eine ungeheim grosse Gefahr bedeutet hätten". Rendulic 1952, p 309.

[27] Ibid., p 309. In Rendulic 1953, a book about his time as a prisoner-of-war and about the tribunal proceedings, he added an extensive legalistic discussion of the term "military necessity" (militärische Notwendigkeit), but otherwise outlined a similar narrative as in his statements to the tribunal and in the 1952 memoir.

[28] Hölter 1977, pp 71–72.

called the 'Lyngen Line' came in mid-September.[29] The outline of the fortifications was based on the premise that Soviet forces would pass through not only Norwegian and Finnish but possibly even Swedish territory.

The Germans were fully aware of the stipulations in the Finnish-Soviet ceasefire and armistice agreements that Finnish, not Soviet, troops should expel the Germans from Finnish territory. Notwithstanding this, they did not take it for granted that Stalin would honour the agreement and that the Red Army would, under no circumstances, enter Finnish territory as part of an operation against German forces in Norway. If they had felt confident that there was no threat from Finnish territory, the configuration of the German fortification would have been different.

The relevant parts of the *KTB des OKW* discuss at some length the situation in the 20th Mountain Army's area of responsibility, including references to some key documents.[30] As a whole, this narrative corresponds and gives additional credibility to the main elements of Rendulic's statements at trial and in his memoir.

The prospect of naval landing operations, involving the Royal Navy and British, US, and Norwegian troops, to block the retreat of the 20th Mountain Army, possibly in coordination with a Soviet offensive over land, was clearly a major concern. Such operations could be of limited size and yet achieve the aim of taking control over crucial coastal areas, and with that, obstruct German movement. On top of this came the increasing threat to German shipping, mainly from the Royal Navy. In the long term, German supplies to Norway were at risk: as Germany had lost its naval bases in Northern France, Norway would be exposed to increased Allied attention as "the only German sea-strategic position" remaining.[31]

According to the *KTB des OKW*, the details of the 20th Mountain Army's retreat from its position in Finland and the Soviet Union were discussed in a correspondence between the *OKW/WFStab* and the *WBH Norwegen*, von Falkenhorst. Terboven was "asked for his opinion".[32]

The *OKW/WFStab*'s position was as follows:

> The WFStab was of the opinion, that the population had to be evacuated, and it was necessary through destructions to make it impossible for the enemy to gain a foothold in the areas evacuated [by the Army]. It was taken into consideration that it was highly likely that Norwegian forces from England would land, something that had to be seen as dangerous in view of the resistance movement in Norway and Sweden's attitude. This opinion was confirmed by the Norwegian King's declaration of 26.10, according to which, in the near future Norwegian forces in cooperation with Russian would intervene.[33]

---

[29] See several documents in NARA, PG 59412/3, microfilm T 312-1060, among them von Falkenhorst's "Befehl für den Ausbau der Lyngenstellung", 22 September 1944, pp 31–35.

[30] Schramm 1961.

[31] "die einzige deutsche see-strategische Position". See ibid., pp 903–904 about a report of 29 September 1944 on the same topic.

[32] "bei dem auch die Stellungnahme des Reichkommissars für Norwegen eingeholt wurde".

[33] "Der WFStab vertrat dabei den Standpunkt, daß die Bevölkerung evakuiert und durch Zerstörungen es dem Feinde unmöglich gemacht werden müsse, in dem geräumten Gelände Fuß zu fassen. Dabei wurde in Rechnung gestellt, daß aller Voraussicht nach von England aus norwegische

The reality of the German concerns about Soviet or Western landing operations in Northern Norway is confirmed by Hitler's 10 October 1944 order to concentrate "as many submarines as possible" to prevent a Soviet landing attempt. For the same reason, on 19 October, Hitler agreed to leave coastal artillery in place behind the retreating 20th Mountain Army, even though this meant that it might be necessary to destroy the cannons instead of bringing them south for possible re-use.[34] On 27 October, the Chief of the *OKW* issued guidelines for defending against British landing operations and a Soviet move towards Narvik.[35]

On several occasions in November and December 1944, the *Wehrmacht* leadership emphasised the need, allegedly for military reasons, to continue and complete the destruction and evacuation according to Hitler's 28 October order. On 16 November, Alfred Jodl sent a message to Bormann, complaining about what he saw as a lack-lustre performance by the German civilian authorities to carry out the evacuation.[36] However, what in October and early November may have been an *expectation* that the Red Army would continue the offensive, possibly along several axes, gradually turned into a *possible*, albeit increasingly less likely, *scenario*:

> From the evidence that was available by mid-November (cf. 14/11), it appeared unlikely that the Russians would leapfrog German forces with landings along Reichsstrasse 50 or that there would be a larger British operation.
>
> In a situation evaluation as seen from Oslo, the *Wehrmachtsbefehlshaber Norwegen* on 19.11 pointed out, that (as expected) the Russian advance had come to a halt and that forces of the Norwegian government-in-exile and Finns would be used as covering force.[37]

When, on 1 December 1944, von Falkenhorst suggested abandoning "the Front on the Lyngenfjord",[38] the *WFStab* disagreed: a Soviet advance was still a possibility and, therefore, remained a threat to the German flank.[39] The *WFStab* most likely had in mind a Soviet move along the Torne Valley and Finnish-Swedish border to attack the Lyngen position from the east.

In December 1944, the *WFStab* concluded that the Soviet forces had not moved forward from the Tana fjord position. Likewise, the Finns showed no signs of continuing their pursuit of the retreating Germans into Finnmark County or attacking the German fortifications on Finnish territory in front of the Lyngen fortifications—the

---

Kräfte gelandet werden würden, was im Hinblick auf die Haltung Schwedens und die Widerstandsbewegung in Norwegen als gefährlich angesehen werden mußte. Diese Auffassung erhielt ihre Bestätigung durch eine Ankündigung des norwegischen Königs vom 26.10., wonach in Kürze norwegische Kräfte im Zusammenwirken mit russischen eingreifen würden", quoted in Schramm 1961, p 905.

[34] Ibid., pp 908–909. This is in accordance with the 19 October 1944 situation report, discussed below.

[35] Ibid., p 915.

[36] See Sect. 3.1 above.

[37] "Nach den Mitte November (vgl. 14.11) vorliegenden Nachrichten war weder damit zu rechnen, dass im Norden die Russen an der Reichsstrasse 50 überholend landeten, noch dass eine grössere britische Operation folgen würde."

[38] "die Front vor dem Lyngen-Fjord".

[39] Ibid., p 906.

only place where German troops remained on Finnish territory.[40] A British landing was still possible, "although there were no clear indications" that such an operation was in the offing.[41] While various documents and participants evaluated the likelihood of Allied landing operations differently, they all kept open the possibility of such undertakings, although of limited scale.[42]

To summarise: until late 1944, the *OKW/WFStab* took into account the possibility of various combinations of Soviet and UK-led operations against Northern Norway. From early on, a Soviet move from the Tana positions was considered less likely than a Soviet offensive over Finnish and possibly Swedish territory towards the Lyngen-Skibotn area combined with landing operations at Hammerfest or elsewhere. The German military leadership also kept open the possibility of a Soviet move along the Ivalo-Lakselv axis and further along *Reichsstrasse 50* southwards towards Narvik.

3.4 The 20th Mountain Army and the *Wehrmachtsbefehlshaber Norwegen*

What can be said about Rendulic's own contemporaneous evaluations or expectations of possible Soviet and Allied moves? No sources have come to light that directly express his personal views at the time of the events under discussion. However, there are several sources that document the information and evaluation that were brought to his attention as Commander of the 20th Mountain Army and that presumably informed his decisions. These include intelligence and situation reports from within the 20th Mountain Army itself and from other parts of the German military that were involved in operations in Norway or Norwegian waters. There are also instructions Rendulic received from his superiors in the *OKW/WFStab*, as well as documents of the *Wehrmachtsbefehlshaber Norwegen*, von Falkenhorst, in Oslo. Unsurprisingly, messages from the uppermost military leadership correspond to the evaluations discussed above on the basis of the *Kriegstagebuch des Oberkommando der Wehrmacht*.

How the *WBH Norwegen* evaluated the situation after the Soviet-Finnish ceasefire appears clearly from von Falkenhorst's aforementioned "Order for the building of the Lyngen line" dated 22 September 1944. I quote the first two paragraphs of the document in full, as they express a reasoning that became prominent in later reports:

> 1.) The Russian (*Der Russe*) will probably follow sharply the retreat of the 20th (Mountain) Army, in order to take control over North-Norwegian space. Their agent activity in the Narvik area makes it seem possible that they will continue their operations there. The main emphasis of the Russian operation will most likely be on the southern flank along the road Karesuando-Skibotn with the aim to cut off the bulk of the 20th (Mountain) Army as well as parts of the LXXI Army Corps.

[40] Ibid., p 910.

[41] "doch lagen keine greifbaren Anzeichen dafür vor".

[42] See inter alia discussion in ibid., pp 915–916.

> One must take into consideration the possibility that the enemy will use Swedish territory to bypass our forces.

It was also possible that the Soviets would pressure the Swedes into letting their army use Swedish railways to transport troops to the Norwegian border to the east of Narvik.[43] In other documents, however, the *WBH Norwegen* appeared to be less concerned about Soviet (or Western) moves against Northern Norway.

On 6 October 1944, Rendulic received formal orders to carry out operation *Nordlicht*—the withdrawal of the entire 20th Mountain Army, including XIX Corps, to the Lyngen positions or beyond.[44] The four-page document mostly concerns tactical and logistical details, but it also says something about possible enemy action that Rendulic needed to take into account. The first point—a retreat to new defences "in the Lyngenfjord—Narvik area",[45] i.e., behind the fortifications that were being built to repel a Soviet move through Finnish or Swedish territory to attack the Germans in Norway—is obvious. The next point—the use of one division "to defend the Swedish border crossings on both sides of Bjoernsfjeld [Bjørnefjell]"—is less so.[46] The latter shows that the Germans took into account the possibility of attacks from Swedish territory either by Soviet troops or by a direct Swedish involvement. The order also notes the need to leave mobile units behind in order to prevent enemy landing operations and tasks the Navy with the removal and transportation of coastal batteries. The 29 batteries should be used to defend the area from Lyngen to Western Lofoten.[47]

The order to change from *Birke* to *Nordlicht* was issued *before* the Soviet offensive against the positions of XIX Corps began the next day, on 7 October 1944. The Germans at this point clearly had no definite information about how and when, or whether, the Soviets would attack the positions held by the 20th Mountain Army, or whether a Soviet offensive would continue into Norwegian territory. A 2 October intelligence report by the 20th Mountain Army suggests that the Germans did not expect a Soviet attack then.[48]

---

[43] "Befehl für den Ausbau der Lyngenstellung", signed by von Falkenhorst, 22 September 1944, NARA, PG 59412/3, microfilm T 312-1060, pp 31–35. "Der Russe wird vermutlich der Absetzbewegung der 20.(Geb.) Armee scharf nachstossen, um sich in den Besitz nordnorwegischen Raums zu setzen. Sein Agenteneinsatz bis in den Raum von Narvik lässt die Ausdehnung seiner Operation bis dorthin möglich erscheinen. Schwerpunkt der russischen Operation wird vermutlich am Südflügel entlang der Strasse Karesuando – Skibotn liegen in der Absicht, Masse 20.(Geb.) Armee sowie Teile Gen.Kdo. LXXI.A.K. abzuschneiden.

Mit Betreten schwedischen Bodens durch den Feind zur Umgehung eigener Kräfte muss gerechnet werden […]".

[44] In the following quoted from the facsimile in Korsnes 2021, which refers to NARA, PG 32162, microfilm T 1022-1719.

[45] "im Raum Lyngenfjord – Narvik".

[46] "zur Verteidigung der schwedischen Grenzübergänge beiderseits Bjoernsfjeld".

[47] It was later decided to leave some batteries in place to counter enemy landing operations—see Sect. 3.3 above.

[48] *Armeeoberkommando 20* (*AOK 20*, i.e., 20th Mountain Army) to *OKW/WFSt* and *OKH/Gen.St.d.H./Fremde Heere Ost*, 2 October 1944, "Betr. Feindberichterstattung und -beurteilung v. 16.-30.9.1944", NARA, PG 65636/2, microfilm T 312-1067, pp 211–213.

In a sign that such an eventuality was clearly taken into account, Rendulic was ordered to thoroughly destroy “all constructions, that can be of use to the enemy”,[49] including communications (roads and railways), industry, military accommodations, and storages. Civilian dwellings or other buildings were not mentioned. The entire able-bodied population[50] was, “in so far as the troop movements allowed it”,[51] to be brought along with the retreating troops and to be handed over to the *Reichskommissar Norwegen* for “work service”.[52] There is nothing in the document to suggest that the scorched earth policy at this point was grounded in anything other than the perceived need to create obstacles to a pursuing enemy or other enemy operations in the areas that were to be abandoned. The construction of the Lyngen fortifications should be pressed forward “by all means”.[53] The plan also included the construction of intermediate positions between the so-called *Sturmbock-Stellung*, on the Finnish side of the border opposite Swedish Karesuando,[54] and Lyngen. A Soviet attack along the Torne Valley was clearly a major concern. Although, in hindsight, we know what soon ensued, the clause about evacuating able-bodied men from an area that could potentially come under enemy control did make military sense.

In the weeks that followed, numerous German military documents continued to anticipate a possible Soviet pursuit on Norwegian territory. On 15 October 1944, Rendulic instructed LXXI Corps to prepare blocking positions along the march route that would make it difficult for the enemy to circumvent: “It should be a basic consideration that a pursuing enemy will use terrain-mobile units to achieve encircling and bypassing movements”. Roads and bridges should be prepared for demolition.[55] Messages that were based on the same premise of a Soviet pursuit with highly mobile forces followed on 18 October,[56] 22 October,[57] 23 October, and 25 October and later. The message of 22 October specifically warned against a Soviet offensive towards Lakselv from Kirkenes and Ivalo, as well as naval landing operations of the Western Allies. The message of 23 October made the point that the Red Army had

[49] “Alle Anlagen, die dem Gegner von Nutzen sein könnten”.

[50] “wehrfähige Bevölkerung”.

[51] “soweit es die Marschbewegungen zulassen”.

[52] “Arbeitseinsatz”. From this point on it seems that Terboven, somehow in collusion with the Quisling “government”, took a special interest in the evacuation of the civilian population that was grounded in other considerations than military necessity. However, Terboven also took as his point of departure the possibility of enemy moves against Northern Norway. Rendulic repeatedly resisted the use of military resources for the evacuation of the civilian population, but it does not appear he resisted forced evacuation as such. On the other hand, Ferdinand Jodl, the Commander of XIX Corps, argued explicitly that a forced evacuation of civilians would be detrimental to military interest.

[53] “mit allen Mitteln”.

[54] In the 6 October 1944 document, as frequently in German sources, called “Karesuando Stellung”.

[55] “Es ist dabei grundsätzlich in Rechnung zu stellen, dass ein nachstossender Feind durch geländegängige Verbände umfassende und überholende Bewegungen anstreben wird”. *Fernschreiben* 15 October 1944, *AOK 20* to LXXI Corps, NARA, PG 65635/7, microfilm T 312-1067, p 428.

[56] NARA, PG 65357/8, microfilm T 312-1063, pp 61–64.

[57] Ibid., pp 184–186. See also another short message the same day, about additional roads that might be used by the enemy to bypass the retreating 20th Mountain Army, p 193; also message on p 197.

already demonstrated its ability to master challenging conditions and successfully conduct long daily marches over the tundra.[58] In the message of 25 October 1944, Rendulic had a list of questions for the retreating corps' commanders: where, along *Reichsstrasse 50*, would the terrain be advantageous for a pursuing enemy to attack the retreating Germans from the rear or by units operating off the road, and where was it possible for ordinary units to move across the terrain off the road, etc.?[59]

A new message of 19 October 1944 from *OKW/WFStab* to the 20th Mountain Army and the *WBH Norwegen* emphasised the threat of an "Anglo-American" landing operation between the North Cape and Narvik. The message referred explicitly to the Soviet border crossing the previous day and envisioned two rationales for such an operation: to obstruct the 20th Mountain Army's retreat, and to prevent Soviet forces from continuing their offensive towards the Norwegian Atlantic coastline and Narvik. The last point reflected the Germans' repeated theorizing about the existence of American and British distrust of Soviet intentions in Northern Norway.[60] While continuing the retreat, the 20th Mountain Army should prepare defences against naval landings. Coastal batteries at the entrances to the fjords, and batteries protecting harbours and covering the *Reichsstrasse 50*, were to be kept in place until the 20th Mountain Army had passed, even if this meant that they would have to be demolished rather than being transported further south for use as was originally stipulated in the order of 6 October.

The 19 October 1944 message also contained instructions for a further extension of the fortifications in the Narvik-Lyngen area, emphasising particularly the need to set up a solid defence on the "flank towards Sweden".[61] A 20th Mountain Army intelligence report, also dated 19 October, envisioned a Soviet intention to launch a "a move over Kirkenes to the West in order to take control over the North-Norwegian Atlantic coast".[62] A similar evaluation a week later foresaw a move by "strong enemy forces" along the *Reichsstrasse 50* "to liberate Norway" and to take control over the Atlantic coastline. Highly mobile units, naval landings and even airborne troops could be used to bypass and cut off the retreating German units. Another possibility was a Soviet attack along the Ivalo-Lakselv axis.[63]

---

[58] NARA, PG 65357/8, microfilm T 312-1063, pp 216–217.

[59] Ibid., p 260.

[60] In reality, while the Norwegian government was concerned about Soviet intentions towards Northern Norway, the Americans and the British were not. See the discussion in Riste 1979, pp 157–237.

[61] "Flanke gegen Schweden", quoted from the facsimile in Korsnes 2021, which refers to NARA, PG 65635/8, microfilm T 312-1063.

[62] "Vorstoss über Kirkenes nach W[esten] zur Gewinnung der nordnorwegische Atlantikküste". *AOK 20* to *OKW/WFStab* and *OKH/Gen.St.d.H./Fremde Heere Ost*, "Betr. Feindberichterstattung und -beurteilung vom 19.10.44", 19 October 1944, NARA, PG 65636/2, microfilm T 312-1067, pp 208–210.

[63] *AOK 20* (Ic), *Feindlagebericht*, 26 October 1944, NARA, ibid., pp 44–86, with attachments.

On 27 October 1944, the 20th Mountain Army Command warned subordinate units of the possibility of Allied actions against the Narvik area, clearly based on the message of 19 October from the *OKW/WFStab*:

> Because of the current military and political overall situation in Northern Norway it is to be expected that there will be a landing operation on the North-Norwegian coast (most likely in the Narvik area).[64]

The 19 October 1944 message also reached the Naval Command in Norway (*Marineoberkommando Norwegen—MOK Norwegen*) that controlled the coastal artillery. On 29 October, the *MOK Norwegen* wired its subordinate units that the German High Command had concluded that "Russia is aiming to break through as far as Narvik". This, in turn, might induce the British to undertake "sea and air landings in the Narvik area, also north and south thereof", which was a serious danger since "even the [Allied] possession of one or more islands in the Norwegian coast could cause the serious dislocation of our supply traffic". This had to be prevented: "It is therefore necessary that any landing operations be recognised as such promptly, so that they may be attacked and driven out whilst still at sea. No coastal sector and not a single battery is to be surprised by the enemy".[65]

On 31 October 1944, the 20th Mountain Army sent a message to subordinate units, the *WBH Norwegen*, and the *MOK Norwegen*. It reflected a new message from *OKW/WFStab*, received two days earlier.[66] The text gives an idea of the wide range of German threat perceptions at this point:

> A reduced enemy pressure on the rear-guard of the XXXVI and XIX Mountain Army Corps should not be interpreted to mean that the Soviets have given up their intention to push through to Narvik. One should expect a continuation of Soviet operations in the Ivalo area and from Kirkenes in the direction of Lakselv.
>
> One is to expect Finnish forces to advance over Muonio in the direction of Skibotn.
>
> A Soviet move through Sweden is possible. Landing undertakings along *Reichsstrasse 50* are likely.
>
> It remains to be seen if and to what degree such Soviet operations run contrary to the Anglo-American plans.
>
> It cannot be excluded, that they [i.e., Soviet operations] if necessary will induce the English to undertake a combined naval and air operation against the Narvik area. However, an English attack on Narvik can be imagined and is possible as an action independent of the Soviet operations.[67]

---

[64] "Auf Grund derzeitiger militärischer und politischer Gesamtlage im nordnorwegischen Raum muss mit einem Landungsunternehmen an der nordnorwegischen Küste (voraussichtlich im Raum Narvik) gerechnet werden". *AOK 20* to subordinate units, 27 October 1944, NARA, PG 65635/8, microfilm T 312-1063, pp 297–298. See also *OKW/WFStab* to *AOK 20* on 29 October 1944, NARA, ibid., p 336.

[65] Here quoted from a facsimile in an e-mail from Kjetil Korsnes of 12 November 2021, with reference to The National Archives UK (hereafter TNA), DEFE 3/474 (High Grade Machine Decrypts) of the Naval Intelligence Division. English translation in the original file.

[66] *OKW/WFStab* to *AOK 20* on 29 October 1944, NARA, PG 65635/8, microfilm T 312-1063, p 336.

[67] "Nachlassen des Feinddruckes gegen des röm. 36 und röm. 19 (Geb.) A.K. darf noch nicht so gewertet werden, dass Sowjets ihre Absicht, nach Narvik durchzustossen, aufgegeben haben. Mit

Through November and December 1944, the perceived threats gradually changed as the Germans realised that the Soviet troops—at least for the time being—showed no signs of moving forward from the Tana positions or from positions further south. As early as 30 October 1944, Major General Hermann Hölter, Rendulic's chief of staff, in one of his "daily reports" (*Tagesmeldung*) characterised the Soviet troops along the Arctic Ocean Road southwest of Nautsi as well as along the *Reichsstrasse 50* as "strikingly restrained".[68] He concluded that their "hesitant behaviour" was most likely "due to political reasons",[69] presumably alleging some sort of intra-Allied deliberations about spheres of operations in Northern Norway. While the possibility of Soviet land offensives and Western Allied landing operations were never discarded, they were gradually perceived as less of an imminent threat. With the approach of winter, the possibility of large-scale enemy action was considered suspended until spring 1945.

However, the possibility of both Soviet land operations and Western landing operations remained part of the 20th Mountain Army's perceived threats. Another message of 30 October 1944, the same day when Hölter signed the *Tagesmeldung*, made it clear that there still was a danger of enemy operations further west: "However, there is still reason to expect landings in the Varanger area and from there an advance to the Tana area".[70] Two days later, Hölter did not exclude the possibility that Soviet or Finnish troops would move "from the Ivalo area in the direction of Lakselv".[71] He noted that Soviet and Finnish troops for the first time occupied neighbouring positions opposite the German front line.[72] On 13 November, XVIII Corps was ordered to prepare to meet a possible Soviet move "over the Kautokeino area to Reichsstrasse 50".[73] A degree of ambiguity is evident in 20th Mountain Army evaluations through

Fortsetzung der sowjetischen Operationen über den Raum Ivalo und von Kirkenes her Richtung Lakselv ist weiterhin zu rechnen.

Nachstosse finnischer Kräfte über Muonio Richtung Skibotn ist zu erwarten.

Möglich ist sowjetischer Durchmarsch durch Schweden. Wahrscheinlich sind Landungsunternehmen an der Reichsstrasse 50.

Ob und inwiefern solche sowjetischen Operationen den anglo-amerikanischen Plänen zuwiderlaufen, bleibt abzuwarten.

Es ist nicht ausgeschlossen, dass sie gegebenenfalls die Engländer zu einer kombinierten See- und Luftlandeunternehmen gegen den Raum Narvik veranlassen. Ein englischer Angriff auf Narvik ist aber auch als von den sowjetrussischen Operationen unabhängige Aktion denkbar und möglich". *AOK 20* to subordinate units and others, 31 October 1944, NARA, PG 65635/8, microfilm T 312-1063, pp 386–388.

[68] "auffallend zurückhaltend".

[69] "durch politische Gründe bestimmt". Hölter's *Tagesmeldung* to *OKW/WFStab* etc., 30 October 1944, NARA, ibid., p 351.

[70] "Mit Landungen im Varangerraum und danach weiterem Vorstoss in den Raum Tana ist jedoch zu rechnen". *Tagesmeldung* 30 October 1944, NARA, ibid., pp 352–353.

[71] "aus Raum Ivalo Richtung Lakselv".

[72] *Tagesmeldung* 4 November 1944, PG 65 635/9, p 70.

[73] "über Raum Kautokeino nach Reichsstrasse 50". *Fernschreiben* 13 November 1944, *AOK 20* to XVIII Mountain Corps and other units, PG 65635/9, microfilm T 312-1063, p 250.

December 1944—large-scale enemy operations, whether Soviet ones on land or landings by the Western Allies, seemed increasingly remote but never remote enough to be excluded.[74]

Intelligence reports, some of them clearly misleading, may have served to bolster the Germans' expectations of Allied moves against Northern Norway. On 1 November 1944, Hölter referred to alleged Finnish-Norwegian talks about the use of Finnish troops in Norway. This, he surmised, could imply joint Soviet-Finnish operations against Northern Norway.[75] No such Finnish-Norwegian talks ever took place. In the same vein, and allegedly based on insights into Norwegian Foreign Minister Trygve Lie's conversations in Stockholm and then in Moscow in October-November 1944, two reports from naval intelligence in the last half of November claimed that Lie expected Northern Norway to be liberated in the near future. Similarly, there was allegedly some kind of understanding that Soviet forces should continue their advance until just north of Narvik, while Norwegian, British, and American troops were to operate to the south of the town. As soon as Soviet troops had reached the allegedly agreed line, the Western Allies would launch a large-scale invasion (*Grossinvasion*) of the rest of the country. This would happen, at the latest, in spring 1945.[76] The Norwegian and Soviet minutes of Lie's conversations in Moscow and Stockholm do not mention such an expectation or understanding on his part.[77] Most importantly, there was never an agreement about a demarcation line between Soviet and Western troops in Norway, and the Western Allies had no plans for a *Grossinvasion* of the country.

During a meeting on 11 November 1944 at Rendulic's preliminary headquarters at Rundhaug, north of Narvik, von Falkenhorst and Rendulic discussed, among other things, the likelihood of "Anglo-American" landing operations in the 20th Mountain Army's area of operations. Von Falkenhorst considered it unlikely, especially not against Narvik: the Allies were focusing their efforts on the continent. Possible Soviet moves were not on the agenda—probably a sign that the two men deemed a

[74] See *AOK 20* to *OKW/WFStab* and *OKH/Gen.St.d.H./Fremde Heere Ost*, *Fernschreiben* 2 December 1944, "Feindberichterstattung und -beurteilung vom 1.12.1944", NARA, PG 65636/2, pp 200-201; *AOK 20* to *OKW/WFStab*, 17 December 1944, including "Feindberichterstattung und -beurteilung", NARA, PG 35636/2, p 199; *AOK 20* to *OKW/WFStab* and *OKH/Gen.St.d.H./Fremde Heere Ost*, *Fernschreiben*, "Betr.: Feindberichterstattung und -beurteilung vom 16.12.1944", NARA, PG 65636/2, pp 203–205.

[75] Hölter's *Fernschreiben* 1 November 1944, NARA, PG 65635/9, microfilm T 312-1063, p 5.

[76] Both documents quoted from a facsimile in Korsnes 2021: OKM intelligence report, 19 November 1944, reference to NARA, PG 33782, microfilm T 1022-2052; naval intelligence report, 26 November 1944, reference to NARA, PG 33782, microfilm T 1022-2052.

[77] Norwegian minutes of Lie's conversations in The National Archives of Norway (Riksarkivet), S-2259, series 25/2 Utenriksministerens samtaler, vol. IX; Soviet minutes in the Foreign Policy Archives of the Russian Federation (Arkhiv vneshnei politiki Rossiiskoi federatsii), f. 05 (Molotov's secretariat), op. 7, d. 573. This and other files from the Molotov collection and other collections are currently (March 2023) available online at https://agk.mid.ru/ [accessed 1 April 2023]. I have not consulted the Swedish minutes from the conversations.

Soviet offensive at this point progressively unlikely.[78] According to a 20th Mountain Army evaluation of 17 November, once Norwegian troops had arrived in Finnmark, the Soviets apparently intended, "for the time being" (*zunächst*), to let them "under Soviet command" take control of areas in Northern Norway abandoned by the Germans.[79] Important here is the qualification "for the time being"—the danger was less imminent, but it was still there.

On 2 November 1944, the same day when Rendulic predicted a Soviet advance from Ivalo towards Lakselv,[80] *OKW/WFStab* ordered the 20th Mountain Army to leave behind "winter mobile units" along *Reichsstrasse 50* to the west of Porsanger fjord in expectation of a Soviet move.[81] To this Rendulic responded by laying out in some detail the measures he had already taken to establish strongholds along the 20th Mountain Army's retreat route.[82] On 19 November, and allegedly based on reports in the US press and instructions from Hitler, Rendulic instructed his troops to be on guard against possible landing operations.[83] A message sent out the following day pointed to the possibility that the enemy could set up an airfield on the island Andøya in the Vesterålen archipelago, with obvious repercussions for the defence of the Narvik area.[84]

Even in late November 1944, Rendulic apparently kept open the possibility that Soviet forces might move into Norway from Finland over Skoganvarre-Kautokeino towards Lakselv and *Reichsstrasse 50*. When the *MOK Norwegen* suggested keeping coastal batteries east of Lyngen in place to ward off naval attacks and landing operations, Rendulic argued against the idea. As he saw it, the danger of a land attack was not over. This meant that strong German land forces would be needed in Finnmark to protect the coastal batteries: they could otherwise be subjected to overwhelming attacks both from the sea and over land by Soviet forces.[85] By this time, a large part of the destruction and forced evacuation had already been carried out. Hammerfest was a major exception: its systematic and total destruction did not occur until as late as February 1945 when the last German units withdrew.

In addition to the range of views that surfaced in 20th Mountain Army documents, there appears to be a consistent difference in the evaluations between Rendulic and his staff on the one hand, and the *WBH Norwegen*, von Falkenhorst, on the other.

[78] "Ergebnis der Besprechung" of a meeting on 11 November 1944 between *WBH Norwegen* and *AOK 20*, dated 18 November 1944, NARA, PG 65635/9, microfilm T 312-1063, pp 256–261.

[79] *Fernschreiben* 17 November 1944, with *Tagesmeldung* of 16 November 1944, NARA, PG 65635/10, microfilm T 312-1064, pp 3–4.

[80] Rendulic's *Fernschreiben* 2 November 1944, PG 65635/9, microfilm T 312-1063, p 30. See also *AOK 20* to *OKW/WFStab* and *OKH/Gen.St.d.H./Fremde Heere Ost*, "Betr. Feindberichterstattung und -beurteilung vom 20.10 – 1.11.44", NARA, PG 65636, pp 206–207.

[81] Jodl (*OKW/WFStab*) to *AOK 20*, 2 November 1944, NARA, PG 65635/9, microfilm T 312-1063, p 56.

[82] Rendulic's *Fernschreiben* 7 November 1944, NARA, ibid., pp 133-135; pp 137–138.

[83] *Fernschreiben* 19 November 1944, NARA, PG 65635/10, microfilm T 312-1064, p 77.

[84] *Fernschreiben* 20 November 1944, NARA, PG 65635/10, microfilm T 312-1064, p 100.

[85] *Fernschreiben* 22 November 1944, NARA, ibid., pp 137–138; also *AOK 20* to *OKW/WFStab*, 7 December 1944, NARA, PG 65365/11, microfilm T 312-1064, pp 116–117.

WBH Norwegen evaluations tended to put less emphasis on the possibility of Soviet or British-led operations against Northern Norway, including a Soviet land offensive through Finnmark County. A report dated 20 September 1944 started by pointing out that Finland's withdrawal from the war against the Soviet Union and the retreat of the 20th Mountain Army would enable the Soviet Union to attain an allegedly "centuries-old [Russian] aim", namely to gain access to ice-free ports in Northern Norway.[86] However, an offensive through Finnmark and *Reichsstrasse 50* would be a much less likely option than an attack on the 20th Mountain Army's right flank. This latter option might involve a Soviet request to Sweden to transport Soviet troops on Swedish railways—possibly as a *quid pro quo* for Germany's use of Swedish railways for troop transports to and from Norway earlier in the war. From this followed the urgency of building strong defences on the Swedish border as part of the Lyngen fortifications.

It was also felt that, since Narvik under Soviet control would be contrary to British interests, the British might attempt a landing pre-emptively. The *WBH Norwegen* considered however that the British prioritised the continental theatre. Consequently, other than a possible move to prevent the Soviets taking Narvik, British landings in Northern Norway were unlikely.[87] This view, expressed in the 20 September 1944 report, reflected the situation before the decision was made to withdraw the entire 20th Mountain Army to the Lyngen Line—in other words, when Finnmark was still in German hands. It was also written before the Red Army launched its offensive against the German XIX Corps. Therefore, at this point, Allied moves to cut off the 20th Mountain Army's retreat through Finnmark and Troms counties may have been something that was not taken into consideration.

A *WBH Norwegen* report of 18 November 1944 noted that the Soviet offensive had stopped, "as expected", presumably a reference to the 20 September document. Instead, Soviet efforts would aim at securing the acquired Petsamo area and the "complete subjugation and russification of the hated Finnish neighbour". Taking control over and securing Finnmark would be left to Norwegian troops, while the Finnish army allegedly had orders not to cross the Norwegian border. Von Falkenhorst's staff concluded that this situation would allow the Soviets to withdraw all of their troops from Karelia—the theatre that extended from the Leningrad front along the Finnish border—for deployment onto more decisive sectors, with the exception of one unit left in place to secure the Petsamo area.

Although this is not said explicitly, von Falkenhorst's command in Oslo apparently no longer saw any serious danger of a Soviet offensive through Finland towards the Lyngen-Skibotn-Narvik area. Moreover, available intelligence allegedly suggested

[86] This idea is a myth rather than reality—neither Tsarist Russia nor the Soviet Union harboured such ambitions. See Nielsen 2002.

[87] *Lagebeurteilung* of *AOK Norwegen*, 20 September 1944, NARA PG 59412/3, microfilm T 312-1060, pp 8–11.

that neither Sweden nor the UK would intervene. The British needed all available resources for the decisive campaign in mainland Europe. Large-scale British interventions in Norway were therefore just as unlikely as a Soviet ground offensive.[88]

An assessment of 24 November 1944 from the *WBH Norwegen* tried to explain why the Soviets had not continued the advance beyond the Tana River. Apart from the difficult terrain and harsh winter conditions, the German scorched earth policy had made it "nearly impossible" to find dwellings for larger troop formations. Once again, the *WBH Norwegen* played down the northern theatre's importance for the Soviets: Finland had become a "secondary theatre of war" (*Nebenkriegsschauplatz*), and the Red Army would most likely transfer units from the North "to the main fronts in the East" (*an den Hauptfronten im Osten*). Land operations in or towards Norway were, by implication, unlikely. The report also downplayed the possibility of large-scale landing operations in Northern Norway: "A rapid capture of Northern Norway would seem unlikely in view of [limited] ship space and because of the lack of sufficient naval support".[89] The deployment of available Norwegian troops to Kirkenes also meant that even minor Allied operations against the German-controlled coastline had become less likely.[90]

In a report from early December 1944, the *WBH Norwegen* continued to play down the risk for large-scale Allied operations in Norway, from the east or west. From the British side, there were no signs of preparations for an invasion. Norwegian troops did not constitute a major threat, although they would continue to build up their strength in Finnmark and could be expected to conduct raids on German communication lines further to the south, including *Reichsstrasse 50*. The Red Army did not, "for the time being" (*z.Zt.*) intend to pursue the retreating 20th Mountain Army: Soviet divisions and significant air force units had been withdrawn from the Murmansk-Kirkenes area for deployment on other fronts. Sweden's intention remained as it had been throughout the war—to avoid being directly involved.[91]

To von Falkenhorst and his staff, this implied that the withdrawal of Rendulic's entire Army (or what was left of it after several units had been sent to mainland Europe) behind the Lyngen fortifications should be reconsidered. A full withdrawal, as planned, would be contrary to German interests:

---

[88] "Beurteilung der Lage in Nordnorwegen von Oslo aus gesehen", von Falkenhorst to Keitel/ *Führerhauptquartier* 18 November 1944, received 19 November, in "Tätigkeitsbericht für den Monat November und Dezember 1944. Abt.: Ia, IIa, N.S.F.O. g.Kdos. AOK 20", NARA, PG 64215, microfilm T 312-1061.

[89] "Eine schnelle Besetzung Nordnorwegens durch eine grössere Landungsunternehmen von See her dürfte schiffraumsmässig und wegen Fehlens ausreichender Unterstützung durch Seestreitkräfte wenig wahrscheinlich sein".

[90] "Beurteilung der Feindlage um skandinavischen Raum im Monat November 1944", Armeeoberkommando Norwegen 24 November 1944, NARA, PG 64215. Quoted from a facsimile in Korsnes 2021, with reference to NARA, PG 64215, microfilm T 312-1061, pp 13–18.

[91] "Feindnachrichtenblatt Nr. 12/44. vom 1.11 bis 30.11.44". *WBH Norwegen*, 6 December 1944, Anlage 5 zum Tätigkeitsbericht für November 1944, NARA, PG 64215, microfilm T 312-1061, pp 97–108.

> The more the 20th Mountain Army retreats, the more space is available to the Norwegian government-in-exile and the less do the Russians worry about securing the Petsamo area. The exile Norwegians will become correspondingly stronger, and the Russians will transfer additional forces to other fronts.
>
> Thus, it seems required to halt the retreat in the north and to keep a rear-guard at Lakselv. It is only interpreted as weakness and works to our disadvantage. In the same way troops should remain at the border to the south of Karasjok.[92]

In winter, the area between Kirkenes-Tana and Banak-Lakselv was allegedly "completely unpassable" (*völlig unpassierbar).* In the meantime, however, the Norwegian troops in the Kirkenes-Tana area could be expanded to a force of up to two divisions with air units. This would mean that "from May 1945 we would have to take this enemy into regard".[93] Based on this interpretation of Allied intentions, von Falkenhorst recommended keeping a force of four divisions with some additional units in Northern Norway.[94] Thus, although the *Wehrmachtsbefehlshaber Norwegen* foresaw no Soviet move during the winter, the threat over land would reappear in spring 1945, with much larger Norwegian forces as part of the scenario.

3.5 Allied Planning and Options—Naval Landings?

As we have seen, Rendulic and other German military and civilian authorities envisioned three main options for continued Allied operations against Northern Norway and the 20th Mountain Army after the Karelian Front's Petsamo-Kirkenes operation came to a halt in early November 1944. The first option would involve a renewed Soviet offensive across Finnmark and Troms counties, from the forward positions of the 14th Army at the Tana River, or along the highway from Ivalo (i.e., from Finnish territory) towards Lakselv. The second option would entail a Soviet move across Finnish (or possibly even Swedish) territory, along the Torne Valley, towards the Lyngen-Skibotn area. The third option would comprise naval landing operations, possibly as a joint endeavour by Soviet and Western forces, to disturb or block the retreat of the 20th Mountain Army to the Lyngen Line.[95] Such landing operations

---

[92] "Je weiter das Geb.AOK 20 sich absetzt, desto mehr Raum fällt der norwegischen Exilregierung zu und desto mehr mindert sich die Sorge der Russen um die Sicherung des Petsamo-Raumes. Die Exil-Norweger werden dadurch entsprechend stärker und die Russen können weitere Kräfte an andere Fronten abbefördern."

[93] "Ab Mai 1945 müsse also mit diesem Gegner gerechnet warden".

[94] "Beurteilung der Lage in Nordnorwegen von Oslo aus gesehen", von Falkenhorst to Keitel/Führerhauptquartier 18 November 1944, received 19 November, in "Tätigkeitsbericht für den Monat November und Dezember 1944. Abt.: Ia, IIa, N.S.F.O. g.Kdos. AOK 20", NARA, PG 64215, microfilm T 312-1061, pp 13–18.

[95] As stated by Rendulic to the tribunal on 31 October 1947 (HLSNTP undated, p 5337), in memoirs and in German contemporary documents. Rendulic speaks about "the Finns" as advancing towards Norway—this may be a mistake in the records, most likely he was speaking about the Red Army. However, as seen from the discussion that follows, the Germans also considered the possibility of a Finnish move into Norway.

could be launched separately or jointly with, or in support of, any of the two envisioned land-based offensives. Before the US military tribunal, Rendulic stressed the danger for the Germans of this third set of options, naval landing operations, repeatedly emphasising that such operations "had to be anticipated" and would have been "considerable [*sic*] more simple" to execute than any of the land-based alternatives.[96]

To what degree did these three main German scenarios of possible Allied moves correspond to actual existing Allied thinking or planning? The last option, naval landing operations, is easily debunked. On the Soviet side, there is no evidence in archival documents or other sources to suggest that the Soviets were, at any point during the war, thinking of landing and holding Norwegian territory west of the Varanger peninsula, or of preparing for such operations. In the spring of 1944, Meretskov, Commander of the Karelian Front, issued instructions to prepare for a battalion-size naval infantry landing operation at Berlevåg on the north-western shore of the Varanger peninsula. This landing was to be followed by an operation to cut the road westwards from Kirkenes, where it crosses the Tana River and follows the narrow passage between the coastline and the Finnish border.[97] However, this was an operation that was never meant to be executed. It was part of an extensive deceptive manoeuvre involving both the Northern Fleet, the 14th Army, and Karelian Front aviation designed to make the Germans believe that the Red Army and Northern Fleet were about to launch a major offensive on the Murmansk sector that would continue into Norwegian territory.[98]

When, in early November 1944, Soviet forces reached the Tana River as the end point of their offensive, they moved by land from the Kirkenes and Sør-Varanger area without attempting any landing operations on the shores of the Varanger peninsula. Moreover, it is unlikely that plans for large-scale Soviet landing operations on the coast of Northern Norway as envisioned by the Germans *could* have existed. The Northern Fleet, with its lack of experience other than on small scale landing operations, would hardly be able to conduct such operations on its own.[99]

---

[96] HLSNTP undated, p 5338, 31 October 1947.

[97] See *Tsentral'nyi Arkhiv Ministertstva Oborony RF* (Central Archive of the Ministry of Defence of the Russian Federation, hereafter TsAMO), f. 214, op. 1437, d. 142, ll. 17–19, "Plan operatsii Karel'skogo fronta i Severnogo flota po godgotovke nastupleniya na raion Petsamo i severnoe poberezh'e Norvegiii s tsel'yu ovladeniya Berlevog, p-ov Varanger", no date. Annotation on the document: "Training exercise in accordance with STAVKA directive of 20.4.1944".

[98] See Krasnaya armiya 2000, pp 572–573, document no. 2 in the chapter "Norvegiya", Stavka's directive of 20 April 1944, without number. See also TsAMO, f. 214, op. 1437, d. 142, ll. 17–19, "Plan operatsii Karelskogo fronta i Severnogo flota po godgotovke nastupleniya na raion Petsamo i severnoe poberezh'e Norvegiii s tsel'yu ovladeniya Berlevog, p-ov Varanger", no date. Annotation on the document: "Training exercise in accordance with STAVKA directive of 20.4.1944", and TsAMO, f. 214, op. 1437, d. 1462, ll. 3–5, Meretskov to 14th Army and Northern Fleet, no. 0019/44/op, 23 April 1944 and ibid., ll. 9–16, Northern Fleet's plan *Grom*, 23 April 1944. The deception may have been related to the Allies' plan *Bodyguard* that aimed at misleading the Germans about the place of the coming Allied invasion of Europe. Cf. Riste 1979, pp 179–180.

[99] For an overview, see Monakov and Rohwer 2001, chapters 8 and 9. As always, when writing about the Northern Fleet, I have benefitted from the generous advice and opinions of Rune Rautio, with his unsurpassed knowledge of Northern Fleet operations and archival sources.

In theory, large-scale joint British-Soviet landing operations in Northern Norway was a more realistic option than a purely Soviet move. Yet, at no point did British military planners seriously consider them, either in 1944 or earlier in the war. Although part of Allied planning since the Casablanca conference in January 1943, Norway became increasingly marginalised. *Rankin B*, the most ambitious scenario for Norway during the end phase of the war, originally envisaged the possibility of Allied operations in Southern and Northern Norway with a division and brigade respectively, but only if the Germans focused their remaining forces on the continent and weakened their presence in more peripheral north-western theatres as a result. This plan was gradually diluted, left with mostly symbolic value in the end.[100] In the weeks and months preceding and following Rendulic's orders to scorch earth in parts of Northern Norway and to forcibly evacuate the population, no British or other Western Allied plans for landing or other offensive operations in Northern Norway were discussed, much less elaborated. Norway was seen as a peripheral theatre of war, while all available resources were used for the campaign on mainland Europe.

3.6 Allied Planning and Options—The Red Army

A recent two-part study of the Karelian Front's 14th Army's Petsamo-Kirkenes operation in October–November 1944, based on Soviet military and Soviet and Western diplomatic archival sources, concludes that that the Red Army's entry into Norway on 18 October 1944, the capture of Kirkenes, and the final move to the Tana River did not reflect a Soviet intention to secure a foothold in Norway to lay the ground for long-term political influence or even a military presence. At no point during the war did Stalin envision Norway as part of a Soviet security zone or sphere of influence after the war. Although crossing the border clearly needed Stalin's approval, the initiative for a decision to pursue the Germans into Norway seem to have originated with the Karelian Front and 14th Army commanders based on operational considerations. The following paragraphs about Soviet thinking and planning build on these earlier contributions.[101]

The Red Army's entry into Norway came on the heels of the 14th Army's failure to capture or destroy, on Soviet territory, the main forces of the German 20th Mountain Army's XIX Corps. The corps, along with the other units of Rendulic's Army, managed to withdraw to Norwegian territory in good order. This situation left the Red Army with an unfinished task. A continued German military presence in the immediate vicinity of the Norwegian-Soviet border was unacceptable. Such a presence would expose Soviet territory to the threat of German attacks and result in

[100] Riste 1979, pp 239–240. Riste's two-volume work is still the most extensive and authoritative discussion of Norway's place in Allied policy and military planning. For a newer, but less comprehensive, discussion, see Mann 2012.

[101] Holtsmark 2021b, c.

another Soviet-German frontline in the north, this time not along the Litsa, but on the Soviet-Norwegian border.[102]

Soviet thinking is explained by the fact that they were not aware of the German decision, a few days before the start of the 14th Army's offensive on 7 October 1944, to bring the entire 20th Mountain Army back behind the Lyngen Line fortifications in Troms county. This meant that the Germans were to abandon not only their positions on Soviet (and previously Finnish) territory, but also their presence in Finnmark county. Thus, the Germans had already decided to leave the entire area that was taken under control by Soviet forces in October and November.[103] Tactical-operational rather than political considerations were the rationale for the Soviet entry into Norway on 18 October 1944. This interpretation corresponds to the fact that the last Soviet troops left Norway as early as 25 September 1945, i.e., less than a year after they arrived and only a few months after the German capitulation.[104]

This benign outcome and interpretation of Soviet motives does not, of course, exclude the existence of Soviet military thinking or even planning along the lines that Rendulic and other German decision-makers allegedly saw as possible Soviet moves in 1944. On the contrary, elements of such thoughts and plans were put on the table (just never realised). Nor does the absence of long-term Soviet ambitions regarding Norway exclude short-term Soviet planning for continuing the fight against German forces on Norwegian territory. Nor, for that matter, does the fact that the Red Army did not continue its offensive in the north beyond the Tana River or move into Norway from positions further to the south necessarily imply that such moves were not, or could not have been, a part of Soviet planning. It is not implausible that, though part of Soviet planning, these southern moves were stopped by German countermeasures—for instance, the scorched earth policy of which Rendulic stood accused at the US military tribunal in Nuremberg.

3.6.1 A Soviet Offensive from the Tana Positions?

Of the three scenarios that the Germans envisaged for Allied moves against Northern Norway, the first—namely, a Soviet offensive through Finnmark county from the Tana positions or along the axis Muonio-Karasjok-Lakselv—*may* have been possible

[102] When, on 15 October 1944, Meretskov sent to Stalin and *Stavka* what seems to be his first request for permission to cross the Norwegian border, he pointed out that the road from Salmijarvi southwards to Nautsi followed the border and could be covered by artillery fire from the Norwegian side. To prevent this, he asked for permission to take control over a limited area on the western side of the Pasvik River. There are several printed versions of this crucial document, with variations between them. A signed, non-published version in TsAMO, f. 214, op. 1437, d. 1998, ll. 2–3.

[103] Hitler made the decision on 3 October 1944, and the 20th Mountain Army was informed on 4 October ("zur vorläufigen Unterrichtung wird mitgeteilt"). See Schramm 1961, p 904. Korsnes 2021 includes a facsimile of a transcript of the message with reference to NARA, PG 32162, microfilm T 1022-1719.

[104] For more about this, see Holtsmark 2021c.

logistically and otherwise. There is no conclusive evidence that it was not, but no sources suggest that the Karelian Front or the 14th Army received orders to prepare for such an operation either before, during, or in the aftermath of the Kirkenes-Petsamo operation.[105] Moreover, it seems that the 14th Army's move into Norway on 18 October 1944 was not part of its plan elaborated before the offensive began eleven days earlier. Rather, the decision to continue the offensive to Kirkenes and then to the Tana River as its end point was apparently made in the last two weeks before the fighting ended.

Both the Germans and the Soviets made their respective decisions with limited knowledge of what their opponents were thinking or planning. Not knowing what the Germans were going to do, the Soviets based their planning on what they thought the Germans *could* do. As a result, instead of planning a continued offensive of their own, the Soviets prepared for the opposite scenario—a German attempt to retake the Petsamo area. On 9 November 1944, immediately after the Petsamo-Kirkenes-operation had come to a halt, *Stavka* ordered the 14th Army to take defensive positions and make preparations to counter German attacks.[106] Plans for this eventuality, from Army level down to individual divisions, continued to be elaborated until the last weeks of the war in Europe in April 1945.

The Soviets envisioned several possible German moves: naval landing operations in the Varangerfjord area, a ground offensive over Finnish Ivalo and northwards over Nautsi and Salmijarvi on the Pasvik River, or a combined attack from both directions.[107] Meanwhile, the Soviet Northern Fleet was assigned purely defensive tasks—securing Soviet and Allied movements, repulsing German assaults, and cooperating with the Norwegian navy. There are no indications of offensive ambitions.[108] The Soviet fear of a German resurgence in the north may seem far-fetched in hindsight, but in hindsight only. Given the uncertainty over German thinking and planning, even as the final defeat seemed certain, the Soviets saw good reasons to keep an

[105] As argued in Holtsmark 2021b, c. In January 1945, General Aleksey I. Antonov, until February 1945 Deputy Chief, and then Chief of the Soviet General Staff, argued in an internal memorandum for the need to reach an agreement with the Norwegian government about a Soviet military presence in Northern Norway after the war. There is nothing in this document, however, about a continued offensive in Norway beyond the Tana River or on other sectors. Related and even more expansionist ideas appeared in the NKID, including proposals in the summer of 1945, i.e., after the end of the war, to order Red Army units in Norway to move forward, "up to and including Narvik". It seems, however, that such ideas were rejected and made no impact on Soviet decisions and diplomatic signalling to Norway. For details and sources references, see Holtsmark 1993, 2004 (revised and extended version in Norwegian).

[106] Stavka 1999, document no. 245, Stavka directive 220260, 9 November 1944.

[107] TsAMO, f. 1023, op. 1, d. 29, ll. 1–4, "Vypiska iz plana oborony voisk 14 Otdel'noi Armii dlya 131 sk", transcript of 31 January 1945, but apparently written in November 1944; same file, ll. 4–8, "Plan oborony i kontratak 131 sk na sluchai nastupleniya protivnika na uchastke: Petsamo-Kirkenes-Ivalo", 12 March 1945; TsAMO, f. 6735, op. 367641, d. 1, ll. 1–10, "Vypiska iz plana boya chastei 45 sd na sluchai nastupleniya protivnika na uchastke Petsamo-Kirkenes-Ivalo. Plany operatsii", 24 April 1945.

[108] TsAMO, f. 363, op. 6208, d. 217, ll. 1–9, "Operativnaya direktiva No-0057/op komenduiushchego Severnym Flotom", 5 December 1944.

armed presence in Eastern Finnmark. After all, the war was still ongoing and strong German forces remained in Norway.

3.6.2 A Soviet Offensive Over Finnish or Swedish Territory Towards Troms County?

There is no evidence in Soviet sources to suggest that a move along the Torne Valley on Finnish or even Swedish territory directly towards the Lyngen-Skibotn area was part of Soviet planning after Finland withdrew from the war against the Soviet Union and broke off relations with Germany. It followed from the terms of the Soviet-Finnish ceasefire, effective from 4 - 5 September 1944, that Finnish, and not Soviet, troops should expel the Germans from Finnish territory. This also implied that Soviet troops should not operate or be stationed in Finland. It is only in hindsight, however, that we know Stalin intended to uphold this part of the arrangement by not sending Soviet forces across the border into Finland.[109]

At that time, there was no reason for the Germans to believe that Stalin would keep his words. Rendulic told the tribunal how he found it an "incomprehensible" mistake for the Soviets not to combine the attack on the Murmansk sector from 7 October 1944 with an offensive in the south, and how this mistake allowed German forces to support the 20th Mountain Army's heavily pressed XIX Corps in the north.[110] Such an offensive, however, would have to be conducted mainly on Finnish, not Soviet, territory, in contravention of the terms of the ceasefire.

The Germans were not alone in seeing the devastating potential of a Soviet move after Finland withdrew from the war against the Soviet Union. Meretskov, Commander of the Karelian Front, was thinking in similar terms from the very start of the planning process that culminated in the 14th Army's offensive from 7 October 1944. The first Karelian Front planning document, from February 1944, for operations later the same year against the German 20th Mountain Army, envisaged an offensive by the 14th, 19th, and 26th Armies against German forces on the line Petsamo-Kuolojarvi-Rovaniemi-Kemi, while at the same time creating a frontline against the Finnish army from Kestenga over Kuusamo to Oulu.[111] A later plan, dated 31 May 1944, was similar in outline, but explicitly envisaged a subsequent attack on the Finnish army in Southern Karelia, by then supposed to be fully separated from their German brothers-in-arms on the northern sectors.[112] In the event,

[109] Apart from archival sources to Soviet decision-making (in Holtsmark 2021b, c), the ultimate evidence of this is simply that Soviet forces did not cross the Finnish border. A further indication of Soviet thinking was the disbandment of the Karelian Front and the transfer of most of its units to other theatres of war.

[110] HLSNTP undated, p 5334, 30 October 1947.

[111] Meretskov's "Soobrazheniya po razgromu nemetskikh voisk", 29 February 1944, TsAMO, f. 214, op. 1437, d. 1481, ll. 38–43.

[112] Meretskov's "Soobrazheniya po vedeniu nastupatel'noi operatsii KarF letom 1944 g.", 31 May 1944, TsAMO, f. 214, op. 1437, d. 1587, ll. 23–30.

the 31 May 1944 plan was rapidly superseded by the decision to attack the Finnish army in Southern Karelia before turning against the Germans in the north. Finnish historian Ohto Manninen has suggested that, in the spring of 1944, after this decision the Soviets may have harboured the idea "to advance through the western arm of Finland to Norway and attack the German rear". However, he provides no references to identifiable sources to substantiate his claim.[113] Thus, the various Karelian Front plans for large-scale operations against Rendulic's Army developed in the first months of 1944 did not suggest a Soviet intent to continue the offensives towards Norway and into Norwegian territory.

In early August 1944, based on the expectation that Finland was to withdraw from the war against the Soviet Union, Meretskov suggested a new set of major operations with the aim of blocking the 20th Mountain Army from retreating into Norway in the north and towards the Finnish Baltic ports in the south. Simply put, the idea was to trap and destroy or take prisoner the larger part of Rendulic's Army on Finnish territory. Arguing for the expediency of the operation, Meretskov outlined to Stalin and *Stavka* what he saw as three possible retreat routes for the Germans from Northern Finland: firstly by rail or road transport to harbours in Southern Finland, secondly to ports in the Oulu-Kemi area in the Bothnian Bay, and thirdly northwards across the Norwegian border and further towards Karasjok-Lakselv or to Kirkenes. If Finland exited the war, broke off relations with Germany and blocked the Germans' access to Baltic Sea ports, the Germans would be left with only the northern escape route to Finnmark, i.e., to Kirkenes or in the direction of Karasjok and Lakselv.

Curiously, Meretskov did not mention a fourth option that was open to the Germans: retreat from Rovaniemi to Muonio, along the Swedish border and the Torne Valley to the Lyngen-Skibotn area in Troms county—the very passage that Rendulic a couple of months later identified as a possible route for a Soviet offensive against the positions of his 20th Mountain Army.[114] Meretskov may have considered that this passage, with its primitive and partly unfinished road, did not have the capacity for large-scale troop movements; he was probably unaware of the work the Germans had done on the road to make it suitable for troop transports. As it turned out, the Torne Valley was one of the routes the Germans used in their retreat to Norway during operation *Nordlicht*.[115]

Meretskov apparently discarded, or may have never even looked into, the possibility of using the Torne Valley passage for exactly the move that Rendulic was preparing to meet. A successful Soviet offensive towards Lyngen-Skibotn would threaten to cut the land-based communications between Southern and Northern Norway, leaving German forces in the north entirely dependent on the maritime transport of not only supplies but also troops—a dire prospect for the Germans in view of British supremacy at sea at this stage of the war. The Germans, for their part, expected the Soviets to be fully aware of the possibility of launching an attack along

[113] Manninen 2004, p 130.

[114] As it turned out, this became a main route into Norway of XXVIII German Corps after its retreat to Rovaniemi from its positions in the area Kuusamo-Oulu-Kemi.

[115] For details, see Thorban 1989, pp 93ff. See also brief discussion in Ziemke 1959, p 302.

the Torne Valley in this direction, and hurriedly started the construction of a system of fortifications in the border area on both Norwegian and Finnish territory.[116]

In early September 1944, it became clear to the Germans that Finland was leaving the war against the Soviet Union, which meant that the 20th Mountain Army's southern flank would be left open. This was exactly the situation Meretskov had foreseen, and he was now eager to launch an operation along the lines he had suggested in August. For days after the implementation of the ceasefire of 4–5 September, Meretskov forcefully argued for, and even took the first step to implement, an offensive deep into Finnish territory to cut of major parts of the retreating 20th Mountain Army from both of their directions of escape, to Norway and the Bothnian Bay ports. The plan included large-scale Red Army operations on Finnish territory, with Soviet troops reaching as far as Rovaniemi in the interior and Kemi and Oulu (Uleåborg) on the Bothnian Bay.

How this initiative evolved is complex, but essentially it illustrates that Meretskov realised, and strongly wanted to take advantage of, the 20th Mountain Army's precarious position. Meretskov was, in other words, thinking of an operation that resembled what Rendulic at Nuremberg, and in his memoirs, presented as an obvious opportunity for the Soviets that they mysteriously failed to realise. Meretskov sought Stalin and *Stavka*'s approval for his move even after he must have become aware of the terms of the 4 - 5 September ceasefire: no Red Army operations on Finnish territory, i.e., to the west of the new border as defined by the ceasefire understanding and further formalised in the armistice of 19 September 1944.[117] The Karelian Front commander's plan for operations on Finnish territory were abruptly stopped as late as 12 September 1944 by a stern rebuke from *Stavka*, reminding Meretskov of the terms of the ceasefire agreement with Finland.[118] Meretskov duly issued orders to the 19th and 26th Armies to discontinue their attacks.[119] However, none of Meretskov's never-to-be-realised plans for operations deep inside Finnish territory included operations to the west of the line Kemijärvi-Rovaniemi-Kemi. In other words, not even Meretskov envisaged an offensive towards the Norwegian border and the Skibotn-Lyngen area.

For the rest of the month, Meretskov's forces seem to have fully respected the new Finnish border as the end point of their operations: as soon as the Germans reached Finnish territory, they were safe from Soviet pursuit. In late September 1944, Meretskov received the order to finalise planning for a more limited operation: the offensive against the German XIX Corps on the Murmansk sector. This operation was far less ambitious than the larger one against the entire 20th Mountain Army

[116] Apart from Rendulic at the Nuremberg tribunal and in his memoirs, see also Hölter 1977, pp 39–40. See also Thorban 1989 and Kaltenegger 2003 for details about German preparations and operations.

[117] The Soviet statement that formed the basis of the 4–5 September 1944 ceasefire did not include the stipulation that the Petsamo area should be returned to the Soviet Union, thereby making Norway and the USSR neighbours. This, however, was at this point taken for granted by both the Finns and the Soviets. In 14th Army documents, therefore, Petsamo was "liberated", not "taken".

[118] *Stavka VGK*, document no. 200, Stavka directive no. 220213, 12 September 1944.

[119] TsAMO, f. 214, op. 1437, d. 2023, ll. 1a-44, "Zhurnal boevykh deistvii voisk 19 A KarF", 13 October 1944, entry for 12 September 1944.

for which he had repeatedly appealed from early August onwards. The Murmansk sector was by then the only place in the north where the Germans had retained their positions on Soviet territory.

Nevertheless, if the aim had been to effectively initiate the entire German Northern Front's collapse, and if foreign policy considerations had not been an issue, an obvious option for the Red Army would have been to attack past Rovaniemi and Muonio along the Torne Valley up to and including the narrow Skibotn-Lyngen area on the Norwegian side of the border. Is this perhaps what Stalin had in mind when, on 14 October 1944, he mentioned Northern Norway during an evening meeting with British Prime Minister Winston Churchill to discuss military affairs?[120]

This episode has been presented as suggesting that, in the autumn of 1944, Stalin did consider exactly this move despite the terms of the Soviet-Finnish ceasefire.[121] Besides Stalin, Churchill, and their military and civilian advisors, W. A. Harriman, US ambassador to Moscow, was also present, together with Major General John R. Dean, head of the US military mission to Moscow, and Edward Page Jr. of the US Embassy.

The British minutes of the conversation suggest that Stalin had no intention of engaging Soviet troops in Northern Norway. I quote the entire fragment of the conversation where Norway was discussed:

> Mr. CHURCHILL enquired whether the German forces in northern Finland could escape.
>
> MARSHAL STALIN said that Soviet troops had broken through in the North, and were now only two kilometres from Petsamo. Three of the German eight divisions were in that area, and the Soviet[s] *[sic]* hope to smash these. The question was, how could the remainder get out? The Finns were reluctant to fight them. They might possibly go through Sweden.
>
> Mr. CHURCHILL thought that the Swedes would certainly not agree to this.
>
> MARSHAL STALIN suggested that co-operation between the British and Russian forces in the North of Norway might be worth considering. If the British get a footing in Norway, they might be able to organise Norwegian forces and increase the sabotage of German communications.
>
> Mr. CHURCHILL said that the Germans had 8 to 10 divisions in Norway, though they were spread over the whole of that large country. No British Divisions *[sic]* were available in the United Kingdom to go to Norway, but it might certainly be possible for British naval forces to co-operate with the Soviet troops. He would very much like to hear any ideas which Marshal Stalin might have on this co-operation. It should be remembered that the Germans had about 150 U-boats in Norwegian ports.
>
> MARSHALL STALIN said that he would think over this question when Petsamo had been captured.[122]

Stalin's suggestion as recorded in this document—"co-operation between the British and Russian forces in the North of Norway"—provides little information about his intentions. One of the least plausible interpretations is that he was thinking of some joint offensive against Norwegian territory, with involvement of Soviet

[120] For more about the Stalin-Churchill meeting, see Holtsmark 2021c, pp 450–453.

[121] Cf. Riste 1979, pp 191f and 229f. Suprun 2020, p 278, gives a completely misleading account.

[122] TNA, PREM 3/434/5, minutes of meeting at 10 pm on 14 October 1944. I am grateful to Professor Patrick Salmon and to Mark Dunn of TNA for providing me with a copy of this file.

ground forces. Stalin's intention is more likely revealed by his suggestion that the British get a "foothold" in Norway. More precisely, they ought to send land forces, and organise Norwegian resistance groups, to "sabotage" German communications.[123]

This is the only fragment of the exchange recorded in the British minutes that is clear and unambiguous about what Stalin had in mind. These minutes suggest that Stalin was not thinking of a joint Soviet-British operation in the Skibotn-Lyngen area or anything remotely similar: an attack on German defences in the adjacent border areas would be a major military undertaking, implying far more than mere sabotage. Presumably, Stalin meant exactly what he said, which made military sense from a Soviet perspective: to get the British involved in Norway, and to support and maximise the strategic effectiveness of the Soviet offensive in the north, by hindering the Germans' transfer of troops from Northern Norway to the south of the country or directly to the continent.

Units of Lieutenant General Vladimir I. Shcherbakov's 14th Army took Petsamo the next day, on 15 October 1944, and, in so far as can be seen from the available sources, Stalin never returned to the issue. Norway is not mentioned in the published Soviet minutes of the meeting;[124] which is a strong hint that Stalin's suggestion, after Churchill's negative response, was not something to be considered further. We know from multiple sources that Stalin corrected draft minutes of his conversations. If the issue of Norway was something he regarded as a substantive part of the conversation, and something to be followed up, it is reasonable to expect that it would have been included.[125] Similarly, in later Soviet documents there are no traces of this Churchill-Stalin exchange about Northern Norway.

The foregoing shows that the Soviets in 1944 or until the German capitulation in May 1945 were not thinking of offensive action against the Germans in Norway—neither against the 20th Mountain Army when it was still on the move, nor against the German positions in the Lyngen-Skibotn area.

3.7 Concluding Remarks

After the end of the Petsamo-Kirkenes operation in early November 1944, the Soviet leadership never considered, or planned to continue the offensive into the Norwegian interior, whether from the Tana River positions, along the axis Ivalo-Lakselv, or along

[123] Stalin's disinterest in Northern Norway and Meretskov's plans for large-scale operations to trap the 20th Mountain Army may be explained also in purely strategic terms: continued operations against the Germans in Finland or Norway would hold back significant Soviet forces that were badly needed on the main theatres of the Eastern Front, while he could leave it to the Royal Navy to limit the transfer of German troops from Norway to mainland Europe. As it turned out, more than 220,000 German troops remained in Norway at the war's end on 8 May 1945.

[124] As published, without a footnote, in Rzheshevskii 2004, pp 459–461. I have not been able to find the original document in Russian archives.

[125] This discussion of the 14 October 1944 meeting is taken from Holtsmark 2021c, with the omission of some remarks on previous interpretations of Stalin's intentions.

the Torne Valley directly towards the Lyngen-Skibotn-Narvik area. Similarly, at this stage of the war, the Western Allies viewed Norway as a marginal theatre, and large-scale landing operations were not on the table. The Norwegian government's pleas for action to halt the German retreat and the destruction of Northern Norway went largely unheeded.

All this, however, was unbeknown to the Germans. The basic assumption at the *OKW/WFStab*, the *WBH Norwegen*, and within the 20th Mountain Army, was that Soviet and Western moves remained a possibility, although not necessarily in the near future. This assumption was the framework for the Germans' military posture in Northern Norway for the remainder of the war. Within this general picture there were visible differences among the German decision-makers—the *OKW/WFStab* and the 20th Mountain Army being more alarmistic about possible Allied moves than the *WBH Norwegen*. Yet, even the latter never discarded the possibility of large-scale Allied action against Northern Norway, by sea or land. However, the *WBH Norwegen* considered that such attacks would not come in winter but that the danger would resurface in spring. Given the Germans' limited knowledge of Allied intentions, there was nothing unreasonable in these German evaluations.

This means that Rendulic spoke the truth in Nuremberg when he emphasised his belief at the time in the danger of both Soviet and Western Allied large-scale attacks on German positions in Northern Norway, not least during the critical phases of the 20th Mountain Army's long march along *Reichsstrasse 50* and its fjord crossings. Moreover, his retelling of how his evaluation of Soviet and Allied intentions gradually changed—from seeing an immediate threat of at least a Soviet move in October and first part of November 1944, to gradually believing that the Allies would not move, at least not until spring 1945—is corroborated by contemporary German sources.

In other words, in so far as the judges based their verdict only on what they accepted as Rendulic's personal perceptions of Allied plans and options when the evacuation and destruction was ordered and then carried out, they reached the right conclusion. Of course, this is not the whole answer, for in other parts of his testimony, as in his memoir, Rendulic told a more ambiguous story.

There is strong evidence for the claim that, at the time, Rendulic did not see the *total* destruction and the forced evacuation of the *entire* population as a military necessity. Indeed, he and some of his subordinate commanders argued *against* these extreme solutions, not for humanitarian, but for strictly military reasons: they would be a burden to the 20th Mountain Army. Thus, when Rendulic at trial fully endorsed the destruction and the evacuation as it was carried out as an absolute military necessity, it may have been contrary to his perception of what constituted 'military necessity' at the time of the actual events.

By focusing too narrowly on the German threat perceptions and the legality of the scorched earth tactics, as such, it appears that the tribunal and judges largely missed this point. Instead, they should have looked closer into the *scale* of the destruction and evacuation. Put simply, the judges missed the crucial point of the *proportionality* of the Germans' actions—whether the *comprehensiveness* and the *geographical extension* of the destruction, and the (attempted) forced evacuation of the *entire* population could be seen as a military necessity. The judges accepted Rendulic's contemporaneous perception of possible Soviet and British moves, the legality *as such* of the scorched earth policy as well as the removal of the civilian population as sufficient grounds for the acquittal.

As a result, when the judges reached their conclusion, some questions were left unanswered: was the scale of the destruction and the order to evacuate by force the entire population motivated by factors other than military necessity? Was the motive for the destruction, including civilian dwellings far away from the likely march routes of an advancing enemy, not to obstruct the enemy's offensive, but rather to force the population to leave?[126]

The judges also somehow overlooked that Rendulic, when pressed, inadvertently admitted in court that he just followed orders. *If* the judges had noticed this element of Rendulic's testimony, the verdict might have been, or even should have been, different: following the verdict in 1946 against the top instigators of Nazi Germany's war of aggression, war crimes and crimes against humanity, just following orders did not relieve the organisers of the responsibility for their actions.

Acknowledgements I would like to thank the following for valuable comments to draft versions of this chapter, in alphabetical order: Nobuo Hayashi, Carola Lingaas, Sigurd Sørlie, Matthew Talbert, and the participants in the project workshop in September 2022.

References

HLSNTP (undated) Harvard Law School Nuremberg Trials Project, https://nbg-02.lil.tools, Transcript for NMT 7: *Hostage* case

Holtsmark SG (1993) A Soviet Grab for the High North? USSR, Svalbard, and Northern Norway 1920–1953. Norwegian Institute for Defence Studies, Oslo

Holtsmark SG (2004) Høyt spill. Svalbard-spørsmålet 1944–47. Norwegian Institute for Defence Studies, Oslo

Holtsmark SG (2021a) Non-Science Fiction on Stalin and Norway. The Journal of Slavic Military Studies 34/1:115–131. DOI: https://doi.org/10.1080/13518046.2021.1923987

Holtsmark SG (2021b) Improvised Liberation, October 1944: The Petsamo-Kirkenes Operation and the Red Army in Norway. Part I. The Journal of Slavic Military Studies 34/2:271–302. DOI: https://doi.org/10.1080/13518046.2021b.1990554

Holtsmark SG (2021c) Improvised Liberation, October 1944: The Petsamo-Kirkenes Operation and the Red Army in Norway. Part II. The Journal of Slavic Military Studies 34/3:426–458. DOI: https://doi.org/10.1080/13518046.2021c.1992707

Holtsmark SG (ed) (1995) Norge og Sovjetunionen 1917–1955. En utenrikspolitisk dokumentasjon. Cappelen, Oslo

Hölter H (1977) Armee in der Arktis: die Operationen der deutschen Lappland-Armee. Schild Verlag, Munich

Kaltenegger R (2003) Krieg in der Arktis. Die Operationen der Lappland-Armee 1942–1945. Leopold Stocker Verlag, Graz/Stuttgart

Kjære landsmenn (1955) Kjære landsmenn. Kong Haakon den VII's taler under krigen 1940 til 1945. Hjemmenes Forlag, Oslo

[126] This interpretation is implied in Korsnes 2021.

Komarov AA et al. (eds) (1997) Sovetsko-norvezhskie otnosheniya 1917–1955. Sbornik dokumentov. Elia-Art-O, Moscow. DOI: http://docs.historyrussia.org/ru/nodes/91745-sovetsko-norvezhskie-otnosheniya-1917-1955
Korsnes K (2021) Brenning og tvangsevakuering i Finnmark 1944. https://actanorvegica.no/2021/02/28/brenning-og-tvangsevakuering-i-Finnmark-1944/
Krasnaya armiya (2000) Krasnaya armiya v stranakh Tsentral'noi, Severnoi Evropy i na Balkanakh. Dokumenty i materialy 1944–1945. Terra 2000, Moscow
Mann C (2012) British Policy and Strategy Towards Norway, 1941-1945. Palgrave Macmillan, Basingstoke
Manninen O (2004) The Soviet Plans for the North-Western Theatre of Operations in 1939-1944. National Defence University, Helsinki
Monakov M, Rohwer J (2001) Stalin's Ocean-Going Fleet. Soviet Naval Strategy and Shipbuilding Programs, 1935–53. Routledge, London
Nielsen JP (2002) The Russia of the Tsar and North Norway. "The Russian Danger" Revisited. Acta Borealia, 19/1: 75–94
Rendulic L (1952) Gekämpft, gesiegt, geschlagen. Welsermühl, Heidelberg
Rendulic L (1953) Glasenbach-Nürnberg-Landsberg. Ein Soldatenschicksal nach dem Krieg. Leopold Stocker Verlag, Graz/Göttingen
Riste O (1979) "London-regjeringa". Norge i krigsalliansen 1940–1940. Vol. 2: Vegen heim. Det norske samlaget, Oslo
Rzheshevskii OA (2004) Stalin, Cherchill. Vstrechi, besedy, diskussii. Dokumenty, komentarii, 1941–1945. Nauka, Moscow
Schramm PA (ed) (1961) Kriegstagebuch des Oberkommandos der Wehrmacht: (Wehrmachtführungsstab) 1940–1945. Volume 4: 1 January 1944–22 May 1945, first half-volume. Bernard & Graefer Verlag für Wehrwesen, Frankfurt am Main
Stavka VGK (1999) Stavka VGK. Dokumenty i materialy 1944–1945. Terra, Moscow
Suprun M (2020) The Liberation of Northern Norway in Stalin's Post-War Strategy. The Journal of Slavic Military Studies 33/2:277–291
Thorban FW (1989) Der Abwehrkampf um Petsamo und Kirkenes 1944. Operationen "Birke" und 'Nordlicht'. Die letzte Schlacht an der Eismeerfront im Oktober 1944 – Die Absetzbewegungen nach Nordnorwegen und das Kriegsende im Raum Lyngen-Narvik. Podzun-Pallas-Verlag, Friedberg
Ziemke EF (1959) The German Northern Theater of Operations 1940–1945. Department of the Army, Washington D.C.

Sven G. Holtsmark Professor of History, Norwegian Institute for Defence Studies, Norwegian Defence University College, Oslo 0150, Akershus Fortress, Norway, e-mail: sholtsmark@mil.no

Chapter 4
Devastation and Forced Evacuation: The Actors and Their Motives

Stian Bones and Gunnar D. Hatlehol

Contents

4.1 Introduction 82
4.2 Terboven's Claw 83
4.3 Military Prerequisites 86
4.4 Organisation of the "Voluntary" Evacuation 89
4.5 Decision to Forcibly Evacuate 91
4.6 Motives 102
References 106

Abstract On 28 October 1944, Adolf Hitler ordered Lothar Rendulic, Commander-in-Chief of the 20th Mountain Army, to evacuate civilians to the east of Lyngen in Norway and destroy their homes. This event was later adjudicated before the International Military Tribunal in Nuremberg in the case against *Generaloberst* Alfred Jodl. Although Jodl claimed that it was Josef Terboven who gave the order, Jodl was found guilty and executed in 1946. The following year, Rendulic was indicted before a US military tribunal for the same facts. He claimed that the scorched earth tactics were necessary for withdrawal of his troops. The judges believed Rendulic and acquitted him. Historical research for this chapter shows that there were strong political motives behind the measures taken and that Terboven played a crucial part. Evacuees in Northern Norway were reluctant to follow instructions from the occupation regime. In Eastern Finnmark, people were threatened into evacuating: they were told what would happen if the "Bolsheviks" arrived. However, most were not intimidated or persuaded. Their resistance imperiled the entire Norwegian occupation regime, and Terboven responded with even tougher measures. Contemporaneous material reveals that Rendulic and his subordinate commanders considered Northern Norway's total devastation and forced evacuation needless distractions. Terboven's actions were likely linked to a power play as the occupation regime in Norway

S. Bones (✉)
UiT The Arctic University of Norway, Hansine Hanssens veg 18, 9019 Tromsø, Norway
e-mail: stian.bones@uit.no

S. Bones · G. D. Hatlehol
Narvik War and Peace Centre, Tromsø, Norway
e-mail: ghatlehol@narviksenteret.no

N. Hayashi and C. Lingaas (eds.), *Honest Errors? Combat Decision-Making 75 Years After the* Hostage *Case*, https://doi.org/10.1007/978-94-6265-611-6_4

headed for its downfall. Terboven attempted unsuccessfully to strengthen his grip on the German army in Norway.

Keywords North Norway · scorched earth tactics · evacuation · Josef Terboven · Lothar Rendulic · Nuremberg · Alfred Jodl · Ferdinand Jodl

4.1 Introduction[1]

On 28 October 1944, Adolf Hitler issued a fateful order. He ordered the Commander-in-Chief of the 20th Mountain Army to forcibly evacuate the civilian population to the east of Lyngen in Norway "for their own safety".[2] At the same time, all homes would be burnt to the ground or otherwise destroyed.

The devastation and forced evacuation of Northern Norway became the subject of adjudication before the International Military Tribunal in Nuremberg in the case against *Generaloberst* Alfred Jodl, Commander of the Operations Staff of the *Oberkommando der Wehrmacht* (*OKW*). Jodl maintained that it was Josef Terboven, *Reichskommissar* for Norway, who had given the order.[3] Jodl was found guilty on all counts, sentenced to death and executed in 1946.

The following year, *Generaloberst* Lothar Rendulic was indicted before the US military tribunal in Nuremberg. He took a different strategy from Jodl, stressing the vested interests of the *Wehrmacht* instead. Rendulic claimed that the *Oberkommando* of the 20th Mountain Army considered it absolutely necessary to execute the scorched earth tactics and forcibly evacuate the population. The German army leadership on the Northern Front agreed that Hitler's directive was a military necessity to ensure withdrawal.[4] The judges, under the leadership of Charles F. Wennerstrum, believed Rendulic and decided that he would not be convicted of the destruction in Finnmark and Northern Troms and the forced evacuation of the population.[5]

As such, the Nuremberg processes provided two different answers as to who on the German side was responsible. In the decades following World War II, all surviving sources relating to this withdrawal have become available for research. The sources show that there were strong political motives behind the measures taken and that Terboven played a crucial part. The Norwegian occupation regime, including

[1] This chapter builds on a study previously published in Norwegian. See Bones and Hatlehol 2022.

[2] Fernschreiben, 29.10.44 from OKW/WFSt, signed Jodl, attached to KTB, 20. (Geb.) AOK, Anlageband 16.10.–31.10.44. NARA, T312/1068, PG65641/4.

[3] *Trial of the Major War Criminals before the International Military Tribunal Nuremberg, 14 November–1 October 1946*, vol. 15 (Nuremberg: International Military Tribunal, 1947), p 555.

[4] *Trials of War Criminals before the Nuernberg Military Tribunals*, vol. 11, pp 1134–1136.

[5] Ibid., pp 1295–1297.

Vidkun Quisling's *Nasjonal Samling* (NS) government, was also heavily involved for political reasons.[6]

Nevertheless, military threat assessments, military planning, and operations were crucial to the outcome as well. Long before October and November 1944, the 20th Mountain Army had developed plans that entailed severe destructions during a retreat through Northern Norway. This chapter will show that military leaders, including Rendulic, were reluctant to the idea of total destruction.

4.2 Terboven's Claw

The idea of evacuating the population did not arise suddenly. Until 1944, around 5,000 Finnmark locals, especially from Eastern Finnmark, had fled the war-torn areas on their own initiative. Soviet bombing raids and other acts of war made life both insecure and dangerous. During the spring of 1943, *Generalleutnant* Curt Ebeling, Commander of the 210th Infantry Division, therefore advocated evacuating women, children, and the elderly. But neither Terboven nor *Generaloberst* Eduard Dietl, then Commander of the 20th Mountain Army, agreed with his assessment. Norwegian labour was precious and needed to be retained in the area. An evacuation would also send an unfortunate political signal that Germany was not in control of the north. Ebeling's proposal was excoriated by Dietl and Terboven, who were on particularly good terms with each other.[7]

The idea of an evacuation was also floated within the Norwegian occupation regime. Gard Holtskog, who was strongly associated with Jonas Lie, Minister of Police, and appointed President of the Finnmark Police Force in October 1943, immediately started drafting a plan on the evacuation of Kirkenes. This plan was met with opposition from several German civilian and military leaders in Eastern Finnmark. Following further extensive bombing raids against Kirkenes, Vardø, and Vadsø in July 1944, Holtskog was eager to initiate a quiet, voluntary evacuation. The occupiers, however, continued to hold back.[8]

It is the realisation that Finland was to withdraw from the war that caused the Germans to implement their retreat and evacuation plans. In order to coordinate the planning of the evacuation, meetings were also held between Terboven and the NS government.[9] At the ministerial meeting on 26 September 1944, Frederik Prytz, Minister of Finance, raised a "secret government matter". The matter related to

[6] Eriksen and Halvorsen 1987 argued this view, which is also evident from Per Kristian Olsen (see Olsen 2019) and Ingunn Elstad (see Elstad 2020).

[7] Eriksen and Halvorsen 1987, pp 39–40; NHM FO II, Div, L0031, 1c No. 1114/44 Secret (inquiry into the evacuation), 29 October 1944, signed by Ebeling.

[8] Copies of Holtskog's report can be found in several archives, here based on SATØ, South Varanger Police Department (Appendix), Eba 1. See also Fosnes 1974; Augestad 2016.

[9] This is according to the statement given by Hagelin during questioning on 7 December 1945. RA, L case, Oslo D 3802 Johan Andreas Lippestad, available from https://media.digitalarkivet.no/view/69762 [accessed 1 April 2023], pp 1484–1486.

Norway's status, especially the relationship between the NS government, the *Reichskommissariat*, and Germany, a contentious issue that had preoccupied the NS leadership throughout the entire occupation. As a result of the military developments, Prytz realised that the occupation of parts of Northern Norway by Soviet or other Allied troops was likely. This would consequently pave the way for the government-in-exile in London to establish authority on Norwegian soil. "When this is achieved," Prytz wrote, "the position of the current national government [...] will become unsustainable. The exiled government's state authority representative on Norwegian soil will use their propaganda and activities to claim that they are the ones who are working for Norway's freedom and independence."[10] In other words: if the government-in-exile managed to gain a foothold on Norwegian soil, the NS state could collapse completely.

The threats facing the German occupying regime were existential. For the NS government, it was essential to obtain German acceptance for a separate peace with Norway. The main purpose was to make Hitler "establish that peace prevails and has always prevailed between the Greater Germanic Reich and Norway, represented by the national government".[11] If approved, the *Reichskommissariat* could be closed down. The NS government hoped that this, in turn, would undermine the government-in-exile's "propaganda" that the NS government was merely "a form of administration under German leadership".[12]

Prytz's proposal at the ministerial meeting, to try and convince Hitler to formally establish peace with Norway, was completely unrealistic and contradicted itself on several points. On the one hand, he referred to the government-in-exile's statements about the NS government as propaganda. On the other hand, he referenced examples that supported the claims made by the Norwegian government in London. Among other things, Prytz mentioned that Norwegian officers were prisoners of war of Germany (precisely because there was a state of war) and that, since 24 April 1940, the *Reichskommissariat* had had the "supreme government authority in Norway". For anyone other than the most delusional NS people, it would also appear completely unrealistic that Hitler or Terboven would now, in the final stages of the war, let go of the real power of governance.

The difficult situation that the occupiers were now facing could also lead to another conclusion: it was politically dangerous to leave behind the Norwegian population in those parts of Norway from which the *Wehrmacht* had to withdraw. A population left behind would inevitably cooperate with the government-in-exile. Beyond the control

---

[10] The active role of the NA was first identified by Knut Einar Eriksen and Terje Halvorsen (see Eriksen and Halvorsen 1987, pp 40ff). For Prytz's speech, see minutes recorded from the ministerial meeting on 26 September 1944, secret state matter, RA/S-4279/Db/L0111, available from https://media.digitalarkivet.no/view/39772/168 [accessed 1 April 2023] (emphasis in the original).

[11] Minutes recorded from the ministerial meeting on 26 September 1944, secret state matter, RA/S-4279/Db/L0111, available from https://media.digitalarkivet.no/view/39772/168 [accessed 1 April 2023].

[12] Minutes recorded from the ministerial meeting on 26 September 1944, secret state matter, RA/S-4279/Db/L0111, available from https://media.digitalarkivet.no/view/39772/168 [accessed 1 April 2023].

of the occupation regime, the civilian population of Finnmark would thereby constitute a propaganda apparatus by virtue of its very existence. Furthermore, there was a risk that civilians would enter the military services in the next phase of the war. The NS government and Terboven stood side-by-side to counteract such a development, that would later become known under the term "autumn of fires" of 1944.

SS *Obersturmbannführer* Hans-Hendrik Neumann, Commander of the *Einsatzstab Norwegen*, was the intermediary and coordinator of discussions between Terboven, the NS government, and the *Wehrmacht*. Neumann had the main responsibility for all issues relating to dialogue with the National Assembly.[13]

On 7 October 1944, shortly after the beginning of the Lapland War in Northern Finland, Terboven tasked Neumann to head north to begin acting as his liaison with Rendulic.[14] Neumann's purpose was to secure the necessary support from the 20th Mountain Army to carry out the so-called "voluntary evacuation". His document folder also contained the authority to lead large parts of the evacuation. All agencies, German as well as Norwegian that fell under the *Reichskommissariat*, had to follow his orders. This would help Terboven secure the interests of Germany's civilian occupation authorities in Finnmark.[15]

The next person to receive directives from Terboven was Quisling, who was to appoint a minister with special authorisation to act alongside Neumann.[16] Quisling followed up by appointing NS minister Lie as *styresmann* of Finnmark, which meant that he was given a special authority. Another NS minister, Johan Lippestad, acted as his deputy. These appointments were based on a temporary act from October 1944. Terboven immediately informed the two NS ministers that the civilian population would have to evacuate itself using its own means of transport.

The fact that the *Wehrmacht* was unable to prioritise logistical support for the evacuation also became clear as soon as Lie and Lippestad arrived in Kirkenes. There they met, among others, Ebeling, Commander of the 210th Infantry Division, and Friedrich Neven, Commander of the *Reichskommissariat* Office in Kirkenes. In Eastern Finnmark, the *Wehrmacht* had seized the vast majority of vehicles and did not want any civilian transport to take place along State Road 50, the main road to the west and south.[17] A major transport operation of civilians would create obstacles for the military withdrawal.

---

[13] Neumann arrived in Norway from his role as adjutant to Reinhard Heydrich, cf. Bohn 2000, p 118. Heydrich was the Commander of the *Reichssicherheitshauptsamt*, one of the main SS departments and was therefore directly subordinate to the powerful SS Commander Heinrich Himmler.

[14] Stated by Heinrich Schnurbusch during questioning on 7 October, von Stackelberg 9 October. But Neumann was with Rendulic on 8 October, so the former is likely to be correct.

[15] Statement from von Stackelberg, given during questioning on 25 November 1945. RA, L case, Oslo D 3802 Johan Andreas Lippestad, available from https://media.digitalarkivet.no/view/69762 (pp 1524–1534) [accessed 1 April 2023].

[16] Statement from Heinrich Schnurbusch, November 1945, RA, L case, Oslo D 3802 Johan Andreas Lippestad, available from https://media.digitalarkivet.no/view/69762 (pp 1535–1539) [accessed 1 April 2023].

[17] Von Stackelberg's statement dated 1 February 1946. RA/S-3138/0001/D/Dg/L0409, folder "G. W. Müller. Forklaringer etc.".

As mentioned earlier, Ebeling had long been attempting to evacuate the civilian population of Eastern Finnmark. By the time he fled with his division at the end of October 1944, he had been working on the matter for more than a year. However, Terboven refused. During the bombings of Vardø, Vadsø, and Kirkenes in August 1944, Ebeling believed that it was time for a forced evacuation. Some voluntary evacuation did take place from these towns, in line with the General's directions. He also attempted, via Rendulic, to influence Terboven to adopt additional measures, but the *Reichskommissar* continued to resist. Ferdinand Jodl, Commander of the XIX Army Corps, equally stressed to Ebeling that evacuation of "the civilians had nothing to do with us, it was being sorted entirely by the *Reichskommissariat* under Terboven".[18]

Terboven thus had a firm grip on the events as well as the formal authority. When he eventually allowed an evacuation, a significant proportion of the civilian population was evacuated from Eastern Finnmark. Boat transport became the solution for most people, who sailed southwest along the coast. Ebeling unhappily stated that the hasty evacuation from Eastern Finnmark would never be successful; the civilian population believed that sea transport was too dangerous and was thus reluctant to travel by sea. Nor was there any transport capacity on land. The civilian population therefore felt that there were greater risks associated with travelling than with remaining.[19]

4.3 Military Prerequisites

Hitler and the *Wehrmacht* had long been preparing themselves for the necessity of a withdrawal in the north. On 28 September 1943, Dietl received Hitler's Directive No. 50, which, among other things, instructed the 20th Mountain Army to prepare new defence measures if Finland withdrew from the war.[20] In February 1944, the staff of the 20th Mountain Army in Rovaniemi had an initial plan ready. It described a withdrawal to Northern Finland and Northern Norway, where forward defence posts were organised in a line running from Petsamo via Ivalo to Karesuando. This line would ensure continued German control of the nickel mines in Petsamo, which was important to Hitler. The withdrawal plan, referred to as *Birke*, entailed critical risk factors, such as problems arising from poor roads, long distances, and the harsh climate. The entire operation could also be undermined if the Allied forces challenged

[18] RA/S-3138/0048/D/Db/L0034, L case Peder J. Berg. Questioning of Ferdinand Jodl, 13 December 1945. Fosnes (see Fosnes 1974, pp 11 and 16) interprets it as though Terboven gradually gained influence over something that was originally a military matter (cf. also Jacobsen 2017, p 323). This description is therefore not comprehensive.

[19] NHM, FO II, Div, L0031, 1c No. 1114/44 Secret (inquiry into the evacuation), 29 October 1944, signed by Ebeling.

[20] OKW, WFSt, KTB II, entries from 28 September 1943, 19 November 1943, with reference to "Führerweisung No. 50"; Ziemke 1959, pp 249–250 and 276ff.

the German control of the Northern Norwegian coast.[21] The risk of lesser Western actions—commando raids, sabotage and other targeted "needlestick operations"—was also imminent.

Both Hitler and his military commanders considered the Western threat extremely serious. During 1941 and 1942, British troops had carried out several raids in Northern Norway. Intelligence reports, including from Stockholm, concerning possible Western landing operations in Norway contributed to raised levels of preparedness on the Northern Front. The *OKW* ordered supply stores at the Northern Cap (*Nordkalotten*) to be sufficiently stocked to last for eight to nine months of warfare.[22]

During the winter of 1943, Nikolaus von Falkenhorst, Commander-in-Chief of the *Wehrmacht* in Norway, believed that an Allied landing could most likely be expected in the region between Trondheim and Narvik. Such a landing would have far-reaching consequences. It would lead to Sweden and Finland amending their war policy and being dragged in a Western direction, which would dramatically weaken the strategic position of Germany in the Nordic region and the Baltic Sea.[23] There was a possibility that the forces in the north would become isolated. This threat perception formed the basis of the German plans, drawn up in 1943, to carry out a military operation against Sweden.[24] This double threat, from both the West and the Soviet Union, had an impact on the German withdrawal from the Northern Cape during the autumn of 1944.

The 20th Mountain Army launched Operation *Birke* on 3 September 1944, the same day that Finland informed Germany of its intention to negotiate a ceasefire with the Soviet Union. Sailing parts of the 20th Mountain Army across the Baltic Sea to Germany was not an option. The entire army would need to withdraw to Northern Norway. Rendulic, Commander of the 20th Mountain Army as of 28 June 1944, was initially convinced that the Red Army would pursue the army as it retreated through Northern Finland.[25] This turned out not to be the case. When Germany's XXXVI Army Corps withdrew from the Kandalaksha Front, the Red Army stopped on the border near Salla. Further south, in the region from which the XVIII Army Corps withdrew, the Soviet forces also stopped at the Finnish-Soviet border.

Both Terboven and von Falkenhorst were consulted in connection with the implementation of Operation *Birke*. On 19 September 1944, the *OKW* in Berlin suggested to Rendulic that the positions in Northern Finland might have to be abandoned that same autumn, with the entire 20th Mountain Army withdrawing behind a defence post in the Lyngen region. On 3 October 1944, Hitler approved a plan to withdraw to the Lyngen Line, known as Operation *Nordlicht*. The following day, Alfred Jodl issued an order to the 20th Mountain Army. The order stated, among other things,

---

[21] The fear was pervasive, cf. OKW, WFSt, KTB II, entries dated 4 July 1943, 8 September 1943. See Chap. 3.

[22] Cf. OKW, WFSt, KTB III A, entry dated 5 January 1943.

[23] Ziemke 1959, pp 252, 276.

[24] See especially Zetterberg 2002.

[25] Ziemke 1959, p 293.

that any physical installations that could benefit the enemy needed to be destroyed: roads, railways, port facilities, airports, *Luftwaffe* installations, industrial facilities, as well as military camps and military structures. Supplies would either need to be seized or destroyed. During the withdrawal, the whole armed Norwegian population in the area should be brought in and handed over to the *Reichskommissar*. Finnish hostages could also be brought in, if required by the situation.[26]

Destructions as well as evacuations of parts of the population were regarded as necessary from a military point of view. Both were a part of Operation *Nordlicht* from the very beginning. However, the Soviet Union's fierce offensive required improvisation. The XIX Army Corps suffered significant loss of troops, equipment and eventually also supplies. It was therefore impossible to follow all the withdrawal plans intended by Operation *Nordlicht*.

On 13 October 1944, Rendulic recommended to the *OKW* that the civilian population to the east of Lyngen should be evacuated, with the exception of those parts of the population that would be useful during Operation *Nordlicht*. Determining who would be useful was up to the Commander of the XIX Army Corps and Terboven. The civilian population would be evacuated using Norwegian vessels.[27]

Rendulic received the *OKW*'s response on 14 October 1944. The order stated that his soldiers would support the *Reichskommissariat* with the evacuation of the civilian population, "at least the parts capable of war and labour".[28] Again, the *OKW*'s clarifications indicate that Terboven had exerted his influence, as the response was entirely in line with Terboven's and Neumann's arrangements. Terboven already contacted Field Marshal Wilhelm Keitel, Commander of the *OKW*, on 12 October 1944, requesting the 20th Mountain Army's support for the evacuation, especially the parts of the population that were capable of labour. Terboven noted the political aspects of the matter: this part of the population should not be left behind. Their continued presence in the region would make it easier for the Bolsheviks or the government-in-exile to seize power and gain popular support.[29] These considerations laid the foundation for the so-called voluntary evacuation.

---

[26] *Trials of War Criminals before the Nuernberg Military Tribunals under Control Council Law No. 10*, Vol XI, p 1114; NOKW-1776. See also Fosnes 1974, pp 7–9; Jaklin 2016, p 60; Jacobsen 2017, pp 212–213. See also more detailed documented dated 6 October from Korsnes 2021, with reference to NARA, PG32162, T1022/1719 and available from: https://actanorvegica.no/2021/02/28/brenning-og-tvangsevakuering-i-finnmark-1944 [accessed 1 April 2023].

[27] Korsnes 2021, with reference to NARA, OKW 138/2, microfilm T77/1419. See also Fosnes 1974, p 8. Regarding "Raum Kirkenes", see KTB (Geb.) AOK 20/la, entries dated 14 and 15 October. At the same time, further clarifications were also issued from OKW/WFSt and (Geb.) AOK 20 concerning physical destruction, which largely followed up on the order from 4 October, cf. also Fosnes 1974, pp 14–15.

[28] Fosnes 1974, p 11.

[29] Fosnes 1974, pp 10–11.

4.4 Organisation of the "Voluntary" Evacuation

From 4 October 1944, there was internal agreement within the occupation regime that an evacuation would take place. This was the background for Terboven instructing Neumann to travel north as a special envoy to coordinate the evacuation. In the first few days, it was up to the military commanders in Eastern Finnmark to determine the extent to which the Norwegian civilian population would be evacuated. At this time, the *Wehrmacht* was mostly concerned with ensuring that civilian evacuees did not get in the way of German movements. The two NS ministers, Lie and Lippestad, arrived in Kirkenes on 11 October 1944 where they were forced to accept Ferdinand Jodl's decision not to announce the civilian evacuation. The so-called voluntary evacuation became known only through "propaganda whispers". The military leaders did not want the evacuation to be announced in public yet, because it would complicate the military operation if civilians made more use of the infrastructure.

By that time, only a very small proportion of the population had evacuated the area. During the summer and autumn of 1944, intense Soviet bombardments of several towns in Eastern Finnmark led most of their inhabitants to relocate within the region. The remaining population was sceptical to evacuation by sea because of the high risks involved.

Terboven displayed his influence by making his special envoy Neumann (*Arbeitsstab* Neumann) organise an important meeting in Billefjord on 14 October 1944, where plans for further evacuation work were made. The meeting split the evacuation into three sections: Eastern Finnmark, Western Finnmark from the Nordkinn Peninsula to the county border, and Northern Troms down to the Lyngen Line. Whilst the evacuation in Eastern Finnmark needed to be largely improvised, there was time for additional organisation in Western Finnmark and Northern Troms.

The Billefjord meeting provided clarity regarding the evacuation's implementation. The population would be evacuated in the order of priority: first NS members and their relatives, followed by German-friendly individuals and their relatives, and finally people who volunteered to evacuate. Other parts of the population would evacuate in the next round but need to "stay in the region until the very end to be evacuated together with the Wehrmacht".[30] This applied to individuals who could, if necessary, bear arms, and key persons required to manage the evacuation. A decision was also made on how boat transport would take place, and Marcus Bull, County Governor of Troms, was tasked with establishing a reception system for evacuees in Northern Nordland and Troms.

The following day, on 15 October 1944, the 20th Mountain Army gave an order to encourage and support the "voluntary evacuation", as it was referred to by the occupation regime.[31] Over the next couple of days, the evacuation plans became known to the public. The measures planned by representatives of the Norwegian

[30] RA/S-3138/0048/D/Db/L0034, L case Peder J. Berg. Minutes, meeting in Billefjord, 14 October 1944.

[31] RA/S-3138/0048/D/Db/L0034, L case Peder J. Berg. Minutes, meeting in Tromsø, 19 October 1944.

occupation regime make it clear that evacuation was not really voluntary. With the support of Terboven, Lie and his people initiated a campaign built on threats, scare tactics, and retaliations.[32]

A plan developed by *Arbeitsstab* Neumann, which was presented to NS Minister Lie on 17 October, said that Norwegians who were considered able to fight ("wehrfähige") would be withdrawn by force.[33] This was intended to have a mobilising effect on the civilian population. Neumann and General Willi Moser, Commander of the LXXI Corps, hoped that this decision would also encourage relatives of armed Norwegians to evacuate. On 20 October, the 20th Mountain Army gave its support for this plan.[34] Thus, it could be argued that these "wehrfähige" Norwegians could be considered hostages. One reason for keeping them under military control was the belief and intention that this would trigger action on the part of others.

Meanwhile, in an effort to encourage people to evacuate, the propaganda machine continued to release information that all homes would be destroyed. In reality, however, Moser agreed with Neumann on 25 October 1944 not to destroy individual homes. Alongside these forcible measures, the coastal population would also be tempted through "promises of new fishing grounds, accommodation, etc. Boathouses are available in Lofoten for provisional use".[35]

In the event, evacuees proved profoundly reluctant to follow instructions from the occupation regime. The occupiers therefore viewed the measure as unsuccessful. In Eastern Finnmark, Lie frightened people into evacuating. In one manifesto, he painted a picture of what would happen when the "Bolsheviks" arrived in Norway: "[i]t means murder and plunder, terror and arbitrariness, rape, godlessness and moral decay". Still, most inhabitants were not intimidated or persuaded. Instead, a widespread resistance characterised the people's attitude.

The only successful part of the evacuation plan was the reception system, which was not controlled by the occupation regime. Within just a few days, a fully functioning reception system was established in the city of Tromsø. It was largely capable of operating without any direct involvement from various NS bodies. As previously mentioned, several thousand people, perhaps even as many as 5,000, were evacuated from Eastern Finnmark before the German withdrawal. When the withdrawal started, the challenges of transporting and receiving arrivals from Finnmark became significant. In Tromsø, Councillor Lars Thøring and Ragnar Hansen, leader of the Evacuation Commission, assumed great responsibility. Significant efforts were initiated to ensure that the evacuees would receive healthcare, food, shelter, and space on a vessel. During October 1944, the Evacuation Commission in Tromsø had gathered seventeen local ships, just over 250 boats and several other vessels for the effort.[36]

---

[32] Eriksen and Halvorsen 1987, pp 41–44; Olsen 2019, pp 44–64.

[33] Elstad 2020, pp 193–194, 216–218.

[34] Fosnes 1974, pp 32–33.

[35] RA/S-3138/0048/D/Db/L0034, Letter dated 25 October 1944 from Neumann to SD Hammerfest.

[36] Augestad 2016, p 31. See also Chap. 5.

When Lie and Lippestad reported on the status for October 1944, the NS considered the results discouraging. Threats and propaganda were supposed to lead to evacuation. When the civilian population reacted to such measures with blatant reluctance—a willingness to resist—a new situation was created. Their resistance now threatened the very occupation regime. Terboven responded with even tougher measures, in the form of coercion and oppression involving military force.

4.5 Decision to Forcibly Evacuate

Terboven was a good friend of Dietl and so interested in his army that the frequency of his visits to its headquarters in Rovaniemi increased. Rendulic, Dietl's successor, was a blank page to Terboven. Yet, just like his predecessor, the golden party emblem adorned Rendulic's uniform, a visible sign of the high position he held in party circles. In order to get to know the new commander better, Terboven eventually sent four men from his inner circle to Rovaniemi. The impression they brought back with them to Oslo was that Terboven and the occupation administration would not have the same cordial relationship with Rendulic as they did with Dietl.[37] Rendulic was a determined officer and less sensitive to the interests of the civilian occupation authorities than Terboven had become accustomed to.

On 26 October 1944, Terboven met with Moser in Narvik and received an initial briefing on the military situation. Moser informed Terboven how the XVIII Mountain Corps, to the very south of the Northern Front, had suffered serious losses. In Tromsø, where Terboven and his entourage arrived in the evening, other high-ranking German officers presented their assessments of the situation. The *Reichskommissar* now appeared to be convinced that the Soviets would advance along State Road 50. Terboven explained, likely for the first time, that he was in favour of completely destroying the Norwegian regions from which the *Wehrmacht* was withdrawing.[38] Immediately after this meeting, Terboven began sending telegrams to Martin Bormann, Hitler's deputy and Commander of the German Nazi Party (*Nationalsozialistische Deutsche Arbeiterpartei*, NSDAP) headquarters.[39] Bormann was the only acquaintance of Terboven who was able to introduce him to Hitler at a time when access to the *Führer* had been restricted to a minimum, even for leading National Socialists directly subordinate to him.

By October 1944, Bormann had long become impatient with Terboven.[40] Nevertheless, Bormann likely sympathised with the content of Terboven's telegrams and

---

[37] RA/S-3138/0001/D/Dg/L0409, L case G.W. Müller. "The retreat of the XX Army through Finnmark and Troms and the evacuation of the Northern Norwegian industry", report by Carlo Otte, November 1944.

[38] L case G.W. Müller, Oslo pkm, Dg L0409. Questioning of Günther Marre, 26/02/1946.

[39] Questioning of Günther Marre, 26/02/1946. L case G.W. Müller, Oslo pkm, Dg L0409.

[40] NHM 153. PWIS no. 80 "Reichskommissariat for occupied Norway"; Gschaid 1995, p 282. Diary entry 27/11/1944.

relayed the *Reichskommissar*'s gloomy proposal for the northernmost part of Norway to Hitler. Hitler's diary shows that Bormann was present with the *Führer* on 27 October 1944 from 6:15 pm.[41] Perhaps this was the point at which Hitler was informed of Terboven's assessment and proposal.[42] According to Alfred Jodl's testimony in Nuremberg in June 1946, Terboven also made direct telephone contact with Hitler on 28 October 1944.[43]

Jodl watched the events on the Northern Front from the *Führer*'s headquarters. Jodl was a technically and tactically competent military professional with little interest in the war's broader military, strategic, and political issues. During the war years, he had developed a loyalty to Hitler that went beyond simple admiration and developed National Socialist ways of thinking. Three conspicuous features of Jodl were his aspirations, his level of ambition, and his obstinacy. Since 23 August 1939, Jodl had been the Commander of the Operations Staff at the *OKW* directly under Keitel but eventually secured greater importance and responsibility in the position. Early in the war, Jodl became Keitel's actual equal and, like Keitel, ended up with direct access to the *Führer*, a privilege other generals were seldom afforded.[44] The *OKW* was Hitler's administrative governing body in his capacity as Commander-in-Chief of the *Wehrmacht*. Whilst Keitel acted as Hitler's Chief of Administration in practice, Jodl grew into the role as Hitler's Chief of Operations and most important military adviser, making him one of the very few generals to whom Hitler would listen respectfully. Jodl could occasionally oppose Hitler, but he would more often take the same stance.[45] Just like Keitel, Jodl had no command authority on his own behalf in relation to equals and subordinate officers outside of the *OKW*. Rather, their authority was based on Hitler's authority. They were, within their respective fields, tasked with turning his whims and decisions into clear, detailed military orders and subsequently ensuring that these orders were implemented.

Jodl managed the operational staff at the *OKW* largely in accordance with the *Führer* principles. This meant that, in practice, the *OKW*'s operational staff acted mostly as his private secretariat. Rather than providing advice and assessments, its staff was expected to design the details of the orders that had already been issued. Nevertheless, Jodl frequently prepared orders based on Hitler's requests and would subsequently assume responsibility for personal communication with field commanders. Jodl rarely paid attention to the views of others, often failed to inform his subordinates at the operations staff of events—even when such events affected them directly—and remained physically absent from the staff for long periods of time.

---

[41] Sander 2017, p 2263. See also Jacobsen 2017, p 325.

[42] The letter from Terboven to Bormann, which has been preserved in the OKW archive, is, however, dated 28 October, cf. Kjetil Korsnes, "Burning and forcible evacuation in Finnmark", available from: https://actanorvegica.no/2021/02/28/brenning-og-tvangsevakuering-i-finnmark-1944/ [accessed 1 April 2023].

[43] *Trial of the Major War Criminals before the International Military Tribunal Nuremberg*, vol. 15, p 555. See also Fosnes 1974, p 44; Elstad 2020, p 246.

[44] Schott 1980, p 67.

[45] An extensive biographical account of Jodl's relationship with Hitler can be found in Scheurig 1999, pp 102–324.

He preferred to stay in the presence of Hitler, a stone's throw away, as part of the *Führer's* inner circle. Only exceptionally would he allow his closest subordinates to accompany him to Hitler's daily situation conferences.[46]

The northern theatre of military operations was the only sector of the Eastern Front situated within the area of responsibility that fell to the *OKW*. Jodl therefore had to pay attention when there were new developments in the 20th Mountain Army's operations. A small subdivision of the operations staff, led by Major Hans Jordan, monitored activities of the German forces in the north and gathered information required by the *OKW*'s operational staff in order to gain an overview of the situation that was now playing out in the north.[47] It was this subdivision that received Terboven's scorched earth proposal for examination on 28 October 1944, after Bormann's office had forwarded the matter to the *OKW*'s operations staff. On the same day, Jordan's subdivision recommended that the proposal be implemented. It argued that the destruction of the evacuated areas would prevent the Norwegian government-in-exile from establishing itself there and gaining access to Norwegian troops from Sweden. The subdivision asked Jodl to decide.[48] However, its evaluation is unlikely to have played a part in Hitler's actual decision, since he had already made up his mind at around 6 pm that same day. Bormann's adjutant informed the subdivision of Hitler's decision the next day and added that it needed to issue the order to the 20th Mountain Army.[49] See Fig. 4.1.

The order was notably not issued by Jodl. If we are to believe his later explanations, Jodl objected to Terboven's proposal. Hitler, however, dismissed the objection. There is no known documentation supporting Jodl's statement. Given his position in the *Führer's* headquarters, it is still fairly clear that Jodl would have discussed the matter with Hitler. It could be that Jodl changed his opinion and agreed with Hitler's assessment in the end. Such a stance would have been more consistent with his narrow military situational understanding, which, unfazed by moral anguish, suggested focusing on what would be tactically appropriate in Northern Norway.

A letter Jodl wrote to Bormann on 16 November 1944 indicates where he stood on the matter. In it, Jodl reacted to the fact that some of Terboven's subordinate agencies had requested suspending or limiting the evacuation efforts. Jodl noted that the evacuation, despite some initial "very significant organisational challenges", could be carried out as intended. The evacuation of the population and the destruction of infrastructure would deprive the enemy of an opportunity to rapidly pursue and attack the retreating 20th Mountain Army before the Lyngen Line's completion.[50] "For these

[46] Megargee 2000, p 81.

[47] The report that the subdivision, Wehrmachtführungsstab/Operationsabteilung (Heer) Nord (WFSt/Op. (H) Nord), drew up during the autumn of 1944 is preserved in BA-MA, RW 4/74.

[48] BA-MA, RW 4/714a. Memorandum "Betr.: Räumungsmaßnahmen in Nord-Norwegen", 28/10/1944.

[49] BA-MA, RW 4/714a. Memorandum WFSt/Qu. 2 (Nord), 29/10/1944.

[50] For more information on the Lyngen Line, see Chaps. 2 and 3.

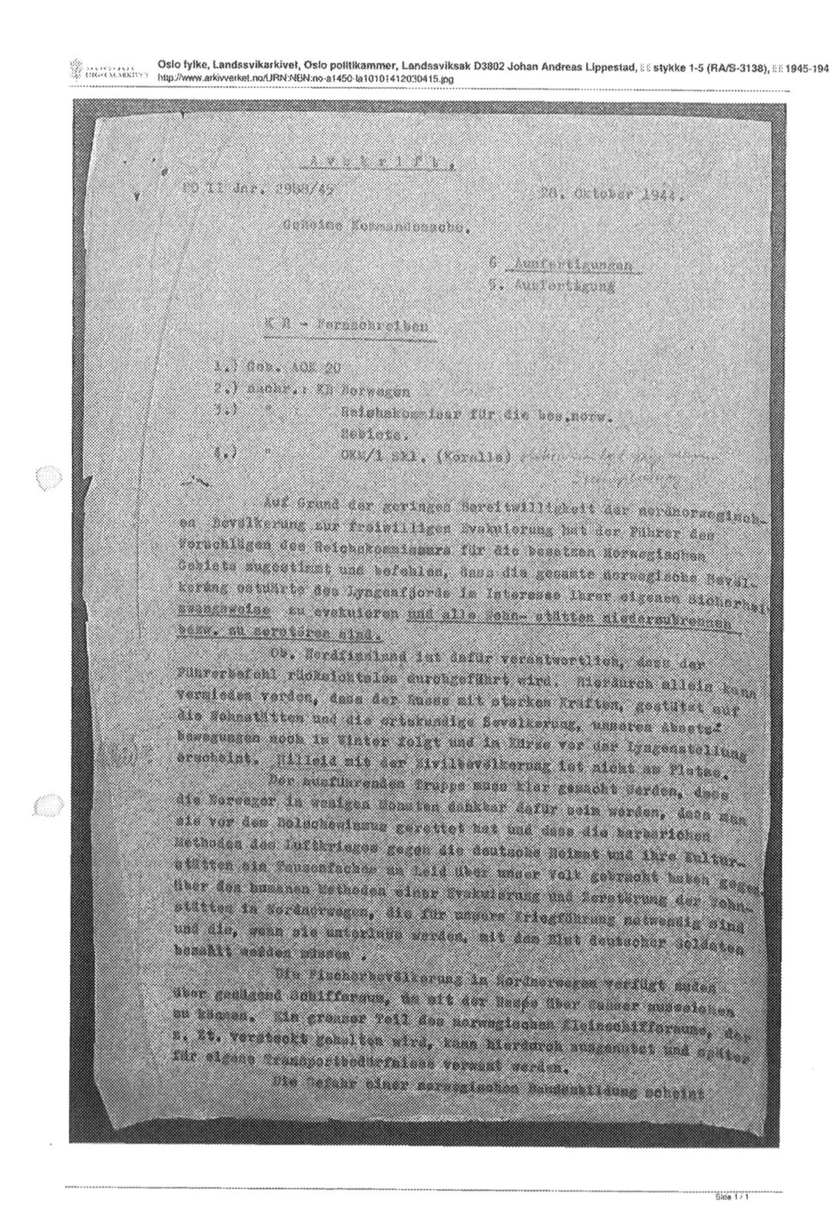

Abschrift.

[illegible] Jnr. [illegible] 28. Oktober 1944.

Geheime Kommandosache.

6 Ausfertigungen
5. Ausfertigung

K R - Fernschreiben

1.) Geb. AOK 20
2.) nachr.: WB Norwegen
3.) " Reichskommissar für die bes.norw. Gebiete.
4.) " OKW/1 Skl. (Koralle)

Auf Grund der geringen Bereitwilligkeit der nordnorwegischen Bevölkerung zur freiwilligen Evakuierung hat der Führer den Vorschlägen des Reichskommissars für die besetzten norwegischen Gebiete zugestimmt und befohlen, dass die gesamte norwegische Bevölkerung ostwärts des Lyngenfjords im Interesse ihrer eigenen Sicherheit zwangsweise zu evakuieren und alle Wohn- stätten niederzubrennen bezw. zu zerstören sind.

Ob. Nordfinnland ist dafür verantwortlich, dass der Führerbefehl rücksichtslos durchgeführt wird. Hierdurch allein kann vermieden werden, dass der Russe mit starken Kräften, gestützt auf die Wohnstätten und die ortskundige Bevölkerung, unseren Absetzbewegungen noch im Winter folgt und in Kürze vor der Lyngenstellung erscheint. Mitleid mit der Zivilbevölkerung ist nicht am Platze.

Der ausführenden Truppe muss klar gemacht werden, dass die Norweger in wenigen Monaten dankbar dafür sein werden, dass man sie vor dem Bolschewismus gerettet hat und dass die barbarischen Methoden des Luftkrieges gegen die deutsche Heimat und ihre Kulturstätten ein Tausendfaches an Leid über unser Volk gebracht haben gegenüber den humanen Methoden einer Evakuierung und Zerstörung der Wohnstätten in Nordnorwegen, die für unsere Kriegführung notwendig sind und die, wenn sie unterbleiben, mit dem Blut deutscher Soldaten bezahlt werden müssen.

Die Fischerbevölkerung in Nordnorwegen verfügt zudem über genügend Schiffsraum, um mit der Masse über Wasser ausweichen zu können. Ein grosser Teil des norwegischen Kleinschiffsraums, der z. Zt. versteckt gehalten wird, kann hierdurch ausgenutzt und später für eigene Transportbedürfnisse verwandt werden.

Die Gefahr einer norwegischen Bandenbildung scheint

Side 1 / 1

Fig. 4.1 This order from the *Oberkommando der Wehrmacht* to the 20th Mountain Army, known in the literature as the *Führerbefehl* of 28 October 1944, was the immediate background for Rendulic's more detailed order to his corps commanders the following day (see Chap. 1, Fig. 1.1). Although signed by Wilhelm Keitel as Chief of the *OKW* or, as here, by Alfred Jodl as Keitel's deputy and Chief of the *Wehrmachtführungsstab*, *OKW* orders conveyed Adolf Hitler's decisions as Commander-in-Chief *Source* The National Archives of Norway (Riksarkivet), landssviksak D3802 Johan Andreas Lippestad, stykke 1-5 (RA/S-3138), courtesy of Ingunn Elstad

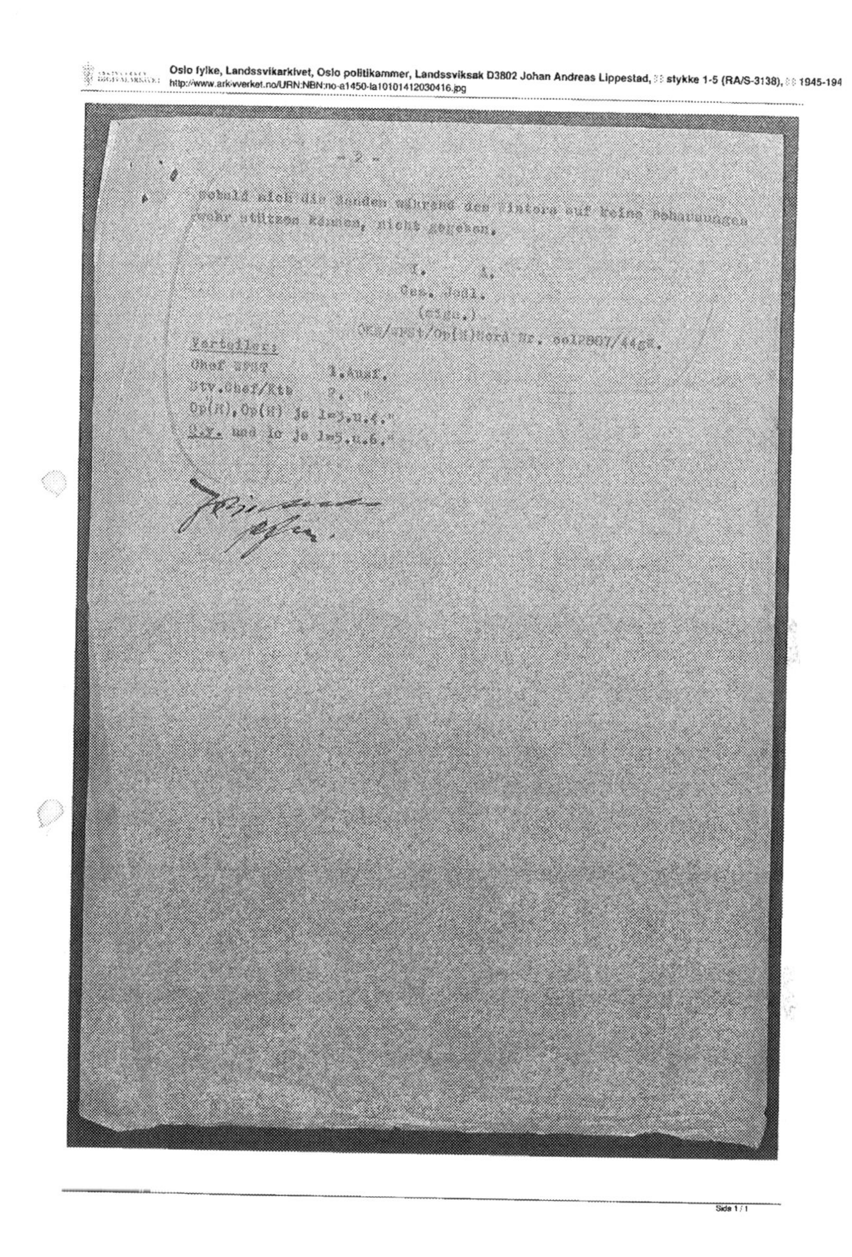
Oslo fylke, Landssvikarkivet, Oslo politikammer, Landssviksak D3802 Johan Andreas Lippestad, stykke 1-5 (RA/S-3138), 1945-194
http://www.arkivverket.no/URN:NBN:no-a1450-la10101412030416.jpg

- 2 -

sobald sich die Banden während des Winters auf keine Behausungen mehr stützen können, nicht gegeben.

I. A.
Gez. Jodl.
(Stgn.)
OKW/WFSt/Op(H)Nord Nr. 0012807/44gK.

Verteiler:
Chef WFSt 1.Ausf.
Stv.Chef/Ktb 2. "
Op(H),Op(M) je 1=3.u.4."
O.V. und Ic je 1=5.u.6."

Side 1 / 1

Fig. 4.1 (continued)

military reasons," he concluded, "the ordered measures in Northern Norway must be upheld."[51]

In his letter, Jodl also referred to German officials in Norway who had expressed objections to aspects of the forced evacuation. They pointed to a lack of Norwegian vessels to carry out the forced evacuation and warned that burning things to the ground could lead to a humanitarian catastrophe with harmful political consequences, especially regarding the reactions in Sweden.[52]

In the end, however, internal oppositions to the forced evacuation and the scorched earth tactics were limited. None of the opponents belonged to decision-making levels or had any major influence to exert in relation to the matter. Finnmark and Northern Troms were destroyed as a result, and the region's population was driven out through a rapidly prepared and initiated operation that was carried out thoroughly and ruthlessly. Moser, one of those who had opposed, lost command over the LXXI Corps on 15 December 1944 and was taken out of active service for a period, allegedly in response to his protests to the scorched earth tactics.[53]

When questioned after the war, von Falkenhorst, *Wermachtsbefelshaber Norwegen*, claimed that it was a strategic mistake to return such large numbers of German troops to Northern Norway during the autumn of 1944, even though that was the only realistic route of retreat for them. Major battles were taking place on the Central Theatre of war, he declared, which was where the German troops belonged. Thus, the Soviets transported their most able troops in the north towards the south. This relocation should have made it clear to the *Wehrmacht* that available forces had to concentrate sufficiently along the most important front sections. "I know the Russians," von Falkenhorst said, predicting that the Soviet forces would not make a considerable effort to penetrate Norway. He also asserted that he informed Keitel in a phone call of his assessment but was ignored. In light of the strategic situation, von Falkenhorst considered both evacuation and destruction meaningless—"sinnlos".[54]

Alas, von Falkenhorst was no longer in command in the far north. His wings had been clipped. When the 20th Mountain Army started to move into Norway, it entered von Falkenhorst's and the *Armeeoberkommando Norwegen*'s area of responsibility, yet without being subordinate to him. The first warning of major upheavals to command came on 15 October 1944, when Alfred Jodl incorporated the LXXI Corps,

[51] BA-MA, RW 4/653. Letter from Alfred Jodl to Martin Bormann, 16/11/1944.

[52] BA-MA, RW 4/714a. Memorandum WFSt/Op (H) Nord, 12/11/1944. These were concerns that Jodl did not share, as stated in the aforementioned letter: Residents who evaded the forced evacuation would run the risk of starvation and hypothermia at their own risk; Sweden still lacked "the military prerequisites" to go to war with Germany and the possibility of a scorched earth operation causing further resentment against the occupation regime could be countered through "timely and savvy" propaganda that communicated "the military necessity" of a forced evacuation, as well as the announcement of "support measures for the population". These statements were made by a man who was completely out of touch with the situation in Norway and the population's relationship with the occupier.

[53] This is according to Oberst Bernhard von Watzdorf, Moser's General Chief of Staff in the LXXI Corps. See Watzdorf 1965, p 347.

[54] NHM, FO II Div, L0031, Questioning of Falkenhorst by Ivar Follestad, 1 September 1947. Per Kristian Olsen has also addressed von Falkenhorst's assessment. See Olsen 2019, p 66.

one of von Falkenhorst's three army corps in Norway responsible for land defence in Northern Norway, into the 20th Mountain Army.[55] For von Falkenhorst, this intervention reinforced the unsustainability of two German *Armeeoberkommandos* acting side-by-side in Norway. He reached out to the *OKW*'s operations staff to ask how this dilemma should be solved. Who would have authority over who? The answer arrived when, on 20 October 1944, Hitler decided that Rendulic would take over as the new military commander in Norway.[56] This decision's formal announcement seven days later made it clear that *Armeeoberkommando Norwegen*, headquartered in Oslo, would be disbanded and replaced by the *Oberkommando* of the 20th Mountain Army.[57]

The actual change in command had to wait until Rendulic was finished with his duties on the Northern Front and large parts of the retreating 20th Mountain Army had passed the Lyngen Line.[58] Meanwhile, von Falkenhorst observed the events in Finnmark and Troms without being able to assert any influence upon them.

What did German field commanders in the north think about these developments? There are rich—and unambiguous—sources available regarding this question: German generals on the Northern Front believed that the total destruction requested by Terboven and ordered by Hitler were unnecessary. These sources show that Moser, Commander of the LXXI Corps, was initially opposed to total destruction. Following a meeting on 25 October 1944, Neumann wrote that Moser agreed with him that homes located beyond key transport routes should not be destroyed.[59] Moser was an important tactical leader, because his corps had primary responsibility for military aspects of the evacuation to the west of Porsangerfjorden.[60]

During questioning by Norwegian authorities after the war, Captain Wolfgang Blell, one of Rendulic's staff officers, explained that both he and other staff officers considered the evacuation order meaningless, since there were no signs of Soviet forces following retreating German troops. Even Major General Hermann Hölter, Rendulic's Chief-of-Staff, indicated during post-war questioning that he was of the same opinion.[61] After the war, Ferdinand Jodl, Commander of the XIX Army Corps, also expressed the same opinion. Once the Soviet forces stopped at Neiden village

[55] BA-MA, RW 4/714. Letter from Alfred Jodl to AOK 20, WBN and Josef Terboven, 15/10/1945.

[56] RA, RAFA-3915, Da, L0077. Report from questioning of Nikolaus von Falkenhorst, 19.9.1945, p 103.

[57] BA-MA, RW 4/714a. Letter from Wilhelm Keitel to AOK 20, WBN, OKM and others, 27/10/1944.

[58] Rendulic 1952, pp 321–324.

[59] Neumann also added: "In der Propaganda ist allerdings nach wie vor restlose Zerstörungsabsicht zu bekunden". RA/S-3138/0048/D/Db/L0034, Letter dated 25 October 1944 from Neumann to SD Hammerfest. See also Fosnes 1974, p 34; Elstad 2020, p 218.

[60] However, during questioning in 1946, Willy Laqua stated that Moser eventually advocated strongly in favour of forced evacuation and total destruction, cf. Elstad 2020, p 459. However, the information from Laqua does not correspond to the information in Watzdorf 1965, p 347.

[61] NHM FO II, Div, L0031, Vernehmungsniederschrift, 28 March 1946. See also questioning of Otto Blank, RA, L case, Oslo D 3802 Johan Andreas Lippestad, available from https://media.digitalarkivet.no/view/69762 (pp 1576–1577). Accessed 1 April 2023. Nevertheless, it can be noted that both Hölter and Rendulic published books after the war in which they defended the burning

at the Norwegian-Finnish border on 26 and 27 October 1944, Jodl did not notice any serious attempts at pursuit. When questioned on 13 December 1945, Jodl said: "At the time, I personally believed that the Russians, for strategic reasons, would never follow across the Tanafjord. This was a belief I also shared with several of my people."[62]

From a German military point of view, a Soviet invasion from Eastern Finnmark was not the most dangerous factor. Rendulic was more fearful of a Red Army pursuit of the German retreat through Finland.[63] An extensive threat assessment carried out in mid-August 1944, signed by Rendulic, makes it clear that this was considered the most dangerous possibility.[64] And yet, other than the Petsamo-Kirkenes operation, the Germans saw Soviet troops stop at the Finnish-Soviet border as well.

Though initially opposed to total destruction and forced evacuation, Rendulic was also adaptable to new realities. On 22 October 1944, he had a meeting with Major Konrad Benze from the *OKW* operations staff. Rendulic informed Benze of the widespread perception among the Norwegian population that the Red Army would stop in the Kirkenes area. Rendulic remained unsure about the intentions and plans of Soviet military leaders; he was unable to have a firm opinion about them at this point. He told Benze that his military actions emphasised the destruction of military facilities, bridges, and roads.[65]

Two days passed. On 24 October 1944, Rendulic wrote a statement to Alfred Jodl, in which he complained that so few Norwegians were willing to be evacuated—"Freiwillig gehen nur wenige Norweger mit"—voluntarily, and that only a few Norwegians had gone along with the evacuation plan. His army neither had nor wished to use the resources to capture fleeing civilians. It was vulnerable while in retreat and had to remain on high alert in case of enemy operations. Rendulic therefore asked Jodl to refrain from forcing Norwegians to evacuate, even if those remaining could be forced by the Soviets to fight against the Germans. Rendulic thereby took a stand on the matter of evacuation.[66] According to Officer Otto Blank, who kept Rendulic's war diary, Rendulic was "personally strongly opposed to *totale Vernichtung*".[67]

We know today, however, that Rendulic eventually complied with decisions made at higher levels. In the announcement issued to the people on the decision to forcibly

---

and forced evacuation. Without any regret, Hölter, in particular, portrayed the forced evacuation virtually as a humanitarian undertaking.

62 RA/S-3138/0048/D/Db/L0034, L case Peder J. Berg. Questioning of Ferdinand Jodl, 13 December 1945 (Norwegian minutes).

63 See Chap. 3.

64 OKW "Studie über die Verteidigungsmöglichkeiten des nordlappländischen Raumes nach Abschluss der Operation 'Birke' und einen anschliessenden Rückzug nach Norwegen", 13 August 1944.

65 KTB (Geb.) AOK 20/Ia, entry 22 October 1944.

66 Rendulic to Jodl, 24 October 1944. In the war diary of (Geb.) AOK, it is clearly stated that this was Rendulic's principled view, cf. KTB (Geb.) AOK 20/Ia, entry 24 October 1944.

67 Questioning of Otto Blank, RA, L case, Oslo D 3802 Johan Andreas Lippestad, available from https://media.digitalarkivet.no/view/69762 (pp 1576–1577) [accessed 1 April 2023].

evacuate them, which was made public on 31 October, Rendulic's name appeared alongside Terboven's.[68] See Fig. 4.2.

Terboven found little support for his plans among those within the *Reichskommissariat* and Neumann who were most involved with the forced evacuation. According to Heinrich Schnurbusch, even Neumann himself, Terboven's special envoy, "passionately objected to the plans".[69] Neumann also tried to stop the total destruction and evacuation through both the SS and Bormann. Other contemporaneous sources also confirm Neumann's objections to the plans.[70] Even Terboven's local leaders in Tromsø and Narvik were opposed to it. The same was true for the *Sicherheitspolizei und Sicherheitsdienst* (Sipo-SD) commanders for Troms and Finnmark.[71]

Neumann appears to have maintained his objections even after Hitler issued the 28 October 1944 order. Objections against the plans also came from the military. For instance, on 29 October 1944, Ebeling, Commander of the 210th Infantry Division, wrote a statement about the evacuation. He made it clear that he opposed total destruction and forced evacuation.[72] As previously noted by Rendulic, Ebeling also stressed that the forced evacuation drew attention away from defence duties. And so indeed it did. In line with the order, the division would gather as much of the population as possible using the resources made available by the *Reichskommissariat*, SS, and the German police. The division would focus on settlements along State Road 50. To ensure that people would obey, they would be told that all homes would be burnt down to the ground.

Ebeling also presented political arguments opposing the order to forcibly evacuate, which were reminiscent of Neumann's objections. Ebeling feared that the *Wehrmacht's* reputation would sink to record low levels among the Norwegians and lead to multiple sabotage operations and partisan warfare further south in the country. His boss, Ferdinand Jodl, ended his letter fully agreeing with Ebeling's considerations.[73] According to Blank, Rendulic's intention was "purely total destruction of all purely military objects in the first place and the settlements along the retreat route, despite the specific *Befehl* mentioned above".[74]

---

[68] Elstad 2020, p 264.

[69] RA/S-3138/0048/D/Db/L0034, L case Peder J. Berg. Reporting by Heinrich Schnurbusch, November 1945. See also Olsen 2019, pp 76–78. Schnurbusch was the successor to Neumann as the commander of the *Einsatzstab* Neumann.

[70] RA/S-3138/0048/D/Db/L0034, Letter dated 25 October 1944 from Neumann to SD Hammerfest.

[71] RA, L case, Oslo D 3802 Johan Andreas Lippestad. von Stackelberg's report, 25 November 1945. Available from https://media.digitalarkivet.no/view/69762 (pp 1524–1534) [accessed 1 April 2023].

[72] 1114/44 Secret (inquiry into the evacuation), 29 October 1944, signed by Ebeling.

[73] Same location. This is consistent with what Ferdinand Jodl explained during questioning on 13 December 1945.

[74] Questioning of Otto Blank, RA, L case, Oslo D 3802 Johan Andreas Lippestad, available from https://media.digitalarkivet.no/view/69762 (pp 1576–1577) [accessed 1 April 2023].

Til befolkningen!

Ved forræderi av en finsk regjeringsklikk er rømningen av en del av Nord-Norge blitt en militær nødvendighet.

I løpet av denne rømning er en evakuering av sivilbefolkningen i dette område utvilsomt nødvendig, idet motstanderen har bevist at han i de av ham besatte områder hensynsløst og brutalt tvinger sivilbefolkningen til innsats for å oppnå sine mål.

Dette medfører at den bolsjevikiske motstander ikke kan overlates noen som helst underbringelses- eller eksistensmuligheter i kampområdet. Alle sådanne innretninger som husly, befordringsmidler og forrådslager av levnetsmidler må ødelegges eller bringes bort.

Dermed blir befolkningen i dette område fratatt eksistensgrunnlaget, slik at den, for å kunne opprettholde livet må evakuere til de norske områder som framdeles blir beskyttet av den tyske vernemakt.

De tyske besetningsmyndigheter erklærte seg av denne grunn beredt til å understøtte med alle til rådighet stående muligheter den tilbakeføring av befolkningen som de norske myndigheter gjennomførte.

I egen interesse er også alle midler til selvhjelp å utnytte i videst mulig utstrekning.

Avgjørende for at en fullkommen gjennomførelse av evakueringsforetagendet skal lykkes er fram for alt en helt gjennomført utnyttelse av alt kuttermateriell som står til disposisjon i dette område for avtransporten. Kuttereiere som forsøker å undra seg denne oppfordring, må rekne med de skarpeste motforholdsregler, som beskytning og senkning av båt og besetning.

Den som ikke følger denne utvetydige anvisning forårsaker selv at han og hans familie derved blir utsatt for den dødelige fare å gå den nordnorske vinter imøte uten husly og ernæringsmuligheter.

Terboven (sign.)
Reichskommissar für die besetzten norwegischen Gebiete.

Rendulic (sign.)
Generaloberst
Oberbefehlshaber der 20. (Geb.) Armee

Fig. 4.2 These posters were produced for distribution in Finnmark and Northern Troms counties immediately after the *Führerbefehl* (see Fig. 4.1) and Rendulic's follow-up order of 29 October (see Chap. 1, Fig. 1.1). The posters blamed the region's destruction and evacuation on the "treachery" of the Finnish government and the "ruthlessness" of the Soviets in occupied territories. They further explained the measures on account of the need to deprive the Red Army of accommodation, communications and supplies in areas that were to be abandoned by the Germans *Source* Alta Museum

An die Bevölkerung!

Durch Verrat einer finnischen Regierungsclique ist die Räumung eines Teiles von Nordnorwegen eine militärische Notwendigkeit geworden, in deren Verlauf die restlose zivile Räumung dieses Gebietes umso unvermeidbarer ist, als erwiesenermassen der Gegner die Bevölkerung in den von ihm besetzten Gebieten rücksichtslos und brutal zum Einsatz für die Erreichung seiner Ziele zu erpressen gewillt ist. Infolgedessen können im Vorfeld des Kampfes dem bolschewistischen Gegner keinerlei Unterbringungs- und Existenzmöglichkeiten überlassen werden. Alle derartigen Einrichtungen, wie Unterkünfte, Beförderungsmittel und Lebensmittelvorräte müssen zerstört bzw. weggeschafft werden.

Damit wird der Bevölkerung dieses Gebietes die Existenzgrundlage genommen, so das szur Erhaltung ihres Lebens eine Evakuierung in den von der deutschen Wehrmacht weiterhin geschützten norwegischen Raum notwendig ist.

Die deutsche Besatzungsbehörde erklärt sich aus diesem Grunde bereit, die von den norwegischen Behörden durchgeführte Rückführung der Bevölkerung mit allen zur Verfügung stehenden Möglichkeiten zu unterstützen.

Im eigenen Interesse sind auch alle Mittel der Selbsthilfe weitestgehend auszunützen.

Entscheidend für das restlose Gelingen der Evakuierungsmassnahmen ist vor allem aber die restlose Nutzbarmachung des dem Gebiet zur Verfügung stehenden Kutterraumes für den Abtransport. Kutter-Eigner, die sich dieser Aufforderung zu entziehen versuchen, haben mit Anwendung schärfster Gegenmassnahmen, wie Beschiessung und Versenkung von Kutter und Besatzung zu rechnen.

Wer dieser eindeutigen Weisung nicht Folge leistet, setzt aus eigenem Verschulden sich und seine Angehörigen dadurch, ohne Wohn- und Ernährungsmöglichkeit, den tödlichen Gefahren des nordischen Winters aus. —

gez.: Terboven
Reichskommissar für die besetzten norwegischen Gebiete.

gez.: Rendulic
Generaloberst
Oberbefehlshaber der 20. (Geb.) Armee

Druck: Deutsche Polarzeitung – Tromsø

Fig. 4.2 (continued)

4.6 Motives

If Rendulic had real ambitions to "modify" Hitler's order in a somewhat more subdued direction, it did not end up being the outcome. Once Hitler had issued the order for destruction, it was largely followed. The military squads responsible for the order's execution were left to their own devices. In this situation, it is reasonable to expect that they interpreted the order literally. It could not have been easy for soldiers and officers to differentiate between propaganda and necessary military measures.[75]

Terboven's actions were based on a combination of military and political threat perception, political ideology, and situational power play. Like the military, Terboven was also anxious to prevent the Soviets from advancing further into Norway and block any Allied landing in the north. Both Rendulic and Terboven believed that the remaining civilian population would support the war efforts of the government-in-exile, either by joining regular military units or by waging a partisan war against the Germans.

Yet, Terboven was more uncompromising than Rendulic when it came to the civilian population. The bells were also tolling for Quisling, who was thinking along similar lines as Terboven. If the government-in-exile managed to gain a foothold in Finnmark and, with the support of locals, re-establish a Norwegian authority there, it would send a strong signal that Quisling's NS government was at risk of collapsing. Despite persistent disagreements, the NS government and Terboven were now intertwined due to a shared perception of threat and a common destiny.

On the Eastern Front, the Red Army inexorably drove the German forces back. On the Northern Front, the "Bolsheviks" would soon be arriving at the Norwegian border and were unlikely to stop there. The propaganda was filled with horror visions depicting the bloodthirsty red hordes. The average Norwegian did not buy into the message, but some National Socialists considered it a reality. This called for action.

While Rendulic accepted more partisan warfare as a consequence of the factual situation in the north, Terboven wanted to strike hard and reduce the threat through unreserved use of force. He reacted strongly to the population's resistance to his evacuation policy and implemented emergency laws and forced measures, as he had done previously in other situations. The remaining civilian population in Finnmark and Northern Troms who had opposed evacuation were treated ruthlessly. Source materials confirm that this was also the intention of German occupiers. At a meeting in Tromsø on 20 November 1944, Hansen, Head of the Evacuation Commission, learned several important things. Firstly, Lie, Minister of the Police, claimed that the Germans estimated a loss of 40 per cent of the local population, while Lie himself had been working on the assumption that 25 per cent of the local population would lose their lives during the evacuation. Secondly, the local commander of the *Reichskommissariat* announced that the Soviet forces had "settled in Kirkenes" and that they were not pursuing. There was therefore plenty of time to complete

[75] Nevertheless, it is difficult to obtain further knowledge of this due to the paucity of sources from lower levels.

the rest of the evacuation. Lastly, Hansen learned that all areas north of Lyngen had been declared war zones and that all Norwegian civilians arrested there would be considered *francs-tireurs*. Hansen's report states that this information came from the *Reichskommissariat*.[76]

Terboven's decision that the civilian population were *franc-tireurs* in a war zone had fateful implications. The term *francs-tireurs* refers to non-uniformed irregular military personnel, often synonymously used with terms such as "partisans" or "guerrillas". *Francs-tireurs* were not considered combatants and could be treated more brutally than prisoners of war.[77] As *Gebietskommissar* Herbert von Stackelberg had said: there was plenty of time, including for systematic and brutal pursuit of the remaining population.

It is also likely that Terboven's actions during the forced evacuation were linked to a power play then under way as the occupation regime in Norway headed for its downfall. Following his involvement in the military retreat plans for Finnmark, and upon realisation that von Falkenhorst's days as Commander-in-Chief were numbered, Terboven attempted, without success, to strengthen his grip on the German army in Norway. Lieutenant General Bruno von Uthmann, Germany's military attaché in Stockholm, said at the time that Terboven made "every effort" to subjugate the *Wehrmacht*.[78] In November, Heinrich Himmler suggested to Keitel that the militarily inexperienced Wilhelm Rediess replace von Falkenhorst. Keitel flatly rejected this suggestion by stating that only one man should fill the posts of Commander of the *Wehrmacht* and the army.[79] Rendulic's appointment for both stood firmly. Admittedly, that autumn and winter Himmler expanded his power at the cost of the *Wehrmacht*. Nevertheless, it is a plausible interpretation that Himmler nominated Rediess with Terboven's understanding. Considering Himmler and Terboven's cooperation in Norway, appointing Rediess to Commander-in-Chief would have provided Terboven with excellent opportunities to take charge of military matters.

As Supreme Commander of all SS and police departments in Norway, Rediess largely surrendered to Terboven's will and became the tool that allowed Terboven to act as the *de facto* Chief of Police. The *Reichskommissar* had virtually free reign to use the SS and police force as instruments of power against the Norwegian civilian population—so much so that he would occasionally initiate police operations himself.[80] The only thing that restrained Terboven's otherwise wilful use of the SS Commander's police and security resources was his fear of getting onto a collision course with Himmler. Terboven made key decisions relating to the SS only after he had obtained consent from Himmler.[81] Terboven and Himmler appear to have reached a tacit understanding. Terboven was at liberty to use the SS and the police force as his own when the need arose, while Himmler had the authority

[76] Ragnar Hansen's report, pp 55–56.

[77] Pictet 1960, p 52.

[78] BA-MA, N619/18. Letter from Bruno von Uthmann to Curt Stumpff, 28/06/1945.

[79] BA-MA, RW 4/651. Letter W. Keitel to H. Himmler, 21/11/1944.

[80] Report Wilhelm Esser, 15/07/1945. RA, L case Wilhelm Esser.

[81] Nøkleby 2003, p 180.

to expand the activities of the SS organisation into other areas in Norway. Both men were committed to maintaining a mutually beneficial arrangement. Himmler's main mission and the expectations of Rediess in Norway may have also involved facilitating such an arrangement.[82]

Himmler, Rediess, and the SS formed part of Terboven's strategies to consolidate his position in Norway. During the final two years of occupation, Terboven expressed concern about Hitler's decision that, in the event of an invasion, defined as "threatening danger", he would need to hand over all political governance authority to the German Military Commander in Norway. In April 1943, Terboven proposed to Hitler the establishment of a civilian-controlled "security area" in Southeast Norway. Terboven would retain supreme authority after a possible Allied landing, while Rediess would function as commander of the occupying forces in the area. Terboven, however, never achieved a final clarification of this proposal.[83]

Despite opposition from von Falkenhorst and the *OKW*, Terboven did not give up. In order to enable the security area's subsequent activation, Terboven approached Himmler via Rediess in May 1944 and managed to convince him to declare Norway a "partisan war zone" (*Bandenkampfgebiet*).[84] This designation had so far been used only in relation to some German-occupied areas in Eastern Europe. It meant that the SS rather than the army would be responsible for fighting any organised guerrilla forces within the territory. The declaration was a startling move on Himmler's part, as there were no guerrilla forces in Norway sufficiently large and active to threaten the occupying powers' communication lines (nor would any arise later). Driven more by opportunism than security concern, the SS obtained authorisation through Norway's status as a partisan war zone to expand its organisation in the country. That status also served Terboven's ambitions of power by providing him with potential protection against any restrictions to his political power.

In October 1944, however, the situation that Terboven had feared became reality: a hostile army arriving in Norway. When the Soviet 14th Army advanced into Finnmark without its offensive plans being clear, the occupying powers could rightly describe the situation as "threatening danger". Nevertheless, neither von Falkenhorst nor Rendulic seized this opportunity to demand full political authority over Norway. It is possible that von Falkenhorst considered Rendulic's army a buffer between the Soviets and his own garrison, so that the Soviet military operation would not directly affect the latter. Or, perhaps, von Falkenhorst was simply too weak-willed to take any initiative on this matter.

Terboven may have been afraid that the new front lines cutting through Finnmark towards the west could raise questions about his continued role as leader of the occupying power. This could explain why, in addition to his constant need to be the

---

[82] Rediess' close associate, Hans Latza, believed this to be the case at any rate. Himmler's wish was Rediess' law, according to a statement made by Latza soon after the war and the instruction was to avoid anything that could spoil the cooperation with Terboven. Report Hans Latza "Verhältnis zu den führenden Persönlichkeiten [...]", 10/12/1945. RA, L case Hans Latza.

[83] BA-MA, RW 4/639. Letter R. Bamler to W. Warlimont, 15/05/1943.

[84] Nøkleby 2003, p 179.

visible strong man, Terboven was so eager to get his way, often by opposing the *Wehrmacht*.

For a *Reichskommissar* in a "partisan war zone" and a man of action who had even expressed concern that resistance groups would emerge in evacuated areas, the next logical step would have been to mobilise security forces. In the event, however, Terboven and Rediess had only very limited police and security resources at hand. In order to seek out and combat a numerically stronger armed enemy in vast areas that lived up to *Bandenkampfgebiet* realities, the SS and Rediess' police force would have needed access to field departments from the *Waffen*-SS. And yet, with three regiments sent to Northern Finland in June 1941 ahead of the launch of Operation *Silberfuchs*, Norway had no *Waffen*-SS departments to speak of. The situation changed with the German retreat in the autumn of 1944, but the bulk of these forces were directed to continue towards the south to the Western Front.[85]

The *Waffen*-SS only had the 3rd Police Company for efforts in the north. This company had barely managed to deploy for a brief period to a quiet front line section of Karelia before the retreat began. The unit returned to Norway largely unscathed, where it became subordinate to the German XIX Army Corps. Repatriations, illnesses, and leaves of absence meant that no more than 70 of the company's approximately 150 men were able to serve when it established a new base at Øyjord outside of Narvik.[86]

These initiatives show how Terboven and Rediess attempted to develop security forces less dependent on the German military. They likely also wanted these forces to take on a greater role in the field in the north. In the balancing of needs against realities, however, resources became the decisive factor and defeating *Milorg* in the south became more important. The 3rd Police Company's deployment was perhaps largely symbolic on the part of Terboven and Rediess. Still, with the military's total destruction of Northern Norway, banishment of its local population and pursuit of anyone who remained, Terboven did get his way in the end.

While the German forces in the north retreated to the Lyngen Line, the Soviets in the east reached East Prussia and the Allies in the west approached the Rhine. Norway's occupying power had a foreboding sense of being under siege. Germany's military control over Norway was challenged, and the *Reichskommissar*'s position came under pressure. When faced with this situation, Terboven acted as a visionary for action. A member of the Nazi party since 1923, he rapidly rose through the ranks to the NSDAP's top echelon and stood out as a tough, cunning, self-serving and hard-nosed political leader.[87] When opportunities presented themselves in Norway and Hitler gave him the freedom to act, Terboven was a man who was willing to take extreme measures in the name of ideology. He entered final combat mode in earnest during the autumn of 1944. And even though the *Wehrmacht* never really came under the control of the *Reichskommissar*, they became his tool of action this particular time.

---

[85] Rusiecki 2010.

[86] Brenden and Thomassen 2013, pp 251–252.

[87] Nøkleby 1992, pp 31–35.

References

Augestad R (2016) Organisering og gjennomføring av tvangsevakueringa hausten 1944: Arbeidet til evakueringskommisjonen i Tromsø. Master's thesis. UiT The Arctic University of Norway, Tromsø
Bohn R (2000) Reichskommissariat Norwegen. Nationalsozialistische Neuordnung und Kriegswirtschaft. R. Oldenbourg Verlag, Munich
Bones S, Hatlehol G (2022) Evakueringens aktører. In: Bones S (ed) Kampen om frihet, Vol 3 of Andre verdenskrig i nord. Orkana akademisk, Stamsund
Brenden G, Thomassen AH (2013) Hitlers norske skijegere. Norske SS-frivillige i Karelen 1941–44. Historie & Kultur, Oslo
Elstad I (2020) Tvangsevakueringa. Orkana akademisk, Stamsund
Eriksen KE, Halvorsen T (1987) Norge i krig. Vol. 8, Frigjøring [Liberation]. Gyldendal, Oslo
Fosnes W (1974) Evakueringen av Finnmark og Nord-Troms. Master's thesis. University of Oslo, Oslo
Gschaid M (ed) (1995) Die Tagebücher von Joseph Goebbels, Teil II, Diktate 1941–1945, Band 14, January–April 1945. De Gruyter Saur, Munich
Jacobsen AR (2017) Skjebnehøst. Aschehoug, Oslo
Jaklin A (2016) Brent jord 1944–1945. Gyldendal, Oslo
Korsnes K (2021) Brenning og tvangsevakuering i Finnmark 1944. https://actanorvegica.no/2021/02/28/brenning-og-tvangsevakuering-i-finnmark-1944
Megargee GP (2000) Inside Hitler's High Command. University Press of Kansas, Lawrence, Kansas
Nøkleby B (1992) Josef Terboven. Hitlers mann i Norge. Gyldendal, Oslo
Nøkleby B (2003) Gestapo. Tysk politi i Norge. Aschehoug, Oslo
Olsen PK (2019) Jevnet med jorden. Brenningen av Finnmark Nord-Troms 1944. Aschehoug, Oslo
Pictet JS (ed) (1960) Commentary III Geneva Convention Relative to the Treatment of Prisoners of War. International Committee of the Red Cross, Geneva
Rendulic L (1952) Gekämpft, Gesiegt, Geschlagen. Welsermühl, Heidelberg
Rusiecki SM (2010) In Final Defense of the Reich. The Destruction of the 6th SS Mountain Division "Nord". Naval Institute Press, Annapolis
Sander H (2017) Hitler. Das Itenerar. Aufenthaltsorte und Reisen von 1889 bis 1945. Band IV 1940–1945. 4. korrigierte Auflage. Berlin Story Verlag, Berlin
Scheurig B (1999) Alfred Jodl. Gehorsam und Verhängnis: Biographie. Verlag Siegfried Bublies, Schnellbach
Schott FJ (1980) Der Wehrmachtführungsstab im Führerhauptquartier 1939–1945. Doctoral dissertation. Rheinische Friedrich-Wilhelms-Universitat, Bonn
Watzdorf B (1965) Zur Taktik der "verbranten Erde" in Norwegen. Zeitschrift für Militärgeschichte No. 4. Militärgeschichtliches Institut der DDR, Potsdam
Zetterberg K (2002) Svensk säkerhetspolitik 1943. En balansakt på slak lina mellan de krigförande. In: Hugemark B (ed) Nya fronter? 1943 – spänd väntan. Svenskt Miliärhistoriskt Bibliotek, Luleå
Ziemke E F (1959) The German Northern Theatre of Operations 1940-1945. Department of the Army Pamphlet 20-271, Washington D.C.

Other Documents

Trial of the Major War Criminals before the International Military Tribunal Nuremberg (1947–1949), 14 November–1 October 1946 ("The Blue Series"), Vols 1–42. International Military Tribunal, Washington. Available at The Library of Congress: https://www.loc.gov/rr/frd/Military_Law/Nuremberg_trials.html

Trials of War Criminals before the Nuernberg Military Tribunals under Control Council Law No. 10 (1950): Nuernberg, October 1946–April 1949 ("The Green Series"), Vols 1–15. United States Government Nuremberg Office, Washington. Available at The Library of Congress: https://www.loc.gov/rr/frd/Military_Law/Nuremberg_trials.html

Stian Bones Professor of History, UiT The Arctic University of Norway; Senior Researcher, Narvik War and Peace Centre. Address: Hansine Hanssens veg 18, 9019 Tromsø, Norway, e-mail: stian.bones@uit.no

Gunnar D. Hatlehol Project Manager, Narvik War and Peace Centre, e-mail: ghatlehol@narviksenteret.no

Part III
Trying Rendulic and Developing the No Second-Guessing Rule

Chapter 5
The Inclusion of Finnmark's Devastation and Forced Evacuation Charge in *Hostage*

Stian Bones and Gunnar D. Hatlehol

Contents

5.1 Introduction ... 112
5.2 Collecting Evidence from a Distance ... 113
5.3 Cooperation and Misunderstandings ... 114
5.4 Preparing the Case ... 117
5.5 Reactions to the Verdict ... 120
References ... 124

Abstract Lothar Rendulic's acquittal by a US military tribunal in Nuremberg for the charges of devastation and forceful evacuation of Northern Norway sent shockwaves through the Norwegian public. How could Rendulic be acquitted when, 500 days earlier, the International Military Tribunal found Alfred Jodl, Rendulic's superior, guilty of the same facts? This chapter shows that the US tribunal did not consider all available information. After the war, two parallel proceedings against Rendulic were initiated: one in Oslo and another by Telford Taylor in Nuremberg. To secure evidence on Rendulic's activities in Finnmark, Taylor collaborated with the Norwegian government-in-exile in London through its envoy to the United Nations War Crimes Commission. This collaboration was not communicated to the public prosecutor in Oslo who later requested Rendulic's extradition to Norway. Once misunderstandings were clarified, a Justice of the Norwegian Supreme Court sent several thousand pages of evidence to Taylor. Only a few were translated to English, however, resulting in an incomplete case for the prosecution. Crucially, Taylor's team did not submit to the tribunal a May 1947 report in which Rendulic admitted to Norwegian interrogators that the destruction of Northern Norway did not appear necessary and could in part have been avoided.

S. Bones (✉)
UiT The Arctic University of Norway, Hansine Hanssens veg 18, 9019 Tromsø, Norway
e-mail: stian.bones@uit.no

S. Bones · G. D. Hatlehol
Narvik War and Peace Centre, Tromsø, Norway
e-mail: ghatlehol@narviksenteret.no

N. Hayashi and C. Lingaas (eds.), *Honest Errors? Combat Decision-Making 75 Years After the* Hostage *Case*, https://doi.org/10.1007/978-94-6265-611-6_5

Keywords *Hostage* Case · Lothar Rendulic · devastation · scorched earth tactics · United Nations War Crimes Commission (UNWCC) · war crimes prosecution · Telford Taylor

5.1 Introduction

When peace finally arrived in 1945, there was a strong public demand to go after and punish war criminals in Norway. Already years before the end of World War II, holding war criminals accountable was an important goal for the Allies, too. It became clear early on that the German leaders, military and civilian alike, would be tried before an international court. During the autumn of 1941, British Prime Minister Winston Churchill said that the Allies prioritised the punishment of war criminals as a war objective. On 13 January 1942, Norway declared, together with eight other Allied countries, that war criminals would be prosecuted.[1]

In the trial against *Generaloberst* Lothar Rendulic, however, the outcome was unexpected. In Norway, it was assumed and even taken for granted that Rendulic would be convicted. "The gallows await General Rendulic," the Norwegian newspaper *Morgenbladet* wrote prior to the trial.[2] The result of the legal proceedings against him was very disappointing to many Norwegians: Rendulic walked free from the devastation charges connected to Norway. Did something go wrong during the legal process since Judge Charles F. Wennerstrum and his colleagues reached this conclusion? Norwegian historians and documentary writers have disagreed on this matter and provided different answers to this question. Some experts aligned their explanations close to the conclusion of US Military Tribunal V in Nuremberg: Rendulic did, in their opinion, overall act in good faith, believing there were urgent military reasons justifying the decision.[3] Other historians and writers hold the view that the evidence in fact supported a different conclusion. In court, several German military commanders stated that they were opposed to the forced evacuation. In fact, evidence suggests that this was the case also for Rendulic himself. Therefore, some writers have argued that the acquittal was the natural result of neglect on the part of the Norwegian government-in-exile. Others believe that the case was not sufficiently prioritised by the Norwegian Director of Public Prosecutions. "The prosecution fell short because the Norwegian investigation failed to obtain the necessary documentation to bring Rendulic down."[4] According to this narrative, a flawed Norwegian investigation explains the disappointing outcome of the case against Rendulic.

---

[1] Known as the St. James declaration of 13 January 1942.

[2] Newspaper clippings in RA/S-1555/D/L0041, folder 2, published 10 July 1947.

[3] Jaklin 2016, pp 360–361, cf. also Eriksen and Halvorsen 1987, p 104; Kjetil Korsnes, *Nordlys* (23 October 2019); Kjell-Ragnar Berge, *Nordlys* (9 November 2019).

[4] Olsen 2019, p 282. See also Jacobsen 2006, pp 242–253.

This chapter analyses how the devastation charge came to be included in the case against Rendulic, how Norwegian and American authorities worked to collect evidence, and how the case was prepared.

5.2 Collecting Evidence from a Distance

The investigation of war crimes in Northern Troms and Finnmark was exceedingly difficult. Seated in London, the Norwegian government-in-exile was a long way from where the events had taken place. The information that reached it was fragmented and not always correct. The organised home front in Norway, on which the exiled government often had to rely for information, was also unable to provide much solid documentation.[5]

These are the circumstances under which the government handed over the charges to the UN War Crimes Commission (UNWCC), of which Norway was a member. The list, which was prepared during the winter of 1945, held *Reichskommissar* Josef Terboven, *Generaloberst* Nikolaus von Falkenhorst, Rendulic, and *Generalleutnant* Curt Ebeling as the German leaders mainly responsible for the war crimes in Finnmark and Northern Troms. The charges against them stated that the "destruction and evacuation was carried out by the retreating Germans with such thoroughness and brutality that it constitutes a major crime against the people of Norway."[6] The document listed many other people who were also responsible, both within the German *Reichskommissariat*, The *Sicherheitspolizei und Sicherheitsdienst* (Sipo-SD), and the 20th Mountain Army.

The charges were based on information that the Norwegian government-in-exile in London had managed to obtain. It also specifically referred to some key documents, such as the proclamation of 31 October 1944 to the people of Finnmark, signed by Terboven and Rendulic. The charges went on to state that "the civil population of Finnmark is being driven from their homes by German soldiers in the most brutal fashion."[7] Those who refused to follow the German evacuation "are hunted down, and if they are found, are shot out of hand." It was also mentioned that "Norwegian civilians, including women and children, have been forced to sleep in the open, exposed to the severe cold of the Arctic winter. It is feared that many will not have survived the experience."[8] The document concluded by stating that the "case is built on the information we have received so far, but we do not consider that it is complete yet."[9]

It is not clear why the Norwegian authorities in Oslo eventually, after the war, chose to drop the charges against leading German officials within the *Reichskommissariat*

[5] Elstad 2020, pp 426–434 and 471–481.

[6] RA/S-1557/Db/Looo9. Charges 1 and 63-289.

[7] Ibid.

[8] Ibid.

[9] Ibid.

and Sipo on this matter. A shortage of hard evidence, along with the fact that Terboven committed suicide on 8 May 1945, probably influenced that decision. The Norwegian authorities in London chose instead to concentrate solely on German military officers, and listed sixteen leading officers in the 20th Mountain Army as responsible for the destruction of the northernmost parts of Norway. A further 210 officers were listed as suspects, all of whom became registered in the Central Registry of War Criminals and Security Suspects, known as CROWCASS.[10]

The Norwegian charges against Rendulic were registered by CROWCASS, and a copy was sent to the court in Nuremberg. Norway charged that those German military officers, and especially Rendulic, had committed crimes such as wanton devastation and destruction of property, forbidden by Article 23(g) of the 1907 Hague Regulations: murder, massacres and systematic terrorism; deliberate starvation of civilians; pillage, which was forbidden under Article 47 of the Hague Regulations; and wanton destruction of buildings belonging to institutions dedicated to public worship and charity, outlawed in Article 47 of the Hague Regulations.[11]

CROWCASS registration was crucial to further processes, as it meant that the case against Rendulic would be managed by the US military tribunal. Rendulic, who was accused and later convicted of more serious war crimes in the Balkans, could not be handed over to the Norwegian authorities for prosecution in Norway. Consequently, his case had to be tried in Nuremberg.[12] As we shall see, however, this was not clear to the legal authorities in Norway.

5.3 Cooperation and Misunderstandings

When the war was over, the Prosecution Authority in Norway began to investigate and prepare the case against Rendulic. Source material in the archives of the Director of Public Prosecutions indicates a lack of overview of all the procedures in Nuremberg, i.e., the processes that followed from international agreements entered by the Norwegian government-in-exile in London. The main reason why this occurred was poor communication between the Norwegian representation at the UNWCC in London and the Norwegian Prosecution Authority in Oslo. This left the latter with an incomplete situational awareness and too high hopes for a Norwegian trial against Rendulic.[13]

Unfortunately, this was not the only misunderstanding that occurred. Norway's Director of Public Prosecution also believed that its Military Prosecution Authority

[10] Soleim et al. 2022, p 363.

[11] RA/S-1555/D/L0041, file 3.

[12] Since much more serious crimes had been committed in the Balkans, Norway did not have a right of priority when it came to extradition. In practice, this meant that the case had to be brought to Nuremberg. See RA/S-1555/D/L0041, folder 2. "Criminal case against Generaloberst Rendulic", 4 October 1948, Asbjørn Bryhn.

[13] RA/S-1555/D/L0041, folder 3. Follestad's letter, 2 March 1948.

was better suited for preparing the case against Rendulic in Norway. This attitude led to a process in which the two bodies exchanged numerous letters relating to expertise and responsibility.[14] Following several months of uncertainty, the Prosecution Authority ended up having to take on the prosecution. By this point, key time and manpower had been lost.[15]

The main reason why the Director of Public Prosecution argued that the case should be brought before a military court was the nature of the crime itself. In his view, only military experts could assess whether the destruction was militarily necessary. Nor would a statement from a military expert alone be sufficient; judges and prosecutors should also have the necessary military expertise.

There were also concerns among the Norwegian authorities about Norway's reputation, which would suffer if Norway chose to handle the case against Rendulic as a civilian matter and not bring it before a military court.[16] The military authorities, on the other hand, argued that if a military jurisdiction were to be invoked, crimes would have had to be committed in a theatre of war. In their opinion, serious doubts could be raised as to whether this had actually been the case.

While Norway's prosecution authorities were discussing matters of jurisdiction, its Military Prosecution Authority managed to prepare a detailed study of the German withdrawal in 1944, which assessed responsibility for the destructions in Finnmark and Northern Troms. The study was prepared by Lieutenant Colonel Harald Wrede Holm who found that the destructions in the eastern parts of Finnmark were based on considerations of military necessity. Destructions in this area were also carried out before the release of the *Führerbefehl* on 28 October 1944.[17]

In the area between Tana and Lakselv, which lies in the middle of Finnmark, German troops still found themselves in an exposed position. In this situation, they could not have predicted whether the Red Army was preparing to follow in their retreat. Contacts did in fact occur between German and Soviet soldiers in the Tana area, however. Furthermore, as the German troops reached the Lakselv area, some 100 kms to the west, they could also clearly see that the Red Army were not following. Had it been the Red Army's intention to continue fighting, it would have made sense to try and attack German troops before they had established more favourable positions in the vicinity of Lakselv. Although the Soviet troops refrained from doing that, Wrede Holm still concluded that the destructions in this area might also have been necessary.[18]

Regarding the destructions in Western Finnmark and Northern Troms, in the area between Lakselv and Lyngen, Wrede Holm could not find any good military reasons for total destruction. He understood, from a military point of view, that some of the

[14] RA/S-1557/Da/L0033, folder "20. Gebirgsarmeé" (several documents).

[15] This loss of time is also raised in Olsen 2019, pp 263–267.

[16] RA/S-1555/D/L0041, file 1, "De tyske ødeleggelser i Finnmark og Nord-Troms vinteren 1944/45", 9 October 1946.

[17] RA/S-1555/D/L0041, file 1. "Ansvarsforholdet for ødeleggelsene i Finnmark og Nord-Troms under den tyske tilbaketrekning 1944", signed Wrede Holm, 27 July 1946.

[18] Ibid.

larger fishing villages and towns on the coast of Finnmark had been burnt down. Burning down every house in the whole area, however, made no sense. This, Wrede Holm felt, had to do with the fact that Terboven, rather than a military leader, had decided to do so. Wrede Holm concluded that, while Alfred Jodl and Rendulic would have to be held accountable, von Falkenhorst had nothing to do with this destruction.

Wrede Holm's study seems to have established a more solid ground for the preparation of the case in Norway. Another important contribution was made by Jakob Bjertnæs, a lawyer and investigator at the Office of Chief of Police in Finnmark. More than anyone else, Bjertnæs was able to clarify how other actors and institutions, such as Terboven's *Reichskommissariat* and Vidkun Quisling's Norwegian Nazi government, shared responsibility for the crimes that had been committed.[19]

At Nuremberg, preparations for the case against Rendulic and eleven other generals charged in *Hostage* began in October 1946. Brigadier General Telford Taylor, Chief of Counsel for the US prosecution in Nuremberg, was dependent on cooperation with the Norwegian authorities and approached the Norwegian envoy to the UNWCC. The envoy was notably based in London and not at the Prosecution Authority in Oslo. A letter from Taylor's office stated that the US prosecution was "anxious to secure whatever evidence you might have available. Particularly, this concerns the activities of Generaloberst Rendulic in Finnmark."[20]

Simultaneously, the Director of Public Prosecutions in Oslo started preparing its own case, unaware of the preparations in which Taylor was involved at Nuremberg. The Supreme Court Justice Ivar Follestad was tasked to lead Norwegian investigations and collect evidence. Police Inspector Asbjørn Bryhn was sent to the American Zone in Germany to track down Rendulic and have him extradited to Norway. Bryhn's dispatch to Germany shows that the Director of Public Prosecutions intended to try Rendulic in Norway before a Norwegian court.

Taylor found Norway's extradition request confusing. Had he not already written to the Norwegian authorities about the process that lay ahead? Taylor wrote another letter on 30 April 1947 to clarify the procedures. He now made it clear that "it would be difficult to comply with the request from the Norwegian authorities to allow Rendulic to be tried in Norway before his trial here," adding: "[w]e are prepared to prosecute Rendulic for crimes committed in Norway".[21] This should not have come as a surprise to the Norwegian authorities, given the letter from Taylor's office in December 1946. There was now little time left before the trial was due to begin, "probably in early June," Taylor wrote.

[19] RA/S-1557/Da/L0033, file "20. Gebirgsarmeé", several documents.

[20] Letter from Clark Denney to Aars Rynning, Norwegian representative, UNWCC, 12 December 1946.

[21] RA/S-1555/D/L0041. Taylor to Springer, 30 April 1947.

5.4 Preparing the Case

From this point on, things progressed quickly. On 16 May 1947, Follestad sent 92 documents over to Taylor's office. These documents amounted to hundreds of pages and constituted a lot of evidence. Follestad was given the impression that the documents would be translated for use during case preparations. Only a few documents were in fact translated, however, and, according to Follestad, many of the most important documents were never translated.[22] The evidence against Rendulic was therefore based on somewhat thin and partly fragmented data, something for which the US prosecution was largely responsible.

The case that the US Chief of Counsel for War Crimes brought against Rendulic for the devastation of Northern Norway did not reflect the evidence that the 92 documents could provide. Instead, it was mainly built on one document, previously unknown to Follestad, that had originated from the Norwegian authorities-in-exile in London.[23] The indictment stated that Rendulic, Commander-in-Chief of the 20th Mountain Army, ordered "the complete destruction of all shelter and means of existence in, and the total evacuation of, the Northern Norwegian province of Finmark *[sic]*". This was "ruthlessly carried out" and resulted in the deaths of hundreds of people, some of whom were shot by German troops, while others froze, starved to death or died of illness.[24]

During the summer of 1947, Follestad returned to Nuremberg for two months to assist the US prosecution. There, he was told that more evidence had to be collected in Norway. In the beginning of August 1947, Walter Rapp, Associate Counsel for the US prosecution team, was especially interested in evidence from witnesses who had been forcibly evacuated. The US prosecution was looking for material in support of the accusation that acts of violence and unnecessary brutality had occurred during the evacuation. In this connection, Follestad also noticed how the German military leaders were changing their narrative. The Nazi conception of a "racial community" between Germanic peoples in the north could no longer serve as an explanation for the less violent acts committed in Norway in contrast to those perpetrated in the Balkans. The Germans now told the story of a peaceful and friendly population in Norway that was more than happy to follow evacuation orders in order to escape Soviet terror. In Follestad's opinion, this totally false narrative had to be refuted in court.[25]

[22] RA/S-1555/D/L0041, folder 3, Follestad's letter to the Norwegian Parliament's Justice Committee, 3 November 1948.

[23] RA/S-1557/Db/Looo9. The document concerns charges 1 and 63-289, "The province of Finnmark in North Norway. October/November 1944".

[24] Ibid.

[25] RA/S-1555/D/L0041, file 3, "Straffesak mot Rendulic", 25 July 1947.

In Norway, the Director of Public Prosecutions did not find it necessary to send eyewitnesses from Finnmark to Nuremberg. Instead, he thought it would be sufficient to record testimony in Finnmark and thereafter make it available to Rendulic's prosecution.[26] Finn Palmstrøm, Magistrate in Tana, was particularly well suited for this task. He managed to collect several statements displaying the brutality that ordinary people had experienced.

One witness, Ove Eriksen, who lived in the vicinity of Lakselv, told the story of how some of the families from his local community had been forced to leave everything behind.[27] All experienced severe brutality. Small children were forced to leave their homes as they burned down. The wind was heavy and cold, and the children froze so much that they were unable to stand straight. After several hours, the families were brought by the Germans to some barracks nearby. Here, the children were put in danger once more. Two German soldiers blew up a couple of hand grenades near some children who were playing, wounding eight to ten of them. Eriksen went on to describe the conditions on one of the two large transportation ships that were used during the forced evacuation, the *Adolf Binder*, where 1,200 people were squeezed together for five days. There were only three toilets on board, and the water was also contaminated. Very soon, people started to become sick, many with dysentery.

The experiences that Eriksen described were supported by many other witnesses. The situation on board the other large transportation ship, the *Carl Arp*, with 1,800 civilians on board, had not been any better. Both the *Carl Arp* and the *Adolf Binder* sailed from Porsanger in Finnmark to Narvik. By the time the *Carl Arp* arrived at the harbour in Narvik, more than twenty people had died because of the severe conditions on board. Even today, it is very difficult to find out how many people died as a result of the forced evacuation. The best estimates that historians are able to establish set the number of evacuation-related deaths somewhere between 200 and 400. According to historian Ingunn Elstad, certainly many more would have died if the evacuation had been carried out in accordance with Rendulic's plan which envisioned more use of large transportation ships such as the *Adolf Binder* and the *Carl Arp*.[28]

The US prosecutors consciously chose not to highlight the brutality towards the civilian population in Northern Norway, since the alleged German war crimes in Finnmark and Northern Troms had to be seen in comparison to the atrocities in the Balkans. Instead, the prosecution chose to focus on the enormous destruction occasioned in Northern Norway.

From Nuremberg, Follestad continuously reported back to Oslo on the preparations for the case against Rendulic, including what kind of evidence was needed to secure conviction. On 24 July 1947, Follestad wrote about a documentary film from Finnmark that had been presented at court the previous day. According to Follestad,

[26] RA/S-1555/D/L0041, file 2, "Straffesak mot general Rendulic for militærdomstolen i Nürnberg", 2 August 1947.

[27] RA/S-1555/D/L0041, file 2,"Rettsbok for Tana forhørsrett, år 1947, den 4. August".

[28] Elstad 2022, p 219.

the US prosecutors were convinced that "the extent of the destructions is sufficiently proven".[29]

In his letter, Follestad also said the US prosecution did not find Wrede Holm's study convincing.[30] Sources indicate that this was partly connected to Wrede Holm's opinion that the German Navy was responsible for the destruction of coastal areas and coastal towns, whereas the US prosecution saw Rendulic as responsible for the whole affair. In another letter, however, Follestad wrote that

> the American Prosecution – and I agree with [the] Prosecution – desires to find in the statement a definite reference that [the Germans'] destructions were at a time when the German defeat was clear to everyone and only a question of time, and a further reference that the terrain at wintertime forbade military operations on a greater scale through Finnmark notwithstanding Troms and Nordland.[31]

To put it differently, the US prosecutors did not want to differentiate between "levels of military necessity"—or lack thereof—as Wrede Holm had done. They therefore did not consider Wrede Holm's study persuasive.

Given these differing opinions, Follestad strongly recommended that Norwegian Major General Arne Dagfin Dahl be sent to Nuremberg to testify as a military expert. This was very important, Follestad wrote, "because, in the opinion of the Americans, the case hinges on the question of whether the evacuation and destruction were necessary or, in any case, justifiable from a military point of view."[32]

Follestad also wanted Terje Wold, former Minister of Justice, and Karl Evang, Director General of Health, as witnesses. From London, they had both provided important information on which the US prosecution had built much of its indictment against Rendulic. Unhelpfully for Norway, however, neither of them was able to testify in Nuremberg. "We must not spare these or other expenses," Follestad wrote. Compared to Yugoslavia and Greece whose representatives had "been present at Nuremberg continuously for three months and had brought with them an enormous amount of evidence," he continued, "Norway paled in comparison."[33]

The indictment was clearly not built on the evidence that the Norwegian side had provided. Nor does the evidence appear to have been presented in the way the Norwegian prosecution desired, either. Judging from documents written in July 1947, one can get the impression that Follestad did not oppose the US critique of Wrede Holm's study. Later, however, he claimed that the view held by Wrede Holm was in full accordance with the view of the Norwegian prosecution. In a letter to the Norwegian Standing Committee on Justice, Follestad claimed that the Norwegian line of reasoning was discarded by the US prosecution because they believed that the destructions would be judged as unlawful acts regardless of time and place.[34]

---

[29] RA/S-1555/D/L0041, file 2,"Straffesak mot General Rendulic", 24 July 1947.

[30] Ibid.

[31] Ibid.

[32] Ibid.

[33] Ibid.

[34] RA/S-1555/D/L0041, file 3, "Straffesak mot generaloberst Rendulic", 20 September 1947.

Follestad was also highly critical of how the US prosecutors had failed to present very solid evidence to the court. Their failure to submit Bryhn's interrogation report of Rendulic dated 6 March 1947 was particularly objectionable. Confronted by Bryhn, Rendulic had openly admitted that had acted on orders and that, to him, the destructions did not appear necessary. Rendulic did in fact admit that the destructions in part could have been avoided.[35] At first, Rapp said to Follestad that it was good to have some valuable evidence in reserve for the last part of Rendulic's trial. Later Rapp stated "that the case was so clear that it would be foolish to express doubt by offering more evidence."[36]

Nor did the US prosecution sufficiently emphasise the destruction's temporal scope. The evidence collected by Follestad unambiguously showed that the destruction continued for several months after 20 November 1944. This was clear from Town Engineer Johannes Kummeneje's report on the destruction of Hammerfest. From around 20 November 1944, the Germans knew that the Red Army was not in pursuit, as documented by Ragnar Hansen, head of the evacuation committee in Tromsø. Furthermore, the documents that Follestad delivered made it clear that the German retreat was largely completed by the end of November or early December. Neither Hansen's nor Kummeneje's reports were presented to the court, despite the fact that the Norwegian authorities had sent these documents to Nuremberg on 16 May 1947.[37]

5.5 Reactions to the Verdict

The trial lasted from 8 July 1947 until 19 February 1948. Rendulic was sentenced to 20 years in prison. Only two of the ten generals charged were given a life sentence, the strictest sentence passed down on this judgment day.

There is no obvious answer to the question why Rendulic got away with a lesser sentence. Just like Generals Wilhelm List and Walter Kuntze, Rendulic was convicted of passing on unlawful orders and for not having stopped unlawful executions in German-occupied Yugoslavia. The judges did not find any extenuating circumstances in relation to these points. However, as the Commander of the 2nd Armoured Army in Yugoslavia during the period of August 1943 to June 1944, Rendulic had been responsible for fewer soldiers and a smaller territorial area than List and Kuntze.[38] This might have had an impact on his sentencing.

---

[35] RA/S-1555/D/L0041, file 3, "Lothar Rendulic – tyskernes ødeleggelser og herjinger i Finnmark og Nord-Troms i 1944–45", 8 November 1948.

[36] RA/S-1555/D/L0041, file 3, "Lothar Rendulic – tyskernes ødeleggelser og herjinger i Finnmark og Nord-Troms i 1944–45", 3 November 1948.

[37] RA/S-1555/D/L0041, folder 3, Follestad's letter to the Norwegian Parliament's Justice Committee, 3 November 1948.

[38] Heller 2011, p 318.

Rendulic was unanimously acquitted of the executions of Yugoslav hostages and captured partisans. The court also rejected criminal charges against him for his role in the forced evacuation and destruction of Finnmark and Northern Troms.

"Military necessity" became the key words for the court. Where the judges found a "reasonable link" between the defendant's actions and the military necessities of the situation, the verdict had to be acquittal of the charges. In Rendulic's case, this link was stretched. The judges did acknowledge that, objectively, there had been no military necessity for Rendulic to ravage Finnmark using the scorched earth tactics. The judges nevertheless chose to place decisive emphasis on the fact that, based on his subjective position and situational understanding, Rendulic had adequate reason to consider the action militarily necessary in order to ensure his army's retreat.[39] In the opinion of the tribunal, the *Generaloberst* was guilty of showing poor judgment rather than committing a criminal act.

When the rulings became known, there was a widespread public perception that the tribunal had been too lenient on the generals on the dock. The outcome caused strong reactions in a number of countries, to such a degree that Taylor's staff issued a press release on 24 February 1948. In response to Norway's indignation with the judgment, the release said:

> We have every understanding for Norwegians being disappointed with General Lothar Rendulic being acquitted of the arbitrary destruction in Finnmark and Northern Norway [...]. The prosecution did its best to prove to the court that the total destruction of Northern Norway and the practice of executing captured partisans were unlawful criminal offences and the prosecution shares the disappointment of these countries that the tribunal proved incapable of reaching a decision on this matter.[40]

At the same time, however, Taylor expressed his understanding of the fact that the verdict was what it was and hoped that *Hostage* would, over time, lead to international law being revised and its rules becoming clearer. As he later put it, the judges applied international law "as we see it," not "the act as it is."[41] The tribunal had become fixated on Article 23(g) of the Hague Regulations, which prohibited "destruction or seizure of the enemy's property, unless such destruction or seizure be imperatively demanded by the necessities of war", interpreting this exemption to cover the destruction of all private and public property in Finnmark.

Taylor was furious with Wennerstrum. Upon his return from Nuremberg to Iowa, Wennerstrum was quoted as saying that "victory in war is not the best judge of war crime guilt."[42] By that, he implied that it had been impossible "to convey to the defence, their counsel and their people that the court is trying to represent all mankind, rather than the country which appointed its members".[43] In response to

[39] Heller 2011, p 311.

[40] Dierl and Stiller 2013, p 247.

[41] Taylor 1949, p 207.

[42] As quoted in *The Stars and Stripes*, 24 February 1948.

[43] Ibid.

these allegations, Taylor charged Wennerstrum with "grave misconduct".[44] Wennerstrum had accused the US prosecutors of being "vindicative" and "pursuing personal ambitions".[45] For Taylor, however, the lowest point of Wennerstrum's behaviour was "the charges you have brought against the conduct of the trial before your own tribunal over which you yourself presided."[46]

Theodore F. Fenstermacher, Taylor's fellow US prosecutor, publicly criticised Wennerstrum as well. Fenstermacher used words such as "utterly disgraceful".[47] According to historian Kim Christian Priemel, Fenstermacher accused Wennerstrum "of bias in favour of the defendants while being 'wholly devoid of sympathy, pity and understanding for […] their innocent victims'."[48] Follestad had also heard Taylor argue that it was inappropriate for Wennerstrum to continue in his role as a judge with the views he had on the process. Taylor told Follestad that there was a slim possibility that General Lucius D. Clay, military governor of the US zone, might overturn the sentence based on the opinions Wennerstrum had expressed.[49]

In the judgment's political repercussions, the Norwegian authorities clung to that straw. Oscar Christian Gundersen, Norwegian Minister of Justice, felt obliged to act when challenged in the Norwegian National Assembly on how the government would respond.[50] Subsequently, Follestad cabled Taylor to notify that an inquiry regarding the possibilities of overturning the verdict were imminent. Meanwhile, United Press International quoted Clay as saying that he would carefully consider such an inquiry, but that he lacked authority to revoke Rendulic's acquittal. The Norwegian authorities took the view that Rendulic had merely been acquitted on account of his order of 29 October 1944 and that the tribunal had not addressed his responsibility for destructions carried out in the latter stages of the retreat, when it was obvious to the Germans that the Soviets were not in hot pursuit.[51] Norway's strategy was twofold: first, to inquire, by contacting Washington officials, whether Rendulic's acquittal could be appealed to the US Supreme Court; and second, to approach Clay, through the Norwegian military mission in Berlin, to establish whether it was within his powers to overturn the verdict.[52]

Both inquiries proved fruitless. On 19 March 1948, the US Army's War Crime Branch, having conferred with the US Justice Department, replied that the case could not be brought before the Supreme Court. Meanwhile, Clay, though sympathetic to the Norwegian position, stated that it was beyond his authority to aggravate punishment. He added that the acquittal covered all the destruction committed during

---

[44] Ibid.

[45] Ibid.

[46] Ibid.

[47] Priemel 2016, p 349.

[48] Ibid.

[49] RA/S-1555/D/L0041, file 3, "Straffesak mot generaloberst Rendulic. - Ødeleggelsene i Finnmark vinter 1944/45", 2 March 1948.

[50] Justice and Police Department, Parliamentary document (Stortingsmelding) No. 44, 1948, p 2.

[51] Ibid., p 2.

[52] Ibid., p 3.

the 20th Mountain Army's retreat, recommending that the matter be taken up with the US government instead. However, when Clay submitted a written statement on 24 March, he did not mention this possibility, which might imply, as the Norwegians believed, that his judicial advisors had convinced him of the futility of that path.[53] Due to Norway's involvement in the trial, and thereby its tacit acceptance of the indictment, Jens Christian Hauge, Minister of Defence and a jurist who had taken an interest in war crimes investigations, concluded that Norway would have to regard the Rendulic judgement as final. As a result, the government decided to let the matter rest. Norwegians were left pondering on the legitimacy of the verdict, however. If Rendulic's acquittal reflected the state of international law at the time, Hauge opined, then perhaps the law would need to be revised.[54] A third option, i.e., of having Rendulic extradited to Norway to face a new trial, was not pursued and seemingly never seriously considered, though it would probably have stood a better chance of success.

One particularly striking feature of the ruling is how little interest the tribunal showed in the details relating to forced evacuations. The judges boiled the civilian suffering associated with forced evacuations in Northern Norway down to a remark that these measures apparently did not cause any deaths. As we have seen, this is partly a result of the priorities made by the US prosecution. What the ruling failed to touch on was the question of how freely an army, faced with the need to retreat from a militarily superior enemy, could be permitted to act in relation to an occupied population. Did "military necessity" provide the belligerent with the right to destroy the population's livelihoods? Was the army free to treat them as movable spoils of war? Was it really the tribunal's assessment that the supposed "necessities of war" on the part of the occupier gave it an unfettered right to commit atrocities against the occupied?

The US military tribunal heard *Hostage* in Nuremberg's Courtroom 600 where, one and a half years earlier, Alfred Jodl had been given a verdict of death by hanging. The judges of the International Military Tribunal (IMT) represented each of the four occupying powers in Germany. They found Jodl guilty on all four charges. Two of the charges, war crimes and crimes against humanity, included Jodl's criminal responsibility for the forced evacuation and damage caused to 30,000 homes in Northern Norway.[55] Jodl had neither ordered nor executed the destruction himself; rather, he had forwarded Hitler's 29 October order to the 20th Mountain Army. This is exactly what Jodl emphasised in his defence: he simply followed Hitler's orders. When forwarding the order, Jodl had made it clear that its initiator was Terboven. According to Jodl, this was his way of distancing himself from the order that had been issued and from the ensuing wrongs. He also argued that no militarily unjustified destruction took place in Finnmark and that cities such as Kirkenes, Hammerfest

[53] Ibid., p 4.

[54] Ibid., p 4.

[55] Trial of the Major War Criminals before the International Military Tribunal ("The Blue Series"), available at The Library of Congress: https://www.loc.gov/rr/frd/Military_Law/Nuremberg_trials.html [accessed 1 April 2023], Vol. 1, p 324.

and Alta had been spared.[56] At the same time, Jodl sought to justify the burning of settlements on the grounds that it prevented a partisan war and the Soviets' continued advance. The burning, he argued, necessitated forced evacuations in turn.[57]

On 1 October 1946, the IMT rejected all of Jodl's explanations, allegations, and attempts to claim legal support for his actions. The judges referred to the destruction of inhabited lands, such as Northern Norway, as a crime.[58] How the IMT treated Jodl's role in forced evacuations stood in sharp contrast to the almost collegial tone used by the US military tribunal when dealing with the same events and treating Rendulic's role in them. Jodl's case was also severely flawed. The IMT did not take the time to further justify Jodl's conviction, other than referencing Article 8 of the Nuremberg Charter according to which a defendant would not be absolved of criminal liability for having acted on the orders of a superior authority.

Without a detailed assessment of the devastation and forced evacuations in Northern Norway, as well as Rendulic's role therein, the judges moved towards a legally unclear ruling and exposed limitations of international law. This left the population of Northern Norway unfulfilled in their need for a legal closure against their wrongdoers and feeling the additional weight of their suffering.

References

Dierl F, Stiller A (2013) Von Generälen und Partisanen: Die Verbrechen der Wehrmacht in Südosteuropa und der "Geiselmord-Prozess" im Kontext des Kalten Krieges. In: Priemel KC, Stiller A (eds) NMT. Die Nürnberger Militärtribunale zwischen Geschichte, Gerechtigkeit und Rechtschöpfung. Hamburger Edition, Hamburg

Elstad I (2020) Tvangsevakueringa. Orkana akademisk, Stamsund

Elstad I (2022) Overleving, død og sjukdom under tvangsevakueringa. In: Bones S (ed) Kampen om frihet, Vol. 3 of Andre verdenskrig i nord. Orkana akademisk, Stamsund

Eriksen KE, Halvorsen T (1987) Norge i krig. Vol. 8, Frigjøring. Gyldendal, Oslo

Heller KJ (2011) The Nuremberg Military Tribunals and the Origins of International Criminal Law. Oxford University Press, Oxford/New York

Jacobsen AR (2006) Nikkel, jern og blod. Krigen i nord 1939–1945. Aschehoug, Oslo

Jaklin A (2016) Brent jord 1944–1945. Heltene. Ofrene. De skyldige. Gyldendal, Oslo

Olsen PK (2019) Jevnet med jorden. Brenningen av Finnmark Nord-Troms 1944. Aschehoug, Oslo

Priemel KC (2016) The Betrayal. The Nuremberg Trials and German Divergence. Oxford University Press, Oxford

Soleim M, Bones S, Hatlehol G (2022) Krigsforbryterne. In: Bones S (ed) Kampen om frihet, Vol. 3 of Andre verdenskrig i nord. Orkana akademisk, Stamsund

Taylor T (1949) Final Report to the Secretary of the Army on the Nuremberg War Crime Trials under Control Council Law No. 10. Washington D.C.

[56] Ibid., Vol. 19, p 35.

[57] Ibid., Vol. 19, p 34.

[58] Ibid., Vol. 21, p 571.

Other Documents

Trial of the Major War Criminals before the International Military Tribunal ("The Blue Series"), Vol. 1–42. Available at The Library of Congress: https://www.loc.gov/rr/frd/Military_Law/Nuremberg_trials.html

Stian Bones Professor of History, UiT The Arctic University of Norway; Senior Researcher, Narvik War and Peace Centre. Address: Hansine Hanssens veg 18, 9019 Tromsø, Norway, e-mail: stian.bones@uit.no

Gunnar D. Hatlehol Project Manager, Narvik War and Peace Centre, e-mail: ghatlehol@narviksenteret.no

Chapter 6
The Adjudication and Findings of Finnmark's Devastation Charge in *Hostage*

Emily Crawford

Contents

6.1 Introduction 128
6.2 Background: The Charges 129
6.3 The Opening Statements 131
6.4 The Prosecution Case: Witnesses and Evidence 134
6.5 Rendulic on the Stand: The Defence Case 135
6.6 The Prosecution's Cross-Examination of Rendulic 138
6.7 Witnesses and Evidence for the Defence 140
6.8 The Judgment on the Devastation Charge 143
6.9 Accounting for the Decision on the Devastation of Finnmark in the Tribunal: Military Necessity in the Law of Armed Conflict of 1947 146
6.10 Critiquing the Decision in *Hostage*: Prosecution Missteps and the Decision-Making Process of the Tribunal 149
6.11 Conclusion 153
References 153

Abstract As part of the post-World War II military trials of Nazi war criminals, General Lothar Rendulic, Commander-in-Chief of the 20th Mountain Army, was put on trial for acts of devastation not justified by military necessity, in the Finnmark region of Northern Norway. In his defence, Rendulic justified the acts on the grounds that the devastation of the territory and the forced evacuation of the region were permissible on the basis of being militarily necessary. Fearful of an imminent Soviet invasion of the territory following the September 1944 armistice agreement between the Soviet Union and Finland, Rendulic and his troops retreated, laying waste to the region and forcibly evacuating the population. These acts were, according to Rendulic's account, necessary to hinder the Soviet forces from advancing. Ultimately, the US Military Tribunal accepted this justification, and found Rendulic not guilty of breaching Article 23(g) of the Hague Regulations—which prohibits the destruction or seizure of enemy property, unless such destruction or seizure is "imperatively demanded by the necessities of war". This chapter will explore how the tribunal came

---

E. Crawford (✉)
The University of Sydney Law School, The University of Sydney, New Law Building F10, Eastern Avenue, Camperdown, NSW 2006, Australia
e-mail: emily.crawford@sydney.edu.au

N. Hayashi and C. Lingaas (eds.), *Honest Errors? Combat Decision-Making 75 Years After the* Hostage *Case*, https://doi.org/10.1007/978-94-6265-611-6_6

to its decision, examining the charges regarding Rendulic's conduct in Finnmark, the prosecution and defence cases, and the decision that eventually saw Rendulic acquitted of the charge of devastation.

Keywords Law of armed conflict · *Hostage* trial · military necessity · Nuremburg tribunals · Lothar Rendulic · Rendulic Rule

6.1 Introduction

The 12 German defendants indicted in what would become known as the *Hostage* case faced an array of charges for acts committed in Greece, Yugoslavia, Albania, and Norway. Those acts included terrorism and intimidation; murder and ill-treatment of prisoners of war and the civilian population; deportation to slave labour of prisoners of war and the civilian population; and "plundering and pillaging public and private property and wantonly destroying cities, towns, and villages for which there was no military necessity."[1] The majority of the case and the judgment focused on the practices carried out by German troops in Greece and Yugoslavia, in particular the taking of hostages, the reprisal measures taken against partisans and civilians in those areas, and the deportation of Jewish civilians to concentration camps.

All the defendants faced the charges of committing the war crimes and crimes against humanity of plundering, pillage, and "other acts of devastation not justified by military necessity"[2] throughout Southeastern Europe. However, only one person—General Lothar Rendulic, Commander-in-Chief of the 20th Mountain Army—was charged with acts of a similar nature in the Northern Norwegian province of Finnmark. The prosecution indicted Rendulic with having ordered the "complete destruction of all shelter and means of existence in, and the total evacuation of the entire civilian population of, the northern Norwegian province of Finnmark."[3] He justified the acts on the grounds that the devastation of the territory and the forced evacuation of the region were permissible on the basis of being militarily necessary: fearful of an imminent Soviet invasion of the territory following the September 1944 armistice agreement between the Soviet Union and Finland, Rendulic and his troops retreated, laying waste to the region and forcibly evacuating the civilian population. The reasoning behind such acts, and the justification given in the Nuremberg courtroom in 1947, was that it was the only way to hinder advancing Soviet forces,

[1] American Military Tribunal sitting at Nuremberg, Germany, *United States of America v Wilhelm List et al.*, Judgment, 19 February 1948, Justice Wennerstrum presiding, p 10419, reprinted from the original typed transcript, http://nuremberg.law.harvard.edu/transcripts/4-transcript-for-nmt-7-hostage-case [accessed 1 April 2023].

[2] American Military Tribunal sitting at Nuremberg, Germany, *United States of America v Wilhelm List et al.*, Indictment, filed 10 May 1947, reprinted at Office of Military Government for Germany (US) (1947), Trial 7—*Hostage* Case, p 9, https://digitalcommons.law.uga.edu/nmt7/1 [accessed 1 April 2023].

[3] Ibid.

to prevent a complete rout of the retreating German army, and to ensure that the Norwegian population was "preserved from Bolshevism".[4]

Ultimately, US Military Tribunal V did not find Rendulic guilty on the devastation charge. It decided that he was justified in reasoning, in the circumstances ruling at the time, that urgent military necessity warranted the decision to carry out the devastation of the Finnmark region. In doing so, the tribunal agreed with Rendulic's argument of military necessity as a basis of justification, permitted under Article 23(g) of the Hague Regulations—which prohibits the destruction or seizure of enemy property, unless such destruction or seizure is "imperatively demanded by the necessities of war."[5] The reasoning outlined in the case would eventually lead to what has become known as the Rendulic Rule—that a commander should only be judged "based on what the commander knew and expected at the time he made his decision."[6]

This chapter will explore how the tribunal ultimately came to its decision, examining the charges regarding Rendulic's conduct in Finnmark, the prosecution and defence cases, and the decision that eventually saw Rendulic acquitted of the charge of devastation. The main thrust of the chapter is largely descriptive, looking at how the charges were laid out, how the defence and the prosecution characterised and either condemned or justified the acts in question, how Rendulic himself defended his acts, and what the tribunal eventually ruled in relation to the charges. This will provide the background for the remainder of the chapter—how to account for the decision, which requires an understanding of the law on military necessity as it existed at the time of trial, how it was defined by both the prosecution and the defence, and how the concept of military necessity more generally was understood at the time of the case. In doing so, the chapter will provide a useful background for the next chapter in this anthology, which looks at how the Rendulic Rule emerged, how it is constituted, and how it has developed in practice in the 75 years since the *Hostage* case.[7]

6.2 Background: The Charges

The Finnmark devastation charge formed part of Count Two of the indictment in *Hostage*. Count Two charged that:

> Between September 1939 and May 1945, all of the defendants unlawfully, wilfully and knowingly committed War Crimes and Crimes against Humanity [...] in that they were principals in, accessories to, ordered, abetted, took a consenting part in, were connected with

[4] American Military Tribunal sitting at Nuremberg, Germany, *United States of America v Wilhelm List et al.*, Evidentiary Document No. NOKW-086, Order for the Evacuation of North Norway, 22 October 1944 (official translation, Office of the Chief of Counsel for War Crimes), https://nbg-02.lil.tools/transcripts/4-transcript-for-nmt-7-hostage-case?seq=92 [accessed 1 April 2023].

[5] Regulations Respecting the Laws and Customs of War on Land, annexed to Convention No. IV Respecting the Laws and Customs of War on Land, 18 October 1907, 36 Stat 2227, TS No. 539 (Hague Regulations of 1907), Article 23(g).

[6] Bill 2009, p 134.

[7] See Chap. 7.

plans and enterprises involving, and were members of organizations or groups connected with, the plundering and looting of public and private property, the wanton destruction of cities, towns and villages, frequently together with the murder of the inhabitants thereof, and the commission of other acts of devastation not justified by military necessity [...].[8]

The indictment went on to note:

The defendants ordered troops under their command and jurisdiction to burn, destroy and level to the ground entire villages and towns, and, on numerous occasions, to execute the inhabitants of such villages and towns. Such arbitrary, inhumane and disproportionately harsh measures of reprisal dislocated hundreds of families, made thousands of peaceful non-combatants homeless and destitute, and brought untold suffering, humiliation, misery and death to vast numbers of innocent civilians.[9]

Furthermore, it was charged that:

This program of wholesale devastation was carried out not only as part of a cruel, senseless pacification-through-terror scheme, wholly unwarranted and unjustified by military necessity and in flagrant violation of the laws and customs of war, but also in furtherance of a long-range plan to despoil and retard for decades the economic and industrial potential of the occupied territories.[10]

The Finnmark devastation charge was the first of the charges to be specified in Count Two, and Rendulic was the first of the defendants to be specifically named. The charge is worth recounting here in its entirety:

On or about 10 October 1944, the Commander-in-Chief of the Twentieth Mountain Army, the defendant RENDULIC, issued an order, to troops under his command and jurisdiction, for the complete destruction of all shelter and means of existence in, amid the total evacuation of the entire civilian population of, the northern Norwegian province of Finmark [*sic*]. During the months of October and November 1944, this order was effectively and ruthlessly carried out. For no compelling military reasons, and in literal execution of instructions to show no sympathy to the civilian population, the evacuated residents were made to witness the burning of their homes and possessions and the destruction of churches, public buildings, food supplies, barns, livestock, bridges, transport facilities and natural resources of an area in which they and their families had lived for generations. Relatives and friends were separated, many of the evacuees became ill from cold and disease, hundreds died from exposure or perished at sea in the small boats and fishing smacks used in the evacuation, while still others were summarily shot for refusing to leave their homeland – in all, the thoroughness and brutality of this evacuation left some 61,000 men, women and children homeless, starving and destitute.[11]

The Finnmark charges are unique in the *Hostage* indictment. *Hostage* was primarily focused on crimes committed against persons and property in Southeastern Europe. The bulk of the charges relating to crimes against persons were in regard to acts of hostage-taking, reprisal killings of hostages, summary executions of partisans, and forced transportation to concentration camps of persons in Greece, Yugoslavia,

---

[8] Indictment, p 9.

[9] Ibid.

[10] Ibid.

[11] Ibid., pp 9–10.

and Albania. Most of the crimes against property included in Count Two of the indictment likewise took place in Southeastern Europe and those acts were usually committed as reprisals against the civilian population. One charge, for example, is that "[o]n or about 16 October 1943, troops of the 187th Reserve Division, under the command and jurisdiction of the LXIX Reserve Corps, arrested the inhabitants of the Croatian villages of Paklonica and Vocarica as 'hostages' and then burned the villages to the ground."[12]

The indictment is not nearly as detailed regarding the acts in the Finnmark region compared to those carried out in Greece, Yugoslavia, and Albania. In the latter cases, specific acts of murder and destruction are recounted, including the dates, the names of towns and villages, and the context. For example, in Count Two, it is charged that "[o]n or about 5 October 1943, in retaliation for the murder of a Regimental Commander and for telephone 'sabotage', troops under the command and jurisdiction of the XXII Mountain Corps destroyed the Greek village of Akmotopos and executed its entire population."[13] No equivalent detail is given, at this stage of the proceedings, regarding the events in the Finnmark region. When arraigned, Rendulic, like his compatriots, pled not guilty.

6.3 The Opening Statements

General Telford Taylor began his opening remarks by detailing how Rendulic came to be in charge of the German 20th Mountain Army, which, in July 1944, was situated in Northern Finland. Soon after Rendulic's arrival in the region, Finland "capitulated to the Soviet forces, and demanded that the Germans promptly withdraw their troops"[14]—a retreat that would take place over the Northwestern Finnish frontier into Northern Norway. After a very brief description of the region's population and geography, Taylor turned to the central issue of the charge: the order given to Rendulic on 28 October 1944 to forcibly evacuate the Finnmark region and to employ scorched earth tactics as the German troops retreated, purportedly to prevent the presumably advancing Soviet forces. Taylor repeated the order verbatim:

> Because of the unwillingness of the north Norwegian population to voluntarily evacuate, the Fuehrer has agreed to the proposals of the commissioner for the occupied Norwegian territories and has ordered that the entire Norwegian population east of the fjord of Lyngen be evacuated by force in the interest of their own security and that all homes are to be burned down or destroyed.
>
> The Supreme Commander, Northern Finland, is responsible that the Fuehrer's order is carried out without consideration. Only by this method can it be prevented that the Russians with strong forces, and aided by these homes and the people familiar with the terrain, follow our withdrawal operations during this winter and shortly appear in front of our position in Lyngen. This is not the place for sympathy for the civilian population.

[12] Ibid., p 10.

[13] Ibid.

[14] Transcript, p 91.

> * * * * * * * * * * *
>
> It must be made clear to the troops engaged in this action that the Norwegians will be thankful in a few months that they were saved from Bolshevism, and that the barbarian methods of the air war against our German country and her cultural shrines have brought a thousand times more misery to our people if compared with the humane evacuation and destruction of homes in northern Norway, which is necessary for our war effort, and which, if it is not done, must be paid with the blood of German soldiers.
>
> The population, whose livelihood is fishing, in northern Norway, furthermore has enough shipping space at its disposal to be able to get out of the way en masse across the water. A large part of the small Norwegian ships which are kept hidden at present can be used for this, and can later also be used for our own transportation needs.
>
> The danger of the formation of guerrilla bands on the part of the Norwegians appears to be negligible since they can no longer use the houses during the winter.[15]

At this point in his opening remarks, Taylor presaged a likely defence argument. He noted that, during the trial of *Generaloberst* Alfred Jodl at the International Military Tribunal (IMT) at Nuremberg, Jodl had purportedly considered the forced evacuation order "unnecessarily far-reaching"[16] and that he had "by various subtle means endeavored to convey to Rendulic that it should not be complied with to the fullest degree."[17] Taylor immediately dismissed this line of argument, noting that "there is little evidence that Rendulic undertook to soften its effect in any material respect."[18] Taylor went on to repeat, verbatim, the orders that Rendulic gave to his subordinates, which followed "very closely the language"[19] of the original order by Jodl. Taylor also recounted parts of the proclamation that Rendulic made to the population of Finnmark:

> The evacuation of a part of northern Norway has been rendered a military necessity as a result of the treachery of a Finnish Government clique.
>
> The evacuation necessitates the removal of the civilian population, as the enemy has proved that, in those territories occupied by him, he ruthlessly and brutally forces the civilian population to give him active assistance in achieving his aims.
>
> This means that no shelter or means of existence of any kind can be left to the Bolshevik enemy in the fighting zone. All such installations as housing accommodation, transport facilities and food stocks must be destroyed or removed.
>
> THE POPULATION IN THESE DISTRICTS WILL THEREFORE BE DEPRIVED OF THE BASIS FOR THEIR EXISTENCE, SO THAT IN ORDER TO BE ABLE TO SURVIVE, THEY MUST EVACUATE TO THOSE NORWEGIAN TERRITORIES WHICH ARE STILL PROTECTED BY THE GERMAN WEHRMACHT.
>
> * * * * * * * * * *
>
> HE WHO DOES NOT COMPLY WITH THESE UNEQUIVOCAL INSTRUCTIONS EXPOSES HIMSELF AND HIS FAMILY TO POSSIBLE DEATH IN THE ARCTIC WINTER WITHOUT HOUSE OR FOOD.[20]

[15] Ibid., pp 92–93.

[16] Ibid., p 93; see also International Military Tribunal 1947, p 324.

[17] Transcript, p 93.

[18] Ibid.

[19] Ibid.

[20] Ibid., pp 94–95 (capitalisation in original).

In closing, the prosecution contended that the devastation of Finnmark under the command of Rendulic was "wholly unjustified from a military standpoint."[21] Taylor stated that the devastation of the region was entirely attributable to "Rendulic's admonition that his order was to be 'carried out ruthlessly'."[22] Beyond the general references to the notion of military necessity, Taylor did not specifically mention the relevant law in relation to Rendulic's acts in Finnmark.

When Dr. Stefan Fritsch, Rendulic's defence counsel, made his opening statement on 16 September 1947, he immediately put forward several bases for either dismissing outright the charges against Rendulic or justifying his acts as being permitted under the law. Fritsch first raised questions about the legality of Control Council Law No. 10, the law enacted by the Allies in 1945 which empowered any of the occupying Allied forces to try suspected war criminals found in their respective zones of occupation. Fritsch criticised this law as a "reprehensible"[23] violation of the principle of *nullum crimen sine lege, nulla poena sine lege*.[24] After noting briefly the legal issues that he believed were at play regarding the purported retroactivity of Control Council Law No. 10, Fritsch then went on to position Rendulic's acts as justifiable within the broader schema of a duty to obey superior orders, or, in the alternative, that Rendulic acted to suitably mitigate any illegality or excess in those superior orders:

> Your Honors, the highest duty of a soldier in the armies of all countries is obedience towards his superiors and to the Laws.
>
> General Rendulic was a soldier of the Austro-Hungarian monarchy; naturally, after the affiliation of Austria to Germany which was universally welcomed by the German people, he did not, and could not, refuse to perform his duty as a soldier, and continued to serve his Fatherland. There is no need to go into details about the fact that he always fulfilled his duty as a soldier and obeyed the orders of his superiors, as far as he could reconcile them with his own general ideas of humanity and the fundamentals of law.
>
> But the defense will also prove that whenever General Rendulic recognized faults in orders from his senior officers, he always carried them out or passed them on in a suitably altered form.[25]

Finally, Fritsch urged that the proceedings be suspended and that this count be stricken from the indictment.[26] Fritsch contended that Rendulic's evacuation and destruction of the Finnmark region were required for reasons of military necessity and were therefore in accordance with Article 23(g) of the Hague Regulations. Fritsch then proceeded to detail, quite extensively, the grounds upon which the charge of devastation should be dismissed.

---

[21] Ibid., p 95.

[22] Ibid.

[23] Ibid., p 3101.

[24] Ibid.

[25] Ibid., pp 3102–3103.

[26] Ibid., p 3111.

The tribunal ultimately ruled that "a prima facie case, at least, has been made against the defendant Rendulic in regard to the evacuation of the province of Finnmark, and the motion of his counsel to dismiss that portion of the count will be overruled."[27]

6.4 The Prosecution Case: Witnesses and Evidence

The prosecution opened its case by offering in evidence Document Book 22, which contained, inter alia, copies of the orders sent to Rendulic and his subordinates for the evacuation and destruction, and Document Book 23, which contained affidavits (undertaken as part of the Norwegian war crimes investigations) from individuals affected by the evacuation and devastation in Finnmark.

The prosecution first called the witness General Ferdinand Jodl (brother to Alfred Jodl). During his testimony, Jodl recounted how he had reservations regarding any possible evacuation of the region, in particular because he did not "believe that the Russians will proceed to the West and will cross the Tana [River]. We are not in touch with them any longer—with the Russians, that is. We know for certain that the bulk of the Russian units have been transported to the East." He went on to affirm that it was clear by November 1944 that the Soviets did not plan to continue west.[28] Jodl agreed that the Finnmark devastation would have been necessary—*but only if* the Soviet invasion had clearly been imminent,[29] which, in his opinion, it was not.

The prosecution also called Arne Dahl to give evidence. Dahl, a major-general of the Norwegian army, testified of his involvement with Soviet troops at the Tana River. In his opinion, it had not been the intention of the Soviets to proceed into the Finnmark region beyond the Tana Fjord.[30] He also testified that the destruction of the region was "wanton, and I could not see that it was a necessity for the German forces so completely to destroy the country as was done."[31] On cross-examination, Dahl acknowledged that, for an invading army to find no shelter, it would hamper an invasion, particularly in such difficult terrain and in such a cold climate as Finnmark. However, Dahl considered the Finnmark devastation to be excessive. He believed that an invasion could have been hampered without destroying the entire country.[32] Moreover, he believed that the devastation was undertaken for reasons other than military necessity—in particular, that Germany wanted to exact revenge on Norway.[33]

Called next was Trygve Schance, a police sergeant-major serving in Vardø, in Finnmark. Schance recalled learning about the devastation and evacuation that were

[27] Ibid., p 3117.
[28] Ibid., p 2583.
[29] Ibid., p 2594.
[30] Ibid., p 2658.
[31] Ibid., p 2659.
[32] Ibid., p 2672.
[33] Ibid., p 2677.

due to take place and recounted watching the destruction of the town of Finnkonjkeila on the afternoon of 31 October 1944.[34] He spoke of his retreat to Skjånes and his flight from the Germans into the mountains surrounding the town. Schance recounted that by 19 November, he had made it back to his place of work in Vardø and had begun to collect information about the devastation that was taking place in Finnmark, primarily by interviewing people who were returning to their homes after escaping German evacuation attempts.[35] When asked if he knew why the devastation was taking place, Schance stated that a German officer had told him that it was being done to save the Finnmark population from "the threatening [S]oviet Russian domination of terror."[36]

The prosecution of Rendulic was concluded with the reading into evidence affidavits and reports detailing the deaths and destruction that occurred in Finnmark.[37] The prosecution rested on 28 August 1947 and reconvened with the opening of the defence case on 15 September 1947.

6.5 Rendulic on the Stand: The Defence Case

Rendulic's defence proper started on 28 October 1947.[38] The first part of the case focused on the activities in Southeastern Europe.[39] The German campaign in Northern Norway was under examination from 30 October. With Rendulic on the stand, the defence spent time discussing the inhospitable terrain of Finnmark and the position of the German forces in the region at the time of Rendulic's command.[40] In his testimony, Rendulic spoke of the aftermath of the Finnish–Soviet armistice and the eventual order to withdraw from Finland.[41] He discussed at length the difficult terrain facing a withdrawing German force, noting that the demand by Finland that German troops be withdrawn within 14 days of the signing of the armistice

> could not be carried out. The demand obviously had the purpose of forcing the Finns to fight against us. In order to evacuate Finland, the troops had to carry out marches of 800 to 1000 km – marches on foot. This would have meant marching unceasingly for 5 to 6 weeks. Such an enormous effort could not be expected of the troops in such a climate and at that time of the year and in such a terrain as I have described. The soldiers would have been able to bear up under this effort, but the horses would not have been able to do it. And the Mountain Army had very many horses because everything had to be carried out on horseback. In addition we have to consider the fact that there were many stores which had to be carried off, and, finally, we have to consider that the troops just didn't march off like that. The enemy would prevent them from marching off and involve them in combat actions which actually did take

[34] Ibid., p 2698.

[35] Ibid., pp 2705–2707.

[36] Ibid., p 2707.

[37] Ibid., pp 2747–2770.

[38] Ibid., p 5124.

[39] Ibid., pp 5124–5328.

[40] Ibid., pp 5328–5332.

[41] Ibid., p 5332.

> place. The combat actions which took place, in order to get the Mountain Army out of that area, took 5 to 6 weeks, and if one is fighting one cannot, after all, march. It was more than three months until finally the last man of the German Army had left Finland, and we tried to expedite matters as much as we possibly could, especially in consideration of the approaching winter.[42]

Rendulic testified that, after the order to commence the evacuation of Finnmark had been received, the late September order to evacuate the region was carried out "very loosely",[43] and only on a voluntary basis, for those who wanted to escape the region.[44]

By the time the second order for evacuation was issued in October 1944, Rendulic testified that his concerns regarding the Soviet forces were profoundly shaping his plans on the ground. The Soviet forces' "numerical superiority, even in that barely negotiable terrain"[45] and orders for four German Mountain Divisions to return to central Europe compelled Rendulic to abandon his plans for what essentially amounted to a limited withdrawal—a retreat, "to concentrate the population in a tolerable area of living space [with] necessary sanitary installations [...] to be left for them."[46] Rather, by the time of the evacuation order of 28 October, Rendulic was convinced that, facing a possible multi-pronged land, air, and sea invasion by Soviet troops, supported by Britain,[47] only a complete evacuation of the area, and the destruction and devastation of the region, could prevent the Soviet advance and save not only the German troops but also the local population of Finnmark.[48]

The defence approach is interesting to examine. Fritsch's opening statements emphasised the legality of Rendulic's acts under Article 23(g) of the 1907 Hague Regulations:

> At that time, on 28 October 1944, the Army had already clearly recognized the entire impact of the superiority of the Russian Forces and the danger, which was constituted by the Fins. The 19th Corps alone had at that time lost more than 6 000 men. Furthermore, on or about this date the first orders to relinquish troops had been received. Under these circumstances it was impossible for the commander-in-chief of the 20th Mountain Army to reject the idea [that] destruction would make it difficult or even impossible for the enemy to advance. In view of this attitude the condition which appears in Article 23 of the Hague Land Warfare Convention must be considered attained, as it states, that the destruction or confiscation of enemy property is permissible, if the necessities of the war should make such action incumbent.[49]

[42] Ibid.

[43] Ibid., p 5334.

[44] Ibid.

[45] Ibid., p 5335.

[46] Ibid.

[47] Ibid., p 5338.

[48] Ibid., p 5346.

[49] Ibid., p 3112.

Fritsch then proceeded to cite relevant scholarly works in international law to date, including by Hersch Lauterpacht, which affirmed the legality of destruction and devastation on grounds of military necessity.[50]

In its opening statement, as throughout the case itself, the defence repeatedly affirms that the acts that took place in Finnmark were not acts of wanton or capricious destruction done for revenge or whim. Rather, they served the dual purpose of delaying the Soviet advance—which was advantageous, obviously, for the German forces—but also of protecting the inhabitants of the region from the Soviets, who would, it was argued, not show similar restraint in their treatment of the population. For example, in his opening statement for the defence, Fritsch argues for the humanity of Rendulic's acts in the evacuation of Finnmark:

> The best proof for the manner in which the defendant General Rendulic wanted the evacuation to be carried out, is his order of 29 Oct. 1944, which has been submitted by the prosecution as exhibit No. 504 [...]. Under point 7 of this order he expressly directs that the evacuation is to be carried out as a welfare measure for the population and that the Norwegians were to be safeguarded. From the report of the evacuation staff, dated 25 Nov. 1944 exhibit No-506 Prosecution Document [...] which cannot be doubted in any manner and the verdict of which is very sincere, it can be seen that the evacuation was carried out very carefully and considerately, and counsel for the defense believes that he can establish that this evacuation was carried out differently from any other of the many evacuations which took place during the war and especially also after the war.[51]

Rendulic himself also takes pains to assert that he acted not just for the purposes of military necessity, but also for the protection of the civilian population. In his testimony, he makes repeated reference to the humanitarian nature of the evacuation and the humanitarian measures that were included in his own order for the evacuation.[52] For example, Rendulic stated that his order, while clearly following the order from Hitler, nevertheless included "quite a number of welfare measures for the benefit of the population."[53] Rendulic made particular note of one directive included in his orders for evacuation, in which he informed his troops that the evacuation should be treated as a relief measure for the Norwegian population, to save them from the Soviets and to keep them alive. Rendulic goes on to say of himself: "A person who orders something like this cannot desire cruelty and ruthlessness."[54] Additionally, he draws the tribunal's attention to the geographical and environmental issues that informed his decision-making. For example, Rendulic positions the evacuation in the broader context of the approaching northern winter:

> Finally, I had to tell myself that it would possibly be better for the population to be transferred to other areas rather than to spend the hard winter in the destroyed country. I participated in both winter battles in Russia. Therefore, I know what flight from cold means. I had to realize that the Russians, if they pushed up on us and if they confronted the choice of either saving themselves by using what remained in the way of shelter or sparing the population, it was

[50] Ibid., p 3114.

[51] Ibid., p 3111.

[52] Order of 29 October 1944, Evidence Code: NOKW-86, Exhibit Code: Prosecution 504.

[53] Transcript, p 5353.

[54] Ibid., p 5354.

> certain that they would not spare the population. Therefore, in the final analysis it was the best thing for the population that they were removed.[55]

6.6 The Prosecution's Cross-Examination of Rendulic

Walter Rapp, associate counsel for the prosecution, began the cross-examination of Rendulic not with questions about the acts in Finnmark, but rather about his membership, however brief, in the Nazi Party, the party's ideology,[56] and the campaign in Southeastern Europe. Rapp finally turned to "the Norwegian picture",[57] beginning his questioning on the practice of hostage-taking in that region.[58] He then focused on the evacuation, asking Rendulic: "did you ever protest to General Jodl of the OKW, WEST, either after the first or the second evacuation order, that you did not consider this to be a military necessity?"[59] Rendulic answered that he believed that both evacuation orders, and the destruction orders that followed, were justifiable:

> The first evacuation order I carried out in such a way as I thought to be necessary. That is, supported those people who wanted to take part in the evacuation to Southern Norway, regard to the second evacuation order, for me there was a conviction of the military necessity of the destructions, but also the destruction of part of the quarters. It was intended that the Norwegian population should be gathered in the necessary living space and then the buildings which were thus made free were to be destroyed; but under all circumstances it had to be prevented that when the enemy arrived he would find any quarters, because in these areas quarters and accommodation meant existence or non-existence.
>
> When the second evacuation order came, which ordered the evacuation of the entire population, then I had to say to myself that the OKW had judged correctly and placed a correct demand.[60]

Rapp directly challenged the defence's attempts to portray Rendulic as having carried out his orders humanely. Rapp queried whether the restraint that Rendulic professed to show was not, as Rendulic had asserted, based on a sense of concern for the Norwegians but rather "because you did not have enough men or material to carry it through one hundred percent?"[61] He also challenged Rendulic's assertion that the German army was acting to save Finnmark from Bolshevism by asking "did any part of the Norwegian population ever come to you or to any representative of the XXth Army and beg them that you save them from the Bolshevists?",[62] or was that "merely an assumption which you more or less put there gratuitously to give

[55] Ibid., p 5346.
[56] Ibid., p 5370.
[57] Ibid., p 5445.
[58] Ibid., pp 5445–5449.
[59] Ibid., p 5452.
[60] Ibid.
[61] Ibid., p 5453.
[62] Ibid., p 5454.

your evacuation a propaganda value?"[63] To this, Rendulic retorted: "I would like to ask whether it is wrong if one tries to save people from Bolshevism?"[64]

At this stage, a particularly interesting exchange takes place between Rendulic and Rapp. Upon Rapp's questions about Rendulic's ability to command the naval and air forces in the region, Rendulic responds that the right of an army general to issue orders to the navy could "only exist in case of danger or invasion."[65] At this, Rapp asks, not unfairly:

> Q. Wasn't that the danger all the time and wasn't the reason this danger existed the very reason that Finnmark was destroyed?
>
> A. Of course there was a danger, but it wasn't acute, when the subordination of the Navy was regulated. The subordination had two parts: first, the preparation for the defense of the coast; and secondly, the carrying out of the defense. The preparations for the defense were being worked on all the time, and in this sphere the Admiral was also instructed to comply with my directives. The acute case of the defense of the coast never occurred during my time, so that subordination did not come into the question here.
>
> Q. I still do not quite understand this, General. If the invasion wasn't acute, then why consider the destruction of Finnmark a military necessity? You can only do one or the other according to your own testimony.[66]

Rendulic went on to explain that the military situation was changeable. Even if there was not an acute threat of invasion, in his view, he was nonetheless justified to prepare for one:

> I can't prepare something today only if I know to one hundred percent that the occasion is going to arrive. This is against every military fundamental, one mus[t]n't work only on the certain; one must also prepare for the probable and the possible. Otherwise every military leadership would just be a game.[67]

Rapp then raised the possibility that operations in the Finnmark region might have been undertaken for reasons beyond military necessity. In particular, Rapp asked whether keeping the Finnmark population from returning, once a Soviet invasion no longer seemed likely, was done to prevent negative propaganda for the Reich. In making this argument, Rapp raised in evidence NOKW 115, a letter from Rendulic to the Commissioner. The letter counsels against allowing civilians to return to Finnmark, as they would "obtain an impression which is only too apt to give further impetus to the inflammatory propaganda which arose on account of the evacuation"[68]—namely, the devastation of the Finnmark region. Rendulic's letter goes on to note that allowing the population to return "is neither in the interests of my army nor in the political interests of the Reich […] I require of my generals and other leaders that, within the sphere of their activities they always take into consideration and represent the political interests of the Reich. It goes without saying that I

[63] Ibid.

[64] Ibid.

[65] Ibid., p 5458.

[66] Ibid.

[67] Ibid., p 5459.

[68] Ibid., p 5464.

myself act according to the same principles."[69] Rapp finally ended his examination of Rendulic, and the case turned to witness testimony.

6.7 Witnesses and Evidence for the Defence

The witnesses called by the defence in relation to the Finnmark charge included Lieutenant General Hermann Hölter, who was Chief-of-Staff of the 20th Mountain Army during Rendulic's posting in Finnmark, and General Emil Vogel, head of the XXXVI Mountain Corps. Under questioning from both Rapp and Fritsch, Hölter and Vogel both spoke of how the Russian forces were dramatically increased in the region, so that "[f]rom Spring of 1944 onwards, the Russians were reinforced so that we were faced by a three-fold superiority on the part of the Russians."[70] Hölter spoke of the difficulties of the planned withdrawal from Finland after the armistice, emphasising the ever-present threat of being overwhelmed by Russian troops, who had "numerical superiority [and] were highly agile in difficult terrain."[71] He then went on to describe how, as the 20th Mountain Army began its withdrawal, it was "pursued ruthlessly"[72] through a difficult terrain as the weather worsened. Hölter made note of the difficulties of fighting during the Arctic winter, especially against a skilled enemy accustomed to winter warfare:

> That country is very sparsely populated. Every soldier who had fought in this arctic area had realized that even a heatable tent presented a means against the cold and against the winter, and solid quarters meant an even greater means of fighting against this winter and climate. Beyond their significance as just quarters, they also represented a means of fighting. Therefore, we had to drive at the following. We had to deprive the enemy of this means in his fight against us, and for this reason we were particularly interested in the destruction of all settlements. The enemy had, above all, on the occasion of the fightings which I have described when I talked about the 19th Corps proved that he could master even the most difficult terrain with the most modern equipment.
>
> [W]e knew from these fights and also from the battles which had taken place in preceding years that the Russians had special units at their disposal which were particularly suitable for the warfare in this desert country. They were organized for this kind of warfare and particularly trained and were specially suitable for this arctic warfare.[73]

Given the geographical impediments of the territory, both Hölter and Vogel were asked whether limited destruction rather than the full-scale devastation could have been carried out, in particular, "if now the bulk of the army marched along one highway only, was it not sufficient then to destroy just that highway?"[74] Hölter noted that such an act would not prevent a Soviet advance, as it was known that

[69] Ibid., p 5465.

[70] Ibid., pp 5551 (Hölter) and p 5618 (Vogel).

[71] Ibid., p 5554.

[72] Ibid., p 5558, though the transcript has it as "rughlesslessly"—obviously a typo.

[73] Ibid., pp 5561–5562.

[74] Ibid., p 5562.

the Soviets "did not merely keep to the highways but instead waged battles away from the highways out in the open in the plains. The Russians used all built-up areas outside of the highway for their purposes."[75] Additionally, Soviet troops included "ski [and] reindeer units, who carried all their equipment on reindeers, and besides they worked with light equipment such as cars etc. All these were special units which had in preceding years trained in the plains, in the Tundra, and had been tested in their organization."[76] Hölter noted that the Finnish army was also a threat which was factored into decision-making regarding the withdrawal and destruction plans:

> The Finns after all were fighting in their own country. That is they were fighting under conditions which they knew well as peasants, foresters, sportsmen and etc. They were particularly masters of battles in the jungles and in deserts, and I don't have to stress that they are particularly well versed in skiing. Every Finnish division and every Finnish brigade is completely mobile on skis. Such an enemy was facing us at this winter-time and was particularly dangerous to us.
>
> [T]he Finns also would have moved very much faster and they could overcome [highway] destructions in summer as well as in winter, because in their whole organization, in their vehicle equipment they were not so much dependent on the highways as was any other Army.[77]

In all, Hölter and Vogel presented a picture of an overwhelming force of highly skilled Finnish and Soviet troops, adept at navigating the extreme terrain and weather of the Arctic.

The defence raised an issue that would prove critical to the eventual decision on the Finnmark devastation: Were the Soviets actually pursuing the retreating 20th Mountain Army?[78] Preventing the Soviet army from advancing was the entire basis of the order for the devastation of the region; if the Soviets were not advancing, then the devastation would not have been required for the purposes of military necessity. Hölter answered in the affirmative: the Soviets had pressed the retreating Germans up to the Tana River. The German army expected the Soviets to pursue, and "we were afraid that the Russians could overtake us by a movement at sea, and this in connection with, and with the help of, allied forces on sea and allied shipping means and also supported by air forces of the Western allies. The overall situation of the 20th Mountain Army was most inviting an Anglo-American-Russian joint operation against us."[79] Both Hölter and Vogel were asked point blank: Was the devastation of Finnmark militarily necessary? Both agreed that it was.[80] Hölter's response is worth repeating verbatim:

> A military necessity can only be judged properly from the circumstances prevailing at the time and according to the particular situation. When this problem was under discussion, the question was this: Were we at the time dealing with an emergency and this is what I would

[75] Ibid., p 5626 (Vogel).

[76] Ibid. (Hölter).

[77] Ibid., p 5568.

[78] Ibid., p 5565.

[79] Ibid. See also concurring testimony by Vogel, p 5627.

[80] Ibid., p 5628 (Vogel).

> now like to talk about; every military situation which one evaluates and judges has to be clearly defined as to three points: What am I to do? What is my task? Our task was at the time to get the 20th Mountain Army as completely as possible out of a desperate situation and to lead as strong and as complete a unit as possible back to the Reich. The second point, which we saw ourselves faced with was: What can the enemy do and what are the enemies *[sic]* intentions. At that time we had to assume that the enemy wanted to destroy us. Could he do that? I believe in my statements of yesterday, I have spoken in detail what the dangers were that threatened us. From the east, from the Ar[c]tic sea superior Russian forces were moving up on us, from the South, the Finns were moving up on us. The Ar[c]tic sea was one large question mark and there at any time the Anglo-American forces could appear with air and sea forces. The third question was: What could we do against that. All we could do was march, march and march again and we had to burn our bridges behind us in the real sense of the word and within this scope the destruction and evacuation has to be considered in what we had to do and that was to rob the enemy of their accommodations and thus keep them away from us. Looking back on it now, what I would like to say is if one considers matters from our armchair point of view and knows everything that has happened, one should not and cannot in my opinion properly evaluate the question of a military necessity.[81]

Rapp, while broadly accepting Hölter's explanation of military necessity, tried to position the order as being motivated for political rather than purely military reasons.[82] Rapp put to Hölter that surely the advancing Soviet forces would have expected a scorched earth policy to be implemented. Therefore, would the Soviets have not made suitable preparations to counter such acts, potentially nullifying a military necessity argument?[83] Finally, Rapp noted that it was obvious that the Soviets were not advancing past the Tana River as early as November 1944, and yet the destruction of Finnmark continued until the spring of 1945. How could the ongoing destruction in Finnmark continue to be justified under military necessity, given "the fact that the fortunes of war had turned considerably against"[84] Germany? Surely, the destruction at this point had some element of "vengeance" in it—"if we can't have Finnmark we want to make sure that nobody else gets it."[85]

After some additional questions from Fritsch following the cross-examinations of Hölter and Vogel, the trial turned to the defence submission of the document books. Tendered into evidence from Fritsch were documents, including maps of the Finnmark region, along with affidavits from army personnel who were stationed in the region before and during the evacuation and devastation. These documents confirmed the generally held belief among the German senior command in the region that the "destructions and evacuations were a military necessity."[86] Other affidavits spoke to Rendulic's humane execution of the evacuation orders.[87] Excerpts from the War Diary of the 20th Mountain Army were submitted, noting the appearance of large

[81] Ibid., pp 5582–5583.

[82] Ibid., pp 5586–5590.

[83] Ibid., p 5592.

[84] Ibid., p 5597.

[85] Ibid., p 5615.

[86] Ibid., p 5652.

[87] Ibid., pp 5656–5659.

convoys of British ships and media reports of imminent US landings in the region.[88] Fritsch, while noting that additional evidence was being sought, then came to the end of his "presentation of evidence".[89] With that, the tribunal turned to the next defendant.[90]

6.8 The Judgment on the Devastation Charge

In February 1948, the closing statements were made. The prosecution noted the accumulated evidence and, in the case of Rendulic, warned the tribunal against the testimony given by Hölter and Vogel, whose "self-interest and bias is so palpable that it merits no extended discussion."[91] The prosecution emphasised that, at the time of the complete evacuation order at the end of October, "none of [Rendulic's] troops had seen a Russian for more than a week. Second, Rendulic knew that the Russians had made no attempt to cross the Tana and that they probably would make none."[92] Attention was drawn to Rendulic's purported awareness that the number of Soviet troops was insufficient to mount a successful invasion and that there was no real risk of a Soviet invasion—a point affirmed in Jodl's testimony.[93] The prosecution presented the acts in Finnmark as "futile, vicious and unreasonable."[94]

In his closing statements, Fritsch reiterated his challenge regarding the competence of the tribunal to rule on the matters at hand, especially for operating in a manner contrary to the maxim *nullum crimen sine lege*. In terms of the specific defence of Rendulic in relation to Finnmark, Fritsch drew the attention of the tribunal to Rendulic's "genuine humanity"[95] and expounded on the military necessity of the destruction of Finnmark:

> No one can doubt the military necessity of such destruction while retreating before a superior enemy. Even in the codification of the rules of warfare, allowance was made for such cases.
>
> Thus the Hague Rules for Land Warfare, in article 23g, declare destruction to be admissible if the necessity of war urgently demands it.
>
> Little proof is needed to show that the destruction of roads and transport installations played a specially important part in the retreat from the Norwegian Finnmark just as for the fact

[88] Ibid., pp 5660–5661.

[89] Ibid., p 5665.

[90] For a full listing of the evidence tendered for Rendulic, see http://nuremberg.law.harvard.edu/search/?q=defendant:%22Lothar+Rendulic%22&f=trial_activities:Norway%2C+evacuation+of+and+destruction+in&page=3 [accessed 1 April 2023].

[91] Transcript, p 9567.

[92] Ibid., p 9662.

[93] Ibid. See further Chap. 3, where Sven G. Holtsmark explores in more detail what Rendulic knew about troop numbers and skirmishes taking place in the region leading up to 25 October.

[94] Transcript, p 9664.

[95] Ibid., p 10071.

> that life in this area is impossible in Winter without billets which can be heated and that the destruction of quarters must have a decisive effect on military operations.[96]

Fritsch also drew attention to the weakness of the prosecution case, relying as it did on "the atrocity stories in dubious Norwegian reports and it omitted or was unable to produce, conclusive evidence concerning the absence of military necessity for the destructions."[97] Fritsch also noted the weakness of the witness testimony, stating that Dahl was "very reticent"[98] to speak because "he realized, beyond a doubt, the relative importance of his own judgment in this matter for after all he mainly knew about the war out of books and was not in charge of any unit in combat with the enemy"[99] and thus could not speak to the legal and military concept of military necessity.[100] Fritsch noted that Jodl understood the concept of military necessity and had stated that the destruction could be justified if the Soviet invasion was feared, which was a genuine concern.[101] After outlining the evidence recounted of Soviet numerical and tactical superiority, as well as the worsening weather conditions and harsh terrain, Fritsch stated: "If there is such a thing as a classic example for a military necessity thus for the justification of destruction, it is this very case."[102] Given the material available to Rendulic on the Soviet army, "all basic conditions for the possibility and the probability of a pursuit existed" and Rendulic was justified in carrying out the evacuation and devastation as ordered.[103]

The tribunal eventually handed down its decision on 19 February 1948. After addressing questions about the legality and competence of the tribunal, the judges turned to the concept of military necessity:

> Military necessity permits a belligerent, subject to the laws of war, to apply any amount and kind of force to compel the complete submission of the enemy with the least possible expenditure of time, life and money. In general, it sanctions measures by an occupant necessary to protect the safety of his forces and to facilitate the success of his operations. It permits the destruction of life of armed enemies and other persons whose destruction is incidentally unavoidable by the armed conflicts of the war; it allows the capturing of armed enemies and others of peculiar danger; but it does not permit the killing of innocent inhabitants for purposes of revenge or the satisfaction of a lust to kill. The destruction of property to be lawful must be imperatively demanded by the necessities of war. Destruction as an end in

[96] Ibid., pp 10080–10081.

[97] Ibid., p 10081.

[98] Ibid.

[99] Ibid.

[100] This seems an unduly harsh and frankly inaccurate assessment. Dahl had served as the commander of Alta Battalion during the fighting at Narvik in northern Norway in 1940 and would have had first-hand experience of wartime strategic decision-making, including the principle of military necessity. See further the history of the Alta Battalion in Norwegian Ministry of Health and Care Services (1998) Alta bataljon: 8 Styrkeforhold og tap (in Norwegian, unofficial translation by the author). https://web.archive.org/web/20101022060708/http://www.regjeringen.no/nb/dep/hod/dok/nouer/1998/nou-1998-12/9.html?id=375470 [accessed 1 April 2023] (archived from the original 22 October 2010).

[101] Transcript, pp 10083–10084.

[102] Ibid., p 10086.

[103] Ibid., p 10087.

> itself is a violation of international law. There must be some reasonable connection between the destruction of property and the overcoming of the enemy forces. It is lawful to destroy railways, lines of communication or any other property that might be utilized by the enemy. Private homes and churches even may be destroyed if necessary for military operations. It does not admit of wanton devastation of a district or the wilful infliction of suffering upon its inhabitants for the sake of suffering alone.[104]

Turning to Rendulic specifically, the tribunal noted the calibre of the Soviet troops that the Germans in Finnmark were facing. The judgment discusses Rendulic's knowledge that a possible invasion could come from several directions, and that the weather and the terrain would make fighting a Soviet invasion force difficult. The tribunal then examined whether Rendulic's orders to evacuate and devastate Finnmark were justifiable. It determined that the legality of Rendulic's actions had to be judged based on what was known at the time, rather than in hindsight:

> There is evidence in the record that there was no military necessity for this destruction and devastation. An examination of the facts in retrospect can well sustain this conclusion. But we are obliged to judge the situation as it appeared to the defendant at the time. If the facts were such as would justify the action by the exercise of judgment, after giving consideration to all the factors and existing possibilities, even though the conclusion reached may have been faulty, it cannot be said to be criminal. After giving careful consideration to all the evidence on the subject, we are convinced that the defendant cannot be held criminally responsible although when viewed in retrospect, the danger did not actually exist.[105]

In acquitting Rendulic on the Finnmark devastation charge, the tribunal drew on Article 23(g) of the Hague Regulations, which prohibited the "destruction or seizure of enemy property except in cases where this destruction or seizure is urgently required by the necessities of war."[106] Applying that law to the events in Finnmark, the tribunal noted:

> The destructions of public and private property by retreating military forces which would give aid and comfort to the enemy, may constitute a situation coming within the exceptions contained in Article 23(g). We are not called upon to determine whether urgent military necessity for the devastation and destruction in the province of Finnmark actually existed. We are concerned with the question whether the defendant at the time of its occurrence acted within the limits of honest judgment on the basis of the conditions prevailing at the time. The course of a military operation by the enemy is loaded with uncertainties, such as the numerical strength of the enemy, the quality of his equipment, his fighting spirit, the efficiency and daring of his commanders, and the uncertainty of his intentions. These things when considered with his own military situation provided the facts or want thereof which furnished the basis for the defendant's decision to carry out the "scorched earth" policy in Finnmark as a precautionary measure against an attack by superior forces. It is our considered opinion that the conditions, as they appeared to the defendant at the time were sufficient upon which he could honestly conclude that urgent military necessity warranted the decision made.
>
> This being true, the defendant may have erred in the exercise of his judgment but he was guilty of no criminal act. We find the defendant not guilty on this portion of the charge.[107]

---

[104] Ibid., pp 10451–10452.

[105] Ibid., pp 10513–10514.

[106] Ibid., p 10513.

[107] Ibid., pp 10514–10515.

Rendulic, though found guilty of those acts making up Counts One, Three, and Four of the charges, was thus acquitted of Count Two of the destruction of the Finnmark region, on the grounds of military necessity under Article 23(g) of the Hague Regulations.

6.9 Accounting for the Decision on the Devastation of Finnmark in the Tribunal: Military Necessity in the Law of Armed Conflict of 1947

Rendulic's acquittal was based on the tribunal's reasoning that military necessity, as outlined in Article 23(g) of the Hague Regulations, justified the devastation in Finnmark. While the laws of war at the time forbade the destruction or seizure of enemy property, an exception to the prohibition existed if "such destruction or seizure be imperatively demanded by the necessities of war."[108] In order to better understand and critique the tribunal's reasoning and its ultimate decision, it is useful to know the origins and development of the concept of military necessity in the international law of armed conflict.

Military necessity was first codified by Francis Lieber, the German-American law academic who assisted the United States in drafting a manual for the application of the law of war during the American Civil War.[109] The Lieber Code,[110] in Article 14, set out the definition of military necessity, which "consists in the necessity of those measures which are indispensable for securing the ends of the war, and which are lawful according to the modern law and usages of war."[111] Military necessity therefore allowed for the destruction of property so long as the destruction was not expressly prohibited by other rules of the law of armed conflict. As outlined further in Article 15 of the Lieber Code:

> Military necessity admits of all direct destruction of life or limb of "armed" enemies, and of other persons whose destruction is incidentally "unavoidable" in the armed contests of the war; [...] it allows of all destruction of property, and obstruction of the ways and channels of traffic, travel, or communication, and of all withholding of sustenance or means of life from the enemy; of the appropriation of whatever an enemy's country affords necessary for the subsistence and safety of the army [...][112]

However, even then, Lieber understood that military necessity had its limits. Article 16 of the Code affirmed:

> Military necessity does not admit of cruelty – that is, the infliction of suffering for the sake of suffering or for revenge, nor of maiming or wounding except in fight, nor of torture to extort

[108] Hague Regulations of 1907, above n. 5, Article 23(g).

[109] See further Hartigan 1995, pp 2–14.

[110] Instructions for the Government of Armies of the United States in the Field, promulgated as General Orders No. 100, April 1863.

[111] Ibid., Article 14.

[112] Ibid., Article 15.

> confessions. It does not admit of the use of poison in any way, nor of the wanton devastation of a district. It admits of deception, but disclaims acts of perfidy; and, in general, military necessity does not include any act of hostility which makes the return to peace unnecessarily difficult.[113]

When, at the end of the 19th century, the international community met with the aim of codifying the customary law of armed conflict, the instruments drafted and adopted were the Hague Regulations of 1899 and 1907. In both instruments, the restrictive approach to military necessity was affirmed, but the Hague Regulations went further than Lieber had, by allowing the destruction or seizure of *property only* for purposes of military necessity.[114] During the drafting at the Hague, the term "necessities of war" was mentioned frequently, but no attempt was made to define it.[115] As historian Isabel Hull has noted, this "omission reflected, but also encouraged, controversial interpretations."[116] One of those "controversial interpretations"—and one that is specifically relevant for our purposes—was commonly found in German military thought and practice of the time. From the late 1800s onwards, German military practitioners and scholars largely took the position that military necessity was to be defined as *anything* that was necessary for the purposes of winning the war. Military necessity, as German General Julius von Hartmann wrote, was dictated by "the great, final purpose of war: *the defeat of the enemy's power, the overcoming of the enemy's energy, the overwhelming of the enemy's will*. This *one* goal commands absolutely, it dictates law and regulation. The concrete form of this law appears as *military necessity*."[117] For von Hartmann:

> War, as compared to peace, is something entirely *abnormal*; it produces exceptional/emergency situations [*Ausnahmezustände* – "declarations of emergency"[118]] in the most decisive sense of that word. Indeed, it is itself an exceptional situation because it contradicts in its innermost nature the foundation on which civilization and culture rest, the laws according to which they have developed. In their stead it returns to conditions that permit the unlimited justification of individual power and might [*Kraft und Macht*].[119]

German dismissiveness of the Hague formulation of military necessity was evident in the fact that the Hague rules on land warfare, and the restrictive view of military necessity, were not included in contemporaneous German programmes of military instruction to personnel, nor even in any standing manuals of instruction for the

[113] Ibid., Article 16.

[114] Regulations Respecting the Laws and Customs of War on Land, annexed to Convention No. II with Respect to the Laws and Customs of War on Land, 29 July 1899, 32 Stat 1803, TS No 403, Article 23(g); Hague Regulations of 1907, above n. 5, Article 23(g).

[115] The term "necessities of war" is mentioned 17 times in the proceedings of the Hague Conference of 1907, during the sessions that discussed what would eventually be the Hague Regulations Respecting the Laws and Customs of War: Ministry for Foreign Affairs 1907.

[116] Hull 2008, p 357.

[117] Von Hartmann 1877, pp 453–454 (emphasis in the original), cited in Hull 2019, p 123.

[118] Hull translates *Ausnahmezustände* as "declarations of emergency"; however, *Ausnahmezustände* better translates to "situations of emergency" or "states of emergency".

[119] Ibid. (emphasis in the original).

armed forces.[120] This dismissive attitude to the law of armed conflict is evidenced by the fact that "whereas other nations' armies drafted their manuals to take the Hague Rules of Land Warfare into account, Germany did not,"[121] something which Hull considers as the basis for Germany's widespread "ignorance or rejection of the writ of positive law in wartime."[122]

The German perspective on military necessity was at odds with the generally accepted position of the time: scholarly writing on military necessity during the inter-war years shows[123] that the German approach to military necessity was not well accepted in the practice of other nations. Rodick in particular rejected any claims to universality of the German belief in *Kriegsräson geht vor Kriegsmanier*—that "military expediency overrules the manner of warfare"[124]—and noted that the German position was not "legally valid,"[125] "has been wholly denied by other states,"[126] and is "clearly untenable":[127]

> It is not a legal method of procedure for a vitally interested party to be able to change the rules of warfare at a moment's notice upon the plea of necessity; it reduces international law from a controlling to a registering agency; and it would appear to be a clear violation of the spirit and letter of the Hague Rules.[128]

Military Tribunal V in Nuremberg acknowledged that German military personnel might have their own conception of military necessity. During *Hostage*, the tribunal noted that "the officer is a child of his time. He is subject to the intellectual tendencies which influence his own nation; the more educated he is the more will this be the case."[129] The tribunal understood that national thought on an issue might deeply shape a person's perspective and that, for a military leader, he might come to believe "that certain severities are indispensable to war, nay more, that the only true humanity very often lies in a ruthless application of them."[130]

However, while the tribunal in *Hostage* accepted that military necessity required whatever is considered necessary by a commander "to protect the safety of his forces and to facilitate the success of his operations,"[131] it was not prepared to accept that a commander had *complete* leeway to be the sole arbiter of what was militarily necessary:

---

[120] Hull 2008, p 362.

[121] Ibid.

[122] Ibid.

[123] See, e.g., Rodick 1928, pp 59–62; Garner 1920, p 195; Westlake 1907, p 117.

[124] Rodick 1928, p 59.

[125] Ibid., p 60.

[126] Ibid.

[127] Ibid.

[128] Ibid. See also Hayashi 2020, in particular pp 261–314, where military necessity as a juridical concept is explored in detail.

[129] Transcript, p 10455.

[130] Ibid.

[131] Ibid.

> It is apparent from the evidence of these defendants that they considered military necessity, a matter to be determined by them, a complete justification of their acts. We do not concur in the view that the rules of warfare are anything less than they purport to be. Military necessity or expediency do not justify a violation of positive rules. International law is prohibitive law.[132]

In particular, the tribunal emphasised that an assessment of military necessity must not be informed by political or personal beliefs. The Hague Regulations, in the view of the judges, did not permit outright devastation of a region for reasons of political vengeance or personal motivation. In this respect, one can see why the defence made repeated references to Rendulic's humanity, his good relations with the Norwegian population, his political opinions regarding the Nazi leadership, and his own purported belief in Nazi ideology. They can be seen as an attempt to portray Rendulic as someone not prone to allow military decisions to be guided by political or personal motivation. Arguably, this approach could ensure that the path to the military necessity defence is all the clearer.

Rendulic was acquitted on the grounds of military necessity, with a key part of the final adjudication noting that the claim of military necessity had to be judged in accordance with the circumstances at the time in which Rendulic determined that the destruction was militarily necessary. Rendulic faced a numerically superior enemy that was well equipped and trained in northern winter fighting conditions. The evidence at the time strongly suggested that the Soviets would follow the retreat. Given those conditions, the tribunal decided that Rendulic's assessment of the situation and his decision to engage in the destruction of the Finnmark region were justifiable.[133]

6.10 Critiquing the Decision in *Hostage*: Prosecution Missteps and the Decision-Making Process of the Tribunal

Unsurprisingly, when the decision was handed down, the exoneration of Rendulic on grounds of military necessity was strongly criticised in some circles. As Taylor noted in his final report on the war crimes trials,[134] the Norwegians were justifiably angry that Rendulic had been acquitted on the devastation charge.[135] Geoffrey Best most convincingly lays out the grounds of the critique, repeating debates that took place in the Norwegian parliament:

---

[132] Ibid.

[133] See Heller 2011, pp 308–311.

[134] Taylor 1949.

[135] Ibid., p 207.

> [T]he justice of Rendulic's acquittal was most convincingly contested on the following grounds. (1) He may indeed have been unable to be sure that the Russians were not close behind him, and his initial devastation of eastern Finnmark (all of it except the very easternmost bit around Kirkenes, which the Russians had seized before winter set in) was excusable in terms of military necessity, but the excuse wore thinner in proportion as the months passed, the German withdrawal continued, and still the Russians did not appear. (2) He pleaded that he was under pressure to act quickly, but plans for such a devastation had been laid well beforehand, and demolition explosives placed in all the predictable places. (3) Uncertainty about Russian intentions was not the only driving idea in his mind. The ruthless and intimidatory way the evacuation was ordered and executed, the frightful totality of the destruction, were of a piece with German policy in general – and, we might add, with the conduct in the Balkans for which he was found guilty [...] Rendulic, a fanatically anti-communist Austrian who, though not apparently a party member, rejoiced in obedience to his Führer, was not one of those easier-going German generals who took risks to moderate the effects of the Führer's extremer orders [...] Far from acting with the understandable temporary wildness of a frightened man in the dark, Rendulic was methodically executing in daylight a preplanned policy of vindictive desertification.[136]

On examining the prosecution case, and the tribunal's own deliberations, one is struck by gaps in the reasoning of the tribunal and by the failure of the prosecution to litigate more effectively the weaknesses in Rendulic's military necessity justification. In reading the transcript, particularly of the prosecution witnesses, there is clearly testimony that could have, were it explored and examined in more detail, undermined Rendulic's justification of his belief in an imminent, devastating Russian invasion, for which there was no other alternative but complete devastation of Finnmark. For instance, Ferdinand Jodl, in his testimony, was adamant that the evacuation and devastation of Finnmark were categorically not justifiable on military necessity grounds. This very point was noted in the judgment against Alfred Jodl at the IMT at Nuremberg. While Alfred Jodl's order of 28 October 1944 called for the "evacuation of all persons in Northern Norway and the burning of their houses so they could not help the Russians,"[137] Ferdinand Jodl was opposed to the order as he did not believe that it was militarily necessary. He carried out the order only because it had been strictly called for by Hitler himself. Surely, the prosecution could have made more of this. What did Ferdinand Jodl know at the time that convinced him that devastation was unnecessary, and did Rendulic know this too? How could two seasoned military commanders reach such essentially opposite positions on the necessity of destruction? Indeed, it seems odd that Alfred Jodl was convicted by the IMT for, inter alia, the destruction of Finnmark, while Rendulic was acquitted by a US Military Tribunal for the exact same conduct. It is remarkable that the prosecution did not make more of Alfred Jodl's conviction on acts originating in the same situation.

The prosecution could have made more of other aspects of the case as well. For example, what exactly had taken place between the first order of late September 1944, which called for a voluntary evacuation, and the order of 28 October 1944, which characterised the evacuation as compulsory? What transpired to effect that change in thinking, such that limited evacuation and destruction were so suddenly

---

[136] Best 1994, pp 329–330.

[137] Judgment of 1 October 1946, in International Military Tribunal 1950, p 517.

transformed into total evacuation and widespread devastation? Were those changed circumstances sufficient to warrant the total destruction that followed? As Sven Holtsmark argues in his own chapter in this anthology,[138] the 28 October order came about not because of Rendulic's own reporting of the situation on the ground, but because of intervention by Josef Terboven to Martin Bormann. Terboven had pushed for a total destruction of the region, when Alfred Jodl had counselled only for a partial destruction.[139] This would suggest that the devastation of Finnmark, though couched in terms of military necessity, was being informed by other, non-military considerations—perhaps a desire for retribution against Norway, in retaliation for its alignment with the Soviet Union. Indeed, as Holtsmark himself notes: "Thus, we may presume that two sets of motives coexisted—a 'rational' one based on military necessity in a traditional sense that could be related to the rules of war in international law, and the other grounded in a mixture of political, ideological and emotive impulses."[140] It seems a missed opportunity that the prosecution did not make more of the origins of the order, and the information on which it was purportedly based.

In addition to the prosecution's missteps, the tribunal itself seemed to accept certain issues at face value, even when there was evidence to suggest that further interrogation was warranted. The tribunal readily accepted Rendulic's subjective interpretation of the facts and evidence, seemingly without question as to whether it was reasonable given what was evident at the time, specifically regarding the Soviets.[141] As noted in the judgment:

> The course of a military operation by the enemy is loaded with uncertainties, such as the numerical strength of the enemy, the quality of his equipment, his fighting spirit, the efficiency and daring of his commanders, and the uncertainty of his intentions. These things when considered with his own military situation provided the facts or want thereof which furnished the basis for the defendant's decision to carry out the "scorched earth" policy in Finnmark as a precautionary measure against an attack by superior forces.

However, these purported "uncertainties", as the tribunal puts it, were arguably not altogether uncertain: the evidence clearly notes that the Germans were aware that the Soviet advance had stopped at the Tana River. Moreover, as noted by Holtsmark, by early November it was unlikely that any purported plans to invade Northern Norway could have eventuated, given the knowledge of the Northern Fleet, "with lack of experience", making the Fleet "hardly […] able to conduct such operations on its own".[142] Surely this fact warranted further examination.

The tribunal also largely failed to examine Rendulic's own contradictory statements on the operation and its military necessity. Initially, Rendulic testified that he had aimed to remove the population only partially—to "concentrate the population in a tolerable area of living space"—and that his "opinion deviated from Hitler's

[138] See Chap. 3. See also Chap. 4.

[139] Transcript, p 5346.

[140] Chapter 3.

[141] See further Chap. 8.

[142] Chapter 3.

opinion in the beginning [...] I did not think it was absolutely necessary to transfer the population to other areas." However, Rendulic then went on to justify the complete removal, noting "I could not close my eyes to Hitler's reasons of military necessity. I could not deny that they were justified."[143] Again, as noted by Holtsmark, this raises the prospect that Rendulic's orders were driven not just by military necessity, but by the desire to comply with Hitler's wishes, regardless of whether such wishes were in alignment with the law on military necessity and the facts on the ground.

Even if the case of military necessity could be made out, the tribunal's failure to consider whether the widespread devastation, as carried out, was warranted in its scope, breadth, and depth, is noteworthy. Ferdinand Jodl made it clear that, by November 1944, a Soviet advance was not forthcoming and seemed increasingly unlikely to eventuate. Indeed, Rendulic himself made a similar statement[144]—and yet, the devastation continued for months and was positioned as something absolutely and immediately necessary for the protection of both the German army and the Norwegian civilian population. As the months passed, Best quite rightly points out that the Germans continued their withdrawal, unimpeded, with no overwhelming Soviet invasion following.[145] This would seem to cast doubt as to the military necessity of the destruction and its positioning as the only available solution—and is something that both the prosecution and the tribunal itself should have made more of. Indeed, as Nobuo Hayashi has noted of Rendulic's claim of urgent military necessity before the tribunal:

> [W]here the purpose was not urgent for the belligerent at the time, it would be appropriate for the trier of fact to assess critically the availability of relevant alternatives and their respective degrees of injuriousness. For example, what would have happened if Lothar Rendulic had genuinely felt the Russian attack less imminent? Such a feeling might not have stopped Rendulic from considering the devastation of Finnmark as a plausible precautionary measure. Nevertheless, he would have considered it – or, in any event, he would have been expected to consider it – against a wider range of reasonably available and materially relevant alternatives. And this wider range of options might very well have included at least one that would be less injurious than devastating Finnmark.[146]

This raises the question of whether there were alternative means for the Germans to achieve the same aim. Could the extent of the destruction, if found to be necessary, have been more limited? The tribunal seemed not to question whether Rendulic could have achieved the same aims with more limited destruction, nor whether Rendulic had himself genuinely and reasonably considered such a path. Indeed, that Rendulic repeatedly spoke of "saving" the Norwegian population from Bolshevism suggests that a key motivation behind the devastation was political rather than military in nature, which, again, would seem to undermine an argument of military necessity.

---

[143] Transcript, pp 5345–5346.

[144] Ibid., p 5341.

[145] Best 1994, p 329.

[146] Hayashi 2020, p 298.

6.11 Conclusion

Rendulic's acquittal on the devastation charge opens avenues for interesting speculation: did the tribunal perhaps consider the acts of devastation in Finnmark less significant than the atrocities carried out in Southeastern Europe? Were the judges, with their non-military backgrounds, less comfortable or less certain questioning the military reasoning of Rendulic and others before the tribunal? Was there any sense that, given Rendulic's conviction on other actions in the Balkans, an acquittal on the devastation charge might make the tribunal less open to charges of victor's justice?

These suppositions are not fanciful. Indeed, in an interview after the trial, the presiding judge, Charles F. Wennerstrum, outright condemned *Hostage* as "victor's justice" and the work of a purportedly craven and vengeful prosecution staff: "The high ideals announced as the motives for creating these tribunals have not been evident [...] the prosecution has failed to maintain objectivity aloof from vindictiveness, aloof from personal ambitions for convictions."[147] Such sentiments go some way to explain the tribunal's ultimate decision. However, blame does not lie with the tribunal alone—as noted above, there were unexplored and underexplored avenues of interrogation that the prosecution could have made more of but did not.

In the years following *Hostage*, the reasoning employed in the charge against Rendulic would develop as a rule bearing his name—the "Rendulic rule"—providing that "commanders and personnel should be evaluated based on information reasonably available at the time of decision."[148] In the chapters that follow, the Rendulic rule will be explored to see how it has evolved in practice and how it has influenced both the law of armed conflict and international criminal law.

References

Best G (1994) War and law since 1945. Clarendon Press, Oxford
Bill B (2009) The Rendulic "Rule": military necessity, commander's knowledge, and methods of warfare. Yearbook of International Humanitarian Law 12:119–155
Garner JW (1920) International law and the World War. Longman Green & Co, London
Hartigan RS (1995) Lieber's Code and the law of war. Legal Classics Library, New York
Hayashi N (2020) Military necessity: the art, morality and law of war. Cambridge University Press, Cambridge
Heller KJ (2011) The Nuremberg Military Tribunals and the origins of international criminal law. Oxford University Press, Oxford
Hull IV (2008) Military necessity and the laws of war in imperial Germany. In: Kalyvas SN et al (eds) Order, conflict, and violence. Cambridge University Press, Cambridge
Hull IV (2019) Absolute destruction: military culture and the practices of war in imperial Germany. Cornell University Press, Ithaca

[147] Faust H (1948) Nazi trial judge rips "injustice": army jumps gun to reply. Chicago Daily Tribune, 23 February, p 1. See further Maguire 2010, pp 133ff.

[148] Judge Advocate General's Legal Center and School, US Army 2022, p 58.

International Military Tribunal (1947) Trial of the major war criminals before the International Military Tribunal: Nuremberg 14 November 1945–1 October 1946. Vol 1. Nuremberg
International Military Tribunal (1950) The trial of German major war criminals: proceedings of the International Military Tribunal sitting at Nuremberg, Germany, part 22 (22nd August 1946 to 1st October 1946). London
Judge Advocate General's Legal Center and School, US Army (2022) Operational law handbook. Charlottesville, Virginia
Maguire P (2010) Law and war: international law and American history. Columbia University Press, New York
Ministry for Foreign Affairs (1907) The Second International Peace Conference, The Hague, June 15–October 18, 1907: acts and documents, Vol III: Second, Third and Fourth Commissions. National Printing Office, The Hague
Rodick BG (1928) The doctrine of necessity in international law. Columbia University Press, New York
Taylor T (1949) Final report to the Secretary of the Army on the Nuremberg War Crimes Trials under Control Council Law No. 10. Washington, D.C.
Von Hartmann J (1877) Militärische Nothwendigkeit und Humanität. Deutsche Rundschau 13:111–128, 450–471
Westlake J (1907) International law: part II. Cambridge University Press, Cambridge

Other Documents

Instructions for the Government of Armies of the United States in the Field, promulgated as General Orders No. 100, April 1863

Emily Crawford Professor, The University of Sydney Law School. Address: New Law Building F10, Eastern Avenue, The University of Sydney, NSW, 2006, Australia, e-mail: emily.crawford@sydney.edu.au

Chapter 7
The Genesis and Significance of the Law of War "Rendulic Rule"

Sean Watts

Contents

7.1 Introduction 156
7.2 The Trial 156
7.3 The Judgment 163
7.4 The Rendulic Rule Legacy 169
7.5 Conclusion 173
References 175

Abstract The notion that in armed conflict commanders are judged only according to information reasonably available to them at the time of decision-making found early and notorious application in the post-Second World War prosecution of *Generaloberst* Lothar Rendulic known as the *Hostage* case. A tribunal of American judges drawn from civilian US legal quarters famously acquitted Rendulic for devastation carried out in the erroneous belief that Soviet forces were pursuing his retreat across Norwegian Finnmark. This chapter traces the legal genesis of the so-called Rendulic Rule and evaluates its modern legal significance. Although the *Hostage* judgment provided little in the way of legal evidence of the rule and traced its source in only very general terms, the Rendulic Rule has since matured into a well-settled aspect of the law of war. States have incorporated it into primary rules of conduct regulating hostilities and rely on it extensively in law of war instruction and implementation.

Keywords war crimes · law of war · international humanitarian law · law of armed conflict · international criminal law · targeting · mistake of fact

S. Watts (✉)
United States Military Academy, West Point, NY, USA
e-mail: sean.watts@westpoint.edu

Lieber Institute for Law and Warfare, 606 Thayer Rd, West Point, NY 10996, USA

N. Hayashi and C. Lingaas (eds.), *Honest Errors? Combat Decision-Making 75 Years After the* Hostage *Case*, https://doi.org/10.1007/978-94-6265-611-6_7

7.1 Introduction

In June 1944, *Generaloberst* Lothar Rendulic took command of the German 20th Mountain Army in Norway. By October of that year, he had ordered a retreat from an anticipated Soviet Army advance across the Northern Norwegian province of Finnmark, leaving much of that territory in ruins. By January 1945, he had returned to Germany to command a series of Army Groups operating in Germany, Austria, and Czechoslovakia. By May of the same year, he had surrendered to Allied forces and was in the custody of the US Army. And by June of 1947 he was facing trial for war crimes in Nuremberg.

Although a US tribunal convicted Rendulic of war crimes relating to operations he commanded in Southeastern Europe, he was notoriously acquitted of charges related to devastation of civilian property in Norway during his 1944 retreat. Among other important holdings related to the law of war, his case acknowledged a rule that prohibits second-guessing commanders' decisions in combat according to information only gained post hoc. The tribunal insisted that commanders could only be judged according to the circumstances as they appeared at the time of a decision. It reasoned that honest battlefield errors cannot be the basis of war crimes convictions. According to the judgment, Rendulic believed that devastation of Norwegian civilian property in the Soviet Army's anticipated path of advance was necessary to preserve his force. Therefore, the judges cleared him of charges that his acts in Finnmark were war crimes.

Far more than an isolated acquittal on a relatively collateral charge, the tribunal's ruling launched a steady and progressive process of international law rule development and incorporation. This chapter traces the legal genesis of the now-eponymous Rendulic Rule respecting honest errors and briefly relates its current content and significance to the law of war and to war fighting. Examination of the judgment reveals that the tribunal did not derive the rule from specialised law of war sources or precedent but rather from far more general, even generic legal sources. And while such general principles of law were at the time and are still today an accepted source of international law, the tribunal's judgment did not build an especially solid evidentiary background for its legal reasoning and conclusion respecting command error and war crimes prosecution. All the same, the tribunal's Rendulic Rule has aged well and now constitutes an established, perhaps even fundamental facet of the law of war. It features prominently in primary rules of the law of war and is a central aspect of law of war implementation by states and commanders.

7.2 The Trial

Conducted in Nuremberg, also the location of the well-known International Military Tribunal (IMT) criminal proceeding that tried the highest-level German political and military leaders, the trial of Rendulic was distinct from the work of the IMT. A US

Army military tribunal tried Rendulic and his eleven co-accused, one of twelve such trials sometimes referred to as the Subsequent Proceedings.[1]

The Subsequent Proceedings adjudicated indictments of senior German military leaders and were carried out contemporaneously with other Allied national prosecutions of German leaders and military commanders.[2]

Under authority granted by the Allied occupying powers' Control Council Law No. 10, the United States convened the case against Rendulic and his co-accused on 28 June 1947.[3] To call the court a military tribunal is in a sense misleading. Its convening order named three civilian American jurists as members, namely Charles F. Wennerstrum, Edward F. Carter, and George J. Burke.[4] Wennerstrum and Carter were judges on the Supreme Courts of Iowa and Nebraska, respectively. Burke was an advisor to US federal district courts on criminal procedure matters and was a member of the Michigan State Bar.[5] Wennerstrum, the tribunal's Presiding Judge, had military experience, having served as a Lieutenant in the US Army during World War I.[6] But he would later criticise the post-war trials of Germans, observing in 1948, "The trials were to have convinced the Germans of the guilt of their leaders [...] They convinced the Germans merely that they lost the war to tough conquerors."[7]

US Army Brigadier General Telford Taylor and Theodore Fenstermacher prosecuted the case against Rendulic and his co-accused, a trial familiarly known as the *Hostage* case (hereinafter *Hostage*).[8] Taylor had been an Army intelligence officer during the war.[9] His assignments included a tour at Bletchley Park, the headquarters of an English team that broke coded German communications.[10] Taylor later helped draft the London Charter, the foundational document of modern international criminal law that established the IMT. By his own admission, neither his legal education nor his prior legal practice had directly prepared Taylor to practice international law or the law of war.[11] Nevertheless, after the war and at the conclusion of the IMT proceedings, he succeeded Justice Robert Jackson as Chief Prosecutor and Head of

---

[1] *See* Heller 2011, p 4. These US proceedings tried 177 defendants over a period of 28 months. Ibid.

[2] Harvard Law School, The Thirteen Nuremberg Trials, Nuremberg Trials Project, https://nuremberg.law.harvard.edu/trials [accessed 1 April 2023]; United Nations War Crimes Commission, United States v. Wilhelm List, et al., Trial Judgment, 1949, XI Law Reports of Trials of War Criminals 757, 761 (*Hostage* Case).

[3] Headquarters, European Command, Order Constituting Tribunal V, General Orders No. 70 by Military Government Ordinance No. 7, 28 June 1947.

[4] *Hostage* Case, above n. 3, p 761.

[5] Ibid., p 762.

[6] Iowa Judicial Branch, Iowa Courts History, Past Supreme Court Justices, https://www.iowacourts.gov/for-the-public/educational-resources-and-services/iowa-courts-history/past-justices/charles-f-wennerstrum/ [accessed 1 April 2023].

[7] Charles F. Wennerstrum, 96; Served on Iowa's High Court, NY Times, 6 June 1986.

[8] *Hostage* Case, p 763.

[9] Taylor 1993, p ix; Parks 1998, p 746.

[10] Taylor 1993, p ix; Parks 1998, p 746.

[11] Taylor 1993, pp x, xi.

the Subsequent Proceedings Division in the US Office of Chief Counsel in Nuremberg.[12] At the US military tribunals, Taylor served as Chief of Counsel for War Crimes and actively litigated many of its cases.[13] Taylor's co-counsel, Fenstermacher, was similarly unpracticed in international law and the law of war. He had worked in private practice at the New York Wall Street law firm Milbank, Tweed, and Hope prior to joining the prosecution team at the Nuremberg military tribunals.[14] Two German jurists, Mr. Stefan Fritsch and Dr. Oskar von Jagwitz represented Rendulic.

Born in Austria, Rendulic came from a military family of Croatian descent. In Vienna, he studied law, then attended a military academy gaining a commission in the Austro-Hungarian Army. He served in World War I and, after further studies in law, joined the German Army following Germany's annexation of Austria. In 1944, Rendulic took command of the German 20th Mountain Army. By early 1945, he was commander of all German forces in Norway and Finland.

The prosecutor's indictment, filed on 10 May 1947, charged war crimes in connection with Rendulic's actions in both Southeastern Europe and in Norway. The portion of the indictment applicable to Rendulic's operations in Norway alleged that he "unlawfully, willingly, and knowingly committed war crimes."[15] Among other offenses, the indictment charged Rendulic with unlawful devastation, "wholly unwarranted and unjustified by military necessity and in flagrant violation of the laws and customs of war."[16] The first specification of the devastation charge alleged:

> On or about 10 October 1944, the Commander in Chief of the 20th Mountain Army, the defendant Rendulic, issued an order, to troops under his command and jurisdiction, for the complete destruction of all shelter and means of existence in, and the total evacuation of the entire civilian population of, the northern Norwegian province of Finmark [*sic*]. During the months of October and November 1944, this order was effectively and ruthlessly carried out. For no compelling military reasons, and in literal execution of instructions to show no sympathy to the civilian population, the evacuated residents were made to witness the burning of their homes and possessions and the destruction of churches, public buildings, food supplies, barns, livestock, bridges, transport facilities, and natural resources of an area in which they and their families had lived for generations. Relatives and friends were separated, many of the evacuees became ill from cold and disease, hundreds died from exposure or perished at sea in the small boats and fishing smacks used in the evacuation, while still others were summarily shot for refusing to leave their homeland-in all, the thoroughness and brutality of this evacuation left some 61,000 men, women, and children homeless, starving, and destitute.[17]

The prosecutor alleged that, rather than reflect a military design to slow an imminent Soviet advance, the scale of devastation proved "a long-range plan to despoil and retard for decades the economic and industrial potential of the occupied territories."[18]

[12] Parks 1998, p 746.

[13] Taylor 1949, p vii.

[14] Barrett 2010, p 586.

[15] *Hostage* Case, above n. 3, p 769.

[16] Ibid., p 770.

[17] Ibid.

[18] Ibid.

It is true that in October 1944, the German High Command had ordered an expansion of devastation tactics. An order to that effect commanded:

> Because of the unwillingness of the northern Norwegian population to voluntarily evacuate, the Fuehrer has agreed to the proposals of the commissioner for the occupied Norwegian territories and has ordered that the entire Norwegian population east of the fiord of Lyngen be evacuated by force in the interest of their own security and that all homes are to be burned down or destroyed.
>
> The Supreme Commander Northern Finland is responsible that the Fuehrer's order is carried out without consideration. Only by this method can it be prevented that the Russians with strong forces, and aided by these homes and the people familiar with the terrain, follow our withdrawal operations during this winter and shortly appear in front of our position in Lyngen. This is not the place for sympathy for the civilian population.
>
> It must be made clear to the troops engaged in this action that the Norwegians will be thankful in a few months that they were saved from bolshevism, and that the barbarian methods of the air war against our German country and her cultural shrines have brought a thousand times more misery to our people if compared with the humane evacuation and destruction of homes in northern Norway, which is necessary for our war effort, and which, if it is not done, must be paid with the blood of German soldiers.[19]

Nonetheless, the prosecutor urged the tribunal to consider the evacuation and devastation to have been "wholly unjustified from a military standpoint."[20]

The trial lasted approximately nine months.[21] Its transcript runs to over 10,500 pages and the tribunal received over 1,700 exhibits from the litigants.[22] Still, and particularly with respect to events in Norway, the facts were clear and relatively undisputed at trial (if not later).[23] Taylor and his team were eager to present a simple case to the tribunal both in factual and in legal terms. In his opening statement for the prosecution, Taylor emphasised that the case should not be understood as a legal or technical debate about the state of the law. The law, Taylor argued, was sufficiently clear to support conviction.

The indictment identified the Regulations annexed to the 1907 Hague Convention (IV) Respecting the Laws and Customs of War on Land as the Finnmark charge's primary source of treaty law.[24] The Hague Conventions were a widely ratified and early, second-round iteration of an effort to codify the laws and customs of war into a multilateral treaty.[25] The indictment also recited the laws and customs of war as well as general principles of law as relevant sources for regulation of the conduct of hostilities.[26]

---

[19] Ibid., p 836.

[20] Ibid., p 839.

[21] Ibid., p 759.

[22] Ibid., p 760.

[23] Ibid., p 786.

[24] Hague Convention (IV) Respecting the Laws and Customs of War on Land, 18 Oct. 1907, 36 Stat. 2247, 1 Bevans 631 [HC IV].

[25] States adopted the first round of the Hague Conventions in 1899. See, e.g., Hague Convention (II) Respecting the Laws and Customs of War on Land with Annex of Regulations, July 29, 1899, 32 Stat. 1803, 1 Bevans 247.

[26] *Hostage* Case, above note 3, p 776.

Although many World War II belligerents, including Germany, were States Parties to the 1907 Fourth Hague Convention, not all were.[27] This would prove a potential obstacle to the convention's operation in World War II. According to Article 2, the so-called *si omnes* or general participation clause of the Fourth Hague Convention, the treaty was inapplicable to any war, such as World War II, that involved a non-State Party as a belligerent.[28] But prior to the proceedings against Rendulic, the IMT had in the view of many effectively negated the *si omnes* clause when it determined that by the beginning of the war, the 1907 Convention reflected customary international law applicable to all states, whether parties to the convention or not.[29] Accordingly, the *Hostage* tribunal would fully apply the Fourth Hague Convention Regulations, particularly its provisions on enemy property destruction.

All the same, Taylor conceded some weaknesses in the law of war as it existed prior to World War II. He observed, "there is a general feeling, not without substantial basis, that some of the laws of war as written in the Hague Conventions are obsolete, and on both sides were honored only in the breach."[30] But in what was likely a legal call to arms to both states and to the tribunal, he continued, "[t]he prosecution fully recognizes that the laws and usages of warfare must be altered and adapted to reflect the developments in this terrible art which man has learned to practice with such appalling proficiency."[31]

Turning to events in Northern Norway, the prosecutor's case highlighted Finland's September 1944 armistice with the Soviet Union. Under that agreement, Finland demanded that Germany withdraw its forces from Finnish territory.[32] Rendulic hastily and with considerable difficulty withdrew his forces, but not without expressing significant resentment toward Finland and the local population for what seemed a betrayal. The Finnish withdrawal from the conflict left the Germans' northern flank in Norway highly exposed to a Soviet advance. It was unsurprising, then, when Soviet forces initially moved into the Norwegian province of Finnmark, an area inhabited by as many as 62,000 nomadic Sámi indigenous people.[33] Advancing Soviet troops at first pursued and kept contact with German forces along an available road. Rendulic's systematic destruction of potential barracks and other facilities was intended to slow the Soviet advance and to cause them to lose contact.[34]

Anticipating the defense teams' legal arguments, the prosecutor rejected any suggestion that Rendulic might be excused from liability for the evacuations and

---

[27] Bulgaria, Greece, Italy, and Yugoslavia, though Second World War belligerents, were not Parties to the Fourth Hague Convention during the war.

[28] HC IV, above note 26, Article 2.

[29] United Nations 1948, p 497. For criticism of this ruling see Watts 2009, pp 402–403.

[30] *Hostage* Case, above n. 3, p 787.

[31] Ibid.

[32] Ibid., p 834. See also Reiter 2010, pp 136–138 (relating circumstance leading to Finland's armistice in the Continuation War with the Soviet Union).

[33] *Hostage* Case, above n. 3, p 834.

[34] Ibid., p 836.

devastation on the basis of superior orders.[35] Taylor's team cited the London Charter, Control Council Law No. 10, as well as the Germany Army Military Penal Code as firm rejections of the superior orders defense. The prosecutors further advised the tribunal that although the extant law might have condoned violations of the law of war as reprisals—responses to enemy violations—they applied only between belligerents and were unavailable against civilian populations or their property.[36] Interestingly, Taylor made no mention of how the tribunal should adjudicate honest errors, nor offered any discussion of a post hoc standard of review of command decision-making. The prosecution's objective assessment that Rendulic had, in reality, lacked military necessity for the Finnmark devastation appears to have been the sole legal theory to support the charge.

Aside from determining the motives and intentions of Rendulic, the defense case focused, as Taylor anticipated, chiefly on law rather than the largely uncontested facts. The defense teams, especially that of Field Marshal Wilhelm List with respect to similar events in other theaters of the war, recited superior orders as a defense.[37] They presented, wisely considering the composition of the tribunal, an Anglo-American-oriented defense. They relied prominently on the work of the renowned British international lawyer Lassa Oppenheim who, in five successive editions of his leading international law treatise, had endorsed the superior orders defense to war crimes.[38] The defense teams were also quick to bring to the tribunal's attention the US War Department *Rules of Land Warfare* and the British Army *Military Law Manual*. Both of these manuals, until amended in 1944 in anticipation of post-war prosecutions, had recited superior orders as an effective defense against war crimes charges.[39]

With respect to the law of war governing devastations, the defense teams emphasised that "only the willful destruction of towns, small towns, and villages, and only devastation not justified by military necessity can be war crimes."[40] The defense cited the US law professor Charles Fenwick, former President of the American Society of International Law, who had observed:

> General devastation of property as a means of covering the retreat of an army was, however, a common practice of belligerents. A more difficult problem was to determine how far the destruction of enemy property was justified, not in connection with direct hostilities, but as a means of cutting off the enemy's lines of communication, eliminating his subsequent sources of supply, or intimidating the civilian population and inducing it to bring pressure upon the government to sue for peace.[41]

---

[35] Ibid., p 839.

[36] Ibid., p 841. The tribunal controversially rejected this argument with respect to executions of civilians as reprisals in the Balkans in another portion of the judgment. Ibid., pp 1252–1253.

[37] Ibid., p 857.

[38] Ibid (citing Oppenheim, International Law).

[39] *Hostage* Case, above n. 3, p 858 (citing United States 1940, para 347; Great Britain 1907, pp 17–18. The copy of the US *Field Manual* uploaded to the United States Library of Congress lines through the superior orders defense language noting "see change".

[40] *Hostage* Case, above n. 3, p 886.

[41] Ibid., p 887 (quoting Fenwick 1934, p 567).

The defense teams featured historical examples of devastation as well, including US Army General William Tecumseh Sherman's 1864 devastation of the state of Georgia in his infamous "march to the sea" and General Philip Sheridan's laying waste to the Virginia Shenandoah Valley during the American Civil War, campaign examples likely familiar to the tribunal members.[42]

Addressing the prosecutor's resort to the 1907 Hague Regulations as the devastation charge's source of international law, the defense acknowledged the Article 23(g) prohibition on destruction of enemy property not "imperatively demanded by the necessities of war". But they emphasised that the law of war "leaves to the determination of the belligerent army the circumstances under which military necessity demands such measures."[43] The defense also noted the ease with which allegations that security measures are unnecessary can be made after armed conflict. Warning of the complexities of second-guessing judgments of military necessity, the defense observed, "Every appraisal of the military-political measures in the southeast area will remain incomplete and inadequate with regard to the actual conditions as long as it is not based on knowledge of the completely abnormal circumstances in occupied territory."[44] Summing up for List, but certainly also relevant to Rendulic's case, the defense team pleaded:

> If in Your Honors' view Field Marshal List surpassed the measure of that which, in retrospect with exact knowledge of the circumstances on both sides, could be designated as justified and tolerable, then you must allow that on the basis of the state of affairs and considering the vagueness of the legal position, Field Marshal List could feel himself justified in ordering the measures he did. The Tribunal cannot pass over these inherent facts in view of the basic principles governing the field of criminal law for all civilized nations for centuries. Reasons of fairness and justice demand that Field Marshal List be treated in this respect exactly as were, for instance, those Allied commanders who gave the orders to attack Dresden and Hiroshima. Both attacks were operations started when the Allies had already clearly won the war, and the officers participating in both operations could have no doubt whatsoever that they would bring a terrible death to tens, nay, hundreds of thousands of innocent civilians.[45]

Finally, turning to the German commanders' motives, the defense teams sought to establish "how things were in reality" between the political and military leadership.[46] Responding to prosecution arguments that the devastation of Finnmark was consistent with the Nazi Party's general "mentality" of harsh reprisal, the defense sought to separate German political motives and those of the military high command from the motives and mentality of its operational commanders like Rendulic. By invoking the firebombing of Dresden and the nuclear attack on Hiroshima, the defense teams offered a clever approach to law of war decision-making. Judged by the prosecution's standards of military necessity, neither Allied attack was strictly necessary

---

[42] *Hostage* Case, above n. 3, p 887. The defense team recounted General Sheridan's observation of the Shenandoah Valley, "A crow flying across it would have had to carry its own rations". Ibid.

[43] Ibid., p 887.

[44] Ibid., pp 889–890.

[45] Ibid., pp 1226–1227.

[46] Ibid., p 1174.

as a measure to win the war. They were only necessary in the specific and peculiar sense that military necessity intends. That is, they were conducive, effective, or contributed to military success and the defeat of the enemy. Finally, rather than a military, wartime, or international law-specific grounding, the defense team looked to general, even universal principles of law to support acquittal. They argued, "it [is] not only a cardinal rule in the procedural law of civilized countries but also a natural commandment of judicial fairness to attribute unfair motives to a man [...] only on the basis of quite definite evidence."[47]

7.3 The Judgment

The tribunal issued its judgment on 19 February 1948. Before turning to the resolution of the charges, it is worth noting two observations the judges made concerning the nature of international law. First, they ascribed a dynamic quality. The tribunal noted the law's "growth by crystallization of generally prevailing custom and practice in law."[48] Second, and no doubt in consideration of the peculiar and in some respects primordial legal landscape from which they worked, they concluded that such growth and adaptation justified articulations of law that lacked unanimous support.[49] Presaging their later conclusions of law, and indeed their general approach to the Finnmark charges, the judges observed, "it is sufficient to say that international law consists of the *principles* which control or govern relations between nations."[50] Meanwhile, addressing how principles should be stated or expressed, the tribunal counseled against "adding rigidity where resiliency is essential."

Turning to the merits of the case, the tribunal began by identifying the international legal sources applicable to the charges. The court observed:

> The sources of international law which are usually enumerated are (1) customs and practices accepted by civilized nations generally, (2) treaties, conventions, and other forms of interstate agreements, (3) the decisions of international tribunals, (4) the decisions of national tribunals dealing with international questions, (5) the opinions of qualified text writers, and (6) the diplomatic papers.[51]

---

[47] Ibid., pp 1174–1175.

[48] Ibid., p 1234.

[49] Ibid., pp 1234–1235.

[50] Ibid., p 1235 (emphasis added).

[51] Ibid. Today the sources of international law are generally agreed to include:

> international conventions, whether general or particular, establishing rules expressly recognized by the contesting states; international custom, as evidence of a general practice accepted as law; the general principles of law recognized by civilized nations; and [with limits] judicial decisions and the teachings of the most highly qualified publicists of the various nations, as subsidiary means for the determination of rules of law.

Statute of the International Court of Justice, June 26, 1945, Article 38, 33 UNTS 993.

Although the tribunal acknowledged the full range of applicable international legal sources, early in the judgment it became clear the judges would rely heavily on the first category, "customs and practices accepted by civilized nations generally". Some may regard this as a reference to customary international law, however, as the judgment later makes clear, the judges may also have intended to refer to what are now commonly known as general principles of law. Today, general principles of law are widely understood to include fundamental concepts of justice and equity recognised and proclaimed in the codes of almost all "civilized nations".[52] One common example of these principles includes the notion that a party in litigation may not cite another party's failure or omission if the asserting party contributed to or caused the failure or omission at issue.[53] Municipal legal systems apply forms of this principle widely as do fora for international litigation.

Wide acceptance notwithstanding, general principles of law remain subject to controversy. For instance, significant debate has emerged at an ongoing UN International Law Commission project on general principles of law.[54] Questions surrounding acceptable methods for discerning precise principles and their normative content have repeatedly plagued efforts to apply general principles of law. Still, the *Hostage* tribunal firmly embraced the concept of general principles of law when it observed, "If [a rule] is found to have been accepted generally as a fundamental rule of justice by most nations in their municipal law, its declaration as a rule of international law would seem to be fully justified."[55]

On one hand, the tribunal's resort to general principles is somewhat surprising. The charges indisputably arose exclusively from military, wartime, and international acts. That a military tribunal would resort to very general legal precepts derived from routine, civilian municipal law to adjudicate that activity is remarkable in light of the military and war-specific international law available at the time.

On the other hand, that these US judges, plucked from domestic courts, resorted to general principles of law rather than delve into the murky and insular territory of military and international law might have been predicted. The defense teams had persuasively steered them toward general legal principles and notions of fairness in their closing arguments. And the tribunal judges were civilian legal professionals and jurists. There are no indications that any of the three judges brought any significant depth in or experience with military or international law to the proceedings. Further, the uncontested facts of devastation and destruction (again excepting Rendulic's intentions and state of mind) naturally led the tribunal's legal considerations away

[52] Akehurst 1976, pp 813–814 (quoting Orinoco Steamship Company, 9 RIAA 180, 200). Although it appears in the text of the Statute of the International Court of Justice, the term "civilized" is no longer an operative aspect of the definition of general principles of law. See Thirlway 2014, p 95.

[53] Gaja 2020.

[54] See, e.g., United Nations, International Law Commission, Third Report on General Principles of Law, Marcelo Vázquez-Bermúdez, Special Rapporteur, A/CN.4/753, 18 April 2022 (noting disagreement whether general principles of law can be developed and drawn directly from international legal contexts).

[55] *Hostage* Case, above n. 3, p 1235.

from the law of war proper and its primary rules of conduct and toward the secondary rules that concern its implementation and enforcement.

The primary or substantive rules of the law of war were not without shortcomings, as the prosecutors had conceded.[56] But the law of war seemed up to the task of judging destructive operations executed outside ongoing contact with enemy forces. It was with respect to secondary rules relating to enforcement and especially concerning processes of implementation that the early and mid-twentieth century law of war was especially underdeveloped. Thus, the tribunal turned to general principles of law to discern these secondary rules.

Drawing from prevailing practice in municipal legal systems, the tribunal dispensed quickly—almost summarily—with the superior orders defense. Clearly applying their previous observation concerning general principles derived from national law, the judges concluded: "The rule that superior order is not a defense to a criminal act is a rule of fundamental criminal justice that has been adopted by civilized nations extensively."[57] In what proved a pattern in the tribunal's legal reasoning, their ruling did not include any significant survey or sounding of global municipal practice. Rather, the ruling was almost entirely conclusory. The defense of superior orders was an issue that had split international lawyers and on which, as the prior section relates, the defense teams had collected considerable contrary authority.[58] One might have reasonably expected the tribunal to have offered a carefully considered and deeply reasoned opinion on superior orders. But the tribunal offered no such work. It seems that, as will be seen momentarily, if the defendants were to profit from the comparatively strict secondary rules of proof in criminal proceedings found in municipal law, they would likewise be subject to similarly strict rules concerning defenses to crimes.

Because the litigants had offered conflicting accounts of military necessity concerning Rendulic's Norway operations as well as other charges, the tribunal addressed that subject directly, though perhaps loosely. The judges offered three relevant observations:

> Military necessity permits a belligerent, subject to the laws of war, to apply any amount and kind of force to compel the complete submission of the enemy with the least possible expenditure of time, life, and money [...] The destruction of property to be lawful must be imperatively demanded by the necessities of war. Destruction as an end in itself is a violation of international law [...] It is lawful to destroy railways, lines of communication, or any other property that might be utilized by the enemy. Private homes and churches even may be destroyed if necessary for military operations.[59]

The excerpt tracks widely accepted notions of military necessity of the period. But it seems not to fully resolve, or for that matter even acknowledge, tension between the relatively unconstrained notion of necessity expressed in the opening and closing passages and the conditioned notion of "imperative necessity" it recites between

[56] Ibid., p 787.

[57] Ibid., p 1236.

[58] See discussion above accompanying nn. 39–41.

[59] *Hostage* Case, above n. 3, pp 1253–1254.

them. The tribunal thus did little to discern or construct the degrees or the hierarchy of military necessity hinted at in its judgment. The full extent to which mere necessity and imperative necessity differ is still not universally agreed.[60]

If the defense teams were eager to showcase permissive *ante bellum* US military legal doctrine as well as both recent and historical military severities, the tribunal was willing to return the favour to the defendants. Elaborating on military necessity, the judgment touted a lengthy excerpt from the 1915 German General Staff *Kriegsbrauch im Landkriege* (*War Book*).[61] Addressing necessity, the *War Book* counseled the German junior officer to study military history to guard "against excessive humanitarian notions, it will teach him that certain severities are indispensable to war, nay more, that the only true humanity very often lies in a ruthless application of them."[62] The tribunal quickly dismissed the *War Book*'s instructions as misguided. Specifically, it rejected the implication that military necessity was a matter to be determined solely by commanders and soldiers as "a complete justification of their acts."[63] Military necessity, the tribunal insisted, did not justify violations of positive law.

Having ruled on other war crimes charges arising chiefly from German operations in the Balkans, the tribunal addressed the Finnmark charges directly. The tribunal began with detailed factual findings on the situation Rendulic confronted in fall and winter of 1944.[64] On the whole, its findings verified the difficult operational situation Rendulic faced. The tribunal first confirmed Rendulic's status as commander of all German forces assigned from the Arctic Ocean to middle Finland and all of Norway.[65] The tribunal also confirmed that, after Finland negotiated a separate peace with the Soviet Union, Rendulic's forces were required to "fight their way out of Finland" over a period of three months across 1,000 km of difficult terrain to reach Norway.[66] The tribunal found that Russia had in fact initially pursued Rendulic into Norway with "very excellent troops" and that their lines of pursuit by both land and sea were highly threatening from an operational standpoint. Importantly, the tribunal also found that Rendulic was aware of the full range of routes available to the Soviets and of the difficulty he would have defending all these axes of advance.[67] However, the tribunal determined that Rendulic's access to intelligence concerning the Soviet force itself was limited. The tribunal also found that poor weather and short winter daylight made

---

[60] The US Department of Defense views imperative necessity as requiring more than the mere convenience or usefulness that unconditioned necessity involves. See United States 2016, para 5.17.2.1.

[61] *Hostage* Case, above n. 3, p 1255 (quoting Germany 1915, p 72). The judgment cites to pp 53–55. The edition consulted for this chapter, which appears to be that cited by the tribunal, finds the quoted passage at p 72.

[62] *Hostage* Case, above n. 3, p 1255.

[63] Ibid., pp 1255–1256.

[64] Ibid., p 1295.

[65] Ibid.

[66] Ibid.

[67] Ibid.

air reconnaissance "almost impossible".[68] Compounding Rendulic's difficulties, and greatly limiting his options to delay or defeat the Soviet advance, the tribunal noted that the German Army had reduced his force by half when it transferred his four best mountain divisions back to Germany.[69]

The tribunal next catalogued the extent of Rendulic's devastation of Finnmark, which it termed a "'scorched earth' policy".[70] It found that Rendulic had in fact removed the entire population of the province, save a few who evaded evacuation. But importantly the tribunal also found, contrary to prosecution arguments, no evidence of any loss of civilian life directly resulted from these evacuations.[71] Property destruction was, however, nearly total. The tribunal observed:

> Villages were destroyed. Isolated habitations met a similar fate. Bridges and highways were blasted. Communication lines were destroyed. Port installations were wrecked. A complete destruction of all housing, communication, and transport facilities took place. This was not only true along the coast and highways but in the interior sections as well. The destruction was as complete as an efficient army could do it.[72]

Still, the tribunal noted a mixed evidentiary record as to whether the devastation was necessary. On one hand, defensive preparations such as foxholes, gun emplacements corroborated that Rendulic had honestly anticipated a Soviet advance through the territory devastated.[73] Had the devastation been merely punitive, opportunistic, or sadistic, Rendulic's units would not likely have invested in such defensive works. Integrated defensive preparations seemed to corroborate the valid operational nature of the devastation to the tribunal. On the other hand, the tribunal noted, "[t]here is evidence in the record that there was no military necessity for this destruction and devastation."[74] Most glaring was the fact that the Soviet Army did not in fact pursue the Germans' retreat across most of Finnmark. In reality, Rendulic need not have devastated Finnmark.[75]

Against these facts, the tribunal then applied the Hague Conventions' devastation rule which requires "destruction or seizure be imperative demanded by the necessities of war."[76] In a literal sense, the destructions proved neither necessary nor imperatively demanded in light of the Soviet decision not to pursue the retreat. Because the Soviets were not in fact in full pursuit, the devastation served no direct military purpose. However, the tribunal insisted:

> We are not called upon to determine whether urgent military necessity for the devastation and destruction in the province of Finmark [*sic*] actually existed. We are concerned with the

[68] Ibid.

[69] Ibid.

[70] Ibid., p 1296.

[71] Ibid.

[72] Ibid.

[73] Ibid.

[74] Ibid.

[75] See Chaps. 3 and 4.

[76] Ibid., pp 1296–1297 (citing HC IV, above n. 26, Article 23(g)).

> question whether the defendant at the time of its occurrence acted within the limits of honest judgment on the basis of the conditions prevailing at the time.[77]

Applying this standard to Rendulic's circumstances, the tribunal highlighted both objective and subjective uncertainty. Concerning the former, the judges noted that military operations in war are inherently "loaded with uncertainties". They acknowledged that enemy strength, equipment, morale, efficiency, risk tolerance, and intentions are rarely clear to commanders. Regarding the latter subjective element, the tribunal noted that Rendulic's precarious military situation as well as his lack of information concerning Soviet capabilities and intentions and his inability to acquire such information required him to develop plans on the basis of limited and imperfect information. These conditions were sufficient for Rendulic to honestly, though erroneously, conclude that "scorched earth" tactics in Finnmark were justified by "urgent military necessity". The tribunal held: "the defendant may have erred in the exercise of his judgment but he was guilty of no criminal act."[78]

There is a clear and basic logic to the tribunal's judgment on honest errors. Although Rendulic's actions produced extensive destruction and suffering, the Finnmark devastation clearly lacked conclusive or even compelling evidence of a *mens rea* on his part. The evidence before the tribunal fell well short of establishing beyond reasonable doubt that a motive other than imperative military necessity informed Rendulic's orders. The tribunal's resistance to the siren's call of victor's justice and the Norwegian victims' understandable demand for redress in the form of conviction is surely commendable as a matter of international criminal law.[79]

Less clear, however, is the judgment's *legal* logic. The tribunal devoted considerable effort at the outset of its judgment to discerning the appropriate international law sources for its rules of decision. In this respect, the judges described a framework that included general principles of law that is passable, if not universally shared, even by today's standards. But when the moment came to give convincing substantive content to the general principles it would use to decide the case, the tribunal foundered. The judgment includes no detailed or empirical assessment of the municipal legal systems that are the agreed sources of general principles of law. Nor is it clear from the judgment that international law had actually incorporated the principle respecting honest errors which the tribunal applied. The judges offered no evidence that any other, much less a preponderance, of adjudications had found the honest errors rule to constitute a general principle of law that correspondingly amounted to international law. But perhaps the tribunal was aware it would fall short in these respects when, early in the judgment, it warned of the comparatively incomplete and uncertain nature of international law and its perception that courts should not "place the principles of international law in a formalistic strait-jacket [that] would ultimately destroy any effectiveness that it has acquired."[80] Overall, the tribunal's Norway judgment is a stark reminder of the relatively rudimentary state of the law

[77] *Hostage* Case, above n. 3, p 1297.

[78] Ibid.

[79] See Chap. 8.

[80] *Hostage* Case, above n. 3, p 1235.

of war, particularly of secondary rules concerning implementation and enforcement, in the mid-twentieth century.

The *Hostage* tribunal was not alone in these respects. Another US Army trial in the Subsequent Proceedings, the so-called *High Command Case*, heard charges similar to those Rendulic faced for his actions in Finnmark.[81] *Generaloberst* Karl Hollidt was charged with "unjustified devastation" for destroying civilian agricultural property during a retreat from Soviet territory. The indictment alleged Hollidt's forces "seized all cattle, poultry, and agricultural machinery in the area, and removed 40,000 tons of corn, of which 4,000 tons were thrown into the Dnepr River."[82] A German order to Hollidt had read, "All land that we have been forced to abandon to the enemy must be made unusable. Each village must be destroyed and burned down, without any regard for the population, in order to make it uninhabitable for the enemy."[83] Eight months after the *Hostage* judgment partially acquitted Rendulic, the *High Command* tribunal acquitted Hollidt, concluding the prosecution had not proved his acts were unjustified "by military necessity under the conditions of war in the area."[84] While Hollidt's case confirmed much of the *Hostage* tribunal's general conclusions concerning devastation, his case did not involve a consideration of honest errors. It seems the devastation Hollidt ordered actually had the intended effect of slowing or deterring advancing Soviet forces.

7.4 The Rendulic Rule Legacy

The *Hostage* judgment's legacy was not immediately favourable. Unsurprisingly, Rendulic's acquittal was not well received in Norway.[85] Meanwhile, later assessments of the *Hostage* tribunal's general work present a mixed bag. A recent comprehensive scholarly treatment of the 12 major US military tribunal cases, including the *Hostage* judgment, assesses that the tribunal's characterisation of civilian executions as reprisals was "misguided".[86] However, that same study highlights absolute separation of the *jus ad bellum* and the *jus in bello* legal regimes among "the tribunals' very progressive" approaches to international criminal law.[87] Interestingly, the work does not identify the honest errors rule as either misguided or progressive. Still, the legacy of the Rendulic Rule, as it came to be called, appears to have improved with

[81] United Nations War Crimes Commission, United States v. Von Leeb, et al., Trial Judgment, Case No. 12, X Law Reports of Trials of War Criminals (1949) [X High Command Case].

[82] Ibid., p 40.

[83] Ibid.

[84] United Nations War Crimes Commission, United States v. Von Leeb, et al., Trial Judgment, Case No. 12, XI Law Reports of Trials of War Criminals 628 (1949).

[85] See Chap. 5.

[86] Heller 2011, p 3.

[87] Ibid.

age. By now it is clear that it extends beyond the narrow facts of the tactical and operational situation faced by Rendulic. The rule—or at least its spirit—has even matured beyond a mere secondary rule of law of war implementation and enforcement into the realm of positive primary rules.

For instance, the Rendulic Rule is now reflected in several primary rules of conduct expressed in law of war treaties. Additional Protocol I to the 1949 Geneva Conventions (AP I), Article 52(2) defines military objectives for purposes of distinction in attacks by belligerents as a matter of both conventional and customary international law.[88] Article 52(2) states:

> Attacks shall be limited strictly to military objectives. In so far as objects are concerned, military objectives are limited to those objects which by their nature, location, purpose or use make an effective contribution to military action and whose total or partial destruction, capture or neutralization, *in the circumstances ruling at the time*, offer a definite military advantage.[89]

A 1996 protocol on landmines, added to an earlier 1980 treaty that regulates the use of conventional weapons, defines military objectives identically to Article 52 of AP I.[90] These articles' explicit references to "the circumstances ruling at the time" are widely understood to reflect incorporation of the Rendulic Rule. It is true that a literal reading might understand "the circumstances ruling at the time" to constitute the *actual facts* involved in an attack, rather than the facts as they honestly appeared to the attacker. However, practice makes clear that the "circumstances" of an attack are to be understood broadly.[91] They include not only the actual conditions of reality at the military objective, but also the informational situation faced by the attacker including limits on the attacker's ability to apprehend conditions and any accompanying honest misconceptions.

The *scienter* elements of many law of war enforcement provisions also subtly incorporate and reinforce the Rendulic Rule. For example, AP I supplements the

---

[88] The US *Department of Defense Law of War Manual* recites verbatim the Additional Protocol I definition of military objective stated in Article 52(2). United States 2016, para 5.6.3. The *Manual* does not expressly identify the Additional Protocol as the source of the customary rule. In fact, it cites instead the 1996 Amended Protocol II to the 1980 Convention on Conventional Weapons. United States 2016, para 5.6.3 (citing Protocol (to the Convention on Prohibitions or Restrictions on the Use of Certain Conventional Weapons Which May be Deemed to Be Excessively Injurious or to Have Indiscriminate Effects) on Prohibitions or Restrictions on the Use of Mines, Booby-Traps and Other Devices as amended on May 3, 1996, Article 2(6), 2048 UNTS 133. However, the latter treaty expresses the rule with respect to landmines identically to the Additional Protocol's more general rule and the *Manual* counsels the military objective standard as applying far more broadly than the limited context of the Amended Protocol II. United States 2016, para 5.6.3.

[89] Protocol Additional to the Geneva Conventions of August 12, 1949, and Relating to the Protection of Victims of International Armed Conflicts, June 8, 1977, Article 52(2), 1125 UNTS 3 (emphasis added) [hereinafter AP I].

[90] Protocol (to the Convention on Prohibitions or Restrictions on the Use of Certain Conventional Weapons Which May be Deemed to Be Excessively Injurious or to Have Indiscriminate Effects) on Prohibitions or Restrictions on the Use of Mines, Booby-Traps and Other Devices as amended on May 3, 1996, 2048 UNTS 133.

[91] United States 2016, para 5.6.7.2.

grave breaches enforcement provisions of the 1949 Geneva Conventions. Article 85 of AP I criminalises disproportionate attacks, but only those attacks made "in the knowledge" that the attack is disproportionate.[92] An attack made under the mistaken belief that civilian harm would not be excessive in relation to the anticipated concrete and direct military advantage would not amount to a grave breach under the article. For that matter, the relevant basis for weighing excessive civilian harm is the "concrete and direct military advantage *anticipated*" by the attacker, rather than the actual military advantage reflected in reality. And the incidental losses addressed by the proportionality rule are described as harm that the attack "may be expected to cause". Similarly, the Rome Statute of the International Criminal Court (ICC) codifies the crime of disproportionate attack as

> [i]ntentionally launching an attack *in the knowledge* that such attack *will* cause incidental loss of life or injury to civilians or damage to civilian objects or widespread, long-term and severe damage to the natural environment which would be clearly excessive in relation to the concrete and direct overall military advantage *anticipated*.[93]

An attack ordered based on honest error concerning collateral harm to civilians or civilian objects could not be said to have been made "in the knowledge" of its unlawfulness.

Meanwhile, the liability theories of international criminal law also feature Rendulic Rule-like aspects. For instance, treaties addressing command or superior responsibility including AP I and the Rome Statute impute war crimes committed by subordinates to their military commanders and civilian leaders.[94] However, they do so only on the basis of information available to the commander or leader in question at the time or as the situation appeared to the commander in the circumstances. AP I assigns command responsibility to individuals when a leader "knew, or had information which should have enabled them to conclude *in the circumstances at the time*, that [a subordinate] was going to commit such a breach and if they did not take all feasible measures within their power to prevent or repress the breach."[95] The subsequent article of AP I provides with respect to states' obligations: "Parties to the conflict shall require any commander *who is aware* that subordinates or other persons under his control are going to commit or have committed a breach of the Conventions or this Protocol, to initiate such steps as are necessary to prevent such violations [...]."[96]

For its part, the Rome Statute differentiates responsibility for commanders and military leaders from that applicable to civilians. Under Article 28 of the Statute, military commanders hold superior responsibility for their subordinates' crimes when, "[t]hat military commander or person either knew or, *owing to the circumstances at the time*, should have known that the forces were committing or about to commit such

[92] AP I, above n. 88, Article 85.

[93] Rome Statute of the International Criminal Court, July 17, 1998, Article 8(2)(b)(iv), 2187 UNTS 90 (emphases added) [hereinafter Rome Statute].

[94] AP I, above n. 88, Articles 86–87; Rome Statute, above n. 91, Article 28(a)–(b).

[95] AP I, above n. 88, Article 86 (emphasis added).

[96] Ibid., Article 87 (emphasis added).

crimes."[97] Civilian leaders are responsible for subordinates' crimes if "[t]he superior either knew, or consciously disregarded information which clearly indicated, that the subordinates were committing or about to commit such crimes."[98] Although the informational or *mens rea* elements of the Rome Statute superior responsibility standards differ between military and civilian leaders, they share a Rendulic Rule-like requirement that assessments be made from the contemporaneous perspective of the leader in question rather than from knowledge gained post hoc.

Defenses available to accused persons also strongly indicate the deeply ensconced status of the Rendulic Rule. The Rome Statute is again reminiscent of the Rendulic Rule at Article 32 concerning mistake of fact. It provides: "[a] mistake of fact shall be a ground for excluding criminal responsibility only if it negates the mental element required by the crime." Although couched in terms of a limitation on the defense, the article clearly endorses mistake of fact as a baseline proposition. Read in conjunction with the relevant mental elements of war crimes within the ICC's subject matter jurisdiction, mistake of fact based on honest errors can be anticipated to operate broadly and effectively at the ICC.[99]

States have also endorsed and incorporated the Rendulic Rule in their domestic processes for ratification of international law instruments. For instance, the US Senate, exercising its constitutionally assigned function to give advice and consent to treaty ratification, has consistently recited the Rendulic Rule. The Senate added to its approval of three relatively recent law of war treaties the following contingency:

> Any decision by any military commander, military personnel, or any other person responsible for planning, authorizing, or executing military action shall only be judged on the basis of that person's assessment of the information reasonably available to the person at the time the person planned, authorized, or executed the action under review and shall not be judged on the basis of information that comes to light after the action under review was taken.[100]

Similarly, Canada's statement of understanding issued when it ratified AP I reads:

> [M]ilitary commanders and others responsible for planning, deciding upon or executing attacks have to reach decisions on the basis of their assessment of the information reasonably available to them at the relevant time and that such decisions cannot be judged on the basis of information which has subsequently come to light.[101]

Other States Parties to AP I submitted similar understandings or statements upon ratification.[102]

Finally, states' military legal manuals resort extensively to the Rendulic Rule. Not long after the *Hostage* judgment, the US Army updated and re-issued its field

[97] Rome Statute, above n. 91, Article 28(a)(i) (emphasis added).

[98] Ibid., Article 28(b)(1).

[99] See Chap. 8.

[100] DeSon 2015, p 116. (citing S. Exec. Rep. No. 110-22, at 13 (2008) (CCW Protocols III (incendiary weapons) and IV (blinding laser weapons)); S. Exec. Rep. No. 106-2, at 20 (2009) (CCW Amended Protocol II (landmines and booby traps)).

[101] Canada 1990, p 464.

[102] See e.g. Australia 1991, p 473; Italy 1986, p 439; Netherlands 1987, p 300; Spain 1989, p 392; Switzerland 1982, p 409; United Kingdom 1998, p 76.

manual, *Law of Land Warfare*.[103] Drafted by the eminent law of war scholar Professor Richard R. Baxter, who would later become a judge on the International Court of Justice, the 1956 US manual, perhaps reflective of the lukewarm immediate legacy of the *Hostage* judgment, included no reference to the Rendulic Rule. That manual's long-awaited replacement, however, the 2015 *Department of Defense Law of War Manual*, repeatedly recites the honest errors rule, even referring to it as "the Rendulic Rule".[104] The US *Manual* advises: "the law of war recognizes that persons must assess the *military necessity* of an action based on the information available to them at that time; they cannot be judged based on information that subsequently comes to light." The Rendulic Rule's operation as a secondary rule guiding the implementation of the law of war is clear. But the *Manual* later expresses the Rendulic Rule in terms of a primary rule, that is, as an obligation of conduct owed by states and commanders under the law of war. The *Manual* provides: "Decisions by military commanders or other persons responsible for planning, authorizing, or executing military action must be made in good faith and based on their assessment of the information available to them at the time."[105]

Finally, the Rendulic Rule is an important confidence building measure for the law of war among its end users, the soldiers called upon to apply the law under the most desperate human conditions. It is essentially a backward-looking provision. It counsels analyses of decisions that exclude information not available at the time of choice. However, it has gained prospective use as well since the *Hostage* judgment. Military legal advisors frequently recite the rule in advice to commanders to remind them of the standard by which their decisions may be judged. Commanders need not be concerned they are strictly liable for what may later prove to be objectively unjustified harm. Nor need they divert or assign resources on that basis. Instead, they are required to act reasonably in the circumstances ruling at the time of their decisions. In this sense, the Rendulic Rule is a sort of legal marketing tool, essential to securing military confidence and faith in the laws of war.

7.5 Conclusion

In a plausible alternate version of events, the holdings of the *Hostage* judgment might have been cabined to the case in question or to their specific factual contexts. But for better or worse, the post-World War II criminal proceedings, especially those conducted in Nuremberg, have had precedential value on the content of the law of war perhaps outsized in light of the scant legal reasoning they offered. For its part, the *Hostage* tribunal's Rendulic Rule emerged from a general principle of law resting on meager legal forensics. But it now has clear and immediate application

[103] United States 1956.

[104] United States 2016, para 2.2.3.3.

[105] United States 2016, para 5.3.2.

as an international law-based defense against allegations of wrongdoing by an individual. Although it operates most clearly in criminal proceedings, it seems relevant to administrative investigations and proceedings as well. In this sense, there is a plausible argument to be made that the Rendulic Rule has matured into a quite broadly applicable adjudicative secondary rule.

The rule's widespread acceptance, of course, does not guarantee ease of application. Tribunals called upon to identify and assess "the circumstances ruling at the time" of combat decisions face significant evidentiary challenges. Disparities between knowledge of the physical effects and aftermath of military operations and knowledge of circumstances of decision-making that produced these effects are common. In light of security considerations and classification of information, it is often difficult, if not impossible, for an outside actor to appreciate what leaders knew and did not know at the time of combat decision-making. The full extent of information that was reasonably available to a commander may never be available to the public or finder of fact. To be sure, *in camera* examination by tribunals may in some circumstances mitigate informational and evidentiary challenges. But evaluations of law of war claims is not limited to judicial proceedings. International organisations such as the UN and civil society including humanitarian organisations are an increasingly influential voice in law of war monitoring and enforcement.

The extent to which the Rendulic Rule operates similarly to and within other rules of the *ius in bello*, that branch of the law of war that regulates the conduct of hostilities, has proved the more surprising development. Outside the contexts of investigation and adjudication, states have widely incorporated the Rendulic Rule into the primary rules of the *ius in bello*. It is a recurring feature in *in bello* treaty law. States have widely integrated the rule's "in the circumstances ruling at the time" notion into *in bello* rules. They have also frequently included it in statements accompanying *in bello* treaty ratifications and in the military legal doctrine that instructs and advises armed forces. So broad is its presence, that it might even be conceived as an overarching theme or sensibility that informs how actual rules of conduct during war should be interpreted and applied. One might go so far even to attribute to it the status of an *in bello* principle.

Despite its settled status in the law of war applicable to individuals, important questions remain concerning the full extent of the Rendulic Rule's operation. The law of war lives two lives. First, it is now widely recognised that the law of war binds and may be enforced against individuals. To be sure, the prospect of enforcement against individuals, particularly on a prominent or wide scale, did not see significant success until the post-World War II Nuremburg, Tokyo, and other national enforcement proceedings. However, states updated the Geneva Conventions treaty regime to include revolutionary provisions on enforcement against individuals. Most significantly, each of the four 1949 Geneva Conventions identifies so-called grave breaches, which states have agreed in concept, if not in practice, to investigate and prosecute universally, without regard to territory or nationality.

But the classic and perhaps primary focus of the law of war has been states as such. The law of war primarily binds the states that form and commit themselves to it. Since the early twentieth century, law of war treaties have largely been multilateral affairs, open to signature, ratification, or accession by any state in the international system. The law of war, in both its conventional and customary forms, expresses obligations owed by and between states. Breaches of the laws of war have long been understood to constitute internationally wrongful acts giving rise to reparation obligations. Yet whether breaches committed on the basis of honest errors may be excused as a matter of state responsibility is unclear.[106] The question presents potential for the Rendulic Rule to extend its maturation from general principles of law, to primary law of war rule of conduct, to an aspect of the law of state responsibility.

References

Akehurst M (1976) Equity and general principles of law. International & Comparative Law Quarterly 25:801

Australia (1991) Australia, Statement on ratification of AP I, Jun. 21, 1991, in 1642 UNTS 473

Austria (1983) Austria, Statement on ratification of Additional Protocol I, Feb. 13, 1983, in 1289 UNTS 303

Barrett J (2010) Henry T. King, at case, and on the Nuremberg case. Case Western Reserve Law Review 60:583

Canada (1990) Canada, Statement on ratification of Additional Protocol I, Nov. 20, 1990, in 1591 UNTS 462, 464.

DeSon J (2015) Automating the right stuff—the hidden ramifications of ensuring autonomous aerial weapon systems comply with international humanitarian law. Air Force Law Review 72:85

Fenwick C (1934) International Law. D. Appleton-Century Company, New York

Gaja G (2020) General principles of law. Max Planck Encyclopedia of International Law

Germany (2015) The war book of the German general staff: being "the usages of war on land" (Morgan JH (trans.))

Great Britain, War Office (1907) Manual of Military Law

Heller K (2011) The Nuremberg Military Tribunals and the Origins of International Criminal Law. Oxford University Press, Oxford

Italy (1986) Italy, Statement on ratification of Additional Protocol I, Feb. 27, 1986, in 1425 UNTS 438, 439

Milanovic M (2020) Mistake of fact. EJIL Talk! (14 January 2020)

Netherlands (1987) Netherlands, Statement on Ratification of Additional Protocol I, Jun. 26, 1987, in 1477 UNTS 300

Parks W (1998) Telford Taylor 1908-1998. International Review of the Red Cross 80:746

Reiter D (2010) How Wars End. Princeton University Press, Princeton

Spain (1989) Spain, Statement on ratification of Additional Protocol I, Apr. 21, 1989, in 1537 UNTS 389, 392

Switzerland (1982) Switzerland, Statement on ratification of AP I, Feb. 17, 1982, in 1271 UNTS 409

Taylor T (1949) Final Report to the Secretary of the Army on The Nuernberg War Crimes Trials under Control Council Law No. 10

Taylor T (1993) The Anatomy of the Nuremberg Trials: A Personal Memoir. Skyhorse Publishing, New York

Thirlway H (2014) The Sources of International Law. Oxford University Press, Oxford

Watts S (2009) Reciprocity and the law of war. Harvard International Law Journal 50:365

[106] See Milanovic 2020 (offering preliminary thoughts on the availability of mistake of fact as a defense in state responsibility).

United Kingdom (1998) United Kingdom, Statement on ratification of Additional Protocol I, Jan. 28, 1998, in 2020 UNTS 75, 76
United States Department of Defense, Office of General Counsel (2016) Law of War Manual
United States, Department of the Army (1956) Field Manual 27-10, The Law of Land Warfare
United Nations War Crimes Commission (1948), Trial of The Major War Criminals Before the International Military Tribunal, Volume 22

Other Documents

United Nations, International Law Commission, Third Report on General Principles of Law, Marcelo Vázquez-Bermúdez, Special Rapporteur, A/CN.4/753, 18 Apr. 2022
United States, War Department, Field manual 27-10, Rules of Land Warfare (Oct. 1, 1940)

Sean Watts Professor, United States Military Academy, West Point; Co-Director Lieber Institute for Law and Warfare. Address: 606 Thayer Rd, West Point, NY 10996 USA, e-mail: sean.watts@westpoint.edu

Chapter 8
The Limits of Honest Judgment: The Reasonable Commander Test and Mistake of Fact

Yasmin Naqvi

Contents

8.1 Introduction 178
8.2 *Hostage* Case 184
8.3 Reasonable Commander Test 190
8.4 Mistake of Fact Defence 196
8.5 Conclusion 210
References 211

Abstract The *Rendulic* case is probably the first demonstration of the link between the so-called "reasonable commander test" in international humanitarian law (IHL) and the defence of mistake of fact in international criminal law (ICL). This chapter analyses the link between the reasonable commander test and the mistake of fact defence. After an outline of the legal reasoning in *Hostage*, it examines the origins, purpose, and operation of the reasonable commander test in IHL. It analyses the mistake of fact defence in ICL. The analysis supports the view that in cases where the reasonable commander test is applicable, mistake of fact will only provide a defence where the mistake is both honest and reasonable. On a policy level, this interpretation best comports with IHL's objective to protect the victims of armed conflict. To hold otherwise would lead to a dilution of the precautionary rules set out in IHL, removing a key incentive for commanders to ensure they have done everything feasible to check the accuracy of the information on which they base their decisions to attack.

Keywords reasonable military commander · mistake of fact · international humanitarian law · precautionary rules · Rome Statute · military necessity · proportionality · mental element · war crimes · devastation · scorched earth · honest judgment · objective standard · wilful blindness · good faith

---

Y. Naqvi (✉)
Office of International Law, Attorney-General's Department, Canberra, Australia
e-mail: ynaqvi1@yahoo.com

Graduate Institute of International and Development Studies, Geneva, Switzerland

Robert Garran Offices, 3-5 National Circuit, Barton ACT 2600, Australia

N. Hayashi and C. Lingaas (eds.), *Honest Errors? Combat Decision-Making 75 Years After the* Hostage *Case*, https://doi.org/10.1007/978-94-6265-611-6_8

8.1 Introduction

In October 1944, Lothar Rendulic, Commander-in-Chief of the German 20th Mountain Army in Lapland, made a mistake. Ostensibly believing that the Soviet army was about to launch a major offensive from the east, Rendulic's forces, under direct order from Hitler, carried out a scorched earth retreat in the northern part of Norway known as Finnmark county and Troms county. Adolf Hitler's order of 28 October 1944 ended with the words "Compassion for the civilian population is uncalled for".[1] The destruction of property and all potentially usable goods, including roads, bridges, food, and dwellings, aimed at stopping or at least slowing down the Soviets. But the Germans were wrong. The Soviets did not launch an offensive to the extent anticipated, and Finnmark and Troms counties were left devastated by Rendulic's forces, apparently without any military justification. The charge of wanton destruction was thus part of the charge sheet against Rendulic before a US Military Tribunal in Nuremberg.[2] However, the tribunal acquitted Rendulic on this charge.[3] The tribunal found that the conditions, as they appeared to Rendulic at the time, were sufficient upon which he could honestly conclude that urgent military necessity warranted the decision made.

The *Rendulic* case is perhaps the first demonstration of the link between the so-called "reasonable commander test" in international humanitarian law (IHL) and the defence of mistake of fact in international criminal law (ICL). The link is that, if a commander is assessed as having acted reasonably in light of the information available to him at the time of his decision-making, and if that negates the mental element of a crime, neither the IHL violation nor the individual liability of the commander can be established, even if his assessment was wrong. On the establishment of the IHL violation, applying a reasonable commander test requires a consideration—not

---

[1] Transcript of Rendulic Trial https://commons.und.edu/cgi/viewcontent.cgi?article=1007&context=nuremburg-transcripts (hereafter "Rendulic trial transcript") p 5352 [accessed 1 April 2023]. At trial, Rendulic explained this as meaning that the Norwegians would be, in retrospect, "thankful for having been saved from Bolshevism, etc., and [would realise] that the whole operation is in the interests of the Norwegians". Ibid.

[2] United States Military Tribunal, Nuremberg, Case No. 47, The *Hostage* Trial, *Trial of Wilhelm List and Others*, 8 July 1947 to 19 February 1948 (hereafter "*Hostage* Case"), p 67.

[3] Rendulic was also charged with murder, torture, and systematic terrorisation, imprisonment in concentration camps, forced labour on military installations, and deportation to slave labour of the civilian populations of Greece, Yugoslavia, and Albania by troops of the German armed forces. For further discussion, see Chap. 6. While acquitted on the charges of wanton destruction, he was ultimately found guilty of the three other charges and sentenced to 20 years' imprisonment. He was ultimately released after 12 years in prison.

of whether military necessity or proportionality actually existed or not—but whether a reasonable commander *could* have believed that they existed at the material time. If the answer is yes, IHL was not violated, even if the commander's belief was based on wrong information or an erroneous assessment. On the liability side, when a perpetrator mistakenly believes that what he was doing was legal, there was no intention to commit a crime and hence responsibility cannot be established.

The *Rendulic* case puts forward a compelling legal framework to analyse international incidents where a mistake of fact is claimed. Consider the following well-known serious international incidents involving a mistake of fact:

- The 2021 missile strike on a car belonging to a civilian working for an American non-governmental organisation in Kabul, Afghanistan, in which the US armed forces targeted the car in the mistaken belief that the vehicle contained an Islamic State of Iraq and Syria (ISIS) bomb and posed an imminent threat to troops at Kabul's airport.[4]
- The 2020 shooting down of the Ukrainian airliner over Tehran, Iran, in which the Iranian Revolutionary Guard Corps mistook the airliner for an American cruise missile.[5]

---

[4] The attack, which occurred in a dense residential block, resulted in 10 deaths, including 7 children, all Afghan nationals belonging to the same family. See Aikins et al., New York Times, 10 September 2022, "Times Investigation: In U.S. Drone Strike, Evidence Suggests No ISIS Bomb". https://www.nytimes.com/2021/09/10/world/asia/us-air-strike-drone-kabul-afghanistan-isis.html/ [accessed 1 April 2023]. The US military originally described the strike as a "righteous strike", which followed hours of surveillance the same day of a vehicle that American officials thought contained an Islamic State of Iraq and Syria (ISIS) bomb. A *New York Times* investigation into the bombing raised doubts about the US version of events, including whether explosives were in the car or whether the driver had a connection to ISIS. A Toyota Corolla, similar to the targeted vehicle, was used to launch an attack against the airport the next morning. In September 2021, the Pentagon acknowledged that the strike was a "tragic mistake" following an internal inquiry which concluded the car posed no threat and the driver had no connection to ISIS. See Schmitt and Cooper, New York Times, 19 September 2021, "Pentagon acknowledges Aug. 29 drone strike in Afghanistan was a tragic mistake that killed 10 civilians". https://www.nytimes.com/2021/09/17/us/politics/pentagon-drone-strike-afghanistan.html [accessed 1 April 2023]. General Kenneth F. McKenzie Jr., head of US Central Command, said the strike was carried out "in the profound belief" that ISIS was about to attack Kabul's airport, as the organisation had done three days earlier, killing more than 140 people, including 13 American service members. General Mark A. Milley, Chairman of the Joint Chiefs of Staff, stated: "In a dynamic high-threat environment, the commanders on the ground had appropriate authority and had reasonable certainty that the target was valid, but after deeper post-strike analysis, our conclusion is that innocent civilians were killed".

[5] The attack resulted in 176 deaths, the majority being nationals of Iran and Canada. See McKernan, The Guardian, 11 January 2020, "Iran admits unintentionally shooting down Ukrainian airliner". https://www.theguardian.com/world/2020/jan/11/iran-admits-shooting-down-ukrainian-airliner-unintentionally [accessed 1 April 2023]. According to an early Islamic Revolution Guards Corps (IRGC) statement, when the airplane seemed to head toward a "sensitive military centre" of

- The 2015 attack against a Médecins Sans Frontières hospital in Kunduz in Afghanistan, in which the US armed forces attacked a hospital based on the mistaken belief that it was in fact a Taliban militia building.[6]

---

the IRGC, controllers mistook it for a "hostile target" and shot it down. See Karimi and Krauss, PBS, 12 January 2020, "Under pressure, Iran admits it shot down jetliner by mistake", https://www.pbs.org/newshour/world/under-pressure-iran-admits-it-shot-down-jetliner-by-mistake [accessed 1 April 2023]. For further details, see "IRGC Releases Details of Accidental Downing of Ukrainian Plane", Iran Front Page, 11 January 2020. https://ifpnews.com/irgc-releases-details-of-accidental-downing-of-ukrainian-plane/ [accessed 1 April 2023]. The Commander of the Aerospace Force of the IRGC explained that: "Given the information sent to this operator—that it is a wartime situation and a cruise missile has been fired—this poor guy identifies it as a cruise missile. Well at such a situation, he was obliged to contact, get approval. This is where this operator makes the mistake; but at that moment, his communication system was apparently disrupted—whether because of jamming systems or the high traffic. For that reason, he fails to contact [his commanders]. He had 10 seconds to decide; he could hit or not hit [the target]. Under such circumstances, he decides to make that bad decision; he engages, the missile is fired, and the plane is hit at this place". On 17 March 2021, the Civil Aviation Organization of Iran concluded that missiles had caused the crash and that "[t]he mitigating measures and defense layers in risk management proved to be ineffective due to the occurrence of an unanticipated error in threat identifications, and ultimately failed to protect the flight safety against the threats caused by the alertness of defense forces". PS752 Accident Investigation Final Report. Civil Aviation Organization. 17 March 2021. Retrieved 18 March 2021. It was reported that 10 officials in Iran had been indicted over the incident. Reuters, 2 April 2021, "Iran indicts 10 over Ukraine plane crash, prosecutor says; Canada demands justice". https://www.reuters.com/article/us-iran-crash-ukraine/iran-indicts-10over-ukraine-plane-crash-prosecutor-says-idUSKBN2BT120?il=0 [accessed 1 April 2023]. In January 2022, Iran announced that it had started paying compensation to the families of those killed. See Motamedi, Al Jazeera, 7 January 2022, "Iran says it has begun paying families over downed Ukraine plane". https://www.aljazeera.com/news/2022/1/7/two-years-on-no-resolution-over-downing-of-flight-ps752 [accessed 1 April 2023].

[6] The attack resulted in at least 42 deaths. The attack from the air lasted for around one hour and consisted of precise and repeated airstrikes on the main hospital. Throughout the airstrikes, Médecins Sans Frontières (MSF) teams repeatedly called military authorities to stop the attack. See MSF undated. On 3 October 2015, US airstrikes destroyed our trauma hospital in Kunduz, Afghanistan, killing 42 people. https://www.msf.org/kunduz-hospital-attack. MSF had provided the GPS coordinates of the trauma hospital to the US Department of Defence, Afghan Ministry of Interior and Defence, and US Army in Kabul just a few days prior to the attack. US and Afghan armies both conducted and released their own investigation and findings. MSF asked the International Humanitarian Fact-Finding Commission to establish the facts of this event, but neither the US nor the Afghan governments consented. The US military investigation found that the "tragic strike" was due to human and technical errors. A US gunship mistook the hospital at Kunduz, run by MSF, for a building that had been seized by Taliban fighters. According to the investigation, the MSF Trauma Centre generally matched the general physical description of the Taliban-controlled target structure which was approximately 400 meters away.16 US service members were disciplined. However, as the error was "unintentional", it did not constitute a war crime. See United States Central Command 2015. MSF also conducted its own internal investigation which found that "the MSF's rules in the hospital were implemented and respected, including the 'no weapons' policy; MSF was in full control of the hospital before and at the time of the airstrikes; there were no armed combatants within the hospital compound and there was no fighting from or in the direct vicinity of the trauma centre before the airstrikes". See MSF 2015.

- The 2014 downing of the MH17 airplane over Ukraine with a Russian Buk missile fired from a rebel-controlled field in eastern Ukraine,[7] in which the civilian aircraft was presumably mistaken for a Ukrainian military aircraft.
- The 1999 NATO bombing of the Chinese embassy in Belgrade, in which the US Air Force apparently mistook it for the Yugoslav Federal Directorate for Supply and Procurement due, inter alia, to reliance on an old map.[8]

[7] All 283 passengers (two-thirds of which were Dutch nationals, the remainder being Australian and Malaysian nationals) and 15 crew (all Malaysian nationals) were killed. A Dutch-led joint investigation team concluded that the airliner was downed by a Buk surface-to-air missile launched from pro-Russian separatist-controlled territory in Ukraine. On 25 May 2018, the Netherlands and Australia issued a joint statement, holding the Russian Federation responsible for the incident. See https://www.government.nl/latest/news/2018/05/25/mh17-the-netherlands-and-australia-hold-russia-responsible [accessed 1 April 2023]. Russia has denied involvement. A criminal investigation into the downing of MH17 was led by the Public Prosecution Service of the Dutch Ministry of Justice. On 19 June 2019, the Dutch Public Prosecution Service charged four people with murder in connection with the shooting down of the aircraft: three Russians and one Ukrainian. On 17 November 2022, the District Court of The Hague found three members of the Donetsk People's Republic in eastern Ukraine guilty (and acquitted another) of destruction of an aircraft and murder, and sentenced them to life imprisonment. As none of the verdicts were appealed, the judgment is now final. *Girkin et al.*, District Court of The Hague, 17 November 2022, English transcript of the judgment summary, https://www.courtmh17.com/en/news/2022/transcript-of-the-mh17-judgment-hearing.html [accessed 1 April 2023]. The court found, in relevant part, that "the firing of the missile at the target in question was intentional and involved premeditation. Given the nature of the weapon and the target at which it was fired, the consequences of firing the missile are abundantly clear: namely, causing the aircraft to crash and the death of all its occupants. The court is of the opinion that although it appears that the Buk missile was launched intentionally, this was done so in the belief that the target aircraft in question was military and not civil. In that respect, it must have been an error. Nevertheless, an error of this kind does not detract from the intent and the premeditation. It is also important to consider that due to the absence of any combatant immunity, just like any other civilian, the accused were not entitled to fire at any aircraft whatsoever, also not a military aircraft, thereby killing the military occupants. The realised criminal act of downing an aircraft and killing the occupants was therefore inherent in the original plan". In 2020, the Dutch government took Russia to the European Court of Human Rights (ECtHR) for "its role in the downing" of Flight MH17. On 30 November 2022, the Grand Chamber of the ECtHR accepted jurisdiction over the case. European Court of Human Rights, *Ukraine and the Netherlands v Russia* (2022) (Applications nos. 8019/16, 43800/14 and 28525/20), Decision, 30 November 2022. A decision on the merits will follow. The Netherlands and Australia also brought the case before the Council of the International Civil Aviation Organization (ICAO). On 18 March 2023, the ICAO Council decided that it had jurisdiction to hear the matter. A decision on the merits will follow. See Lambert, Reuters, 18 March 2023, "U.N. aviation council votes to hear MH17 case against Russia", https://www.reuters.com/world/un-aviation-council-votes-hear-mh17-case-against-russia-2023-03-17/ [accessed 1 April 2023]. A proposal to create an international tribunal to investigate the incident failed at the UN Security Council. United Nations Security Council, Draft Resolution (with Annex "Statute of the International Criminal Tribunal for Malaysia Airlines Flight MH17 (ICTMH17)", S/2015/562, 29 July 2015. United Nations Meetings Coverage, "Security Council Fails to Adopt Resolution on Tribunal for Malaysia Airlines Crash in Ukraine, Amid Calls for Accountability, Justice for Victims", 7498th Meeting (SC/11990), 29 July 2015, https://www.un.org/press/en/2015/sc11990.doc.htm [accessed 1 April 2023].

[8] Three Chinese nationals were killed. President Bill Clinton apologised for the bombing, stating it was an accident. Central Intelligence Agency (CIA) Director George Tenet testified before a congressional committee that the CIA had identified the wrong coordinates for a Yugoslav military target on the same street. It was reported that from the grainy aerial photographs that were used the

One could cite more recent examples of potential alleged war crimes perpetrated in Ukraine by Russian armed forces, in which conflicting accounts of military necessity to justify devastation of civilian infrastructure have been posited by various actors. For instance, Russian forces claimed that there was military necessity to bomb a children's hospital and maternity ward in Mariupol, Ukraine on 9 March 2022, citing the supposed presence of Ukrainian armed forces.[9] A report by the Organization for Security and Co-operation in Europe concluded that no mistake in this regard was possible. It noted that:

> A media report trying to corroborate this military use shows a photograph of a tank and armed persons in front of a building alleged to have been the maternity hospital, but this

two buildings looked very similar in terms of size, shape and height, and that the distance between them is about 200 yards (180 m). Multiple checks designed to prevent attacks on sensitive targets each failed as the location of the embassy had not been updated since the embassy moved to New Belgrade three years earlier. As a result, the bombers took to the air with the coordinates of the Chinese embassy programmed into the bombs on board. See Pickering, US Department of State, 6 July 1999, "Oral Presentation the Chinese Government Regarding the Accidental Bombing of The P.R.C. Embassy in Belgrade". According to officials interviewed by *The New York Times*, the target was checked against a "no-strike" database of locations such as hospitals, churches, and embassies, but the embassy was listed at its old address. Officials said a similar list in the UK also had the same error. However, a joint investigation by Observer/Politiken reported that a NATO flight controller in Naples said that on this "don't hit" map the Chinese embassy was listed at its correct location and that the coordinates of the Chinese embassy were correctly listed in a NATO computer. See Sweeney et al., The Guardian, 17 October 1999, "Nato bombed Chinese deliberately". https://www.theguardian.com/world/1999/oct/17/balkans [accessed 1 April 2023]. The International Criminal Tribunal for the Former Yugoslavia (ICTY) report entitled "Final Report to the Prosecutor by the Committee Established to Review the NATO Bombing Campaign Against the Federal Republic of Yugoslavia" after the Kosovo War concluded that the Office of the Prosecutor should not undertake an investigation concerning the bombing. In reaching its decision, it observed "[t]hat the root of the failures in target location appears to stem from the land navigation techniques employed by an intelligence officer in an effort to pinpoint the location of the FDSP [Federal Directorate for Supply and Procurement] building at Bulevar Umetnosti 2. The officer used techniques known as 'intersection' and 'resection' which, while appropriate to locate distant or inaccessible points or objects, are inappropriate for use in aerial targeting as they provide only an approximate location. Using this process, the individual mistakenly determined that the Chinese embassy was the FDSP headquarters". The ICTY further noted that the aircrew involved in the attack should not be assigned any responsibility for the fact they were given the wrong target and that it would be inappropriate to attempt to assign criminal responsibility for the incident to senior leaders because they were provided with wrong information by officials of another agency. See UNICTY, "Final Report to the Prosecutor by the Committee Established to Review the NATO Bombing Campaign Against the Federal Republic of Yugoslavia", paras 82–85. Amnesty International concluded that a genuinely accidental attack would not imply legal responsibility, but further noted that "the very basic information needed to prevent this mistake was publicly and widely available at the time" and that, "[i]t would appear that NATO failed to take the necessary precautions required by Article 57(2) of Protocol I". See Amnesty International 2000.

[9] Ukrayinska Pravda, 10 March 2022, "Lavrov confirms Russia deliberately bombed maternity hospital in Mariupol". https://www.pravda.com.ua/eng/news/2022/03/10/7330042/ [accessed 1 April 2023]. This account contradicted the version by the Russian Defence Ministry, that stated that the attack on the hospital was staged by the Ukrainian government. See Interfax, 10 March 2022, "Russian troops don't hit hospital in Mariupol, it's Kyiv's information provocation—Russian Defense Ministry". https://interfax.com/newsroom/top-stories/76302/ [accessed 1 April 2023].

> building does not align with any of the buildings within 1 km of the hospital when compared with satellite imagery. The shape of the building is quite unique and would be detectable from above. Likewise, a video embedded in the article depicting what appears to be a soldier with an antitank guided missile on the roof of a building does not match any buildings within 1 km of the hospital.[10]

The report concluded that the attack on a protected medical facility was deliberate, without military justification, and could amount to a war crime.

The Rendulic approach to analysing the above-mentioned events would require an assessment of what the decision-makers knew when deciding to launch these attacks, and whether those conditions were sufficient to allow an honest, albeit erroneous, conclusion that the use of force was legal. The approach involves both objective and subjective considerations. On the one side, it requires an objective test of reasonableness: were the known facts such that a reasonable decision-maker would conclude the action was justified by the exercise of judgment? On the other side, it requires a subjective test: how did the situation appear to the defendant at the time? Both considerations hinge on evidence adduced at trial that shed light on the information available to the defendant at the material time.

For Rendulic, the US Military Tribunal, basing its assessment on the evidence before it, found that he could have honestly believed that the Soviet army was about to launch a massive multi-sided offensive and that the devastation of Finnmark was militarily necessary in those circumstances. It is possible therefore that the tribunal would have found differently had evidence been presented that Rendulic had more accurate information about the Soviet plans.

This chapter analyses the link between the reasonable commander test and the mistake of fact defence. After an outline of the legal reasoning in *Hostage*, it examines the origins, purpose, and operation of the reasonable commander test in IHL. It then turns to the mistake of fact defence in ICL, focusing on its articulation under the Rome Statute of the International Criminal Court (ICC).

It is often stated that the mistake of fact need only be honest using a purely subjective test—to successfully absolve responsibility under ICL.[11] The analysis in this chapter supports the contrary view that in cases where the reasonable commander test is applicable, mistake of fact will only provide a defence where the mistake is both honest and reasonable. On a policy level, this interpretation best comports with IHL's objective to protect the victims of armed conflict. To hold otherwise would lead to a dilution of the precautionary rules set out in IHL,[12] removing a key incentive

---

[10] OSCE 2022, p 47 (internal footnotes omitted).

[11] See, e.g., Milanovic 2020: "[with respect to crimes with a specific mental element with regard to certain conduct] The standard is purely subjective; there is no requirement that the belief be both honest and reasonable. An objective lack of reasonableness might, however, make it more likely for the court to conclude on the facts that the purported subjective belief was not actually honestly held—but this is then simply an evidentiary inference". See also Heller 2011, p 375 ("[t]he Rome Statute's reliance on a subjective mens rea for the war crime of 'excessive incidental death, injury, or damage', [...] reflects the Hostage tribunal's problematic acquittal of Lothar Rendulic"); Schabas 2016, p 657.

[12] See Article 57, Protocol Additional to the Geneva Conventions of 12 August 1949, and Relating to the Protection of Victims of International Armed Conflicts of 8 June 1977, 1125 UNTS 3 (hereafter,

for commanders to ensure they have done everything feasible to check the accuracy of the information on which they base their decisions to attack.

8.2 *Hostage* Case

Chapter 6 of this volume provides a detailed outline of the *Hostage* case and the way that the tribunal dealt with the Finnmark charge. It suggests that the tribunal gave Rendulic quite some latitude in the case he set out in his defence. At trial, Rendulic testified that on 3 September 1944, Finland, which had been occupied by Germany since 1940, signed a peace agreement with the Soviet Union and demanded that German troops withdraw from Finland in 14 days—a demand impossible to comply with.[13] The tribunal accepted that Rendulic knew that the Soviets had ships that could use landings behind German lines as well as access to land routes. According to the tribunal, he had very little information about the Soviets' intentions, especially as air reconnaissance was almost impossible due to the short autumn days. The tribunal found that what the Germans anticipated was a huge Soviet breakthrough into Norway. So, the German Army, commanded by Rendulic, decided on a scorched-earth retreat. It was October 1944, and with no shelter, food or supplies, the plan was for the Red Army to starve and freeze to death. The Germans removed the population from Finnmark. There was no evidence in the trial about any loss of life directly due to the evacuation. However, towns were burned, roads were wiped from the map, telegraph poles were chopped down and communication lines destroyed. The harbours lay ravaged, mines were laid in the towns, and the entire population of the surrounding municipality were left homeless. 10,000 buildings in one town—Hammerfest—were razed to the ground. When the war was over, more than 70,000 people were left homeless in Finnmark. In the end, the Soviets did not follow up the retreat to the extent anticipated.

Rendulic was charged with "the commission of acts of devastation not warranted by military necessity in Norway by troops of the German Armed Forces acting at the direction and order of the defendant; and ordering troops to burn, level and destroy entire villages and towns [...] without any recognized military necessity for so doing".[14] The basis for this crime was Article 23(g) of the 1907 Hague Regulations, which provides that: "[...] it is especially forbidden [t]o destroy or seize the

"Additional Protocol I") which has been identified as a customary rule of IHL (Rule 15 Henckaerts and Doswald-Beck 2005 (hereafter "ICRC Customary Law Study").

[13] Rendulic trial transcript, p 5332. Rendulic's depiction of events is not entirely accurate, however. As described in Chap. 3, a Soviet-Finnish cease-fire went into effect on 4 or 5 September and was formalised with the armistice agreement of 19 September 1944. According to the agreements, Finnish, not Soviet troops should expel the Germans from Finnish territory. This suggests that Soviet troops should not operate or be stationed in Finland.

[14] Office of Military Government for Germany (US), "Indictment" (1947). Trial 7—*Hostage* Case. 1, https://digitalcommons.law.uga.edu/nmt7/1 [accessed 1 April 2023], p 9.

enemy's property, unless such destruction or seizure be imperatively demanded by the necessities of war".[15]

In *Hostage*, the US Military Tribunal found that the prohibitions of Article 23(g) of the Hague Regulations "contained control and are superior to military necessities of the most urgent nature except where the Regulations themselves specifically provide the contrary".[16] The tribunal found that the destruction of public and private property by retreating military forces, which would give aid and comfort to the enemy, might constitute a situation falling within the exceptions of Article 23(g).[17] The tribunal noted that, while the Soviets did not follow up the retreat to the extent anticipated, there were physical evidences that they were expected to do so, citing gun emplacements, fox-holes, and other defence installations perceptible in the territory.[18] In other words, "there are mute evidences that an attack was anticipated".[19] The tribunal further noted evidence in the record that there was no military necessity for this destruction and devastation. However, while "[a]n examination of the facts in retrospect can well sustain this conclusion [...] we are obliged to judge the situation as it appeared to the defendant at the time".[20]

The tribunal concluded that:

> If the facts were such as would justify the action by the exercise of judgment, after giving consideration to all the factors and existing possibilities, even though the conclusion reached may have been faulty, it cannot be said to be criminal. After giving careful consideration to all the evidence on the subject, we are convinced that the defendant cannot be held criminally responsible although when viewed in retrospect, the danger did not actually exist.[21]

The tribunal further held that:

> We are not called upon to determine whether urgent military necessity for the devastation and destruction in the province of Finmark [*sic*] *actually existed*. We are concerned with the question whether the defendant at the time of its occurrence acted within the limits of honest judgment on the basis of the conditions prevailing at the time. The course of a military operation by the enemy is loaded with uncertainties, such as the numerical strength of the enemy, the quality of his equipment, his fighting spirit, the efficiency and daring of his commanders, and the uncertainty of his intentions. These things when considered with his own military situation provided the facts or want thereof which furnished the basis for the defendant's decision to carry out the 'scorched earth' policy in Finmark [*sic*] as a precautionary measure against an attack by superior forces. It is our considered opinion that *the conditions, as they appeared to the defendant at the time were sufficient upon which he could honestly conclude that urgent military necessity warranted the decision made.* This

[15] Convention (IV) respecting the Laws and Customs of War on Land and its annex: Regulations concerning the Laws and Customs of War on Land. The Hague, 18 October 1907, USTS 539 (hereafter "Hague Regulations").

[16] *Hostage* Case, p 69.

[17] Ibid.

[18] *Hostage* Case, p 68.

[19] Ibid.

[20] Ibid.

[21] Ibid., pp 68–69.

> being true, the defendant may have erred in the exercise of his judgment but he was guilty of no criminal act. We find the defendant not guilty on this portion of the charge.[22]

The *Hostage* judgment stated in effect that the plea of mistake of fact could, in suitable cases, be successfully pleaded in conjunction with the plea of military necessity. The tribunal pointed out that the offensive feared by Rendulic did not materialise. Nonetheless, it was obliged to judge the situation as it appeared to the defendant at the time. From that perspective, the tribunal assessed that when Rendulic ordered the destruction of Finnmark, he acted within the limits of honest judgment based on the conditions prevailing at the time.

A similar finding was made by the same tribunal in the *High Command* case, where it also dealt with the charge of wanton destruction that it referred to as "spoliation".[23] In the *Hostage* case, the tribunal had found that "[m]ilitary necessity or expediency do not justify a violation of positive rules [...]. The rules of international law must be followed even if it results in the loss of a battle or even a war".[24] In *High Command*, the tribunal considered that the contrary view "would eliminate all humanity and decency and all law from the conduct of war and it is a contention which this Tribunal repudiates as contrary to the accepted usages of civilized nations".[25] The tribunal nonetheless noted that:

> The devastation prohibited by the Hague Rules and the usages of war is that not warranted by military necessity. This rule is clear enough but the factual determination as to what constitutes military necessity is difficult. The defendants in this case were in many instances in retreat under arduous conditions wherein their commands were in serious danger of being cut off. Under such circumstances, a commander must necessarily make quick decisions to meet the particular situation of his command. A great deal of latitude must be accorded to him under such circumstances. What constitutes devastation beyond military necessity in these situations requires detailed proof of an operational and tactical nature. We do not feel that in this case the proof is ample to establish the guilt of any defendant herein on this charge.[26]

While *High Command* did not deal with mistake of fact in conjunction with military necessity, it underlines some of the core aspects of the reasonable commander test, analysed in the next part, as well as the need for "detailed proof of an operational and tactical nature" to show intention behind acts of devastation.

The *Hostage* tribunal's consideration of the core issue of what Rendulic knew about the Soviets' movements (and therefore whether he honestly thought there was military necessity) is rather oblique. The tribunal did not discuss the merit of the prosecution's submissions or supporting evidence, so it is difficult to assess if

---

[22] Ibid., p 69 (emphases added).

[23] US Military Tribunal, Nuremberg, Case No. 72, *The German High Command Trial: Trial of Wilhelm von Leeb and thirteen others*, Judgment of 27 October 1948, in: Trials of War Criminals Before the Nuremberg Military Tribunals, Vol. IX (hereafter "High Command Case").

[24] *Hostage* Case, p 67.

[25] *High Command* Case, p 540.

[26] Ibid.

the judges considered them credible or not.[27] Nor did the tribunal overtly consider the testimony of General Ferdinand Jodl, one of the corps commanders in the 20th Mountain Army, who testified that the order to evacuate Finnmark and to apply the scorched earth policy was so plainly unnecessary from the point of view of military necessity that if he were given the order to do it again, he would resign his commission before carrying it out.[28] Alfred Jodl, Ferdinand Jodl's older brother who was chief of the Operations Staff of the German Armed Forces High Command, was in fact convicted by the International Military Tribunal (IMT) at Nuremberg for exactly the same conduct in Norway for which Rendulic was acquitted by the US Military Tribunal. The IMT's judgment is cursory on this matter and does not discuss the military necessity exception or mistake of fact. This did not prevent the International Criminal Tribunal for the Former Yugoslavia (ICTY)'s *Orić* Trial Judgment relying on the ruling by the IMT against Alfred Jodl for the view that "the principle must be upheld that the destruction of civil settlements, as a rule, is punishable as a war crime". The ICTY noted that "[a] policy of 'scorched earth', i.e., the destruction of any facilities that might be useful to the enemy while withdrawing from an area, was not recognised at the Nuremberg Tribunal to be justified by military necessity".[29] The ICTY did not make mention of the contrary holding of the US Military Tribunal in *Hostage*.

In *Hostage*, the prosecution also argued that military necessity could only have justified the destruction of roads and communications but that—despite there being only one highway which ran from north to south—Rendulic's order went far beyond this to destroy "every dwelling place, barn and other evidence of civilization" throughout an area 40 miles on either side of the highway. Moreover, this destruction, which began in October 1944, continued until the German surrender to the Allies on 8 May 1945. The prosecution characterised this devastation as "completely unjustifiable", "futile, vicious and unreasonable".[30]

According to Rendulic's own order, the evacuation should be carried out "in the sense of a relief action for the Norwegian population. Though it will be necessary here and there to be severe all of us must attempt to save the Norwegians from

[27] The historical analysis of events, as described in Chaps. 3 and 4, suggests that the prosecution's submissions, for instance, that by the time Rendulic issued his devastation order on 28 October 1944, "none of his troops had seen a Russian for more than a week", was not in fact accurate. See Rendulic trial transcript, p 9662. In fact, fighting with the Soviet forces continued until early November 1944.

[28] Rendulic trial transcript, p 9663.

[29] ICTY, *Prosecutor v Naser Orić*, IT-03-68-T, 30 June 2006, p 207 n.1581. The relevant passage of the IMT ruling reads as follows (International Military Tribunal, *France and ors v Göring (Hermann) and ors*, Judgment and Sentence, [1946] 22 IMT 203; Law Reports of Trials of Major War Criminals, Vol. XXII, 1949, p 517): "By teletype of 28 October 1944, Jodl ordered the evacuation of all persons in northern Norway and the burning of their houses so they could not help the Russians. Jodl says he was against this, but Hitler ordered it and it was not fully carried out. A document of the Norwegian Government says such an evacuation did take place in northern Norway and 30,000 houses were damaged".

[30] Rendulic trial transcript, p 9664.

Bolshevism and to keep them alive".[31] (One cannot help but note the resemblance to current day Russian President Putin's proclaimed reasons for the armed invasion of Ukraine in 2022, the purpose of which is officially "to protect people who, for eight years now, have been facing humiliation and genocide perpetrated by the Kiev regime. To this end, we will seek to demilitarise and denazify Ukraine".[32])

Contrarily, Major-General Arne Dahl of the Norwegian Army testified that "it was not the Russian intention to follow the German forces". In his view, the destruction was wanton and motivated by a desire for revenge.[33] Dahl's testimony is corroborated by Ferdinand Jodl's, who testified that at the relevant time in late October 1944 he did not "believe that the Russians will proceed to the West and will cross the Tana". Jodl stated that the Germans knew for certain that the bulk of the Soviet units had been transported to the east and, had the Soviets wanted to pursue the Germans, they would have been acting differently. He testified that when he shared this opinion with General Hermann Hölter, he answered: "The A.O.K. [Army Higher Command] is roughly of the same opinion as you but just now the order [from Hitler] […] has arrived, according to which destruction has to be carried out[…] and nothing can be done now".[34] According to Jodl, "[d]uring the last days of October, in any case, there was no indication whatsoever that the Russians should keep on pursuing us across the Tana River to the west, or that he [*sic*] intended to do so". Further, as time went on, "everyday showed more and more that the Russians were for the time being not advancing with stronger forces". By mid-November 1944, it was "quite evident" that the Soviets would not proceed. And yet the destruction proceeded. While Jodl expressed the view that the destruction would have been militarily necessary had the Soviets advanced, he described the destruction and evacuation as "a highly unpleasant and awkward matter" in view of the absence of any Soviet advance. Jodl testified that due to its lack of justification, "[t]his destruction of the North of Finnmark was one of the hardest tasks I had ever been given throughout the war".[35]

Rendulic, for his part, testified that he had become convinced that the Soviets would not push up on the land route via Northern Finnmark towards the latter part of November 1944. He stated that reconnaissance was not possible in mid-November as the airbases had all been transferred further south, combined with the short amount of daylight each day. Taking into account the great distance for a flight, he claimed that it was not possible to reconnoitre the movements thoroughly. Rendulic said that he became certain that the Soviet Union had withdrawn forces only towards the beginning of December 1944, having received a communication from the Army Group North that was stationed near the East Prussian frontier. Rendulic further testified that "everything we did was dictated by the needs of the enemy. That was

[31] Ibid., p 2557.

[32] Address by the President of the Russian Federation, 24 February 2022. http://en.kremlin.ru/events/president/news/67843 [accessed 1 April 2023].

[33] Rendulic trial transcript, p 2668.

[34] Ibid., p 2579.

[35] Ibid., p 2586.

its necessity".[36] Rendulic did not, however, agree with the necessity of evacuation but testified that it was "quite impossible not to obey this evacuation order" and that he managed to convince himself that "it was the best thing for the population that they were removed".[37]

The verdict on Rendulic's acquittal on this charge brought indignation in Norway in early 1948. Norwegian parliamentary debates contested the acquittal on the basis that, while Rendulic's initial devastation of Eastern Finnmark might have been excusable on grounds of military necessity, this excuse "wore thinner in proportion as the months passed, the German withdrawal continued, and still the Russians did not appear".[38] The obligation of commanders to suspend or cancel an attack when it becomes apparent that it is no longer justified or proportionate was codified in 1977 with Article 57(2)(b) Additional Protocol I (API). However, even in 1944, as a matter of law, military necessity no longer excused the devastation once Rendulic knew the Soviets were not in hot pursuit. By Rendulic's own admission, this was by the beginning of December 1944, yet the destruction continued for another five months. The Norwegian parliamentarians also noted that the plans for devastation had been laid well beforehand, which put in doubt Rendulic's claim of acting under pressure. Further, the ruthless and extreme totality of destruction were in line with German policy and similar measures were taken in Finnish Lapland in late 1944,[39] which suggested to them that "Rendulic was methodically executing in daylight a preplanned policy of vindictive desertification".[40] The Norwegians tried but failed to get a rehearing of the case against Rendulic, a retrial in Norway or an appeal before the US Military Tribunal. According to Best's reading of the legacy of the case, Rendulic was "metamorphosed into the patron saint of commanders who plead ignorance or error for doing more 'incidental' harm to civilians than others may think necessary".[41] For Best, the Norwegians' arguments make the Rendulic Rule "a shaky pillar to lean on".[42]

A review of the evidence in the case on the question of Rendulic's knowledge of Soviet movements indicates that the tribunal was faced with competing considerations, at least as far as the situation from the end of October to mid-November 1944 was concerned. While a lot of deductions about what Rendulic knew can be made from the situation at the time, there did not appear to be conclusive proof at trial that Rendulic knew that the Soviets were not advancing and would not advance further with sufficient troops, at least in the initial period. This raises the question on the one hand of the quality of evidence adduced at the trial,[43] and on the other hand whether Rendulic's own assumptions about the situation—based as he himself

[36] Ibid., p 5345.

[37] Ibid., p 5346.

[38] Best 1994, p 329. See also Chap. 5.

[39] For a historical analysis of the broader regional strategic context, see Chaps. 2 and 5.

[40] Best 1994, p 330.

[41] Ibid., p 330.

[42] Ibid.

[43] See Chap. 5.

stated on a lack of proper intelligence—were within the limits of honest judgment. As argued in the following section, both objective and subjective elements must be considered to assess whether Rendulic's judgment was reasonable and done in good faith or, alternatively, whether his plea of military necessity was merely a cover for the decision to carry through Hitler's order regardless of its necessity due to the changed situation on the ground.

8.3 Reasonable Commander Test

In setting out the test of "whether the defendant at the time of its occurrence acted within the limits of honest judgment on the basis of the conditions prevailing at the time", the *Hostage* judgment essentially applied to the issue of military necessity what is known in contemporary parlance as the "reasonable commander" test. This test is a tool to assess if the standards set out in IHL requiring the exercise of judgment by a commander in a specific situation were met. The reasonable commander test has been commonly applied to assess decisions on proportionality.[44] This assessment entails, according to Yoram Dinstein, "a mental process of pondering dissimilar considerations—to wit, civilian losses/damage and military advantage—and is not an exact science". This means that "[t]here is no objective possibility of quantifying the factors of the equation, and the process necessarily contains a large subjective element".[45] In other words, the test has both objective and subjective elements.

There is no mention of the reasonable commander test in IHL treaties or in the Rome Statute. The term—while grounded in the rules of IHL—finds its genesis in the final report to the ICTY Prosecutor by a committee established to review the NATO bombing campaign against the Federal Republic of Yugoslavia in its discussion of what standard should apply to assessing proportionality.[46] The committee contended that:

> the determination of relative values must be that of the 'reasonable military commander'. Although there will be room for argument in close cases, there will be many cases where reasonable military commanders will agree that the injury to noncombatants or the damage to civilian objects was clearly disproportionate to the military advantage gained.[47]

Interestingly, the committee's final report explicitly references the Rendulic Rule in discussing the allegation of environment harm, noting:

[44] The principle of proportionality, codified in Additional Protocol I, prohibits attacks that "may be expected to cause incidental loss of civilian life, injury to civilians, damage to civilian objects, or a combination thereof, which would be excessive in relation to the concrete and direct military advantage anticipated". See Articles 51(5)(b), 57(2)(a)(iii), 57(2)(b).

[45] Dinstein 2010, para 326.

[46] Final Report to the Prosecutor by the Committee Established to Review the NATO Bombing Campaign Against the Federal Republic of Yugoslavia, https://www.icty.org/en/press/final-report-prosecutor-committee-established-review-nato-bombing-campaign-against-federal [accessed 1 April 2023] (hereafter "ICTY Final Report").

[47] ICTY Final Report, para 50.

> the requisite *mens rea* on the part of the commander would be actual or constructive knowledge as to the grave environmental effects of a military attack; a standard which would be difficult to establish for the purposes of prosecution and which may provide an insufficient basis to prosecute military commanders inflicting environmental harm in the (mistaken) belief that such conduct was warranted by military necessity. (In the Hostages case before the Nuremberg Military Tribunals, for instance, the German General Rendulic was acquitted of the charge of wanton devastation on the grounds that although Rendulic may have erred in believing that there was military necessity for the widespread environmental destruction entailed by his use of a 'scorched earth' policy in the Norwegian province of Finnmark, he was not guilty of a criminal act…).[48]

The committee seemed to conclude on the basis of the Rendulic precedent that it would be too onerous to prove the knowledge of the commander for the charge of environment harm.[49] This is somewhat different to the assessment made by the US Military Tribunal in *Hostage*, which accepted that Rendulic knew the extent of the harm caused by the scorched earth retreat but found that Rendulic honestly believed the military necessity exception applied because he mistakenly thought the Soviet Union would attack. The committee instead emphasised the difficulty of applying a reasonableness standard to proving that a commander knows the extent of harm which might be caused by a particular attack. This seems to conflate evidentiary issues related to knowledge with the legal standard.

The reasonable commander test is apt in cases involving the military necessity exception since the principles of necessity and proportionality are deeply connected. It has been posited that the proportionality rule may be "deduced from the general principle of military necessity provided by customary law".[50] Others have argued that "the law of armed conflict obliges those who plan or decide on an attack to adopt an integrated approach" which takes both necessity and proportionality into account.[51] Moreover, the crime of wanton destruction of property not justified by military necessity, with which Rendulic was charged, involves a consideration of proportionality. In this case, the principle of proportionality dictates the limits on the legality of an attack on, or the seizure of, enemy property, and when it is not imperatively militarily necessary, it is considered excessive. Frits Kalshoven has explained the link between proportionality and military necessity in the context of Article 23(g) of the Hague Regulations in the following way:

---

[48] Ibid., para 23.

[49] The committee noted that "[i]n order to fully evaluate such matters, it would be necessary to know the extent of the knowledge possessed by NATO as to the nature of Serbian military-industrial targets (and thus, the likelihood of environmental damage flowing from their destruction), the extent to which NATO could reasonably have anticipated such environmental damage (for instance, could NATO have reasonably expected that toxic chemicals of the sort allegedly released into the environment by the bombing campaign would be stored alongside that military target?) and whether NATO could reasonably have resorted to other (and less environmentally damaging) methods for achieving its military objective of disabling the Serbian military-industrial infrastructure […]. It is therefore the opinion of the committee, based on information currently available to it, that the [Office of the Prosecutor] should not commence an investigation into the collateral environmental damage caused by the NATO bombing campaign". Ibid., paras 23–25.

[50] Oeter 2020, p 358.

[51] Heintschel von Heinegg 2020, p 325.

> the military necessity of pursuing the attack will not in all cases outweigh the combined import of the other values at stake. The cut-off line beyond which the collateral damage is no longer regarded as acceptable may be found with the aid of the principle of proportionality…[this] was implicit in the Hague Regulations of 1899/1907. Reflecting the first step [identifying the military necessity of the attack], Article 23(g) states that it is forbidden 'to destroy or seize the enemy's property, unless such destruction or seizure be imperatively demanded by the necessities of war.' Logically, one may add, it is not just 'unless' but 'to the extent' that the destruction or seizure is so demanded.[52]

Some observers have interpreted the Rendulic Rule as establishing that "whenever a commander is invested with the power to make a judgment, or put another way, is granted a measure of discretion, his decision should be assessed in light of the information available to him at the time".[53] However, applying the rule to contemporary situations must take into account developments in IHL since the issuance of the *Hostage* judgment in 1948. The IHL rule on precautionary measures, codified in Article 57 of API in 1977 and since identified as a customary law rule, demands more of commanders than to simply rely on information they happen to have at hand.[54] The International Committee of the Red Cross (ICRC) Commentary on Article 57 makes clear that this provision was drafted to respond to the history of the Second World War—no doubt including the campaign in Finnmark and Troms counties—and subsequent conflicts which "contains numerous cases of attacks which were launched in error against non-military objectives, or against objectives whose destruction produced only an insufficient military advantage compared with the losses inflicted on civilians".[55]

The ICRC Commentary—written ten years after *Hostage*—specifies that, consistent with the Rendulic Rule, "those who plan or decide upon such an attack will base their decision on information given them, and they cannot be expected to have

[52] Kalshoven 1992, p 41.

[53] Bill 2009, p 137.

[54] Article 57 of Additional Protocol I, which has been identified as a customary rule of IHL (Rule 15 of the ICRC Customary Law Study) provides, in relevant part: "1. In the conduct of military operations, constant care shall be taken to spare the civilian population, civilians and civilian objects. 2. With respect to attacks, the following precautions shall be taken: (a) those who plan or decide upon an attack shall: (i) do everything feasible to verify that the objectives to be attacked are neither civilians nor civilian objects and are not subject to special protection but are military objectives within the meaning of paragraph 2 of Article 52 and that it is not prohibited by the provisions of this Protocol to attack them; (ii) take all feasible precautions in the choice of means and methods of attack with a view to avoiding, and in any event to minimizing, incidental loss of civilian life, injury to civilians and damage to civilian objects; (iii) refrain from deciding to launch any attack which may be expected to cause incidental loss of civilian life, injury to civilians, damage to civilian objects, or a combination thereof, which would be excessive in relation to the concrete and direct military advantage anticipated; (b) an attack shall be cancelled or suspended if it becomes apparent that the objective is not a military one or is subject to special protection or that the attack may be expected to cause incidental loss of civilian life, injury to civilians, damage to civilian objects, or a combination thereof, which would be excessive in relation to the concrete and direct military advantage anticipated […]". While Article 85 of API makes failure to comply with Article 57 a grave breach, this is not included in the war crimes list of the Rome Statute of the International Criminal Court UNTS 2187, p 3 (hereinafter "Rome Statute").

[55] Sandoz et al. 1986, paras 2193–2194.

personal knowledge of the objective to be attacked and of its exact nature". However, the Commentary goes on to clarify that

> *this does not detract from their responsibility, and in case of doubt, even if there is only slight doubt, they must call for additional information and if need be give orders for further reconnaissance* to those of their subordinates and those responsible for supportive weapons (particularly artillery and airforce) whose business this is, and who are answerable to them. In the case of long-distance attacks, information will be obtained in particular from aerial reconnaissance and from intelligence units, which will of course attempt to gather information about enemy military objectives by various means. *The evaluation of the information obtained must include a serious check of its accuracy.*[56]

Further, "[e]ven if this system is based to some extent on a subjective evaluation, the interpretation must above all be a question *of common sense and good faith* for military commanders".[57]

Kalshoven has similarly observed that such rules mean that

> the attacker [...] cannot simply turn a blind eye on the facts of the situation; on the contrary, he is obliged to take into account all available information. Negligence in this respect makes him responsible [...] these rules apply on all levels of military action and at all stages of the planning and execution of attacks.[58]

Furthermore,

> this clause in Article 57 [...] may perhaps best be seen as an appeal to the good faith of the normal, responsible military man or woman. For those who fail to meet this standard of responsible behaviour, there are always the references to 'indiscriminate attack' in Article 51 and to Article 85, which makes this a 'grave breach'.[59]

Other commentators have noted that "[t]his requirement [in Article 57(2) API] of doing everything feasible underlies the Rendulic Rule. Once a commander has done everything feasible to gather information and learn those specific circumstances of the object of this attack, he can rely on those facts in taking action".[60] Hampson has characterised Articles 51(5)(b) and 57(a)(iii) and (b) of API as codifying the Rendulic Rule.[61] According to Bill, "[the Rendulic Rule] is applicable in any case where the commander is invested with judgment or granted discretion".[62] A contemporary application of the Rendulic Rule as part of the reasonable commander test, taking into account IHL rules, therefore must assess both objective (good faith) and subjective (information known) elements.

Perceptively, Bill observes that "[t]he ultimate impact of the Rendulic Rule [...] is in the post hoc decision to assign responsibility to an individual for a decision that

---

[56] Ibid., para 2195 (emphasis added).

[57] Ibid., para 2208 (emphasis added).

[58] Kalshoven 1992, p 44.

[59] Ibid., p 44. He further notes that "the greater the military advantage anticipated, or in other words, the more imperative the elimination of the target, the greater will be the level of collateral damage that need not be regarded as excessive".

[60] Jensen 2003, p 1183.

[61] Hampson 1992, p 46.

[62] Bill 2009, p 138.

in hindsight turn out to be wrong". In his view, "[t]he rule reflects a reluctance to characterize as a crime conduct for which the individual acted in substantive *good faith*. In the context of war crimes, a similar sentiment is evident in the positive conventional law that emerged after Rendulic".[63] As Bill puts it, since the exception for military necessity is explicitly included in the definition of the war crime of destruction of property ("unlawfully and wantonly"), "[m]aking an incorrect judgment with the intelligence on hand is not a grave breach; knowing that the attack is disproportionate, and launching it anyway, is".[64] It is further argued here that, in view of the requirements of Article 57 of API, failing to check the accuracy of the intelligence on the basis of which an incorrect judgment is made may render the commander's mistake of fact unreasonable and made in bad faith.

The argument that there should also be an objective reasonableness test in assessing crimes involving the military necessity exception is supported by the work of GIAD Draper, who himself was a former military prosecutor for the UK Military Tribunals in Nuremberg. In his commentary on Article 53 of the Fourth Geneva Convention, which prohibits the destruction of public or private property by an Occupying Power, "except where [...] rendered absolutely necessary by military operations", Draper argued that "[t]his is a matter of *objective determination* and is not decided by the opinion of the military commander at the time of the destruction".[65] Draper concluded that the "decisions of US Military Tribunals in such cases as the High Command Trial [...] and Wilhelm List and others [*Hostage*] [...] indicating that the subjective view of the commander is decisive, cannot, it is thought, be supported [...]".[66]

The ICRC Commentary on Article 53 of the Fourth Geneva Convention puts it somewhat differently, stating that "it will be for the Occupying Power to judge the importance of such military requirements" but emphasising that

> *bad faith* in the application of the reservation may render the proposed safeguard valueless; for unscrupulous recourse to the clause concerning military necessity would allow the Occupying Power to circumvent the prohibition set forth in the Convention. The Occupying Power must therefore try to interpret the clause in a *reasonable* manner: whenever it is felt essential to resort to destruction, the occupying authorities must try to keep a sense of proportion in comparing the military advantages to be gained with the damage done.[67]

While the ICRC Commentary varies from Draper's on this point, it nonetheless follows that, in order to judge *post hoc* whether a commander has acted in good faith and in a reasonable manner, an objective standard needs to be employed together with the subjective analysis.

Both Article 51(5)(b) and Article 57(2)(b) of API have in common that they do not depend upon the "actual outcome of the attack but [on] the initial expectation and

---

[63] Ibid., pp 144–145. Emphasis added.

[64] Ibid., p 146.

[65] Draper 1958, p 41. Emphasis added.

[66] Ibid., p 42. He further cites in support of his view the judgment of the IMT in relation to Jodl: Cmd 6964 (1946), p 118.

[67] Pictet 1952–60, p 302. Emphasis added.

anticipation".[68] There is no "hindsight rule".[69] Accordingly, there is an expectation of excessive collateral damage only if "a reasonably well-informed person in the actual circumstances [...], making reasonable use of the information available to him or her, could have expected excessive civilian casualties to result from the attack".[70] As stated in the Declaration of the United Kingdom to API, "military commanders and others responsible for planning, deciding upon, or executing attacks necessarily have to reach decisions on the basis of their assessment of the information from all sources which is reasonably available to them at the relevant time".[71]

This reasonableness standard has been applied in war crimes cases. In *Galić*, the ICTY Trial Chamber held that

> [i]n determining whether an attack was proportionate it is necessary to examine whether a reasonably well-informed person in the circumstances of the actual perpetrator, making reasonable use of the information available to him or her, could have expected excessive civilian casualties to result from the attack.[72]

At the national level, in the *Beit Sourik Village Council v The Government of Israel* case before the Supreme Court of Israel, which concerned whether the building of a security wall in the West Bank was proportionate in respect of its effects on the civilian population, President Barak noted that "[a]ll we can determine is whether a reasonable military commander would have set out the route as this military commander did".[73] Or, as put by another judge, "we examine the question whether, in light of all of the facts, the employment of the means can be viewed as reasonable".[74] Similarly, in *Public Committee against Torture in Israel v Government of Israel*, which concerned the policy of targeted killings of alleged terrorists, the court asked itself

> whether a reasonable military commander would have made the decision that was actually made [...] It is true that 'military considerations' and 'state security' are not magic words that prevent judicial scrutiny. But the question is not what I would have decided in the given circumstances, but whether the decision that the military commander made is a decision that a reasonable military commander was entitled to make.[75]

---

[68] Dinstein 2010, p 326.

[69] Heintschel von Heinegg 2020, p 335, citing Germany Declaration, Australia Declaration, Belgium Declaration, Canada Declaration; Italy Declaration; Netherlands Declaration; New Zealand Declaration; Spain Declaration.

[70] Dinstein 2010, p 327.

[71] Declarations and Reservations of the UK Regarding Additional Protocol I to the Geneva Conventions, Treaties, State Parties And Commentaries, https://ihl-databases.icrc.org/applic/ihl/ihl.nsf/Notification.xsp?action=openDocument&documentId=0A9E03F0F2EE757CC1256402003FB6D2 [accessed 1 April 2023].

[72] ICTY, *Prosecutor v Stanislav Galić*, Case No. IT-98-29-T, Judgement and Opinion, 5 December 2003, para 58.

[73] Israel Supreme Court, *Beit Sourik Village Council v The Government of Israel et al.*, HCJ 2056/04, 20 June 2004, para 46.

[74] Ibid.

[75] Israel Supreme Court, *The Public Committee against Torture in Israel et al. v The Government of Israel et al.*, 14 December 2006, para 57.

The US Military Tribunal's articulation of the Rendulic Rule in *Hostage* reflects the reasonable military commander test. When the tribunal referred to its obligation to judge the situation as it appeared to the defendant at the time, this is very much akin to the "circumstances of the actual perpetrator", both in terms of the position and status of the commander, and the information that was available to him. When the tribunal examined whether the defendant acted within the limits of honest judgment based on the conditions prevailing at the time, and whether the facts would justify the action by the exercise of judgment, this is another way of asking if he made reasonable use of the information reasonably available to him. When the tribunal found that the conditions, as they appeared to the defendant at the time, were sufficient upon which he could honestly conclude that urgent military necessity warranted the decision made, the tribunal was essentially finding that Rendulic could have expected that the military advantage of the devastation of Finnmark would not be excessive in relation to the damage to civilian objects. Seen from this perspective, there is clearly an objective reasonableness standard that applies in conjunction with a subjective assessment in cases where commanders exercise judgment. As examined below, this objective standard logically forms part of the operation of the mistake of fact defence.

8.4 Mistake of Fact Defence

In a mistake of fact defence, an accused is not criminally responsible since he or she did not have the intent to commit a crime because he or she was under a mistaken belief about a particular fact. The defence is aimed at demonstrating the lack of the criminal mind,[76] or the *mens rea*, which is a requirement of a crime.[77]

There is no uniform practice at the national level, and a variety of approaches are used. Common law jurisdictions base the mistake of fact defence on lack of *mens rea*, while civil lawyers tend to base it on lack of culpability.[78] Since the lack of culpability has a wider scope than the lack of *mens rea*, the mistake of fact defence has a wider application. Most civil law systems adopt an objective test for this defence by applying the requirements of reasonableness.[79] In several common law jurisdictions, a mistake of fact also operates as a defence only when it is reasonable.[80] Furthermore,

---

[76] UK House of Lords, *Haughton v Smith* (1975) AC 476, at 491 f.): "An act does not make a person guilty of a crime, unless the person's mind be also guilty".

[77] Woodruff 1959, p 319.

[78] Van Sliedregt 2012, p 326.

[79] Ibid., p 280.

[80] See, e.g., Commonwealth Criminal Code 1995 (Australia), Part 2.3, Division 9.1, para 2 ("In determining whether a person was under a mistaken belief about, or was ignorant of, facts, the tribunal of fact may consider whether the mistaken belief or ignorance was reasonable in the circumstances"); Cornell Law School, Legal Information Institute ("In criminal law, a mistake of fact can usually operate as a defense so long as it is reasonable"); Justia ("Mistakes of fact arise when a criminal defendant misunderstood some fact that negates an element of the crime. [...] One important qualification, however, is that this mistake of fact must be honest and reasonable").

it is often the case that the want of knowledge must not be the result of carelessness or negligence.[81]

An instructive example at the domestic level where the legislature decided to impose a condition of reasonable belief is the Sexual Offences Act 2003 (UK), which provides that a person (A) will be guilty of an offence if B does not consent to engage in sexual activity and A does not reasonably believe that B consents.[82] This legislation was passed in response to the House of Lords judgment in *Morgan*.[83] The facts of the case involved the violent gang rape of the wife of one of four assailants. All three men[84] pleaded that they honestly believed that the victim had consented. The House of Lords held that mistaken belief that the victim was consenting would provide a complete defence; the basis for that belief did not need to be objectively reasonable, so long as the jury were satisfied that the defendant honestly believed it.[85] Although the men were ultimately convicted, the decision prompted widespread anger, with critics pointing out that, in most other areas of English criminal law, mistaken belief must be held on a reasonable basis to found a defence.[86] Under the Sexual Offences Act, the test of reasonable belief is a subjective test with an objective element. Two questions are asked to establish if the test is met:

- Did the suspect genuinely believe the complainant consented (the subjective element of the test)?
- If so, did the suspect reasonably believe it (the objective element)?[87]

Deciding whether a belief is reasonable is to be determined having regard to all the circumstances, including any steps A has taken to ascertain whether B consents. Although rape is a different type of criminal offence from conduct-of-hostilities war crimes, the framework of analysis established by the Sexual Offences Act is remarkably similar to the reasonable commander test outlined in the previous section. In both scenarios, there is: (1) the subjective element of personal belief of the accused;

[81] See, e.g., United States Alabama Supreme Court, *Gordon v State*, 52 Ala. 308, 23 Am. Rep. 575 (1875) ("The criminal intent being of the essence of crime, if the intent is dependent on knowledge of particular facts, a want of such knowledge, not the result of carelessness or negligence, relieves the act of criminality").

[82] Sexual Offenses Act 2003 (UK), Sections 1–4, https://www.cps.gov.uk/legal-guidance/rape-and-sexual-offences-chapter-6-consent [accessed 1 April 2023].

[83] UK House of Lords, *DPP v Morgan* [1976] AC 182.

[84] Only three men were charged with the rape. The husband was not charged as at the time it was believed that a husband had an absolute defence in law by virtue of being married to the victim. He was instead charged with aiding and abetting the others to commit rape.

[85] While the defendants won their legal argument, their convictions were nonetheless upheld. The judges found that no reasonable jury would have ever acquitted the defendants even had they been correctly directed by the trial judge as to the law, and so applying "the proviso" they upheld the convictions.

[86] Dolly 1995, pp 207–246.

[87] See the guidance provided at https://www.cps.gov.uk/legal-guidance/rape-and-sexual-offences-chapter-6-consent [accessed 1 April 2023].

(2) the objective element to be assessed by examining whether the belief was reasonable; and (3) the requirement that the accused checked the accuracy of information on which the decision to engage in the conduct was made.

At the international level, mistake of fact was not mentioned as a possible defence in the IMT Statute, Control Council Law No. 10 or the Statutes of the ICTY or the International Criminal Tribunal for Rwanda (ICTR), although this did not prevent the defence being invoked and sometimes accepted by the respective tribunals.[88] In the1947 *Hans* trial, the Supreme Court of Norway acquitted German policeman Oscar Hans, who was charged with the execution of numerous Norwegians without trial, but mistakenly believed that he was carrying out regular court sentences. In *Hans*, the Court stated that "it was not sufficient for a conviction for wilful murder that the accused ought to have known the circumstances which made his act illegal".[89] In the opinion of the Supreme Court, the defendant could not be held guilty unless it had been shown that he was actually aware that the victims had not been tried and sentenced according to law; constructive knowledge was not sufficient. Since the evidence was unclear as to the actual (not constructive) knowledge of the accused, he was acquitted. Notably, the Court still implicitly assessed whether Hans' purported mistaken belief that the executions had been judicially sentenced was reasonable. The Court took into consideration: (1) that he received for each execution a document stating that the person had been "sentenced"; and (2) the secrecy of Hitler's order that had abolished tribunals in occupied countries, which allowed the court to assume that Hans was ignorant of this fact.[90]

---

[88] In the case of the ICTY and ICTR, the defence could qualify as a "special defence" pursuant to Rule 67(A)(ii)(b). In *Erdemović*, the ICTY judges demonstrated a willingness to apply generally accepted legal rules on defences not explicitly provided for in the Statute. See ICTY, *Prosecutor v Drazen Erdemović*, Sentencing Judgment II, IT-96-22-T, 29 November 1996, para 16. There was surprisingly little use made of this defence at the ad hoc tribunals. At the ICTY, in the *Hartmann* contempt case, the defence raised mistake of fact and mistake of law to allegations that the accused was in contempt of court for revealing allegedly confidential information in a book written by the accused. It argued that public discussions in the media, prior to the publication of the accused's book, of the information she was charged with improperly disclosing thereafter, could have reasonably led the accused to believe that the information in question was no longer confidential. Hence the defence argued the accused was not aware that her conduct was illegal. See ICTY, *In the Case Against Florence Hartmann*, IT-0254-R77.5, Judgement on Allegations of Contempt, 14 September 2009, para 63. The chamber rejected the accused's defence of mistake of fact based on its findings as to the knowledge and intent of the accused in publishing the confidential information in violation of an order. Ibid., para 67.

[89] Trial of Hauptsturmfuehrer Oscar Hans (Eidsivating Lagmannsrett, January 1947 and Supreme Court of Norway, Aug. 1947), 5 Law Reports of War Criminals 82, 87 (UN War Crimes Commission, UNWCC, 1948); *In re* Hans 14 ILR 305, p 306.

[90] Hans gave evidence that he received execution orders from his superior, Fehlis (a lawyer, as noted by the court), which stated that the persons had been "sentenced". In June/July 1944, a decree was issued on Hitler's orders from Berlin which abolished tribunals in occupied countries, thereby giving the discretion to issue executions directly to the police. However, evidence indicated that the execution orders received by Hans nonetheless stated that the persons were "sentenced". Since the 1944 order was secret, the Norwegian Supreme Court reasoned that it could therefore be assumed that the defendant's superiors had not acquainted him with it. Ibid.

In the *Almelo* trial, which also involved executions without trial, the British Military Court clearly used an objective reasonableness standard in acquitting the defendant, finding that: "[t]he circumstances were such that a reasonable man might have believed that this officer [i.e., the victim] had been tried according to law, and that they were carrying out a proper judicial legal execution, then it would be open to the court to acquit the accused".[91] In *von Lewinsky*, which, like Rendulic's case, dealt with destruction by German forces during retreat (this time in Ukraine), the British Military Court at Hamburg found, as summed up by the Judge Advocate, that:

> In coming to a conclusion on this question as to whether the destruction caused by the accused was excusable upon this ground [of military necessity], it is essential that you should view the situation through the eyes of the accused and look at it at the time when the events were actually occurring. It would not be just or proper to test the matter in the light of subsequent events, or to substitute an atmosphere of calm deliberation for one of urgency and anxiety. You must judge the question from this standpoint: whether the accused having regard to the position in which he was and the conditions prevailing at the time acted under the honest conviction that what he was doing was legally justifiable.[92]

Although it seems at first glance that the court applied a purely subjective test, it would appear that it used an objective standard to assess the reasonableness of the personal belief, finding that the evidence did not support the assertion of honest mistaken belief of military necessity.[93] Rather than being imperatively required by military necessity, the court found that the destruction was part of a preconceived policy planned a considerable time before and which had nothing to do with military necessity.[94] Notably, this is precisely one of the arguments the Norwegian parliamentarians raised in objecting to Rendulic's acquittal.

By contrast to its predecessor statutes, Article 32(1) of the Rome Statute explicitly includes mistake of fact as a possible defence in providing that "[a] mistake of fact shall be a ground for excluding criminal responsibility only if it negates the mental element required by the crime". The provision makes no further elaboration on the scope of the defence, or whether such mistake need be honest, reasonable, or merely asserted, so long as it negates the *mens rea*. It is therefore an open question as to how the defence operates in the context of a mistaken belief about military necessity.

First, it should be noted that Article 30 of the Rome Statute, which sets out the required mental element, applies to all crimes defined under the statute. It establishes that criminal responsibility is possible only if the material elements of the act are

---

[91] British Military Court at Almelo, *Trial of Otto Sandrock and Three Others*, TWC, Vol. I, at 41. See also the trial of Rath & Thiel, by a British Military Court at Hamburg, UNWCC, Vol. I, at 50–51, in which the defendant was found to have honestly believed that the executions were lawful.

[92] British Military Court at Hamburg, *Von Lewinski (called von Manstein)*, 19 December 1949, 16 AD 509. Case-513 at 522.

[93] See the passage: "If, in regard to any particular instance of seizure or destruction, you are left in doubt upon the matter, then the accused is entitled to have that doubt resolved in his favour. But, in deciding on this question, you will have to take into consideration also the facts as disclosed from the documents themselves".

[94] *Von Lewinski*, n. 92, at 521–523.

committed with intent and knowledge unless the statute provides otherwise.[95] Given that the Rome Statute also recognises the affirmative defence of a mistake of fact when such mistake "negates the mental element required by the crime", commentators have noted the

> interesting and difficult academic issue regarding the Rendulic Rule: were Rendulic charged under the Rome Statute, would he prevail because the prosecution would be unable to prove one of the elements of the offense (i.e. that he did not act with intent and knowledge, as required by Article 30, as to the lack of military necessity in his attack), or because he could interpose the affirmative defence of mistake of fact (i.e. his mistake negated the very same mental element)?[96]

While, as Bill notes, the answer to this question may not have any practical effect since the accused's knowledge will be assessed either way,[97] this question illustrates why the mistake of fact defence in the Rome Statute has sometimes been characterised as redundant.[98] This is because the same result could be produced by simply applying the mental element requirement in Article 30 as by using the affirmative defence in Article 32(1).

The drafting history of Article 32(2) indicates that, while the common law approach of linking mistake of fact to *mens rea* ultimately prevailed, there remained a lack of consensus on the exact scope of the defence. Nonetheless, the concept of reasonable mistaken belief was prevalent in various proposed iterations. The 1951 and 1954 Draft Codes of Offences against the Peace and Security of Mankind by the International Law Commission (ILC) did not mention defences or extenuating circumstances. The issue was, however, extensively debated by the ILC at the 1986 session revising the Draft Code as drafts from non-governmental organisations had dealt with the defence. Draft 1987 Article 9 included "[e]xceptions to the principle of responsibility" (formerly Article 8) and referred in a subparagraph (d) to "error of law or of fact". Both were mentioned as grounds that would not "relieve the perpetrator of criminal responsibility unless, in the circumstances in which it (the crime) was

[95] Article 30 of the Rome Statute provides: "1. Unless otherwise provided, a person shall be criminally responsible and liable for punishment for a crime within the jurisdiction of the Court only if the material elements are committed with intent and knowledge. 2. For the purposes of this article, a person has intent where: (a) In relation to conduct, that person means to engage in the conduct; (b) In relation to a consequence, that person means to cause that consequence or is aware that it will occur in the ordinary course of events. 3. For the purposes of this article, 'knowledge' means awareness that a circumstance exists or a consequence will occur in the ordinary course of events. 'Know' and 'knowingly' shall be construed accordingly".

[96] Bill 2009, p 147.

[97] Ibid.

[98] See Eser 2002, p 891 ("If, for instance, according to Article 32(1) a mistake of fact shall exclude criminal responsibility (only) 'if it negates the mental element', this paragraph simply repeats what is already stated in Article 30(1) by requiring a certain mental element. Instead of this repetition which seems to have been acceptable to the Preparatory Committee as a mere clarification of a generally accepted principle, it would have been much more interesting to have clarified under which conditions a mistake of fact may negate the mental element"). Schabas explains that the purpose of codifying defences in the Rome Statute was not to authorise them, but rather to confine them. Schabas 2016, p 657.

committed, it was unavoidable for him".[99] It was considered that a defence would be permitted where there was a negation of "the mental element required by the crime charged provided that said mistake is not inconsistent with the nature of the crime or its elements, and provided that the circumstances he reasonably believed to be true would have been lawful".[100]

It was proposed to include in the ILC Draft Statute for an International Criminal Court with Suggested Modifications (referred to as the Updated Siracusa Draft) the following formula: "If an individual would not be held guilty of the crime if the circumstances were as he reasonably believed, he is not punishable".[101] No agreement, however, could be reached on this question during the work on the 1996 Draft Code. The Ad Hoc Committee on the Establishment of an ICC proposed guidelines "for consideration of the question of general principles of criminal law", which contained a list of possible defences including "error of fact" but did not contain any further details. The Preparatory Committee (PrepCom) discussed proposals by Japan to formulate an article on "mental element" and by The Netherlands concentrating on avoidability and consistency of errors with the nature of the alleged crimes. The report on the first and second sessions of the PrepCom suggests that the majority held the opinion that mistakes should be a defence and not "a ground for exemption from criminal responsibility". Some delegates questioned whether "this defence needs to be explicitly mentioned as it is merely one example of the various factors that could negate the existence of the required mental element".[102] As a result of this situation, the PrepCom in its third session in 1997 noted that "there were widely divergent views on this matter". According to some delegations, a regulation for "mistake of fact was not necessary because it was covered by mens rea". The first of two proposals treated both mistakes as defences if they were unavoidable or as mitigating circumstances if they were avoidable, adding: "provided that the mistake is not inconsistent with the nature of the alleged crime". The Consolidated Draft from 15 April 1998 repeated the two options and noted that there remained "widely divergent views on this article".[103]

Given the lack of consensus on the scope of the mistake of fact defence even as the Rome Statute was adopted,[104] defining the scope of mistake of fact under

[99] Triffterer 2008, p 897, citing (1987) YBILC, Part I, 7.

[100] Ambos 2022, p 1385, citing Appendix—General Part, Article IX, section 7 A.I.D.P. Draft 1980, reprinted in Bassiouni, ICL Draft (1980), p 164; for the Bassiouni Draft 1987, see Part I—General Part, Article IX, Section 7, reprinted in Bassiouni, ICL Draft (1987), p 110; see also Updated Siracusa Draft, Article 33-15(1)

[101] ILC Draft Statute for an International Criminal Court with Suggested Modifications (Updated Siracusa-Draft) prepared by a Committee of Experts for consideration by the Preparatory Committee on the Establishment of a Permanent International Criminal Court pursuant to General Assembly Resolution A/Res 50/46 (18 December 1995), 15 March 1996. Ibid., p 1386.

[102] Ibid., p 1386, citing Preparatory Committee II 1996, p 96.

[103] Ibid., p 1387. The discussion expressly referred to the decision of the German Federal Court defining "the concept of insurmountable error". Triffterer, n. 99, p 897, citing BGHSt 2, 194, 18 Mar. 1952.

[104] Eser 2002, n. 98, p 892 (noting that since the "political struggle about what errors to tolerate or not was never really solved but rather continued 'behind the scenes' by arguing with partially

it is left open for the decision of the ICC. Since Article 21(b) of the Statute[105] requires the court to apply, where appropriate, applicable treaties and the principles and rules of international law, including the established principles of armed conflict, it may be argued that—at least for those war crimes involving a value judgment—the reasonable commander test should apply to mistaken belief when involving a value judgment. When interpreting the mistake of fact defence and whether an objective reasonableness standard is part of it, it is therefore incumbent on the court to take into account IHL rules including the reasonable commander test. Failing that, per Article 21(c) of the statute, the court can apply general principles of law derived by the court from national laws of legal systems of the world. As noted above, these principles also commonly incorporate a reasonableness standard when assessing the mistake of fact defence.

The use of a reasonableness standard would also help ensure that the mistake of fact defence under the Rome Statute can fully encapsulate complex notions of culpability. Albin Eser has criticised the singular *mens rea* focus of the mistake of fact defence:

> With regard to the required awareness that a circumstance exists, the wording is one-sided in its solely thinking of the presence of positive constituents of the crime [...] while the knowledge of the absence of circumstances which would negate the crime (such as for instance [...] necessities of war justifying the destruction or seizure of the enemy's property) seem to have been forgotten.[106]

Eser notes that, since it is difficult to define knowledge in a way that comprises both the presence of positive circumstances and the absence of negative circumstances of the crime, national codes, such as those of Germany and Poland, are more cautious. By avoiding the reference to the "existence" of a circumstance, they merely require the knowledge of the circumstances which are part of the crime definition and leave it open whether these circumstances are of a positive or negative nature.[107] In Eser's view, the PrepCom failed to take into account the mental requirement where it would concern the absence of a ground excluding the wrongdoing or culpability, as with the absence of a military justification in the case of displacing civilians.[108] This means that the awareness of the absence of grounds excluding responsibility is basically determined by the same requirements of factual knowledge and normative evaluation as positive material elements of the crime. As awareness seems to suggest positive knowledge, Eser asks whether the perpetrator can be held liable if he lacked this only because he had wilfully shut his eyes to what he had otherwise become aware of. The PrepCom had suggested to close this loophole of "wilful blindness" by means

irreconcilable national propositions of mistake of fact and law, it was impossible to agree on a consistent concept").

[105] Ibid., p 892 (noting that "in view of Article 21 of the ICC Statute it will be all the more necessary, though extraordinarily difficult, to construe Articles 30 and 32 of the ICC Statute in a way that is adequately applicable").

[106] Ibid., p 920.

[107] Ibid., p 921.

[108] Ibid., p 930.

of an additional clause: in offering two alternatives, knowledge should also mean "to be aware that there is a substantial likelihood that a circumstance exists and deliberately to avoid taking steps to confirm whether this circumstance exists" or "to be wilfully blind to the fact that a circumstance exists or that a consequence will occur".[109] However, as these recommendations were dropped, it could be concluded that the Rome Statute does not cover cases of "wilful blindness". Eser posits that this conclusion

> is not cogent though, as an offender shutting his eyes to the truth is at least aware of possible, or even obvious, facts he merely does not want to see. Whether this may be called 'implied knowledge', 'constructive knowledge' or, as occasionally suggested, the 'second degree of knowledge' does not matter as long as it is considered sufficient knowledge.[110]

Similarly, Robert D. Sloane notes that Kalshoven's reference to the attacker who "turn[s] a blind eye on the facts of the situation"[111] does not imply negligence as the law conventionally understands it; rather, it implies something more like wilful blindness or perhaps even recklessness.[112]

Where a commander makes a value judgment, for instance, in deciding that an attack is proportionate or justified by military necessity based on a mistaken belief, assessing whether that mistaken belief is reasonable would be consistent with IHL and the objective of protecting victims of armed conflict. Jefferson D. Reynolds, a Major in the US Air Force, has pointed out that "many attacks are launched with the knowledge that they will result in some civilian casualties".[113] He points out that, under a purely subjective test, "[a] defendant would not be criminally liable if an attack was executed under the personal belief that any collateral damage was not excessive compared to the military objective achieved".[114] Notably, the general introduction to the final version of the ICC's Elements of Crimes states that "[w]ith respect to mental elements associated with elements involving value judgement […] it is not necessary that the perpetrator personally completed a particular value judgement […]".[115] However, the drafters of the Elements, in footnote 37 accompanying the war crime of excessive incidental death, injury or damage—in a vein reminiscent of the Rendulic Rule—state that:

> [a]s opposed to the general rule set forth in […] the General Introduction this knowledge element requires that the perpetrator make the value judgement as described therein. An evaluation of that value judgement must be based on the requisite information available to the perpetrator at the time.[116]

---

[109] Article H (Proposal 1) (3) (b) Report of the Preparatory Committee, 51st Sess., Vol. II, p. 92 (in Bassiouni 1998, p 488).

[110] Ibid., p 932.

[111] Kalshoven 1992, p 44.

[112] Sloane 2015, p 299.

[113] Reynolds 2005, p 70.

[114] Ibid., p 71.

[115] No. 4 General Introduction of the Elements of Crimes, ICC-ASP/1/3 (part II-B), adopted and entered into force on 9 September 2002.

[116] Ibid., p 13.

This could suggest that liability is based solely on the attacker's subjective normative assessment regarding the "excessive" nature of the collateral damage, rather than an objective assessment of whether the belief was reasonable. For instance, Kevin Jon Heller has lamented that "[t]he Rome Statute's reliance on a subjective mens rea for the war crime of 'excessive incidental death, injury, or damage,' [...] reflects the Hostage tribunal's problematic acquittal of Lothar Rendulic".[117] However, this interpretation fails to take into account the IHL dimensions of the crime encapsulated in the reasonable commander test. Thus, the interpretation by the authoritative Commentary on the Rome Statute of the mistake of fact defence is that:

> [i]t is clear that the evaluation must be made with reference to information that was available to the attacker, but the evaluation clearly calls for an objective standard. If the alternative interpretation were accepted, it would not accord with the spirit of the Rome Statute preamble and its stated goal of preventing impunity, but would instead further impunity for those persons who launch attacks 'in the knowledge that they will result in some civilian casualties'.[118]

The purely subjective approach is dangerous because it frustrates the law's goal of fostering compliance with IHL, as Reynolds ultimately concludes:

> Under this interpretation a defendant's culpability depends entirely and exclusively on that individual's own value judgement. If the defendant believed the collateral damage was not excessive, then there could not be a finding of guilt. The court's own evaluation of the defendant's value judgement as to the excessive character of the damage is irrelevant. Defendants are able to make an independent value judgement that ultimately determines their own criminality and rewards wilful ignorance.[119]

As noted, certain specific rules of IHL, such as the duty to take all feasible precautions in attack and in particular the duty to do everything feasible to verify that the objectives to be attacked are neither civilians nor civilian objects, encapsulate an objective reasonableness requirement and require commanders to check the information on which they base their decisions to use force. This logically means that a mistake of fact that is both honest and reasonable would mean there is no IHL violation and no criminal culpability. The European Court of Human Rights has explained this in the following terms:

> the reasonableness of the use of force has to be decided on the basis of the facts which the user of force honestly believed to exist: this involves the subjective test as to what the user believed and an objective test as to whether he had reasonable grounds for that belief. Given that honest and reasonable belief, it must then be questioned whether it was reasonable to use the force in question.[120]

In contrast to this reasoning, the Rendulic Rule is sometimes characterised as having "effectively transformed military necessity into a purely subjective test".[121]

---

[117] Heller 2011, p 375.

[118] Ambos 2022, n. 100, p 1402.

[119] Reynolds 2005, n. 113, p 71.

[120] European Court of Human Rights, *McCann et al. v United Kingdom* (1996) 21 E.H.R.R. 97 (hereafter "McCann case"), para 134.

[121] Heller 2011, n. 11, p 311.

The reasoning is that, although the tribunal acknowledged that the evidence indicated that, objectively, there had been no military necessity for Rendulic's scorched earth policy, it nevertheless acquitted him, concluding that "the conditions as they appeared to the defendant at the time were sufficient upon which he could honestly conclude that urgent military necessity warranted the decision made".[122] However, focusing only on the subjective aspect is not a complete picture of the tribunal's reasoning. The tribunal identified the pertinent question as "whether the defendant at the time of its occurrence acted within the limits of honest judgment on the basis of the conditions prevailing at the time".[123] It found that the conditions, as they appeared to Rendulic at the time were sufficient upon which he could honestly conclude that urgent military necessity warranted the decision made. The words "limits of honest judgment", "sufficient" and "could honestly" demonstrate that the tribunal was not concerned merely with honest error, purely subjectively held. These words and the context in which they were used show that the tribunal looked into whether it was possible for a person in that situation—i.e., a reasonable commander—to have made such an error honestly. In other words, the tribunal examined whether such an error could have objectively and reasonably been made. It suggests that the mistake of fact must be both honest and reasonable.

Marko Milanovic has contended that, if the definition of a particular crime under the Rome Statute requires specific mental elements with regard to certain conduct or circumstances, an honestly held mistake of fact would negate the mental element even if it was unreasonable.[124] However, while he interprets the standard as purely subjective, he acknowledges that an objective lack of reasonableness might make it more likely for the court to conclude on the facts that the purported subjective belief was not actually honestly held.[125] In other words, he construes this as a matter of credibility. Similarly, William Schabas has noted that "the Court will always need to assess the credibility of such claims in the light of the circumstances, and would be unlikely even to consider a defence of mistake of fact that did not have an air of reality to it, with some credible evidence in support".[126] This exercise in assessing the credibility of the purported mistaken belief is essentially the same as utilising a reasonable commander test. This is because the only way to judge post hoc a commander's claim to have acted in good faith and in a reasonable manner is to use an objective standard together with the subjective analysis.

The *Pistorius* case before the South African Supreme Court of Appeal provides a domestic example of this type of reasoning.[127] The case involved the defence

[122] *Hostage* Case, p 69.

[123] Ibid.

[124] Milanovic 2020, n. 11.

[125] Milanovic paraphrases the ICC's possible reasoning as: "in view of all this information at the commander's disposal, he could not possibly have honestly believed that the attack was imminent".

[126] Schabas 2016, p 657.

[127] South Africa Supreme Court of Appeal, Director of Public Prosecutions, *Gauteng v Pistorius* (96/2015) [2015] ZASCA 204; [2016] 1 All SA 346 (SCA); 2016 (2) SA 317 (SCA); 2016 (1) SACR 431 (SCA) (3 December 2015) (hereafter "*Pistorius* case").

of putative self-defence[128] against a murder charge. The defendant, a well-known professional sprinter, had fired his gun at the door of the bathroom in his house, killing his girlfriend who was inside the bathroom. He argued that he had genuinely but erroneously believed that his life was in danger. The court noted that "[t]he test for private defence is objective–would a reasonable man in the position of the accused have acted in the same way".[129] The court found that, although Pistorius may have been anxious, "it was inconceivable that a rational person could have believed" he was entitled to fire at this person with a heavy calibre firearm without taking even that most elementary precaution of firing a warning shot.[130] This constituted prima facie proof that the accused did not entertain an honest and genuine belief that he was acting lawfully. Just as in *Hostage*, the question boiled down to whether the perpetrator could honestly believe their actions were lawful and that question is answered by applying an objective reasonableness standard.

As noted above, similar reasoning was used by the European Court of Human Rights in *McCann v United Kingdom*, a case dealing with UK Special Air Service special forces who killed several Irish Republican Army terrorists in Gibraltar, having been told by their superiors that the terrorists posed an imminent threat to the lives of others as they could remotely detonate a car bomb.[131] There was, in fact, no such bomb. The court accepted that the soldiers honestly believed, in the light of the information that they had been given, that it was necessary to shoot the suspects in order to prevent them from detonating a bomb and causing serious loss of life. The actions they took, in obedience to superior orders, were thus perceived by them as absolutely necessary in order to safeguard innocent lives. The court considered that the use of force by agents of the state in pursuit of one of the aims delineated in Article 2(2) of the European Convention on Human Rights may be justified under this provision where it is based on an honest belief which is perceived, "for good reasons", to be valid at the time but which subsequently turns out to be mistaken.[132] For the court, it was necessary to use the subjective test as to what the user believed and an objective test as to whether he had reasonable grounds for that belief.

The standard has been applied more broadly in civil cases. In the *Bici* case, which concerned three British soldiers in a UN peacekeeping operation in Kosovo shooting and killing two Kosovar Albanian men travelling in a car, the England and Wales High Court of Justice stated that it was not necessary to assess whether, in the heat of the moment, the soldiers could conceivably for some reason have been acting under the honest but mistaken impression that one of the men was threatening to shoot them. It is enough for the purposes of civil liability that the court reaches the clear conclusion that any such belief was not reasonable.[133]

[128] For an analysis of how putative self-defence is treated in the context of mistake of fact, see Ghanayim 2007.

[129] *Pistorius* case, n. 127, para 52.

[130] Ibid., para 53.

[131] *McCann* case, n. 120.

[132] Ibid., para 134.

[133] England and Wales High Court of Justice, *Bici and Another v Ministry of Defence*, [2004] EWHC 786 (QB).

The consideration of reasonableness is also reflective of the more fundamental operation of the law, summarised in the opinion (of Coke and Blackstone) that "[r]eason is the soul of the law [...]. The centerpiece of this preoccupation with reasonableness is the reasonable man[...] reasonable is what a reasonable man would do".[134] Using a reasonableness standard in the context of mistake of fact does not equate to using strict liability standard, which was clearly rejected as a general principle of liability under the Rome Statute, except in the limited case of command responsibility.[135] The question is not whether the defendant "should have known" a material element of the crime, for instance in the case of command responsibility, but rather "could (honestly or in good faith) have known" using the reasonable commander test. In the second case, the consciousness of unlawfulness which underlies the principle of culpability, and is absent in strict liability, is retained.

Finally, there are strong policy grounds for interpreting the mistake of fact defence as requiring an honest and reasonable mistaken belief where a commander makes a value judgment to use force. Without any reasonableness standard attached to mistake of fact in the context of conduct-of-hostilities war crimes, the constraints on the use of force become weaker or lost. The balance that should be struck between military necessity and humanity will inevitably bend toward the former, even when the military justification never even existed. Honest but unreasonably held mistakes based on faulty intelligence and confirmation bias that exculpate perpetrators of criminal liability will—and do—lead to more civilian casualties and damage.[136]

This has been documented in a recent Pulitzer prize-winning *New York Times* report that showed that US Special Forces (operating in Afghanistan, Syria, and Iraq) justified 80% of their strikes as "self-defence".[137] The report found that "military teams counting casualties rarely had the time, resources or incentive to do accurate work. And troops rarely faced repercussions when they caused civilian deaths".

---

[134] Fletcher 1988, pp 39ff; see also Ripstein 1999, pp 6ff.

[135] Eser 2002, p 890 ("the Rome Statute not only removes itself from older notions of 'result liability' which punished the wrongful deed without consideration of the actor's mind, but it also dissociates itself from notions of 'strict liability', as they are still practised in certain areas of common law"). It has been posited that "[g]iven that international criminal tribunals are mandated with the task of prosecuting 'the most serious crimes of concern to the international community as a whole' and the corresponding severity of the criminal charges, it would be disproportional [*sic*] and thus incompatible with the rights of the accused to introduce a form of strict liability in international criminal law". Bock 2013, p 184. But see the use of the "should have known" standard used in Article 6(e) (genocide by forcibly transferring children); Article 8(2)(b)(vii)-1 (war crime of improper use of a flag of truce); Article 8(2)(b)(vii)-2 (war crime of improper use of a flag, insignia or uniform of the hostile party); Article 8(2)(b)(vii)-4 (war crime of improper use of the distinctive emblems of the Geneva Conventions); Article 8(2)(b)(xxvi) (war crime of using, conscripting or enlisting children); and Article 8(2)(e)(vii) (war crime of using, conscripting and enlisting children).

[136] For more discussion on this point, see Chap. 11.

[137] Khan, 19 December 2021, "Airstrikes allowed America to wage war with minimal risk to its troops", The New York Times Magazine. https://www.nytimes.com/2021/12/19/magazine/victims-airstrikes-middle-east-civilians.html (hereafter "NYT report on Airstrikes"). Accessed 1 April 2023. See also Chap. 11.

Civilian deaths were undercounted even in classified reports.[138] In one example, the US military made a strike on 5 March 2016 in Mosul, Iraq, which killed a family of 21, with no military justification. The family had been monitored for just 95 minutes over the course of several weeks before the target was authorised. There was evidence of confirmation bias since "no overtly nefarious activity was observed". Instead, the normal activity of the household which was under surveillance was viewed through an incriminating lens, for instance, that when the gate was opened to allow a guest to enter, this was considered consistent with the tactics, techniques and procedures of a headquarters; the apparent absence of women was used as confirmation that this was an ISIS facility. Ultimately, the official report acknowledged that perhaps the target may have been confused for a compound next door.[139]

In another example, a 2019 Baghuz strike by the US armed forces against a group of women and children in Syria during the last days of the battle against ISIS, which killed 80 people, was justified as self-defence.[140] The strike was ordered after a Special Forces Group officer looked at drone footage with only a standard-definition camera and did not see any civilians. However, a high-definition drone was available at the Combined Air Operations Center at Al Udeid Air Base in Qatar. Those watching that footage saw two or three men armed with rifles wander through the frame near the crowd, but "do not appear to be maneuvering, engaging coalition forces or acting in a way that would seem to justify a self-defense strike with 2,000-pound bombs".[141] When the strike fell, the chat log registered one analyst asking, "[w]ho dropped that?" and another responding, "[w]e just dropped on 50 women and children".

A legal officer flagged the strike as a possible war crime that required an investigation. The Defense Department's independent inspector general began an inquiry, but the report containing its findings was stalled and stripped of any mention of the strike. The only assessment done immediately after the strike was performed by the same ground unit that ordered the strike. It determined that the bombing was lawful because it killed only a small number of civilians while targeting ISIS fighters in an attempt to protect coalition forces. No formal war crime notification, criminal investigation or disciplinary action was therefore warranted, it said, adding that the other deaths were accidental.[142] In both these examples, it appears that an honest mistake may have been made in deciding that the targets were military objectives and/or proportionate. To not require further consideration of whether those mistakes

[138] As a result of the *Times* investigation, US lawmakers put forward the bill for the Protection of Civilians in Military Operations Act (POCIMO). The proposed POCIMO bill enhances investigations into civilian harm resulting from US military operations to get to the bottom of how, when, where, and why civilians were harmed.

[139] NYT report on Airstrikes, n. 137.

[140] Khan, 18 December 2021, "Hidden Pentagon Records Reveal Patterns of Failure in Deadly Airstrikes", New York Times. https://www.nytimes.com/interactive/2021/12/18/us/airstrikes-pentagon-records-civilian-deaths.html [accessed 1 April 2023].

[141] Ibid, citing witness testimony of those who watched the footage.

[142] Ibid.

were reasonable removes the incentive for military commanders to check the intelligence they are using before making a strike, which in hindsight was not justified by military necessity or was disproportionate.

In this respect, the Dutch District Court of The Hague in its 2022 judgment on the criminal responsibility of the four members of the armed group—the Donetsk People's Republic (DPR)—charged with the destruction of the civilian airline MH17 over Ukraine in 2014 and the murder of all those onboard missed an opportunity.[143] The court found that an international armed conflict existed at the time and place of the incident (due to Russia exercising "overall control" of the DPR which was fighting the Ukraine government) and that, therefore, "the provisions of international humanitarian law governing combatant status apply". It also held, however, that members of the DPR were not combatants under Article 43 of API since Russia had denied that they had any control or involvement over the DPR in that period. According to the court, this meant that members of the DPR lacked combatant immunity, which allowed the court to exercise jurisdiction over the alleged crimes and removed the need for the court to consider whether the accused complied with IHL.

Apart from its questionable reliance on Russia's denial of involvement with the DPR,[144] the court's failure to consider whether firing upon the aircraft was lawful from an IHL perspective was a missed opportunity for clarifying how mistake of fact applies in such cases.[145] Notably, the court found:

> A Buk weapon system is designed to shoot down aircraft and cannot simply be used at random. Such deployment requires preparation, including determination of and transport to a launch site. Firing the missile needs to be very deliberate and carefully considered in accordance with a technical procedure and requires a highly trained crew.[146]

This type of evidence would arguably have supported the conclusion that the mistake was not reasonable. Had the court taken an alternative approach and found that the DPR members were lawful combatants entitled to combatant immunity but that this immunity does not cover war crimes, it could have decided that the requisite mental element for the crimes charged was whether the accused honestly believed that the aircraft (and its occupants) was military in character and whether the basis for such belief was reasonable. Such an approach—while no doubt presenting a more

---

[143] *Girkin et al.* judgment summary, n. 7.

[144] This conclusion, somewhat contradictory to its "overall control" finding, has been criticised, and could complicate ongoing efforts by the Netherlands and Australia to hold Russia accountable for its role in the downing of MH17 in other fora, namely, the ECtHR and ICAO. See n. 7. For commentary on this finding, see Yanev 2022 (arguing that had the Court taken the alternative approach, "the judges would have been pushed to engage in complicated factual analyses about the extent to which the downing of MH17 was an accident caused by the perpetrators' genuine belief that they were shooting at a Ukrainian military aircraft (which they would have had the right to do, had they been lawful combatants under IHL). The decision to altogether reject combatant status for the DPR, based on Russia's denials that this group is fighting on its behalf is, in this respect, a pragmatic way out of this conundrum."); de Hoon 2022; Trampert 2022.

[145] The court itself acknowledged that "[t]he crew appears to have thought the missile was being fired not at a civilian but at a military aircraft". *Girkin et al.* judgment summary, n. 7.

[146] Ibid.

complex case—would arguably comport better with basic notions of culpability. It would also have reinforced the precautionary rules requiring commanders to double-check the available information before deciding to launch an attack on an aircraft that is destined to kill all those onboard.

Be that as it may, the court's point about the highly technical and sophisticated nature of the weapon that was used, the impact this had on planning and the decision to use it, and what this demonstrates about the mental element, was cogent. For instance, Bill has observed that

> without doubt, advances in intelligence collection, and the advanced means by which it is possible to document its delivery to the commander, may, in the long-term, render his immunity to act mistakenly less likely. For example, a present-day Rendulic would know within days, if not much sooner, that the Russians were not following up their attack.[147]

Given that modern intelligence gathering and surveillance techniques are now available for commanders, assessing whether the mistaken belief was reasonable as well as honest would not only allow the criminal standard to be interpreted in a manner consistent with IHL rules, but also further the objective of both regimes of law, to protect the victims of armed conflict.[148]

8.5 Conclusion

The international community stands to gain by learning the lessons from Rendulic's mistake. The *Rendulic* case illustrates the relationship between the reasonable military commander test and mistake of fact and demonstrates how they can be considered together to assess if liability attaches to the commander exercising judgment under a mistaken belief about a material fact.

The purpose of the mistake of fact defence is to ensure that people are only held accountable for unlawful behaviour that they knew was unlawful at the time. Both objective and subjective elements must be considered to assess whether a commander's judgment was reasonable and done in good faith. Whether reasonableness will be read into mistake of fact in Article 32 of the Rome Statute in cases where the reasonable military commander standard applies is yet to be seen. But if so, this would arguably narrow the scope of this defence, which from a policy perspective would serve to further protect civilians and their property from harm. It could also serve as a deterrent against commanders using faulty information without checking its accuracy or motivate commanders to use all feasible precautions prior to attacking.

Given the enormous damage (including on an international scale) from the numerous cases in which an alleged mistake of fact has occurred, a reasonableness standard could arguably help to define the scope of the mistake of fact defence

---

[147] Bill 2009, p 148.

[148] For further discussion on this point, see Chap. 10.

while ensuring that individuals are liable only for behaviour they know is criminal. In summary, applying a test of whether the exercise of judgment fell within "the limits of honest judgment" using the reasonable commander standard would ensure consistency with IHL rules related to precautionary measures, deter decision-making based on incomplete intelligence or confirmation bias, better protect civilians from harm, and avoid impunity for war crimes.

Acknowledgements All views expressed here are the author's and should not be understood to reflect the views of any past or present employer.

References

Ambos K (ed) (2022) Rome Statute of the International Criminal Court: Article-by-Article Commentary, 4th edn. Beck/Hart/Nomos, Oxford/Baden-Baden

Amnesty International (2000) 7 June 2000, "NATO/Federal Republic of Yugoslavia 'collateral Damage" or Unlawful Killings? Violations of the Laws of War by NATO during Operation Allied Force", available at: https://amnesty.no/natofederal-republic-yugoslaviacollateral-damage-or-unlawful-killings.

Bassiouni MC (ed) (1998) The Statute of the Criminal Court, A Documentary History. Transnational Publishers, Ardsley, NY

Best G (1994) War and Law Since 1945. Clarendon Press, Oxford

Bill BJ (2009) The Rendulic "rule": military necessity, commander's knowledge, and methods of warfare. Yearbook of International Humanitarian Law 12:119

Bock S (2013) The prerequisite of personal guilt and the duty to know the law in the light of Article 32 ICC Statute. Utrecht Law Review 9 4:184–197

de Hoon M (2022) Just Security, 19 December 2022 "Dutch Court, in Life Sentences: Russia Had "Overall Control" of Forces in Eastern Ukraine Downing of Flight MH17", available at: https://www.justsecurity.org/84456/dutch-court-in-life-sentences-russia-had-overall-control-of-forces-in-eastern-ukraine-downing-of-flight-mh17/

Dinstein Y (2010) The Conduct of Hostilities under the Law of International Armed Conflict, 2nd edn. Cambridge University Press, Cambridge

Dolly A (1995) Twenty years of Morgan: a criticism of the subjectivist view of mens rea and rape in Great Britain. Pace International Law Review 7:207–246

Draper GIAD (1958) The Red Cross Conventions of 1949. Frederick A. Praeger, New York

Eser A (2002) Mental elements–mistake of fact and mistake of law. In: Cassese A et al. (eds) The Rome Statute of the International Criminal Court, Vol. I. Oxford University Press, Oxford, pp 889–946

Fletcher G (1988) A Crime of Self-Defense. University of Chicago Press, Chicago

Ghanayim K (2007) The Role of Reasonable and Unreasonable Mistake in Justified Defences – A Comparative and Analytical Study. 3 Oxford University Comparative Law Forum, available at https://www.ouclf.law.ox.ac.uk

Hampson FJ (1992) Proportionality and necessity in the Gulf Conflict. ASIL Proceedings 86:45-53

Heintschel von Heinegg W (2020) Considerations of necessity under Article 57(2)(a)(ii), (c), and (3) and proportionality under Article 51(5)(b) and Article 57(2)(b) of Additional Protocol I: is there room for an integrated approach? In: Kreß C, Lawless R (eds) Necessity and Proportionality in International Peace and Security Law. Oxford Scholarship Online

Heller KJ (2011) The Nuremberg Military Tribunals and the Origins of International Criminal Law. Oxford University Press, Oxford

Henckaerts J-M, Doswald-Beck L (2005) Customary International Humanitarian Law, Vol. I. Cambridge University Press, Cambridge

Jensen ET (2003) Unexpected consequences from knock-on effects: a different standard for computer network operations. Amer. Univ. ILR 18 5:1145–1188

Kalshoven F (1992) Implementing limitations on the use of force: the doctrine of proportionality and necessity. ASIL Proceedings 86:39–44

Médecins Sans Frontières (MSF) (undated) "On 3 October 2015, US airstrikes destroyed our trauma hospital in Kunduz, Afghanistan, killing 42 people", available at: https://www.msf.org/kunduz-hospital-attack-depth

Médecins Sans Frontières (MSF) (2015) Initial MSF internal review: Attack on Kunduz Trauma Centre, Afghanistan November 2015, available at: https://www.msf.fr/sites/default/files/review_final_041115_for_public_release.pdf

Milanovic M (2020) EJIL: Talk!, 14 January 2020, "Mistakes of Fact When Using Lethal Force in International Law: Part I", available at: https://www.ejiltalk.org/mistakes-of-fact-when-using-lethal-force-in-international-law-part-i/

Oeter S (2020) Specifying the proportionality test and the standard of due precaution: problems of prognostic assessment in determining the meaning of "may be expected" and "anticipated". In: Kreß C, Lawless R (eds) Necessity and Proportionality in International Peace and Security Law. Oxford Scholarship Online, available at Necessity and Proportionality in International Peace and Security Law, Oxford Academic (oup.com)

OSCE (Organization for Security and Co-operation in Europe Office for Democratic Institutions and Human Rights) (2022) Report on Violations of International Humanitarian and Human Rights Law, War Crimes and Crimes Against Humanity Committed In Ukraine Since 24 February 2022 by Professors Wolfgang Benedek, Veronika Bílková and Marco Sassòli, 12 April 2022, available at: https://www.osce.org/files/f/documents/f/a/515868.pdf

Pictet J (ed) (1952–60) Commentary to Geneva Convention IV of 1949. ICRC, Geneva

Reynolds JD (2005) Collateral damage on the 21st century battlefield: enemy exploitation of the law of armed conflict, and the struggle for a moral high ground. Airforce Law Review 56:1-108

Ripstein A (1999) Equality, Responsibility, and the Law. Cambridge University Press, Cambridge

Sandoz Y et al. (1986) Commentary on the Additional Protocols of 8 June 1977 to the Geneva Conventions of 12 August 1949. ICRC, Geneva

Schabas W (2016) The International Criminal Court: A Commentary on the Rome Statute, 2nd edn. Oxford University Press, Oxford

Sloane RD (2015) Puzzles of proportion and the "reasonable military commander": reflections on the law, ethics, and geopolitics of proportionality. Harvard National Security Journal 6:299–343

Trampert J (2022) EJIL: Talk!, 12 December 2022, "Possible Implications of the Dutch MH17 Judgment for the Netherlands' Inter-State Case before the ECtHR", available at: https://www.ejiltalk.org/possible-implications-of-the-dutch-mh17-judgment-for-the-netherlands-inter-state-case-before-the-ecthr/

Triffterer O (ed) (2008) Commentary on the Rome Statute of the International Criminal Court: Observers' Notes, Article by Article, 2nd edn. CH Beck/Hart/Nomos, Baden-Baden

United States Central Command (2015) Summary of the Airstrike on the MSF Trauma Center in Kunduz, Afghanistan, on October 3, 2015; Investigation and Follow-on Actions, 29 April 2016, available at: https://hrvoices.org/assets/attachments/documents/Oct-3-2015-Kunduz-Trauma-Center-Strike.-CENTCOM-Summary-Memo.pdf

van Sliedregt E (2012) Individual Criminal Responsibility in International Law. Oxford University Press, Oxford

Woodruff Jr. OE (1959) Mistake of fact as a defense. Dickinson Law Review 63:319–333

Yanev L (2022) EJIL: Talk!, 7 December 2022, "The MH17 Judgment: An Interesting Take on the Nature of the Armed Conflict in Eastern Ukraine", available at: https://www.ejiltalk.org/the-mh17-judgment-an-interesting-take-on-the-nature-of-the-armed-conflict-in-eastern-ukraine/

Other Document

UNICTY, Final Report to the Prosecutor by the Committee Established to Review the NATO Bombing Campaign Against the Federal Republic of Yugoslavia.

Yasmin Naqvi Principal Legal Officer, Office of International Law, Attorney-General's Department, Canberra, Australia; Visiting Professor, Graduate Institute of International and Development Studies, Geneva, Switzerland. Address: Robert Garran Offices, 3-5 National Circuit, BARTON ACT 2600 Australia, e-mail: ynaqvi1@yahoo.com

Part IV
Assessing an Error's Reasonableness

Chapter 9
The ICT Revolution, 21st Century Warfare, and Honest Errors

Tae Hoon Kim

Contents

9.1 Introduction 218
9.2 C4ISR, RMA and a New Type of Warfare—USA's Dominant Battlefield Knowledge (DBK) and Russia's Non-Contact Warfare 219
9.3 Case Studies 222
9.3.1 Iraq and Afghanistan: Limits of Achieving DBK and "Honest Errors" 222
9.3.2 Russia's ICT Warfare: The Ukrainian Disaster and Systemic Failures 225
9.4 Conclusion 229
References 230

Abstract Since the 1990s, proponents of a so-called revolution in military affairs (RMA) have argued that the tremendous development in information communications technology (ICT) would revolutionise warfare through enhanced intelligence capabilities. This would reduce the scope of battlefield uncertainty of the kind in which Rendulic had claimed to have found himself in late 1944. The difficulty of gaining accurate intelligence of the battlefield at the time of the evacuation and destruction of Finnmark was one of the reasons why Rendulic's action was considered an honest error. This chapter examines whether the ICT revolution has reduced battlefield uncertainty and honest errors in 21st-century warfare by examining two case studies: the US invasions of Afghanistan and Iraq, and Russia's invasion of Ukraine. The chapter shows that the relationship between ICT, intelligence, uncertainty, and honest errors is far more complex than argued by RMA advocates and is influenced by several factors. In particular, this chapter argues that the ICT revolution has not reduced the sense of uncertainty, fear, and other psychological constraints of combatants.

Keywords Information communications technology (ICT) · revolution in military affairs (RMA) · network-centric warfare (NCW) · battlefield intelligence · human judgment · uncertainty

---

T. H. Kim (✉)
Swedish Defence University, Drottning Kristinas väg 37, 114 28 Stockholm, Sweden
e-mail: taehoon.kim@fhs.se

N. Hayashi and C. Lingaas (eds.), *Honest Errors? Combat Decision-Making 75 Years After the* Hostage *Case*, https://doi.org/10.1007/978-94-6265-611-6_9

9.1 Introduction

One reason why Rendulic's destruction of Finnmark was judged to be an honest error was his inability to gain accurate intelligence on Soviet troop movements. Rendulic's lawyer, Stefan Fritsch, sought to emphasise this when he probed Rendulic whether he had had the means to reconnoitre Soviet positions at the time. Rendulic replied that this was impossible due to the lack of air reconnaissance assets in the vicinity and the inclement weather. Rendulic further highlighted that, despite receiving news of a Soviet withdrawal from the Lapland area, this did not give him "any information concerning the real interests of the Russians in Finnmark".[1] The withdrawal itself did not preclude the possibility that the Soviets would later advance. In any case, Rendulic had been confronted with thirty Soviet divisions which were "far too strong". Faced with this uncertain and probable Soviet threat, the destruction of Finnmark had been necessary on military grounds.[2]

Since the events at Finnmark, intelligence collection methods have undergone enormous changes, especially in the last thirty years with the advancement in information communications technology (ICT). Nowadays, combatants supposedly have access to technologies that provide unprecedented levels of intelligence that enable them to dominate opponents through information superiority and to execute precise and effective attacks. These arguments were particularly prevalent amongst military thinkers from the 1990s to the 2000s. These advocates of a so-called revolution in military affairs (RMA) claimed that warfare was experiencing fundamental changes, a process through which battlefield uncertainty greatly diminished.

This inquiry aims to examine whether such a vision amongst RMA enthusiasts can be substantiated on the battlefield by analysing two 21st century conflicts. These are the US invasions of Afghanistan and Iraq and Russia's ongoing invasion of Ukraine. They were chosen for three reasons: first, both the Russian and US militaries have been prominent articulators of an ICT-driven modern war that emphasises information superiority, precision strikes, and network-based capabilities. Second, both conflicts reveal how large conventional militaries deploy their ICT capabilities in combat. Third, they reveal a gap between the vision of ICT-enabled warfare that is often couched in a futuristic and techno-centric language on the one hand, and the reality on the ground on the other.

This chapter's analytical scope is limited to kinetic warfare in the operational and tactical domains. Strategic considerations and non-kinetic warfare have been deliberately omitted. This is because the Rendulic Rule is primarily concerned with operational and tactical uncertainties on the battlefield, not strategic policy issues. Non-kinetic warfare, such as cyber warfare and psychological operations, is a central element in modern warfare. Unfortunately, it is not governed or constrained by an enforceable international legal framework in the way that kinetic warfare is.[3]

[1] International Military Tribunal, Hostage, 1947, Nuremberg Transcripts 5, p 5342.

[2] Ibid., p 5343. See also Piątkowski 2013, p 74.

[3] For an attempt to delineate and define legal mechanisms to govern non-kinetic warfare, see Tsagourias 2016; Tsagourias and Farrell 2020.

This chapter is organised as follows. The first section gives a brief overview of how the ICT revolution has impacted military and military thinking, especially amongst US and Russian RMA proponents. The second section contains the case study which looks into the US military's experience in Afghanistan and Iraq and Russia's invasion of Ukraine. The conclusion summarises key findings from the previous sections and highlights some further areas of research.

9.2 C4ISR, RMA and a New Type of Warfare—USA's Dominant Battlefield Knowledge (DBK) and Russia's Non-Contact Warfare

One hallmark of military thought from the 1990s was the impact that advanced ICT would have on warfare. The advent of the World Wide Web, the explosion of computing power, the accessibility of personal computers, and the general trend towards economic globalisation have all contributed to the rise of the information age. These have led to pervasive technological, organisational, and doctrinal changes (or attempts to institute such changes) throughout different militaries. The US military is by far the most prominent among them.

One of the most prominent officials who articulated how these changes were shaping warfighting was Vice Admiral William Owens, Vice-Chairman of the US Joint Chiefs of Staff between 1994 and 1996. Owen argued that an RMA was taking place with three characteristics. The first was intelligence, surveillance, and reconnaissance (ISR), which consisted of sensors and other technologies related to intelligence collection, surveillance, and reconnaissance. The second was an advanced command, control, communications, computers and intelligence processing (C4I), which involved converting intelligence from ISR to a "dominant understanding of the battlespace" and "mission and assignments".[4] The combination of these two has become popularly known as C4ISR. The third was precision force, the ability to execute missions and assignments accurately and precisely.

According to Owens, these changes enabled war-fighters to achieve what he called dominant battlefield knowledge (DBK). DBK "involves everything from automated target recognition to the knowledge of an opponent's operational plans and the networks relied on to pursue them".[5] Having DBK will allow the US military to "know more about the flow of conflict than an opponent and to operate well within the decision cycle of that opponent". Owens did admit that battlefield uncertainty or the fog of war would persist. He nevertheless claimed that the fog would be reduced to a point where it would allow US information superiority and dominance over its opponents.[6]

---

[4] Owens 1996, p 2.

[5] Ibid.

[6] Ibid., p 3.

Owens' arguments were echoed by others within the US defence establishment. David Alberts, Director of Research for the Office of the Assistant Secretary of Defence for Networks and Information Integration, took a more radical line. Instead of being "preoccupied with reducing the fog of war", RMA would enable the US military to be in a position where it would be "preoccupied with optimizing a response to a particular situation".[7] In other words, RMA would lead to a shift from a situation where decisions have to be made under uncertainty to "a situation in which decisions are made with near-perfect information".[8] Alberts further argued that this would bring fundamental changes to command and control. Commanders "will be more focused on strategic issues; the role of staffs will be diminished, and organizations will be flattened".[9] Rather than a top-down form of command and control, decision-making and command would be decentralised yet synchronised between units that would be connected via ICT-based networks. This network-based or network-centric warfare (NCW) would complement and strengthen DBK.[10]

Owens and Alberts were two of the best-known RMA advocates in the US following the end of the Cold War. The changes taking place in the military in the 1990s were perhaps not as revolutionary as Owen and Alberts might have made them appear. Throughout history, there had been numerous instances where warfare had been significantly transformed to the point of being considered revolutionary. These instances include Sweden's sweeping military reforms under Gustavus II Adolphus in the 17th century, the *levée en masse* in the French Revolutionary Wars, and the use of indirect fires and airpower in World War I.[11]

What was perhaps unique about RMA advocates in the late 20th century is their belief that the fog of war and friction would be greatly reduced thanks to technologies such as C4ISR. In other words, they suggested that the very nature of warfare, which had been punctuated by uncertainty, was changing. *Operation Desert Storm* (ODS), a stunning US military success, seemed to corroborate this unprecedented development. ODS involved the pervasive application of C4ISR, electronic warfare, a devastatingly effective air campaign, and the successful execution of precision-guided missiles. One specific system that perhaps exemplified all these characteristics was the joint surveillance and target acquisition radar system (JSTARS), which was used extensively to locate and track enemy units, especially those dug in along the Iraqi and Kuwaiti borders with Saudi Arabia.[12]

The success of ODS, combined with the dissolution of the USSR, the end of the Cold War, and the overall mood of US global supremacy, helped popularise the futuristic visions of warfare advanced by Owens. This was not lost on Soviet and then later Russian military thinkers. Soviet observers were shocked that the US was able to defeat a much larger Iraqi army by using technologies such as new cruise missiles,

[7] Alberts 1995, p 80.

[8] Ibid., p 80.

[9] Ibid., p 88.

[10] Alberts and Hayes 2003, p 137.

[11] Murray and Knox 2009, p 13. See also Farrell and Terriff 2002.

[12] Gray 2002, p 15.

aircraft, and C4I. They were especially surprised by the speed of the war, the low number of casualties, and the precision with which Iraqi command centres, communications systems and infrastructure were targeted. For Russian military thinkers, ODS was the success of the United States' "overwhelming superiority in combat and information support systems".[13] Ivan Vorobyov and Valery Kiselyov argued that it portended the emergence of a "next-generation warfare based on information and networks".[14] This view was echoed by General Vladimir Slipchenko, who described it as a victory of informatised precision weapons over the massed industrial army of the Cold War.[15] In a similar vein to their US counterparts, these Soviet/Russian thinkers understood that warfare was about to transform itself profoundly. They were also convinced that these changes would consign existing Soviet doctrine, concepts, and technology into obsolescence.

The demise of the Soviet Union meant that Russia had little means to implement anything similar to counter the Americans in the years immediately after ODS. The subsequent wars it fought in Chechnya and Georgia were not of this new kind. Nevertheless, the lessons of ODS and its implications were not lost on Russian military thinkers. They embraced, adapted, and went about developing a Russian-style NCW throughout the military reforms of the 2010s. Despite much attention being put on Russia's so-called hybrid warfare capabilities as articulated in the so-called Gerasimov doctrine, the core of Russia's conventional military doctrine is NCW.[16] For example, Russia's 2010 Military Doctrine stressed networked command and control systems as an integral part of modern conflict. General Nikolai Makarov, Chief of General Staff between 2007 and 2021, echoed this priority, stating that the armed forces were shifting to a "network-centric principle" of command and control.[17] General Sergei Bogdanov and Colonel Sergei Chekinov, who together penned thirteen influential articles on Russian military thinking in the 2010s, highlighted that NCW would be implemented in an integrated combat environment under a single command structure with shared and synchronised information and communication.[18]

One particular feature in the Russian discourse on NCW from ODS to the present day has been the continued focus on non-contact, remote kinetic warfare through precision munitions. Compared to US RMA theorists, Russia's NCW architects have been less expressly preoccupied with achieving a more comprehensive form of information dominance such as DBK or encouraging decentralisation of command and control. What interested them foremost was the ability to launch long-range precision guided munitions (PGM) accurately into the opponent's depth from a remote command centre, supported by C4I systems and an integrated command structure that accelerates target acquisition, dissemination and execution. To some degree,

[13] Grau and Thomas 1996, p 510.

[14] Jonsson 2019, p 106.

[15] Kipp 2007, p 150.

[16] Revaitis 2018, p 289.

[17] McDermott 2011, p 5.

[18] Jonsson 2019, p 107.

one could argue that Russia's vision of an ICT-based high-tech war has been less comprehensive and much narrower than that envisioned by their US counterparts.

Despite these differences, both US and Russian proponents of NCW agree on the importance of information superiority to enable effective, agile, and accurate attacks, all supported and driven by the latest ICT. Both were in agreement that ICT was the medium of future warfighting. The US was the pioneer of this type of warfare, which it pushed ahead confidently in what people believed to be a period of Pax Americana. The Russians studied and emulated these doctrines in their attempt to revive the Russian military from its post-Cold War doldrums, with an emphasis on precision strikes. How they went about implementing these visions on the battlefield is the topic of the next section.

9.3 Case Studies

9.3.1 Iraq and Afghanistan: Limits of Achieving DBK and "Honest Errors"

For the US military, Operation Enduring Freedom (OEF) and Operation Iraqi Freedom (OIE) were the first testing grounds of the ICT-driven RMA in the 21st century. Both started with sweeping US/coalition victories. The Taliban was removed from power, while Saddam Hussein was toppled. The C4ISR systems deployed by the Americans proved their worth, especially during OIE. OIE demonstrated the US military's ability to produce and employ imagery from satellites and Predator drones, while further highlighting the efficacy of JSTARS. OIE was also the first conflict where the Global Positioning System (GPS) became a central feature in tactical intelligence. General John Abizaid, Deputy Commander of the US Central Command during the invasion, stated that the US had an outstanding picture of the enemy's dispositions and intentions and that the intelligence picture at both the operational and tactical levels was one of the most accurate.[19]

Not everything was smooth sailing, however. Despite being efficient in some aspects, the latest C4ISR did little to help US troops in others, especially human intelligence (HUMINT).[20] HUMINT is the oldest form of intelligence collection, and the one least affected by technological developments. Unlike other forms of intelligence, it is the only one that has the potential to reveal real human intentions.[21] For soldiers on the ground fighting against a foe whose thinking and culture they did not always understand, the lack of HUMINT was a serious issue.[22] As

[19] Nomination of LTG Abizaid to be Appointed to the Rank of General and Commander of USCENTCOM, Hearing before the Senate Armed Services Committee, 25 June 2003, https://irp.fas.org/congress/2003_hr/062503abizaid.html [accessed on 1 April 2023].

[20] Ferris 2003, p 160.

[21] Althoff 2016, p 45. See also Warner 2014, pp 11–36.

[22] Murray 2004, p 7.

opposed to the lack of accurate HUMINT, units were often saddled with a plethora of other technology-based intelligence. This led to information bottlenecks, making it difficult to analyse and process information properly. In addition, the speed with which information and intelligence could be shared between different echelons posed particular problems. For example, a chat function within the United States' classified military internet system, the SIPRNET, that connected Tactical Operations Centres (TOCs) at the brigade level to the national level, allowed anyone to participate and ask questions. This, however, risked information and communication overload.[23]

As the wars in Afghanistan and Iraq evolved into long and unconventional conflicts, US troops found it more difficult to assert battlefield dominance using their advanced C4ISR. For example, militants in both Afghanistan and Iraq, though heavily outgunned and without the same technological prowess, adapted smartly and adeptly.[24] They sought to neutralise the US military's C4ISR advantage and hinder its effort to execute pinpoint airstrikes by avoiding direct open combat.[25] Instead, they concealed, dispersed, and covered themselves using the terrain and urban environment.[26] As the insurgencies intensified, the US military was compelled to adopt what could be called more traditional fighting methods. Much like their opponents, they had to use cover, concealment, and camouflage and engage their enemies in ground combat.[27]

ICT also had little effect in addressing basic errors arising from negligence, improper judgment, or fatigue. The US Air Force's bombing of a hospital in Kunduz operated by Doctors Without Borders which killed 42 is a case in point. The US military initially claimed that the attack was executed to defend US forces on the ground. It then argued that the airstrike was requested by its Afghan allies who had been under Taliban fire. An internal investigation later showed that the bombing was the result of an error in judgment and equipment failure. The aircraft crew had misidentified the hospital as a Taliban-controlled building, based on the physical description given to them by their Afghan allies. They did not consult their no-strike list that included the coordinates of the hospital. Moreover, there were problems with the electronic equipment on the aircraft that prevented the crew from receiving or sending emails and transmitting video footage.[28]

Such avoidable mistakes were not only made against civilians but also against one's own. In December 2001, an American B-52 bomber mistakenly bombed US special forces and their Afghan allies, killing three Americans and dozens of Afghans. This was alleged to have been caused when the targeteer erroneously provided

---

[23] Ferris 2003, p 164.

[24] Porter 2013, pp 160–169.

[25] Betz 2006, p 512; see also Press 2001.

[26] Biddle 2004.

[27] Biddle 1996.

[28] Schulberg (2015) U.S. Bombing of Doctors Without Borders hospital result of "human error". HuffPost, https://www.huffpost.com/entry/msf-kunduz-human-error_n_5655d5c8e4b079b28189cf5b [accessed 1 April 2023].

the bomber with his own coordinates rather than the enemy's.[29] Another instance involved a US F-16 fighter jet bombing Canadian soldiers taking part in a live-fire exercise, killing four and injuring eight. The pilot believed that he was bombing enemy positions and claimed that he had not been informed of the exercise. It was later claimed that the pilot had been suffering from fatigue and was taking amphetamines to help him stay alert.[30]

Perhaps the greatest limitation of NCW was that it did little to clear away the combatants' sense of uncertainty and insecurity, especially in an armed engagement. In 2007, a US Army helicopter shot a group of unarmed Iraqi civilians in Baghdad, including two employees of Reuters. The footage of this shooting came from another helicopter and was later released by Wikileaks. One of the crew members claimed to have identified six people with AK-47s. The shadow from a camera that one of the Reuters employees held was mistaken as a rocket-propelled gun. Another crew member said that the men were shooting and moving in the direction of US soldiers. The crew believed that an attack was imminent, given that they had been engaging with their enemy the entire day. It later turned out that none of the civilians had been armed.[31] Despite the outcry of many, some came to the defence of these men. Defence Secretary Robert Gates argued that the footage did not show the entire picture of the situation.[32] The implication was that this was a heat-of-the-moment incident, where calm and imperturbable thinking was difficult.

In a similar and more controversial case, Lieutenant Clint Lorance killed unarmed Afghans in July 2012. Lorance had ordered his men to shoot three Afghans on a motorbike while on patrol in a Taliban-controlled area of Zhari District in Kandahar Province, an area where US troops had previously come under fire. Lorance believed that these were armed Taliban, although it turned out they were unarmed civilians. Lorance was later convicted and sentenced to 20 years in prison for breaking the law of war. His soldiers testified against him and highlighted what they described as Lorance's generally abusive behaviour toward ordinary Afghans.[33] In 2019, however, he was pardoned by Trump.

One could argue that, had Lorance and the helicopter pilots been equipped with better technology that enabled them to realise that their victims were unarmed, such incidents might not have occurred. Yet, even if these attackers had clear visual evidence that their targets were unarmed, they might have still acted similarly, albeit

---

[29] Betz 2006, p 517.

[30] (2005) Friendly fire case: The legal saga. CBC News, https://www.cbc.ca/news2/background/friendlyfire/ [accessed 1 April 2023].

[31] (2010) Leaked U.S. video shows deaths of Reuters' Iraqi staffers. Reuters, https://www.reuters.com/article/idUSTRE6344FW20100406 [accessed 1 April 2023].

[32] Farley (2010) Gates said leaked military video of shooting in Iraq doesn't show the broader picture of Americans being fired upon. PolitiFact, https://www.politifact.com/factchecks/2010/apr/12/robert-gates/gates-said-leaked-military-video-shooting-iraq-doe/ [accessed 1 April 2023].

[33] Londoño (2013) Army officer convicted in shooting deaths of 12 Afghans. The Washington Post, https://www.washingtonpost.com/world/national-security/army-officer-convicted-in-shooting-deaths-of-2-afghans/2013/08/01/6ec9aca6-fae0-11e2-a369-d1954abcb7e3_story.html [accessed 1 April 2023].

not killing them. Given the unpredictability of the battlefield, they could have believed that unarmed Iraqis and Afghans could potentially harm US soldiers later. This is a similar argument to Rendulic's, who pointed out that the retreat of Soviet soldiers did not confirm that the Soviets had no intentions of advancing across Finnmark.

The examples above suggest that not even the most advanced C4ISR systems could replace the human element in war, such as the occurrence of basic errors and the sense of uncertainty and fear. The US experience with NCW in these two wars did not correspond to the triumphalist vision portrayed by RMA enthusiasts. If anything, it betrayed the limits of techno-centric visions of war that predicted battlefield clarity. The fact that the US did not leave these two wars as victors, and that its opponents eventually made a comeback, further calls into question the assumptions of RMA proponents.

It is important not to exaggerate the problems, however. Despite not achieving their strategic objectives, US forces on the ground were never seriously defeated in a tactical or operational sense. Its NCW capabilities, while not perfect, were not entirely ineffective either, especially since the United States was fighting an unconventional war in difficult and unfamiliar terrain. This is all the more so if one compares the US military's ability to execute NCW to that of the Russian armed forces in the war in Ukraine.

9.3.2 Russia's ICT Warfare: The Ukrainian Disaster and Systemic Failures

Before it invaded Ukraine, the Russian military had the opportunity to test its NCW and remote warfare doctrine in practice in Syria. For the Russian military, the Syrian War was a low-risk operation where it engaged technologically backward opponents. One of Russia's achievements during this time, as noted by Russian military experts, was the development and operation of an integrated intelligence command strike system, similar to the one envisioned by Chekinov and Bogdanov. These simultaneously coordinated missions and operations of the air force, army, and navy enhanced operational jointness and intelligence sharing, and they streamlined the process between target acquisition and execution. The Russian military also tested the capabilities of its PGM assets and satellite system, as well as its unmanned aerial vehicles and fighter aircraft, while also enhancing its electronic warfare capabilities.[34]

Whether the Russian military had intended to further test its NCW capabilities in Ukraine is difficult to know. In some respects, its foray into Ukraine had never been meant to be a full-scale war. The Kremlin had believed that Ukraine would swiftly fall and that most Ukrainians, except for "Nazis", would welcome Russian forces.

[34] Revaitis 2020, pp 33–50. See also McDermott (2020) Tracing Russia's path to network-centric military capability. The Jamestown Foundation Global Research & Analysis, https://jamestown.org/program/tracing-russias-path-to-network-centric-military-capability/#_ftnref25 [accessed 1 April 2023].

The fact that Russia sent in its riot police, the OMON, to take over and restore order in Kyiv at the beginning of the war is evidence of this misjudgement.[35] Part of this belief might have to do with the cultural, linguistic, historical, and ethnic proximity between the two countries. It is not implausible to assume that such proximity would have provided the Kremlin with good intelligence assets. Another reason could be attributed to the Kremlin's confidence in its capabilities, based on what it considered a successful military campaign in Syria.

Whatever confidence the Russians might have had in conquering Ukraine, it was soon shattered on the battlefield. One surprising aspect has been Russia's difficulties in employing its ICT capabilities. In general, there were four interrelated problems. The first was deficient situational awareness. As opposed to using the latest C4ISR systems, as Russian doctrine stipulates, some units had been given Soviet-era maps made over thirty years ago.[36] Many soldiers did not even know where they were or what they were meant to be doing, never mind synchronising the operational picture.

The second was poor communication. Russia's main secure phone system, the ERA, which handles both secure and non-secure communication, proved vulnerable to jamming. This meant that the Russians often had to use non-secure Ukrainian mobile networks, with fatal consequences for some.[37]

The third was poor satellite technology and imagery intelligence (IMINT), which are crucial for launching precision strikes. The Russians do not use GPS developed by the United States. Instead, it has developed its own positioning called GLONASS. Unfortunately, many of Russia's satellites needed to make GLONASS functional are outdated. Furthermore, the maximum resolution of Russia's Persona satellites is 50 centimetres per pixel, while the American spy satellite, the Keyhole, has a maximum resolution of 5 centimetres per pixel.[38]

The fourth is the Russian air force's deficiencies, and the lack of joint effort with the army.[39] The inability of the Russian air force to dominate the skies has been a constant talking point in this war. Despite years of modernisation and experience in

---

[35] McMillan (2022) Know no mercy: The Russian cops who tried to storm Kyiv by themselves. The Debrief, https://thedebrief.org/know-no-mercy-the-russian-cops-who-tried-to-storm-kyiv-by-themselves/ [accessed 1 April 2023].

[36] Cecil (2022) Putin's troops using "antiquated" maps from 1970s are missing targets in Ukraine, say western officials. Evening Standard, https://www.standard.co.uk/news/world/putin-s-troops-antiquated-maps-1970s-missing-targets-ukraine-western-officials-b997218.html [accessed 1 April 2023].

[37] Bryen (2022) The fatal failure of Russia's ERA cryptophone system. Asia Times, https://asiatimes.com/2022/05/the-fatal-failure-of-russias-era-cryptophone-system/ [accessed 1 April 2023].

[38] Krutov and Dobrynin (2022) In Russia's war on Ukraine, effective satellites are few and far between. Radio Free Europe Radio Liberty, https://www.rferl.org/a/russia-satellites-ukraine-war-gps/31797618.html [accessed 1 April 2023]. See also Grossfield (2022) What does the war in Ukraine tell us about Russian intelligence?. The War on Ukraine Explained: Hear from Our Experts, King's College London, https://www.kcl.ac.uk/what-does-the-war-in-ukraine-tell-us-about-russian-intelligence [accessed 1 April 2023].

[39] Corfield (2022) How Ukraine gave Putin a bloody nose—and rewrote the future of air power. The Telegraph, https://www.telegraph.co.uk/business/2022/06/19/ukraine-gave-putin-bloody-nose-rewrote-future-air-power/ [accessed 1 April 2023].

Syria, Russian fighter jets, most notably the SU-34, still lack many of the capabilities that Western jets have. These include the ability to conduct electronic warfare, provide command and control support to units on the ground, and refuel on air.[40] Some fighter jets had to attach rudimentary GPS receivers on their dashboards because their navigation system was so poor.[41] Despite their capability to launch precision-guided munitions, most have been using old Soviet-era missiles. The failure rate of air-launched precision guided missiles is said to be as high as 60%.[42]

Russia's military performance stands in stark contrast to Ukraine's. In terms of the battlefield intelligence picture, it could be argued that the Ukrainians have an advantage against the Russians given that they are fighting on their territory. They have also benefited hugely from Western intelligence, weapons such as drones and anti-tank guns, and commercial satellites. The Ukrainian armed forces had adopted tactics along NATO lines, encouraging decentralised command, tactical agility, and local initiative.[43] Such changes, together with ICT from the West, have enabled Ukraine to carry out precise strikes against Russian targets. The recent deployment of long-range HIMAR missiles has further strengthened this capability, enabling the Ukrainians to do what the Russians were perhaps meant to be doing according to their doctrine. The Ukrainians' recent successes in the Kharkiv counteroffensive and their steady progress in the Kherson region further attest to their military competence.

The problems bedevilling the Russians in terms of C4ISR are of a different magnitude from those experienced by the Americans. US soldiers had certain problems in employing their advanced C4ISR in difficult and foreign terrain. Some Russian units do not even have properly functioning technologies to begin with, never mind an updated map of Ukraine. Furthermore, American soldiers fought against unfamiliar opponents with whom they had little in common. Ukrainians, if the propaganda from the Kremlin is to be believed, are practically Southern Russians, or at least similar to Russians. They would have surely benefited from the large pool of HUMINT in the form of pro-Kremlin Russian-speaking minorities in Ukraine in a way that the Americans could not. The fact that they have fought in a semi-intelligence vacuum shows just how poorly they are performing.

In a similar way to the United States, Russia's inability to wage NCW might be attributed to techno-centrism amongst its military and political elite. This can also be seen in Russia's NCW concept that is more materially oriented and less expansive

[40] O'Brien and Stringer (2022) The overlooked reason Russia's invasion is floundering. The Atlantic, https://www.theatlantic.com/ideas/archive/2022/05/russian-military-air-force-failure-ukraine/629803/ [accessed 1 April 2023].

[41] Bostock (2022) Downed Russian fighter jets are being found with basic GPS "taped to the dashboards," UK defense minister says. Insider, https://www.businessinsider.com/russia-su34-jets-basic-gps-receivers-taped-to-dashboards-uk-2022-5?r=US&IR=T [accessed 1 April 2023].

[42] Stewart (2022) Exclusive: U.S. assesses up to 60% failure rate for some Russian missiles, officials say. Reuters, https://www.reuters.com/business/aerospace-defense/exclusive-us-assesses-up-60-failure-rate-some-russian-missiles-officials-say-2022-03-24/ [accessed 1 April 2023].

[43] Herszenhorn and McLeary (2022) Ukraine's "iron general" is a hero, but he's no star. Politico, https://www.politico.com/news/2022/04/08/ukraines-iron-general-zaluzhnyy-00023901 [accessed 1 April 2023].

in scope than the United States'. Some have noted that Russia's preoccupation with remote precision strikes has led it to overlook the importance of seizing and holding ground.[44] One could also point to the Russian military's organisational and tactical backwardness and excessive centralisation, which do not sit well with the waging of NCW. Perhaps the bigger reason for Russia's inability to execute NCW is the wider systemic deficiencies within the Russian state.[45] One of the most debilitating factors has been corruption. Some estimate that, every year, around one-quarter of Russia's defence budget gets pocketed by others.[46] The fact that so many of the technologies deployed by the Russians have shown to be defective or simply absent seems to be a manifestation of this.

Russia's failure to conduct its vision of NCW in Ukraine has compelled it to revert to Soviet-style mass artillery. Along with the deliberate execution-style massacres in Bucha, indiscriminate artillery barrage has been the main cause of civilian casualties.[47] However, the fact that many Russian soldiers have refused to fight, have voluntarily turned themselves to the Ukrainians, or have expressed anger at the war, does betray that not all have been supportive of the deliberate killings of fellow Slavs.[48] At any rate, it is not unreasonable to assume that there would have been numerous cases of honest errors.

If one takes into account that some of these men were forced to fight despite their poor training, lack of food and intelligence vacuum, the likelihood of errors would increase. Unfortunately, it is not easy to pinpoint such examples. Compared to the US military, little of what goes on within the Russian armed forces is published or admitted officially. Nevertheless, the recent indictment of Vadim Shimsharin, a Russian tank commander, by a Ukrainian court offers some clues as to the type of mistakes that have been made. Sergeant Shimsharin had been separated from his unit and was coming under fire from the Ukrainians. While escaping in a hijacked car with other soldiers, Shimsharin was told by one of the passengers to shoot an unarmed man who was on the phone. The soldier told Shimsharin that civilians might report their location to Ukrainian forces, which would have put them in danger. Shimsharin duly shot the man. Whether the soldier who told Shimsharin to shoot was a superior commanding officer remains unclear. Following his capture and trial, Shimsharin

---

[44] Cranny-Evans and Kaushal (2022) The intellectual failures behind Russia's bungled invasion. Commentary, The Royal United Services Institute for Defence and Security Studies, https://rusi.org/explore-our-research/publications/commentary/intellectual-failures-behind-russias-bungled-invasion [accessed 1 April 2023].

[45] Mittal (2022) Russian strategy relied on technology: It appears inadequate. Forbes, https://www.forbes.com/sites/vikrammittal/2022/02/27/russian-strategy-relied-on-technology-it-appears-inadequate/?sh=691a58d614fb [accessed 1 April 2023].

[46] Beliakova (2022) Russian military's corruption quagmire. Politico, https://www.politico.eu/article/russia-military-corruption-quagmire/ [accessed 1 April 2023].

[47] Gunter (2022) Bucha killings: "I wish they had killed me too". BBC, https://www.bbc.com/news/world-europe-61003878 [accessed 1 April 2023].

[48] See, e.g., Chance, Picheta and Krebs (2022) "All of it is a lie": Russian paratrooper condemns his country's war in Ukraine. CNN, https://edition.cnn.com/2022/08/22/europe/pavel-filatyev-ukraine-russia-paratrooper-interview-intl/index.html [accessed 1 April 2023].

was found guilty largely for two reasons. First, he was not subject to an order, given that there were no clear superiors to direct one. Second, his actions were not deemed proportional. Instead of shooting the man on the phone, he could have simply gotten out of the car and taken away the phone.

Could Shimsharin have judged whether the civilian on the phone had been reporting on his and his fellow soldiers' location? What means did Shimsharin have to discern this? Could he have simply walked out of the car and asked the civilian, at the risk of being fired on by Ukrainian forces nearby? Even if Shimsharin had the technical means to verify that the civilian on the phone was just having a normal conversation with a friend, could he have been sure that the civilian would not later report on him? One could argue that, much like the case of Rendulic or Lorance, the US helicopter pilot, Shimsharin's actions were driven by fear and uncertainty. He told the court that he did not want to kill the civilian, but that he somehow ended up doing so. His lawyers argued that it was a genuine error of judgment, not an execution-style killing as Bucha.[49]

At present, it is difficult to know how many more cases like Shimsharin will receive publicity. The lurid evidence of mass murder and indiscriminate artillery strikes against civilians is bound to focus the public's mind more on clear-cut war crimes. This does not mean that grey zone cases such as Shimsharin's should be overlooked. Distinguishing such types of error from war crimes in this chaotic war will no doubt be a great challenge to legal scholars.

9.4 Conclusion

The Russian and American war experiences show that the relationship between ICT, information superiority, and battlefield dominance is far less straightforward than RMA proponents envisaged. These experiences do not support the case that advanced ICT provides battlefield clarity and reduces the scope of human errors, whether they are honest or not.

There are three interlinked reasons. The first concerns the limitations of technology in providing information clarity. Russia's technologies simply did not work and were outdated or faulty from the start. While ICT greatly advanced intelligence collection such as SIGINT and IMINT for the US military, it has had less of an impact on HUMINT, much to the dissatisfaction of some combatants. The second involves larger systemic factors. Political, social, institutional and economic settings all shape how ICT is prepared and implemented within the military. These factors become particularly acute when considering the Russian debacle in Ukraine, where

[49] Tondo (2022) Russian soldier says he will accept punishment for Ukraine war crime. The Guardian, https://www.theguardian.com/world/2022/may/20/russian-soldier-will-accept-punishment-ukraine-war-crime-vadim-shysimarin [accessed 1 April 2023]. See also Jenks (2022) Ukraine symposium: The atrocity crimes advisory group & Ukrainian prosecutions of Russian POWs—Part I. Articles of War, https://lieber.westpoint.edu/atrocity-crimes-advisory-group-ukrainian-prosecutions-russian-pows-part-1/ [accessed 1 April 2023].

systemic corruption and pervasive authoritarianism impeded Russia's NCW capabilities from the beginning. Similar factors can also be seen in the United States with its tendency towards techno-centrism. The third and perhaps the most important is the persistence of the human element, namely the psychological, physical, and cognitive strains to which war-fighters are subject. The latest C4ISR assets might be able to collect a plethora of information, but they do not address these inherent strains.

This chapter is a small contribution to the bigger question surrounding the relationship between information technology and the Rendulic Rule. Several other areas, which could be explored in future research, have not been examined here.

One such area concerns how ICT has been used by militaries or armed groups other than the US and Russian armed forces. This would provide a broader, more diverse and geographically balanced picture. A quantitative analysis of the relationship between ICT and battlefield mistakes or successes is another area. This could entail a comparison between recent wars fought with military ICT and past wars where such technologies were not present. Yet another area may involve investigating what distinguishes a battlefield error that is honest from a battlefield error that is not honest and what role, if any, ICT can play in that distinction. Russia's invasion of Ukraine will surely be a rich source of inquiry on this matter.

References

Alberts D (1995) The future of command and control with DBK. In: Johnson SE, Libicki MC (eds) Dominant Battlespace Knowledge: The Winning Edge. National Defence University Press, Washington D.C., pp 77–102

Alberts DS, Hayes RE (2003) Power to the Edge: Command... Control... in the Information Age. Command and Control Research Program Publication Series, Washington D.C.

Althoff M (2016) Human intelligence. In: Lowenthal MM, Clark RM (eds) The 5 Disciplines of Intelligence Collection. CG Press. Thousand Oaks, California, pp 45–79

Betz DJ (2006) The more you know, the less you understand: The problem with information warfare. Journal of Strategic Studies 29:505–533

Biddle S (1996) Victory misunderstood. International Security 21:139–179

Biddle S (2004) Military Power: Explaining Victory and Defeat in Modern Battle. Princeton University Press. New Jersey

Farrell T, Terriff T (2002) The Sources of Military Change. Culture, Politics, Technology. Lynne Rienner Publishers, Boulder, Colorado

Ferris J (2003) A new American way of war? C4ISR, intelligence and information operations in Operation "Iraqi Freedom": a provisional assessment. Intelligence and National Security 18:155–174

Gray CS (2002) Strategy for Chaos: Revolutions in Military Affairs and the Evidence of History. Routledge, London

Grau LW, Thomas TL (1996) A Russian view of future war: theory and direction. Journal of Slavic Military Studies 9:501–518

Jonsson O (2019) The Russian Understanding of War : Blurring the Lines between War and Peace. Georgetown University Press. Washington D.C.

Kipp JW (2007) A review of 'Vladimir Slipchenko and Makhmut Gareyev'. Journal of Slavic Military Studies 20:147–158

McDermott RN (2011) Russian Perspectives on Network-Centric Warfare: The Key Aim of Serdyukov's Reform. Foreign Military Studies Office. http://www.dtic.mil/docs/citations/ADA549119

Murray W (ed) (2004) A Nation at War in an Era of Strategic Change. United States Army War College Press, Carlisle, Pennsylvania

Murray W, Knox M (2009) Thinking about revolutions in warfare. In: Knox M, Murray W (eds) The Dynamics of Military Revolution 1300–2050. Cambridge University Press, Cambridge, pp 1–14

Owens WA (1996) The Emerging U.S. System-of-Systems. https://apps.dtic.mil/sti/pdfs/ADA394313.pdf

Piątkowski M (2013) The Rendulic Rule and the law of aerial warfare. Polish Review of International and European Law 2:69–85

Porter P (2013) Military Orientalism: Eastern War Through Western Eyes. Oxford University Press, New York

Press DG (2001) The myth of air power in the Persian Gulf War and the future of warfare. International Security 26:5–44

Revaitis A (2018) Contemporary warfare discourse in Russia's military thought. Lithuanian Annual Strategic Review 16:269–301

Revaitis A (2020) Russian perception of its network-centric warfare capabilities in Syria. Journal on Baltic Security 6:33–50

Tsagourias N (2016) Non-state actors, ungoverned spaces and international responsibility for cyber acts. Journal of Conflict & Security Law 21:455–474

Tsagourias N, Farrell M (2020) Cyber attribution: Technical and legal approaches and challenges. European Journal of International Law 31:941–967

Warner M (2014) The Rise and Fall of Intelligence: An International Security History. Georgetown University Press, Washington D.C.

Tae Hoon Kim Associate Senior Lecturer in Military History, Swedish Defence University. Address: Drottning Kristinas väg 37, 114 28 Stockholm, Sweden, e-mail: taehoon.kim@fhs.se

Chapter 10
Empathy at War: The Distinction Between Reasonableness and the Reasonable Military Commander Standard

Valentin Jeutner

Contents

10.1 Introduction 234
10.2 Honest Errors in *Hostage* 234
10.3 The Sentimentalist Origins of Anthropomorphised Legal Standards 238
10.4 The Identity of the Reasonable Military Commander 243
10.5 Empathy and Killing 250
10.6 Conclusion 256
References 257

Abstract There is a distinction between asking whether a military commander's act was reasonable and asking whether a military commander acted in the manner in which a reasonable military commander would have acted. The difference is that only the second question compels a person assessing a given state of affairs to engage in empathetic perspective-taking. Accordingly, this chapter argues that the reasonable military commander test is a legal device which invites those who apply it to engage in empathetic perspective-taking. Construing the reasonable military commander test as a perspective-taking device brings into focus the crucial question of whose views and whose interests influence the legal evaluation of a commander's behaviour. Understanding the reasonable military commander test in this way also directs attention to the role of empathy in the battlefield. It is important to be clear about this rationale of the reasonable military commander test in the battlefield in order to ensure that the conduct of military commanders is assessed accurately.

Keywords Reasonable person · Reasonable military commander · Empathy · Sentimental enlightenment · International law of armed conflict · Proportionality

V. Jeutner (✉)
Faculty of Law, Lund University, 22100 Lund, Sweden
e-mail: valentin.jeutner@jur.lu.se

N. Hayashi and C. Lingaas (eds.), *Honest Errors? Combat Decision-Making 75 Years After the* Hostage *Case*, https://doi.org/10.1007/978-94-6265-611-6_10

10.1 Introduction

When military commanders make mistakes, one could assess their behaviour by asking whether the mistake was based on a reasonable, honest error. Alternatively, one could ask whether the mistake was an error that a reasonable military commander would have made.

In practice and in scholarly discussions, these two questions are frequently conflated. This is problematic because, similar though they seem, they are different questions. The first question calls for an assessment of a commander's behaviour with reference to a general notion of honesty or reasonableness. The second question calls for an assessment of a commander's behaviour with reference to the perspective of a hypothetical legal creature: the reasonable military commander.

I will explain the nature of this distinction in Sect. 10.2 of this chapter. In Sect. 10.3, I will address the distinction's conceptual implications, and in Sect. 10.4, I will explore the distinction's practical consequences. I will conclude with the observation that, while both questions are suitable means for assessing the legality of a commander's behaviour, it is in the interest of legal certainty for all actors in a theatre of war to be clear about which test is applied because they rest on different metaphysical foundations.

Before turning to these matters, however, I consider the *Hostage* case since it is frequently identified as one of the first cases applying the reasonable military commander test despite the term's absence from the decision.

10.2 Honest Errors in *Hostage*

When the German *Wehrmacht* left the Norwegian town of Hammerfest on 10 February 1945, the cemetery chapel was the only building left standing. Having forcibly evacuated the town's inhabitants, the *Wehrmacht* burned their homes to the ground and destroyed their hospitals, schools, the waterworks, the power station, every shop, and every factory. Foundations that survived the fires were blown up. Bridges were blasted, electricity cables cut, telegraph posts capped. As the German forces departed from the town, they mined the ruins.[1] The destruction was later described as being "as complete as an efficient army could do it".[2] Hammerfest was just one of many towns in Finnmark—that part of Northern Norway bordering

[1] For a comprehensive account of Hammerfest's destruction, see the report "The Devastation of Hammerfest after the Compulsory Evacuation of the Population at the Beginning of the Month of November 1944" dated 20 April 1945 by the city's engineer, Johannes Kummeneje. Excerpts of the report were cited by the prosecution during the *Hostage* case, see US Nuremberg Tribunal, "Transcript for NMT7: *Hostage* Case" 2761–2769 (27 August 1947), http://nuremberg.law.harvard.edu/transcripts/4-transcript-for-nmt-7-hostage-case [accessed 1 April 2023].

[2] United States Military Tribunal at Nuremberg, *United States v. Wilhelm List et al.* ("*Hostage* Case"), Judgment, 19 February 1948, (1950) Trials of War Criminals Before the Nuernberg Military Tribunals under Control Council Law No. 10, p 1296.

the Soviet Union—which the German forces destroyed in the winter of 1944–1945. Confronted with the threat of quickly advancing Soviet troops in the north of Norway, the *Wehrmacht* was retreating and attempted to slow down the Soviets by pursuing a scorched earth policy. Implementing a decision by Adolf Hitler, Alfred Jodl, Chief of the Operations Staff of the German Armed Forces High Command (*Oberkommando der Wehrmacht*), had decreed that:

> the entire Norwegian population east of the fjord Lynge [must] be evacuated by force […] all homes are to be burned down or destroyed. […] Only by this method can it be prevented that the Russians with strong forces, and aided by these homes and the people familiar with the terrain, follow our withdrawal operations during this winter and shortly appear in front of our position in Lyngen. This is not the place for sympathy for the civilian population.[3]

The decree was addressed to Dr. Lothar Rendulic, Chief of the *Wehrmacht* in Northern Norway. Rendulic, in turn, instructed his troops to carry out the order "ruthlessly". He reiterated that "[p]ity for the civilian population is out of place"[4] and that "no shelter or means of existence of any kind"[5] was to be left for the advancing Russian troops. The subsequent actions by the German armed forces resulted not only in the destruction of towns such as Hammerfest. It also led to the complete devastation of remote fishing villages and settlements in the interior of Norway. In early December 1944, the destruction of Finnmark being well under way, Rendulic received the news that Soviet troops were withdrawing from the northern front and that they were no longer expected to advance further into Northern Norway.[6]

After the end of the war, Rendulic appeared as a defendant before US Military Tribunal V at Nuremberg. In what came to be known as the *Hostage* case,[7] US prosecutors charged Rendulic, among other things, with "wanton destruction of private and public property in the province of Finnmark, Norway, during the retreat of the 20th Mountain Army commanded by him".[8] The applicable legal norm was Article 23(g) of the 1907 Hague Convention (IV) Respecting the Laws and Customs of

---

[3] Jodl A (1944) Teletype, dated 28 October 1944, from Chief of the Operations Staff of the German Armed Forces High Command to Armed Forces Commander in Chief, Norway Concerning the Evacuation of Northern Norway. Reproduced as document 754-PS by United States Military Tribunal at Nuremberg (1950) *Hostage* Case, p 836.

[4] Rendulic L (1944) Teletype from 20th (Mountain) Army to Subordinate Units Concerning the Evacuation of Northern Norway. Reproduced as document NOKW-086 by United States Military Tribunal at Nuremberg (1950) *Hostage* Case, pp 1114–1117

[5] Rendulic L (1944) Teletype from 20th (Mountain) Army to Subordinate Units Concerning the Evacuation of Northern Norway. Reproduced as document NOKW-086 by United States Military Tribunal at Nuremberg (1950) *Hostage* Case, p 1117.

[6] Rendulic's testimony reproduced by US Nuremberg Tribunal, p 5542 (31 October 1947).

[7] According to the tribunal's own law report, the case was so called since "the greater part of the trial was concerned with alleged hostage or reprisal actions of one kind or another", United States Military Tribunal at Nuremberg (1950) *Hostage* Case, p 759. The official designation of the case is, however, *United States of America vs. Wilhelm List et al.* (Case No. 7).

[8] Ibid., p 1295.

War on Land.[9] According to this provision, it is forbidden to "destroy or seize the enemy's property unless such destruction or seizure be imperatively demanded by the necessities of war".[10] Rendulic argued in his defence that the scorched earth policy that he had carried out with respect to towns like Hammerfest was demanded by the necessities of war. His actions were mandated by "military necessity".[11] The tribunal accepted that "the destruction of public and private property by retreating military forces which would give aid and comfort to the enemy may constitute a situation coming within the exceptions contained in Article 23g".[12]

The key point of contention concerned the definition of "military necessity" and the extent to which this concept was informed by a commander's own assessment. In Rendulic's case, it was clear, based on the evidence presented to the tribunal, that "there was no military necessity for [the] destruction and devastation" of Finnmark since the Soviet troops "did not follow up the retreat [of the German forces] to the extent anticipated".[13] Retrospectively, Rendulic himself acknowledged that the scorched earth policy was unjustified. But, he argued, at the time when he gave the order to destroy Finnmark, he believed that these actions were necessary to hinder Soviet advances.[14]

The tribunal agreed with Rendulic that it was not asked to assess the situation retrospectively but to consider "the situation as it appeared to the defendant at the time".[15] The question, the tribunal said, was whether the defendant "acted within the limits of honest judgment" in light of the knowledge and conditions available to the defendant at the time the decision was made.[16] If the defendant's decision fell within the limits of an honest judgment, the action taken in consequence of such a decision was not unlawful.[17] This understanding applies even to decisions based on mistaken assumptions—such as that of Rendulic with respect to the anticipated advance of Soviet troops that did not occur. Applying the test to Rendulic, the tribunal determined that, in light of the information available to Rendulic in November 1944, he could have "honestly conclude[d] that urgent military necessity warranted"[18] the adoption of the scorched earth policy. Thus, Rendulic was acquitted.[19]

---

[9] Hague Convention (IV) respecting the Laws and Customs of War on Land and its Annex: Regulations concerning the Laws and Customs of War on Land, opened for signature 18 October 1907, (1907) 3 Martens (3d) 504, entered into force 26 January 1910.

[10] Ibid., Article 23(g).

[11] United States Military Tribunal at Nuremberg (1950) *Hostage Case*, p 1295. See also Rendulic's testimony reproduced by US Nuremberg Tribunal, p 5536 (30 October 1947).

[12] United States Military Tribunal at Nuremberg (1950) *Hostage* Case, p 1296.

[13] Ibid.

[14] US Nuremberg Tribunal, p 5345 (31 October 1947). See also Rendulic 1965, p 374.

[15] United States Military Tribunal at Nuremberg (1950) *Hostage* Case, p 1296.

[16] Ibid., p 1297.

[17] Ibid., p 1296.

[18] Ibid., p 1297.

[19] Rendulic was convicted, however, on counts one, three and four relating respectively to the "murder of hundreds of thousands of civilians", to the "drafting, distribution, and execution of illegal

The judgment's passage concerning the "limits of honest judgment" is often cited as one of the first examples of the "reasonable military commander" test.[20] In the course of the seventy-five years that have passed since the US Military Tribunal delivered its judgments at Nuremberg, the concept of the "reasonable military commander" has become an established standard for assessing the conduct of military personnel in times of war.[21]

Most frequently, this standard is used to evaluate a commander's assessment of the proportionality of an attack—that is, when assessing whether a commander struck a reasonable balance between the anticipated military advantage of a given operation and the expected civilian casualties and damage to civilian property that the operation entails. The standard is enshrined in military manuals,[22] applied by NATO,[23] the United Nations[24] and non-governmental-organisations, including the International Law Association[25] and Human Rights Watch.[26] Both domestic[27] and international[28] courts frequently refer to it. The standard also featured prominently in a report concerning NATO's bombing campaign against the Federal Republic of Yugoslavia commissioned by the International Criminal Tribunal for the Former Yugoslavia (ICTY) in 2000.[29] The authors of that report stipulated that the balance between the "relative values to be assigned to the military advantage gained" as a result of a given military operation and "the injury to non-combatants and or

---

orders", and to the "murder, torture, and systematic terrorization, imprisonment in concentration camps, forced labor" of civilians, ibid., pp 1233–1234.

[20] Clarke 2012, p 78; Merriam 2016, pp 111–112; Johansen 2019, p 77.

[21] See Chap. 8.

[22] USAF JAG Department 2014, p 19; Ministry of Foreign Affairs (Israel) 2009, para 125; Office of the Judge Advocate General (Canada) 2001, para 418(3). For an overview of the state practice in this area, see the International Humanitarian Law Database of the International Committee of the Red Cross, available at: https://ihl-databases.icrc.org [accessed 1 April 2023].

[23] Montgomery 2002, p 189.

[24] Human Rights Council 2009, paras 42, 700, 1922.

[25] International Law Association's Study Group on the Conduct of Hostilities in the 21st Century 2017, p 369.

[26] Human Rights Watch 2016, p 7.

[27] Supreme Court of Israel Sitting as a High Court of Justice, *Hassan Khalaf Ali el Hamri v. Commander of the Judea and Samaria Region*, Merits, 10 August 1982, [1982] HCJ No. 361/82, 1984 (1) Palestine Yearbook of International Law 129 (1982), p 133; The Supreme Court of Israel Sitting as the High Court of Justice, *Beit Sourik Village Council v. The Government of Israel and the Commander of the IDF Forces in the West Bank*, Merits, 30 June 2004, [2004] HCJ 2056/04, para 46. See also Supreme Court of Israel Sitting as High Court, *Public Committee against Torture in Israel and Palestinian Society for the Protection of Human Rights and the Environment v Israel*, Merits, 13 December 2006, [2006] HCJ 769/02, para 57.

[28] International Criminal Court (Office of the Prosecutor) (2014), paras 26, 75, 81; International Criminal Tribunal for the Former Yugoslavia (ICTY) (Trial Chamber 1), *Prosecutor v. Stanislav Galić*, Judgment and Opinion, 5 December 2003, IT-98-29-T (2003), paras 55, 58, 719.

[29] ICTY Review Committee 2000. The authors of this report are at times credited with having created the standard of the "reasonable military commander", see Henderson and Reece 2018, p 840. In fact, the expression dates back at least to the 1970s. See, for instance, Mallison and Mallison 1977, p 56.

the damage to civilian objects" should be struck with reference to the view of the "reasonable military commander".[30]

While it is possible to construe *Hostage* as one of the first examples of the judicial application of the reasonable military commander test, the tribunal did not explicitly establish such a test. Instead, it asked whether Rendulic "acted within the limits of honest judgment". One way of answering this question is to consider whether a reasonable military commander would have acted in the same manner as Rendulic did. However, it is also possible to answer the question whether Rendulic "acted within the limits of honest judgment" by considering whether Rendulic's behaviour conformed to a general standard of honesty and reasonableness. Thus, the conflation of the two tests can be traced to the very beginning of the line of cases that established international law's reasonable military commander test. If one considers both tests to be essentially the same, their interchangeable use might be deemed unproblematic. As I will argue in the next section, however, the two tests are categorically different with significant conceptual and practical consequences.

10.3 The Sentimentalist Origins of Anthropomorphised Legal Standards

The question whether a military commander acted reasonably or made an honest error can be answered with reference to general notions of reasonableness. However, the question whether a commander acted in the way a reasonable military commander would have behaved, calls for an assessment of a commander's behaviour with reference to the perspective of a hypothetical legal creature: the reasonable military commander.

For the purposes of explaining the difference between the two tests, let us briefly consider the history of the reasonable military commander's domestic counterpart and predecessor: common law's reasonable person. The modern concept of the reasonable person emerged at the turn of the 18th century. The legal climate at the time was shaped by two variants of the European enlightenment: rational enlightenment, prevalent mostly on the European continent, and sentimental enlightenment, prevalent mostly on the British Isles and in Scotland in particular. As I have argued in detail elsewhere,[31] the difference between the two questions concerning a reasonable military commander's behaviour corresponds to the difference between the way in which rational enlightenment thinkers on the one hand and sentimental enlightenment thinkers on the other sought to identify moral principles.

[30] ICTY Review Committee 2000, paras 49–50.

[31] Jeutner forthcoming.

Representatives of rational enlightenment, such as Christian Wolff or Immanuel Kant,[32] argued that moral principles could be identified by reason alone.[33] They considered that moral truths were "built into the universe independent of human psychology".[34] These truths merely had to be discovered by means of rational deductions. To a rationalist, the "criterion of truth is not sensory but intellectual and deductive".[35] The image that emerges from this approach is that of a singular individual directly confronting the universe from which the individual attempts to deduce principles of rightful conduct.

This image stands in contrast to the view advanced by sentimental enlightenment thinkers. For them, enlightenment was not just the "age of reason" but also the "age of feeling".[36] They agreed that the cognitive, analytical faculty of the mind is important. Yet, crucially, they maintained that moral principles are not deduced by reason alone but also by emotional responses to experiences and observations. More specifically, moral sentimentalists argued that individuals possess a "moral sense"[37] that allows them to determine whether a given characteristic or a given action is morally desirable. This moral sense responds not only to the feelings of the individual who is assessing a given situation, but, importantly, connects to "feelings shared among individuals".[38]

David Hume was one of the first sentimentalists. According to Hume, "the minds of men are mirrors to one another", they reflect "each others [*sic*] emotions [...] passions, sentiments and opinions".[39] Hume explains:

> When I see the *effects* of passion in the voice and gesture of any person, my mind immediately passes from these effects to their causes, and forms such a lively idea of the passion, as is presently converted into the passion itself.[40]

For Hume, the assessment of whether or not a given act or characteristic is morally desirable "proceeds entirely from moral taste, and from certain sentiments of pleasure or disgust, which arise upon the contemplation and view of particular qualities or characters".[41] To ensure that an individual's subjective preferences do not unduly influence that individual's "moral taste", Hume writes that an individual must

> depart from his private and particular situation, and must choose a point of view, common to him with others: He must move some universal principle of the human frame, and touch a string, to which all mankind have an accord and symphony.[42]

---

[32] Notably, Immanuel Kant rejected the ideas of the sentimental enlightenment only in the last quarter of his life. See Frazer 2010, p 112.

[33] Ibid., p 8.

[34] Ibid., p 34.

[35] Bourke 1951, p 263.

[36] Moyn 2006, p 399.

[37] Or "moral taste", as David Hume calls it. See Hume 1896, p 581.

[38] Frazer 2010, p 4.

[39] Hume 1896, p 365.

[40] Ibid., p 576 (emphasis in original).

[41] Ibid., p 581.

[42] Hume 2006, p 75.

We must, says Hume, "fix on some *steady* and *general* points of view; and always, in our thoughts, place ourselves in them, whatever may be our present situation".[43] In the 18th century, the taking of this general point of view—the touching of a string connected to all mankind—placing oneself in the shoes of another, would have been described as an act of sympathy. If sympathy is defined as "the active will to identify with others",[44] it is nowadays most accurately described as an act of empathy.[45]

The connection between the thoughts of sentimentalists like David Hume and the concept of the reasonable military commander becomes clearer when one considers that Hume and his successors did not merely advocate the assumption of a general point of view, but that they anthropomorphised this point of reference. In doing so, they encouraged individuals to engage in acts of perspective-taking when assessing a given situation. They encouraged individuals to consider a given situation not from their own but from some other person's point of view. Hume himself proposed that one should strive to conform one's conduct to "the model of a character of which [one] approves".[46]

However, it is Adam Smith, Hume's Scottish compatriot, who presented the most refined account of a personified standard for judging the behaviour of oneself and others. In *Theory of Moral Sentiments*,[47] first published in 1759, Smith develops a comprehensive theory of how our moral sense influences our judgments. Smith begins by explaining that humans must judge the propriety of their own and of the behaviour of others[48] with reference to an imaginary "impartial spectator". Adopting the perspective of an impartial spectator when assessing our own or others' actions means removing ourselves

> from our own natural station, and [to] endeavour to view them as at a certain distance from us. But we can do this in no other way than by endeavouring to view them with the eyes of other people, or as other people are likely to view them. Whatever judgment we can form concerning them, accordingly, must always bear some secret reference, either to what are, or to what, upon a certain condition, would be, or to what, we imagine, ought to be the judgment of others. We endeavour to examine our own conduct as we imagine any other fair and impartial spectator would examine it.[49]

The impartial spectator is meant to facilitate the forming of judgments by providing a point of reference that allows us to look at a given situation from an imaginary external point of view. In order to be able to adopt this point of view, individuals must do two things: use their imagination and empathise.

---

[43] Hume 1896, pp 581–582 (emphasis in original).

[44] Hunt 2007, p 65.

[45] On the etymology and the relationship between the terms sympathy and empathy, see Moyn 2006, pp 399–400. See also Stueber 2019.

[46] Hume 1889, p 158.

[47] Smith 1976.

[48] At times, Smith focusses on self-assessment, at times he focusses on passing judgment on others. But he maintains that both types of assessment are governed by the same principle, ibid., p 109.

[49] Ibid., p 110.

Imagination is important, because the impartial spectator is not an actual third party whose views one could try to gauge.[50] The impartial spectator is a creation of the mind of an individual attempting to gain an accurate understanding of a given situation.[51] As Karsten Stueber explains, in assuming the perspective of the impartial spectator, "we put ourselves in his situation and imagine how he would respond to the situation, how he would think and feel about it".[52] Thus, we imagine not only what the impartial spectator might think about a given state of affairs but also what the impartial spectator would feel about it.

Empathy becomes important here, because what is morally required is judged not with reference to some independent abstract standard, but rather with reference to those concrete sentiments that an impartial spectator would deem appropriate for any other individual and for society to feel in a given situation.

Using imagination and empathy in this manner, the spectator's perspective can be invoked *ex post* to judge a given act or circumstance that has already occurred, for example when assessing a defendant's conduct in court. It can also be used to generate standards of behaviour *ex ante* with respect to acts or circumstances that have yet to occur, for example, when an individual is deliberating how to behave in a given situation.[53]

One might wonder what Smith's impartial observer has to do with the contemporary concept of the reasonable military commander. After all, Smith aimed to develop a theory of how to make moral judgments,[54] a theory that would be an alternative to the rationalist accounts of morality mentioned at the beginning of this section.[55] In his *Lectures on Jurisprudence*, however, Smith explicitly applies the concept of the impartial observer to the field of law.[56] With respect to property law, for example, Smith observes:

> an injury was done one when an impartial spectator would be of opinion he was injured, would join with him in his concern and go along with him when he defended the subject in his possession against any violent attack, or used force to recover what had been thus wrongfully wrested out of his hands.[57]

This would be the case, Smith explains, if one person "wrestles" an apple from another person who had just picked said apple from a tree.[58] And thus, in light of an impartial spectator's disapproval of such an act, it would be proper to conclude that it is not permissible to wrestle apples from other people. Note that the impartial spectator's empathy with the owner of the apple is not itself the foundation of the

[50] See, generally, Del Mar 2018.

[51] Raphael 2007, p 35.

[52] Stueber 2019.

[53] Del Mar 2018, p 64.

[54] Raphael 2007, p 10.

[55] Ibid., p 49.

[56] See also, generally, ibid., Chapter 12.

[57] Smith 1978, p 17.

[58] Ibid., pp 16–17.

apple picker's right to the apple. The impartial spectator's empathy merely "confirms the apple picker's judgment".[59] The ground for the apple picker's right to the apple is their reasonable expectation to acquire title to property by occupying it.[60] However, it is by empathising with the apple picker that this foundation becomes apparent. Apart from property law, Smith also demonstrates the applicability of the impartial spectator doctrine to the areas of criminal law[61] and contract law.[62]

It did not take long before the views of Smith and his fellow sentimentalists began influencing the practice of law. In the late 18th and early 19th century, they led to the emergence of the reasonable person, the reasonable military commander's domestic counterpart.

The reasonable person, the reasonable military commander, and Smith's impartial spectator are not identical. Each of these legal creatures has its own history and context. Nevertheless, considering the scholarship of sentimentalists like Smith helps us answer the question posed at the beginning of this section, namely, whether there is a difference between asking whether (a) a given action is what a reasonable military commander would have done, or (b) whether a given action was reasonable.

In light of the brief introduction to sentimentalist thought, I argue that there is a significant difference that corresponds to the difference between the rationalist and sentimentalist enlightenment thinkers. Asking whether a given action conformed to the behaviour of a reasonable military commander necessarily forces one to engage in an act of perspective-taking. It compels us to consider our own situation from an external point of view and from a distinctly social point of view. Since the idea of an imaginary figure necessarily invokes the image of others (real or imaginary), it reminds the person who is assessing a given situation of that person's connectedness to a specific kind of social context. Even a person alone on an island, when asked to entertain what a reasonable person might do in a given situation, must reflect not just on their role as a single individual but as a member of humanity.

These implications are absent from the question whether a given act was reasonable. It is therefore misleading to equate references to reasonableness standards with references to the reasonable military commander standard. Of course, the question of what it means to be reasonable could be answered by means of perspective-taking, but the abstract notion of reasonableness appeals more obviously to objective truths built into the universe that are accessed not by empathy but by rational deductions.

The argument in favour of understanding the concept of the reasonable military commander as an empathy-based perspective-taking device is not merely an argument about the concept's history. The argument also brings to the fore two crucial questions concerning the concept's contemporary application. The first question concerns the identity of the imaginary reasonable military commander to whose views commanders and courts alike appeal when evaluating conduct at times of war.

---

[59] Raphael 2007, p 110.

[60] Smith 1978, p 17.

[61] Ibid., p 104.

[62] Ibid., p 87.

The second question concerns the manner in which empathy operates on the battlefield and, specifically, the way in which empathy appears to undermine a soldier's preparedness to kill. I will address the first question in the next section and the second question in Sect. 10.4.

10.4 The Identity of the Reasonable Military Commander

If the concept of the reasonable military commander is understood as an empathetic perspective-taking device, its accurate application presupposes that it is clear whose perspective the imaginary reasonable military commander is intended to represent. Legal practice and academic commentaries traditionally focus on two alternative answers to this question. Some maintain that the reasonable military commander is no more than a military avatar of its domestic counterpart. In other words, the perspective of the reasonable military commander is that of a civilian character in uniform. Others argue that the reasonable military commander is a categorically different kind of character, one who subscribes to the logic of waging war and possesses military training.

This question matters, since the standard of behaviour expected of an ordinary reasonable person might differ from that expected of an ordinary military person.[63] In the polemic words of one military officer, the former might be "in the business of saving lives", while the latter is "in the business of killing".[64] It matters also because the answer to the question determines the range of people whose views are relevant when evaluating the standard of behaviour in question. If a reasonable person in the battlefield is understood as an ordinary reasonable person in uniform, then ordinary persons should be able to meaningfully judge whether the decision of a given commander met a given standard of behaviour. By contrast, if the reasonable person in the battlefield is assumed to possess specialised knowledge and particular military competences, the relevancy of the views of ordinary persons who lack such knowledge and competences is precluded.

In *Hostage*, the US Nuremberg Tribunal appeared to favour the latter option. When evaluating whether Rendulic failed to comply with the rules protecting prisoners of war in Southeastern Europe, the tribunal held that the standard of assessment with respect to the conduct of military personnel was based on persons "trained in military science"[65] as opposed to ordinary reasonable persons. Many commentators

---

[63] While it might be presumed that civilians are less likely to commit war crimes, Noel Trew points out that the opposite can also be the case: Trew 2017, pp 124–125.

[64] This account by an anonymous military lawyer is related by Luban 2013, p 315. The lawyer in question described the difference between the perspective of civilians and of military officers. Luban himself distinguishes the two camps by reference to their starting point: one "begins with armed conflict" assigning "military necessity […] axiomatic status" while the other "begins with humanitarianism" assigning "human dignity […] primary status". Ibid., p 316. See also Benvenisti 2010, p 348.

[65] United States Military Tribunal at Nuremberg (1950) *Hostage* Case, pp 1245–1246.

and courts share this view.[66] Ian Henderson and Kate Reece, for example, argue that the standard applicable to commanders in the battlefield is explicitly not that of a "reasonable person", supposedly with a more civilian worldview, but rather that of a "reasonable military commander" standard.[67]

The view of the reasonable person, with which Henderson and Reece contrast the perspective of the reasonable military commander, is often equated with the assumed stance of a human rights lawyer. For instance, the authors of a report prepared for the ICTY concerning NATO's bombing campaign against the Federal Republic of Yugoslavia begin by observing that it is "unlikely that a human rights lawyer and an experienced combat commander would assign the same relative values to military advantage and to injury to noncombatants".[68] They then conclude, however, that the "determination of relative values must be that of the 'reasonable military commander'".[69] Sigrid Redse Johansen, too, maintains that, when assessing a commander's conduct, "the comparison is to be done with a commander, not a 'human rights lawyer'".[70] Yoram Dinstein rejects the idea that the views of civilians, human rights lawyers or otherwise, matter on the battlefield in particularly forceful terms. In a speech delivered at the US Naval War College in Newport on 24 June 2010, Dinstein made an impassioned argument in favour of construing the reasonable military commander in military terms. Dinstein is concerned by the evolving "menace" of "human rights zealots and do-goodniks"—"human rights-niks" for short.[71] These people, he says, present a danger to civilised nations "equally acute"[72] as that posed by the "barbarians",[73] which civilised nations fight. The human rights-niks "would prefer a non-violent solution to every conflict"[74] and are motivated by pacifist motives that resonate "with the lay (and basically uninformed) public at large".[75] They would like to introduce a "system of warfare characterized by zero collateral damage to civilians".[76] Fearing that too much attention is paid to these views when assessing a military commander's conduct, Dinstein asserts that, "in Afghanistan, airstrikes essential to mission accomplishment—and legally unimpeachable—have been scrapped, so as to avoid altogether lawful collateral damage to civilians".[77] As a consequence of

[66] Notably, Rendulic himself observed that he found it particularly irritating that he was asked to justify his conduct during wartime before people who "by their own admission" had not "the slightest idea of war", Rendulic 1965, p 444.

[67] Henderson and Reece 2018, p 841. For similar interpretations of the report, see Holland 2004, pp 48–49; Groeben 2010, p 480.

[68] ICTY Review Committee 2000, para 50.

[69] Ibid.

[70] Johansen 2019, p 86.

[71] Dinstein 2011, p 488.

[72] Ibid.

[73] Ibid., p 484.

[74] Ibid., p 488.

[75] Ibid. See also Sloane 2015, p 319.

[76] Dinstein 2011, p 488.

[77] Ibid., p 486.

construing the reasonable military commander in too civilian terms, the "command echelons" on the side of civilised nations "bend over backward in the application" of the norms governing armed conflicts.[78] According to Dinstein, this is problematic because it weakens civilised nations in the fight against "modern barbarians",[79] who conduct hostilities "in an utterly lawless fashion" and "slaughter civilians on a large scale".[80] Consequently, a "hostile takeover" of the laws of armed conflict by human rights-niks must be "resisted"[81] in the interest of preventing complete "lawlessness"[82] on the battlefield. Reiterating once more his argument in favour of seeing the battlefield as the exclusive domain of the reasonable person construed as a military commander, Dinstein concludes by encouraging the military lawyers gathered at the Naval War College "to keep poachers"—presumably human rights-niks and uninformed reasonable people—"off the grass".[83] Paraphrasing a passage from a text by Michael A. Newton, one could summarise Dinstein's speech by saying: "the reasonable person in the battlefield belongs to the armed forces of the world".[84]

As the defensive tone of Dinstein's speech foreshadows, his view is not undisputed. Many deem the reasonable military commander to be a functional equivalent of domestic law's reasonable person. They argue that the reasonable person in the battlefield is the "reasonable person in the most general sense—the person on the Clapham Omnibus, subject to the normal vagaries of everyday life, not the military commander subject to the completely abnormal vagaries of armed conflict".[85] William O'Brien, for example, calls the "'reasonable colonel' […] the law of war counterpart to the common law 'reasonable man'".[86] Thomas Franck refers to the "reasonable military commander" as "an international version of the common law's reasonable man".[87] Robert D. Sloane connected the standard to "that old favorite of the law, the reasonable person".[88] For Laurie R. Blank, the reasonable military commander fulfils functions "[a]nalogous to the 'reasonable person' in domestic law".[89]

---

[78] Ibid.

[79] Ibid., p 484. For a sceptical view of such a portrayal of the enemy, see Noll 2012, pp 223, 225.

[80] Dinstein 2011, p 485.

[81] Ibid., p 488.

[82] Ibid., p 489.

[83] Ibid., p 493.

[84] Newton 2007, p 900.

[85] McLaughlin 2010, p 237. McLaughlin contrasts this understanding of the reasonable person's identity with a narrower construction of the reasonable person as the reasonable military commander to which the "common law 'reasonable person' […] is irrelevant", ibid., p 232.

[86] O'Brien 1972, p 629. See also O'Brien 1957, p 55. Both times O'Brien attributes the term "reasonable colonel" to Ernst Feilchenfeld. Attempts to verify this attribution were unsuccessful. Paul Ramsey used the same expression (and also attributes it to Feilchenfeld), Johnson and Smith 1974, p 192.

[87] Franck 2008, pp 737, 765.

[88] Sloane 2015, pp 317–318.

[89] Blank 2011, p 717.

Not all of these authors use the term "reasonable person" in contradistinction to the term "reasonable military commander". Others, however, leave no doubt that they are referring to a civilian standard. William H. Boothby, for instance, argues that a reasonable military commander must not do what "all fair-minded people, including the well-known 'man on the Clapham omnibus', would regard [...] as being so excessive as to require prosecution of the person making the decision".[90] In the context of trying Stanislav Galić for besieging the city of Sarajevo, the ICTY also construed the standard in broad terms by stipulating that the perspective that matters is that of the "reasonably well-informed person". The ICTY held:

> In determining whether an attack was proportionate it is necessary to examine whether a reasonably well-informed person in the circumstances of the actual perpetrator, making reasonable use of the information available to him or her, could have expected excessive civilian casualties to result from the attack.[91]

David Luban, too, while offering a very balanced assessment of the debate, rejects restrictive constructions of the identity of the reasonable military commander. To say that "military professionals ought to own the laws of war" (or, for that matter, that they ought to own the reasonable person in the battlefield) is "like saying that Wall Street ought to own securities regulation".[92] "Militaries", he says, "are not the only people in the battle space or the only ones"[93] affected by war. Due in part to the close scrutiny of armed conflicts by the media and by private users of social networks, Luban argues, the "laws of war are now common property".[94] If this is the case, the perspective of the reasonable military commander cannot be limited to that of a person with military experience alone but must also account for the multifaceted perspectives of everyone else affected by armed conflict.

Incidentally, it is also in the context of a colloquium held at the US Naval War College in Newport—the same place where Dinstein shared his concern about human rights-niks kidnapping the reasonable person in 2010—that Michael Bothe advanced one of the most sustained arguments in favour of a civilian identity of the reasonable military commander. Bothe says the decision of the authors of the ICTY Report to describe the reasonable military commander in military terms is "problematic"[95] and "not really a satisfactory solution",[96] unless one defines the "reasonable military commander [...] in more civilian terms".[97] Bothe's plea for a more civilian identity of the reasonable person in the battlefield is rooted in his belief that:

> In democratic systems, the values pursued by the military and those by society at large cannot be far apart. The value system on the basis of which the military is operating has to

[90] Boothby 2012, p 190.

[91] ICTY (Trial Chamber I), *Prosecutor v. Stanislav Galić*, Judgment and Opinion, 5 December 2003, IT-98-29-T (2003), para 58.

[92] Luban 2013, p 338.

[93] Ibid.

[94] Ibid.

[95] Bothe 2002, p 184.

[96] Bothe 2001, p 535.

[97] Ibid.

> conform to that of the civil society, not vice versa. What is necessary in this respect is the dialogue between civil society and the military, which then has to be reflected in military decision-making.[98]

The proceedings of the colloquium[99] which reproduce the discussions following Bothe's presentation reveal that his proposal was met with immediate criticism. While Dinstein, who was also in the audience, remained silent, Harvey Dalton, a captain of the US Navy and a Judge Advocate General, declared that he was "a bit worried" by Bothe's view. "A military commander knows how to employ the Tomahawk land attack missile […] better. I'm going to defer to his judgment in terms of weaponizing and employing" it.[100] Leslie Green agreed. He, too, was "worried about this 'reasonable civilian'—this idea of the ordinary civilian and the ordinary soldier".[101] He asked:

> What was the thought of a reasonable man? A reasonable man is the man on a downtown bus; that is not the reasonable soldier. One of the reasons that I don't like civilian judges trying military offences is that they don't know the circumstances that were prevailing at the time that led to the soldier's actions. The question of what is reasonable in times of conflict depends on what is reasonable in the eyes of the man who is involved in that conflict. That would only be accepted by those who have similar background knowledge, not by one who has been securely moved up in some Inn of Court.[102]

Bothe responded to these comments by pointing to the particular developments in West Germany after World War II. One of the lessons the Federal Republic drew from its history was that it is important

> to integrate the military into a civilian system of values, not to have the military as a state within the State. Arguing that military matters are something which the military knows and the civilian doesn't is utterly a step in the wrong direction.[103]

This exchange concerning the identity of the reasonable person in the battlefield might seem highly specific to the context of the law of armed conflict. At an elementary level, however, the issues raised here engage at least two existential questions of passing legal judgments.

The first concerns the extent to which it is possible for one person (belonging to a community) to pass judgment upon another (belonging to a different community). For the purposes of the law of armed conflict, Natalino Ronzitti suggested that the gap between the civilian and the military perspective could be bridged by inviting military staff to participate in the legal evaluation of military matters by civilian courts.[104] Others suggested that civilian courts could use "expert witnesses to assess what

[98] Ibid.

[99] Wall 2002b.

[100] Wall 2002a, p 211.

[101] Ibid.

[102] Ibid., p 212.

[103] Ibid.

[104] Ibid.

reasonable conduct" of a military commander "might look like"[105] or, conversely, that military staff could consult civilian advisors who are "likely to possess more empathy than the powerful commander".[106] If adopted, such proposals could help integrate and unify the double life that the reasonable military commander currently leads on the battlefield.

The second existential issue facing the reasonable military commander in the battlefield has thus far only been touched upon implicitly. It relates to one of the credos of the Scottish sentimentalists, namely the unity and equality of all humans. It is the assumed—the stipulated—equality of humans that is a cornerstone of Hume's and Smith's theory about the possibility of deriving truth and norms from empathetic engagement with others.[107] This is so, because a person's ability to accurately imagine the perspective of another presupposes at least a rudimentary familiarity of that person with the person whose perspective is being imagined. Stipulating that all humans are ultimately the same with similar senses and faculties thus implies that we can actually reasonably accurately relate to the views of other humans. Transporting the reasonable person to the battlefield has the potential to seriously shake this foundation of the figure.

The problem arises most poignantly with respect to the relative value that the reasonable military commander is expected to assign to civilian lives of the different warring parties. Some argue that a reasonable military commander embedded within a given state's armed force should give priority to protecting the lives of civilians of that state. Sloane observes, for example, that "[n]o state military force that is or has ever been treats enemy civilians and its own civilians equally [...] it is implausible as law [and] would render disproportionate the vast majority of strikes that cause collateral damage".[108] "States", he says, "like people, may—and perhaps should—assign greater weight to the welfare of those with whom they have a morally, socially, or politically salient relationship".[109]

Others vehemently disagree. Gregor Noll argues that in the law of armed conflict, "civilians appear as unqualified civilians. The proportionality rule relates not to 'enemy civilians', but to civilians at large, regardless of nationality or political allegiance".[110] To speak of proportionality in the context of the law of armed conflict, he says, presupposes that there exists a relationship between a given military commander and "enemy civilians" who might die as a result of the former's decision. They form part of the same *demos*, in fact everyone belongs to the same *demos*.[111] Consequently, a distinction between one's own civilians and enemy civilians is not possible; already "the first civilian casualty" injures this common *demos*.[112] A reasonable

[105] Trew 2017, pp 122–123, 125–126. See also Olásolo 2008, pp 229–230.

[106] Adams 2019, p 178.

[107] See also Frazer 2010, p 142.

[108] Sloane 2015, p 330.

[109] Ibid., pp 328–329.

[110] Noll 2012, pp 225–226. See also Traven 2021, p 274.

[111] Noll 2012, pp 227–228.

[112] Ibid., p 228. See also Chap. 11.

military commander would be expected to act as an agent of all humanity when it comes to making proportionality decisions. Thus understood, a reasonable military commander in Rendulic's position could not reasonably have subordinated the interests of the civilian population in occupied Norway to the military interests of the *Wehrmacht*.

While this is not the place to determine which image of the reasonable military commander is to be preferred, it should be noted that the expectation that a reasonable military commander would distinguish between civilians and enemy civilians and/or that it would treat them unequally is asking a lot from an empathy-based standard.

It is evident that some favour an image of the reasonable military commander construed in military terms whose common sense is accessible only to military staff, while others prefer to construct the reasonable military commander as a reasonable person in uniform but rooted in civilian values which are accessible to members of civil society at large. The first alternative represents an understanding of the reasonable military commander standard that is the exclusive preserve of a select group of people. The second alternative would be in keeping with the more egalitarian connotations that the reasonable person, the reasonable military commander's domestic counterpart, has. The point and the appeal of common law's (ideal) man on the Clapham omnibus was precisely the concept's ordinary and accessible character, which was meant to allow everyone to identify the right course of action in a given situation by imagining what the man on the Clapham omnibus would do. Both of these different manifestations of the reasonable military commander exist. However, considering that the utility of the figure of the reasonable person relies on its connection to "common sense",[113] one should note that the smaller the class of people is whose views are permitted to inform the content of that "common sense", the more the standard's ability to offer relatable and predictable guidance in concrete situations is undermined.

This section addresses two existential and unresolved questions facing the reasonable military commander. First, is the figure accessible to civilian persons or is it the exclusive preserve of military personnel? Second, is the reasonable military commander embedded in human society as a whole, or within a particular national context that allows it to distinguish between civilians and enemy civilians?

The foundational nature of these questions, combined with the fact that their answers are the subject of fierce debates, impairs the utility of the reasonable military commander standard in the battlefield. Even if these questions could be resolved, however, there is yet another existential problem confronting this imaginary legal creature: namely, that empathy makes killing difficult.

---

[113] For the question of common sense in the context of war, see, for example, Lieblich and Benvenisti 2016, pp 253–254; Johansen 2019, pp 403–404.

10.5 Empathy and Killing

Towards the end of the first wave of the destruction of Northern Norway by the *Wehrmacht* in late November 1944, Kurt Herrmann, the officer overseeing the evacuation of the civilian population on the ground, prepared a report for Rendulic concerning the measures taken and the results achieved. In that report, Herrmann informed his superior that there are certain forms of conduct that make the evacuation of civilians more difficult. These include: "the separation of the men from their families to be deported and [...] guarding [them] like prisoners [and the] burning down of houses in the presence of the inhabitants even where an immediate destruction was not necessary".[114] Herrmann also noted that the "shelling of the locality Kjoellefjord by units of the navy" while the evacuated population looked on from ships anchored off the town "hinder[ed] the readiness of the population to follow the officially prescribed way".[115]

Herrmann's reflection is entitled "Experiences"—a standard section of these reports meant to help improve the implementation of military missions in the future. One might think that it would be obvious to a reasonable military commander that the needless destruction of homes before the eyes of their former inhabitants might not make the mission, already difficult enough, any easier.

The officer's conclusions are less intriguing if one considers that it is more difficult for persons in positions of power to empathise. Thus, what might be obvious to many might not be obvious to a military commander focussed on turning Northern Norway into an uninhabitable wasteland.

The fact that power impairs its holder's ability to empathise—to understand the views and feelings of others—confronts an empathy-based standard like that of the reasonable military commander with a considerable challenge. The challenge is complicated by the fact that a lack of empathy actually enhances a military commander's ability to implement missions, especially lethal ones, efficiently. Against this background, one might argue that the utilisation of the reasonable military commander test, an empathy-based standard after all, is misguided. Or one might argue that there are few places where an empathy-based standard is more urgently needed than the battlefield.

Before we consider this question and the inherent suitability of the reasonable military commander standard to assist with decision-making in the field towards the end of this section, however, we will first address the relationship between power and empathy. Numerous studies have shown that the possession of power significantly influences how a person relates to others. Findings derived from experiments include that power creates a "psychological distance" between the powerful person and others[116] and that power "leads to reduced processing of others' actions

[114] Herrmann K (1944) Report from Evacuation Staff to 20th Mountain Army Concerning Evacuation of Northern Norway. Reproduced as document NOKW-090 by United States Military Tribunal at Nuremberg (1950) *Hostage* Case, pp 1118–1123.

[115] Ibid.

[116] Galinsky et al. 2006, p 1069.

and emotions".[117] Powerful persons struggle to take the perspectives of others into account and, where they attempt it, they reach less accurate conclusions.[118] Summarising the results of numerous experiments and studies, Adam Galinsky and others have observed that power is "associated with a reduced tendency to comprehend how other individuals see the world, think about the world, and feel about the world".[119] Possessing power makes persons "less likely to spontaneously adopt another person's visual perspective, less likely to take into account that another person did not possess their privileged knowledge, and less accurate in detecting the emotional states of other people".[120]

This relationship between power and perspective-taking has numerous consequences, including a tendency to think in stereotypes,[121] to neglect the interests of less powerful individuals,[122] to objectify others,[123] and to treat them as a means to an end.[124] Deborah Gruenfeld and others observed, for example, that participants of an experiment who were primed to feel powerful reported that they tend to reach out to others when they need something from them and that they were less likely to like a person that was not useful to them.[125] When asked to write the letter "E" on their forehead, power-primed participants tended to write the letter as if they were looking at it (resulting in an illegible mirrored "E"), whereas participants not power-primed wrote the "E" in a manner that other persons looking at them could read it.[126]

Most significantly for our purposes, the possession of power has been linked to a lack of empathy.[127] "[A]s [a powerful person's] empathy wanes", notes Dacher Keltner,

> so does [their] capacity for moral sentiments that depend on empathy – namely, concern for others' suffering (compassion), reverence for what others give (gratitude), and inspiration experienced in appreciating others' goodness (elevation).[128]

Scott Adams counsels a degree of caution when treating the conclusion that power necessarily results in a lack of empathy, since the ability of experiments to simulate the behaviour of people might be limited.[129] Galinsky and others also point out that some studies contradict the findings presented above.[130] As a general

---

[117] Hogeveen et al. 2014, p 759; Adams 2019, pp 168, 169.

[118] Galinsky et al. 2006, p 1068.

[119] Ibid., p 1072.

[120] Ibid. The authors note that the lack of perspective-taking is not necessarily the result of a conscious decision but rather that power "makes perspective-taking less likely".

[121] Galinsky et al. 2006, pp 1069, 1072.

[122] Hogeveen et al. 2014, p 760.

[123] Galinsky et al. 2006, p 1072; Gruenfeld et al. 2008, p 124.

[124] Robertson 2013, p 187.

[125] Gruenfeld et al. 2008, p 127; Robertson 2013, p 187.

[126] Galinsky et al. 2006, p 1070.

[127] Ibid., p 1072; Robertson 2013, p 187. See also Adams 2019, p 152.

[128] Keltner 2016, p 101.

[129] Adams 2019, p 172.

[130] Galinsky et al. 2016, p 92.

phenomenon, however, it appears universally accepted that power tends to result in a loss of empathy. According to Michael Frazer, already David Hume had noted that "oppressive social institutions may successfully shield the feelings of certain others from our view, or may cultivate our own characters so that we are insensible to their feelings".[131] With respect to slavery, for instance, Hume spoke of the "little humanity commonly observed in persons accustomed from their infancy to exercise so great authority over their fellow creatures and to trample upon human nature".[132] In other words, great authority can lead to a lack of humanity and to a lack of empathy.

This conclusion is a problem for the concept of the reasonable military commander, since great authority is certainly one of the distinguishing features of military commanders. Indeed, if power is defined as an "individual's relative capacity to modify others' states by providing or withholding resources or administering punishments",[133] there are few individuals more powerful than commanders with the capacity to modify others' states in quite existential terms from "alive" to "dead". The commander's power coupled with their tendency to lack empathy is problematic, because the standard of the reasonable military commander—which is meant to guide their decision-making-processes—presupposes both the ability to engage in perspective-taking and to empathise. In concrete terms, there is a risk that the distinct character of the relationship between a soldier and a civilian distorts the accuracy of the soldier's interpretation of the context within the soldier must make a decision.

One response to this problem could be to attempt to improve a military commander's ability to empathise. Some studies indicate this possibility, for example, by appealing to a commander's sense of responsibility and accountability.[134] Other studies appear to suggest that a capacity for empathy, once lost, cannot be recovered.[135] The question concerning the utility of empathy training presupposes that armies would be interested in enhancing the capacity of their military commanders to emphasise.

In fact, however, the opposite appears to be the case. This is due to the phenomenon that empathy undermines a person's ability to harm another. Indeed, studies suggest that the closer a soldier gets to their adversary, and the stronger the soldier's identification with that opponent, the more difficult it is for the soldier to kill that person. An episode from the 1831 Polish-Russian War related by the French colonel Ardant du Picq illustrates the phenomenon:

> [T]wo Russian and two Polish regiments of cavalry charged each other. They went with the same dash to meet one another. When close enough to recognize faces, these cavalrymen slackened their gait and both turned their backs. The Russians and Poles, at this

---

[131] Frazer 2010, pp 53–54.

[132] Hume 1889, p 383.

[133] Keltner et al. 2003, p 265. The exact definition of the concept of power is disputed. For a similar though slightly different definition, see Galinsky et al. 2016, p 91.

[134] Galinsky et al. 2006, p 1073. A similar argument had been advanced earlier by Marshall 1978, pp 160–161.

[135] Adams 2019, p 170.

> terrible moment, recognized each other as brothers, and rather than spill fraternal blood, they extricated themselves from a combat as if it were a crime.[136]

A similar pattern of behaviour emerged when Samuel Lyman Atwood Marshall, Chief US Combat Historian of World War II, studied the actions of US troops across numerous battles in the Pacific region and in Europe. In his book, *Men Against Fire*,[137] Marshall presents findings that suggest that "out of an average one hundred men along the line of fire during the period of an encounter, only fifteen men on the average would take any part with the weapons".[138] Even in the most aggressive units, "the figure rarely rose above 25 per cent".[139] The soldiers who did not fire did not desert the scene or hide, "they simply would not fire their weapons at the enemy".[140] Analyses of soldiers' behaviour during World War I,[141] the American Civil War,[142] and even from wars in ancient Greece and Rome,[143] reach similar conclusions.

Studies across these different theatres of war suggest that it is the distance to one another that conditions the likelihood of killing. Jesse Glenn Gray, a philosopher with war experience, noted how "destroying is easier when done from a little remove. With every foot of distance there is a corresponding decrease in reality. Imagination flags and fails altogether when distances become too great".[144] Ardant du Picq likewise concludes: "[t]o fight from a distance is instinctive in man. From the first day he has worked to this end, and he continues to do so".[145]

At one end of the spectrum are long-range weapons that allow a soldier to "slay hundreds and never see their blood flow".[146] At the other end is hand-to-hand combat where a soldier's weapon "becomes a natural extension of his body"[147] that must physically penetrate their adversary. To illustrate this difference, Dave Grossmann ponders whether the pilots who bombed Hamburg in July 1943 causing "horrible deaths, burning and suffocating"[148] to more than 30,000 people would have carried out their mission if instead they would have had to "turn a flamethrower on each one of these […] women and children, or worse yet slit each of their throats".[149] Killing is easier, it seems, when a distance between the soldier and the person the soldier fights limits the extent to which a soldier empathises with the latter.[150]

---

[136] Ardant du Picq 1921, pp 45–46.

[137] Marshall 1978.

[138] Ibid., p 57.

[139] Ibid., p 56.

[140] Grossman 1996, pp 3–4.

[141] Ibid., p 27.

[142] Adams 2019, p 176.

[143] Ardant du Picq 1921, p 110.

[144] Gray 1999, p 178. See also Adams 2019, p 176.

[145] Ardant du Picq 1921, p 112.

[146] Strozzi-Heckler 2003, p 127. See also Grossman 1996, p 97.

[147] Grossman 1996, p 121.

[148] Ibid., pp 100–101.

[149] Ibid.

[150] Fromm 1973, p 123.

Apart from physical distance, the threshold for killing can be lowered further by dehumanising the persons one fights based on their cultural, ethnic or class background.[151] With respect to the act of killing itself, Erich Fromm notes that there is "good clinical evidence for the assumption that destructive aggression occurs, at least to a large degree, in conjunction with momentary or chronic emotional withdrawal".[152] This circumstance is also reflected in the language used to describe the act of killing. Persons killed do not die, but are "engaged", "knocked over", "wasted", "greased", "taken out", or "picked up".[153] Killed soldiers "fall" or "remain" in the field or at sea,[154] enemies are pejoratively called "Kraut", "Jap", or "Reb",[155] and weapons of mass destruction like the nuclear bombs dropped by US forces on Hiroshima and Nagasaki receive nicknames like "Little Boy" or "Fat Man".[156]

Just how considerable the distance brought about by these linguistic conventions is becomes apparent in the comparison of the benign terms given to the atomic bombs with a poet's description on the ground. In a poem entitled "Little Child", Sankichi Tōge describes a scene in Hiroshima after the US had visited "Little Boy" upon the city:

little child, dear child
where can you be?
like a stone stumbled on accidentally
that clear morning, parting
from your eyes, open so wide
you have no mother
suddenly
behind your pupils, which sharply reflect the sky
a dark red cloud rises
and up above is turned inside out and spreads
the disaster of that light with no sound
in front of your endless questions
who will tell you of that day?

little child, dear child
where could you have gone?
leaving you with the neighbors, she went off to work detail
thinking of you
supported only by that devotion
your mother raced to you through burning streets
not strong enough to be bothered

[151] Ibid., p 121; Grossman 1996, pp 160, 161.

[152] Fromm 1973, p 123.

[153] For more examples, see Holmes 1989, p 364; Grossman 1996, p 92.

[154] Ardant du Picq 1921, p 99.

[155] Holmes 1989, p 364; Grossman 1996, p 92.

[156] Holmes 1989, p 364; Grossman 1996, p 92.

by even the maggots beginning to fester on the putrefying soles of her feet
in the darkness of a temporary aid station
silently died[157]

Confronted with these existential horrors of war, captured by Tōge's poem, and lacking the distancing tools discussed above—social, cultural, physical, linguistic or otherwise—human beings do what comes naturally to them: "[s]ome load, some pass weapons, some tend the wounded, some shout orders, a few run, a few wander off in the smoke or find a convenient low spot to sink into, and a few, a very few, shoot".[158] Similarly, Marshall concluded that:

> [T]he average and healthy individual—the man who can endure the mental and physical stresses of combat—still has such an inner and usually unrealized resistance towards killing a fellow man that he will not of his own volition take life if it is possible to turn away from that responsibility.[159]

Consequently, if the armies of the world want their soldiers to shoot, they must actively train these average and healthy individuals, the "ordinary men, who do not like combat at all",[160] specifically to kill. For Ardant du Picq, the French colonel, the entire purpose of an army is to "make men fight in spite of themselves".[161] Otherwise, the "civilized man, in war, which is opposed to civilization returns... to his"[162] peaceful instincts.

One of the first to act in this regard appears to have been the German Army whose 1915 *War Book* already noted that "sentimentality"[163] and "humanitarian considerations"[164] undermine a soldier's fighting spirit and must be kept in check. Rendulic's own order to implement the "scorched earth" policy "ruthlessly" and without "pity" for the civilian population equally reflects an awareness of the potential of empathy to undermine the successful implementation of a mission. The US Army, too, confronted with Marshall's findings, took action after World War II.[165] By taking measures including "rehearsing and mimicking"[166] the act of killing or replacing abstract target circles with human-shaped targets[167] during shooting practice, it was able to increase the firing rates of soldiers from "15 to 20 percent in World War II to 90 to 95 percent in Vietnam".[168]

---

[157] Tōge 2012, pp 38–39.
[158] Grossman 1996, p 20.
[159] Marshall 1978, p 79.
[160] Dyer 1985, p 118.
[161] Ardant du Picq 1921, pp 111, 110.
[162] Ibid., p 112.
[163] Great General Staff of the German Army 1915, pp 71–72.
[164] Ibid.
[165] For a general overview of the manner in which Marshall's studies influenced the US Army and of the most important criticisms of his theories, see Williams 1999, Chapters 4–5.
[166] Grossman 1996, p 132.
[167] Ibid., p 253.
[168] Ibid., p 132.

With this, we now return to the question of the reasonable military commander in the battlefield. Rather than focussing on countering the de-empathising effect of power on military commanders discussed above, armies specifically desire and nurture a soldier's distance and non-empathic engagement with those they are fighting. This might be problematic for many reasons. But it is also a challenge to the utility of an empathy-based standard like that of the reasonable military commander. If it is the case, as the discussion above aims to show, that the reasonable person as such does not kill and that a military commander's power impairs the commander's ability to empathise, one could argue that the application of the reasonable military commander standard in the battlefield is misguided.

Instead, one could operate with less empathy-charged concepts like reasonableness per se or general notions of proportionality and banish the reasonable person from the battlefield. The outcomes of such a course of action do not necessarily have to be disastrous. Some have argued, for instance, that reducing empathy in the field furthers the swift conclusion of hostilities.[169]

Conversely, one might say the fact that the reasonable person is naturally opposed to killing makes it uniquely suited for deployment on the battlefield and that the world would be a better place if battlefields were exclusively populated by reasonable military commanders with a sharpened sense of empathy.

10.6 Conclusion

I have argued throughout this chapter that there is a difference between an abstract reasonableness standard and a personified reasonableness standard. The former evaluates a commander's conduct with reference to abstract notions of reasonableness, whereas the latter complements abstract principles with insights gained by means of empathetic perspective-taking.

I have also shown that this difference is not only a matter of legal history but matters in practice for at least two reasons. First, construing the reasonable military commander test as a perspective-taking device brings into focus the crucial question of whose views and whose interests influence the legal evaluation of a commander's behaviour. Second, understanding the reasonable military commander test in accordance with its rationale directs attention to the role of empathy in the battlefield. It is problematic if modern armies train their commanders and soldiers to overcome their natural empathetic instincts and at the same time subject these commanders and soldiers to a legal standard that explicitly relies on that very sentiment that the commanders and soldiers are trained to disregard.

The most straight forward reply to my argument, and to the problem of empathy in the battlefield more generally, is to suggest that any reference to the reasonable military commander standard be read as a reference to general reasonableness. The second of the two questions posed at the beginning of this chapter—namely, whether

[169] Great General Staff of the German Army 1915, pp 71–72. See also Adams 2019, pp 175–176.

a military commander acted in the way in which a reasonable military commander would have acted—would then be equated with the first question, i.e. whether a military commander acted reasonably. This would introduce a degree of terminological imprecision into the legal analysis of the behaviour of commanders. A more serious consequence of this approach is, however, the sacrifice of the most important function of the concept of the reasonable military commander construed as an empathetic perspective-taking device, namely, the reminder that one's own perspective is always only one amongst many. Indeed, asking oneself whether a proposed course of conduct corresponds to what another hypothetical person would do compels us to engage with views other than our own and thereby subjects our own convictions to a (self-)critical review process.

It is of course difficult to determine the extent to which such a (self-)critical review process would make a difference in practice. Perhaps a (self-)critical review process would not have inhibited Rendulic from giving the order to implement the scorched earth policy in Northern Norway; perhaps it would have been difficult for a person like Rendulic, so embedded within the logic of the German *Wehrmacht*, to consider his own behaviour from an external point of view.

Nevertheless, the mere potential that military commanders subjected to empathetic perspective-taking test may adopt more considered and more empathetic decisions is sufficient justification for construing the reasonable military commander standard in accordance with its original rationale. That is so even if, and maybe especially because, thus construed, the reasonable military commander test could reduce the lethality of combatants in the field.

References

Adams RS (2019) Power and proportionality: The role of empathy and ethics on valuing excessive harm. AF L Rev 80:149–182

Ardant du Picq CJJJ (1921) Battle Studies: Ancient and Modern Battle. Macmillan, New York

Benvenisti E (2010) The legal battle to define the law on transnational asymmetric warfare symposium: war bound by law: non-state actors and the law of armed conflict in the twenty-first century. Duke Journal of Comparative and International Law 20:339–360

Blank LR (2011) A new twist on an old story: lawfare and the mixing of proportionalities AGORA: classic international legal maxims in a modern world. Case Western Reserve Journal of International Law 43:707–738

Boothby WH (2012) The Law of Targeting. Oxford University Press, Oxford

Bothe M (2001) The protection of the civilian population and NATO bombing on Yugoslavia: comments on a Report to the Prosecutor of the ICTY. European Journal of International Law 12:531–535

Bothe M (2002) Targeting. In: Wall AE (ed) Legal and Ethical Lessons of NATO's Kosovo Campaign. Naval War College, Newport, Rhode Island, pp 173–188

Bourke VJ (1951) Rationalism. In: Runes DD (ed) The Dictionary of Philosophy. Philosophical Library, New York

Clarke B (2012) Proportionality in armed conflicts: a principle in need of clarification? Journal of International Humanitarian Legal Studies 3:73–123

Del Mar M (2018) Common virtue and the perspectival imagination: Adam Smith and common law reasoning. Jurisprudence 9:58–70
Dinstein Y (2011) Concluding remarks: LOAC and attempts to abuse or subvert it. In: Pedrozo RA, Wollschlaeger DP (eds) International law and the Changing Character of War. Naval War College, Newport, Rhode Island, pp 483–496
Dyer G (1985) War. Crown, New York
Franck TM (2008) On proportionality of countermeasures in international law. American Journal of International Law 102:715–767
Frazer ML (2010) The Enlightenment of Sympathy: Justice and the Moral Sentiments in the Eighteenth Century and Today. Oxford University Press, Oxford
Fromm E (1973) The Anatomy of Human Destructiveness. Holt, Rinehart and Winston, New York
Galinsky AD, Magee JC, Inesi ME, Gruenfeld DH (2006) Power and perspectives not taken. Psychological Science 17:1068–1074
Galinsky AD, Rucker DD, Magee JC (2016) Power and perspective-taking: a critical examination. Journal of Experimental Social Psychology 67:91–92
Gray JG (1999) The Warriors: Reflections on Men in Battle. University of Nebraska Press, Lincoln
Great General Staff of the German Army (1915) The War Book of the German General Staff. McBridge, Nast & Company, New York
Grossman D (1996) On Killing: The Psychological Cost of Learning to Kill in War and Society. Little, Brown and Co., New York
Gruenfeld DH, Inesi ME, Magee JC, Galinsky AD (2008) Power and the objectification of social targets. Journal of Personality and Social Psychology 95:111–127
Henderson I, Reece K (2018) Proportionality under international humanitarian law: the "reasonable military commander" standard and reverberating effects. Vanderbilt Journal of Transnational Law 51:835–855
Hogeveen J, Inzlicht M, Obhi SS (2014) Power changes how the brain responds to others. Journal of Experimental Psychology: General 143:755–762
Holland J (2004) Military objective and collateral damage: their relationship and dynamics. Yearbook of International Humanitarian Law 7:35–78
Holmes R (1989) Acts of War: The Behaviour of Men in Battle. Simon & Schuster, New York
Human Rights Council (2009) Human Rights in Palestine and Other Occupied Arab Territories: Report of the United Nations Fact-Finding Mission on the Gaza Conflict, UN DOC A/HRC/12/48
Human Rights Watch (2016) Making the Case: The Dangers of Killer Robots and the Need for a Preemptive Ban. Available at https://www.hrw.org/sites/default/files/report_pdf/arms1216_web.pdf
Hume D (1889) Essays: Moral, Political, and Literary. Lewis, London
Hume D (1896) A Treatise of Human Nature (Selby-Bigge LA (ed)). Clarendon Press, Oxford
Hume D (2006) An Enquiry Concerning the Principles of Morals: A Critical Edition (Beauchamp TL (ed)). Clarendon Press, Oxford
Hunt L (2007) Inventing Human Rights: A History. W. W. Norton & Company, New York
ICTY Review Committee (2000) Final Report to the Prosecutor by the Committee Established to Review the NATO Bombing Campaign Against the Federal Republic of Yugoslavia, ICTY, The Hague
International Criminal Court (Office of the Prosecutor) (2014) Situation in the Republic of Korea (Article 5 Report), ICC, The Hague
International Law Association's Study Group on the Conduct of Hostilities in the 21st Century (2017) The Conduct of Hostilities and International Humanitarian Law: Challenges of 21st Century Warfare. International Law Studies 93:322–388
Jeutner V (forthcoming) The Reasonable Person: A Legal Biography. Cambridge University Press, Cambridge
Johansen SR (2019) The Military Commander's Necessity: The Law of Armed Conflict and Its Limits. Cambridge University Press, Cambridge

Johnson J, Smith D (1974) Love and Society: Essays in the Ethics of Paul Ramsey. Scholars' Press
Keltner D (2016) The Power Paradox: How We Gain and Lose Influence. Penguin, London
Keltner D, Gruenfeld DH, Anderson C (2003) Power, approach, and inhibition. Psychological Review 110:265–284
Lieblich E, Benvenisti E (2016) The obligation to exercise discretion in warfare: why autonomous weapon systems are unlawful. In: Bhuta N, Beck S, Geiß R, Liu H-Y, Creß C (eds) Autonomous Weapons Systems: Law, Ethics, Policy. Cambridge University Press, Cambridge, pp 245–283
Luban D (2013) Military necessity and the cultures of military law. Leiden Journal of International Law 26:315–349
Mallison WT, Mallison SV (1977) The juridical status of irregular combatants under the international humanitarian law of armed conflict. Case Western Reserve Journal of International Law 9:39–78
Marshall SLA (1978) Men Against Fire: The Problem of Battle Command in Future War. Peter Smith, Gloucester, Mass.
McLaughlin R (2010) The law of armed conflict and international human rights law: some paradigmatic differences and operational implications. Yearbook of International Humanitarian Law 13:213–243
Merriam JJ (2016) Affirmative target identification: operationalizing the principle of distinction for US warfighters. Virginia Journal of International Law 56:83–146
Ministry of Foreign Affairs (Israel) (2009) The Operation in Gaza: Factual and Legal Aspects. Ministry of Foreign Affairs, Jerusalem
Montgomery T (2002) Legal perspective from the EUCOM targeting cell. In: Wall AE (ed) Legal and Ethical Lessons of NATO's Kosovo campaign. Naval War College, Newport, Rhode Island, pp 189–197
Moyn S (2006) Empathy in history, empathizing with humanity. History and Theory 45:397–415
Newton MA (2007) Modern military necessity: the role and relevance of military lawyers symposium. Roger Williams U L Rev 12:877–903
Noll G (2012) Analogy at war: proportionality, equality and the law of targeting. Netherlands Yearbook of International Law 43:205–230
O'Brien WV (1957) The Yearbook of World Polity. Praeger, Westport
O'Brien WV (1972) Law of war, command responsibility and Vietnam, The. Geo L J 60:605–664
Office of the Judge Advocate General (Canada) (2001) Joint Doctrine Manual, Law of Armed Conflict at the Tactical and Operational Levels, B-GJ-005-104/FP-021
Olásolo H (2008) Unlawful Attacks in Combat Situations: From the ICTY's Case Law to the Rome Statute. Brill Nijhoff, Leiden
Raphael DD (2007) The Impartial Spectator: Adam Smith's Moral Philosophy. Clarendon Press, Oxford
Rendulic L (1965) Soldat in stürzenden Reichen. Damm Verlag, Munich
Robertson IH (2013) How power affects the brain. The Psychologist 26:186–189
Sloane RD (2015) Puzzles of proportion and the "reasonable military commander": reflections on the law, ethics, and geopolitics of proportionality. Harvard National Security Journal 6:299–343
Smith A (1976) The Theory of Moral Sentiments (Raphael DD, Macfie AL (eds)). Clarendon Press, Oxford
Smith A (1978) Lectures on Jurisprudence (Meek RL, Raphael DD, Stein PG (eds)). Clarendon Press, Oxford
Strozzi-Heckler R (2003) In Search of the Warrior Spirit: Teaching Awareness Disciplines to the Green Berets. North Atlantic Books, Berkeley
Stueber K (2019) Empathy. In: Zalta EN (ed) The Stanford Encyclopedia of Philosophy. Metaphysics Research Lab, Stanford University, Stanford
Tōge S (2012) Little Child. In: Tōge S (author) Poems of the Atomic Bomb. University of Chicago, Chicago, pp 38–41
Traven D (2021) Law and Sentiment in International Politics: Ethics, Emotions, and the Evolution of the Laws of War. Cambridge University Press, Cambridge

Trew N (2017) Dead Letter Law Arising from Strategic Choices: The Difficulty of Achieving Accountability for the Jus in Bello Rules on Proportionality and Precautions in Attack. University of Exeter, Exeter

USAF JAG Department (2014) Air Force Operations and the Law, 3rd edn. United States Air Force, Maxwell AFB

von der Groeben C (2010) Criminal responsibility of German soldiers in Afghanistan: the case of Colonel Klein. German Law Journal 11:469–491

Wall AE (ed) (2002a) Discussion: Reasonable Military Commanders and Reasonable Civilians. Legal and Ethical Lessons of NATO's Kosovo Campaign. International Law Studies. Naval War College, Newport, Rhode Island, pp 211–212

Wall AE (2002b) Legal and Ethical Lessons of NATO's Kosovo campaign. Naval War College, Newport, Rhode Island

Williams FDG (1999) SLAM - The Influence of S.L.A. Marshall on the United States Army. In: Canedy S (ed) Office of the Command Historian, United States Army Training and Doctrine Command, Washington, D.C.

Other Documents

US Nuremberg Tribunal, "Transcript for NMT7: Hostage Case" 2761–2769 (27 August 1947). Available at: https://nuremberg.law.harvard.edu

Valentin Jeutner Associate Professor of Law, Lund University Faculty of Law. Address: 22100 Lund, Sweden, e-mail: valentin.jeutner@jur.lu.se

Chapter 11
Drone Warfare, Civilian Deaths, and the Narrative of Honest Mistakes

Matthew Talbert and Jessica Wolfendale

Contents

11.1 Introduction 262
11.2 The Narrative of Honest Mistakes and the Acceptance of Civilian Casualties 263
11.3 Moral Responsibility, Blame and Honest Mistakes 266
11.3.1 Blame and Blameworthiness 266
11.3.2 Blame and Collateral Damage 268
11.4 Are Honest Mistakes Possible in the US Drone Programme? 272
11.4.1 Knowledge and Intention in the Military Institution 275
11.4.2 Errors and the Suppression of Knowledge 276
11.4.3 Suppression and Denial of Knowledge in the Military 277
11.4.4 Knowable Recognised Unknowns 278
11.5 Conclusion 280
11.5.1 The Moral Risk of Joining the Military 281
11.5.2 Punishing and Preventing Unintended Civilian Harm 282
References 284

Abstract In this chapter, we consider the plausibility and consequences of the use of the term "honest errors" to describe the accidental killings of civilians resulting from the US military's drone campaigns in Iraq, Syria, Afghanistan, and elsewhere. We argue that the narrative of "honest errors" unjustifiably excuses those involved in these killings from moral culpability, and reinforces long-standing, pernicious assumptions about the moral superiority of the US military and the inevitability of civilian deaths in combat. Furthermore, we maintain that, given the knowledge-distorting practices within the US military's organisational structure, few if any civilian deaths from drone strikes meet the criteria of a genuinely morally excusing "honest mistake". Instead, these accidental killings often reflect objectionable attitudes of relative disregard

M. Talbert (✉)
West Virginia University, Morgantown, WV 26506, USA
e-mail: matthew.talbert@mail.wvu.edu

Lund-Gothenburg Responsibility Project, Lund, Sweden

J. Wolfendale
Case Western Reserve University, Clark Hall 211, 11130 Bellflower Road, Cleveland, OH 44106, USA
e-mail: jessica.wolfendale@case.edu

N. Hayashi and C. Lingaas (eds.), *Honest Errors? Combat Decision-Making 75 Years After the* Hostage *Case*, https://doi.org/10.1007/978-94-6265-611-6_11

for the safety of civilians. These attitudes are, we argue, sufficient to warrant the attribution of blame and moral responsibility, both with respect to certain individual actions and with respect to the US military as an institution. In light of this, we propose incorporating a *principle of the moral equality of non-combatants* into military assessments of what counts as "acceptable risk" to civilians. This would go some way, we argue, to redressing the ongoing injustice inflicted on the victims of civilian killings by the failure of the US military and US political leadership to take moral responsibility for unjustified civilian deaths.

Keywords Rendulic rule · drone warfare · war crimes · moral responsibility · honest mistakes · blame · military ethics

11.1 Introduction

On 29 August 2021, a US drone strike in Kabul killed 10 Afghan civilians, including seven children. As reported by the *New York Times* in a series of articles in late 2021, this strike was one of many drone strikes that have mistakenly killed civilians.[1]

The causes of these mistakes are controversial.[2] Our goal here is not to further elucidate the causes of these drone strikes. Instead, in this chapter we focus on the legal and moral narrative of "tragic mistakes"[3] or "awful but lawful" outcomes, to use the military's own parlance,[4] that has consistently accompanied media, military, and political reportage of civilian deaths from drone strikes. In what follows, we show how this narrative replicates and reinforces long-standing and entrenched assumptions about the moral superiority of the US military and the inevitability of civilian deaths in combat, and cultivates a denial of individual and collective moral and legal responsibility for civilian deaths. Drawing on the account of moral responsibility and

[1] Khan (2021) Hidden Pentagon records reveal patterns of failure in deadly airstrikes. The New York Times, https://www.nytimes.com/interactive/2021/12/18/us/airstrikes-pentagon-records-civilian-deaths.html [accessed 1 April 2023].

[2] For example, some commentators argue that a contributing factor to the high number of civilian deaths from US drone strikes are the targeting guidelines adopted by the US military. In particular, the US has refused to adopt the First Additional Protocol (API) to the Geneva Conventions from 1977, which requires that belligerents "do everything feasible" (Article 57) to verify that targets are not civilians or civilian objects, and states that "in case of doubt whether a person is a civilian, that person shall be considered a civilian" (Article 50) (Protocol Additional to the Geneva Conventions of 12 August 1949, and relating to the Protection of Victims of International Armed Conflicts (Protocol I), opened for signature 8 June 1977, 1125 UNTS 3 (entered into force 7 December 1978)). Instead, the US military "only acknowledges a duty to take feasible precautions in 'good faith' to avoid civilian casualties". Rosen 2021.

[3] U.S. Central Command (2021) https://www.centcom.mil/MEDIA/Transcripts/Article/2781320/general-kenneth-f-mckenzie-jr-commander-of-us-central-command-and-pentagon-pres/ [accessed 1 April 2023].

[4] Rosen 2021.

blameworthiness developed in our book *War Crimes: Causes, Excuses, and Blame*,[5] we argue that this narrative reflects and reinforces an unjustified and morally blameworthy acceptance of preventable civilian deaths. Put simply, due to the combination of knowledge-distorting practices within the military's organisational structure and unique features of the drone programme, few if any civilian deaths from drone strikes meet the criteria of a morally excusing "honest mistake". In light of this, we propose incorporating a new principle—the *principle of the moral equality of noncombatants*—into decision-making procedures around acceptable risk to civilians as well as into military training and education around collateral damage mitigation. This would go some way, we argue, to redressing the ongoing injustice inflicted on the victims of civilian killings by the failure of the US military and US political leadership to take moral responsibility for unjustified civilian deaths. In our conclusion we consider the implications of our argument for the morality of enlisting in a military force that is known to engage in practices that impose morally blameworthy degrees of risk to civilians. Secondly, we explore the implications of our view for assessments of institutional and individual legal and moral culpability for collateral damage and consider concrete steps that may be taken to reduce the risks that US combat operations pose to civilians.

11.2 The Narrative of Honest Mistakes and the Acceptance of Civilian Casualties

The narrative of "honest" or "tragic" mistakes is consistently used to describe cases of civilian deaths caused by drone strikes and is often accompanied by assertions that the US military is committed to protecting civilians. For example, a Pentagon investigation determined that the 29 August 2021 strike in Kabul "was an 'honest mistake'"[6] and Pentagon spokesperson John Kirby stated that "[n]o military in the world works as hard as we do to avoid civilian casualties".[7] Similarly, according to the *New York Times*:

> Capt. Bill Urban, the spokesman for the U.S. Central Command, said that "even with the best technology in the world, mistakes do happen, whether based on incomplete information or misinterpretation of the information available. And we try to learn from those mistakes." He added: "We work diligently to avoid such harm. We investigate each credible instance. And we regret each loss of innocent life."[8]

The description of civilian deaths as honest mistakes in conjunction with the affirmation of the US military's commitment to protecting civilian lives creates the

[5] Talbert and Wolfendale 2019.

[6] Borger (2021) "Honest mistake": US strike that killed Afghan civilians was legal--Pentagon. The Guardian. https://www.theguardian.com/world/2021/nov/04/us-afghanistan-strike-killed-civilians-legal-pentagon [accessed 1 April 2023]

[7] Quoted in Rosen 2021.

[8] Khan (2021), n. 1 above.

impression that civilian deaths are unfortunate events for which no one is to blame. But, once we unpack the narrative of honest mistakes more carefully, we see that this narrative relies on a toxic combination of assumptions that combine to unjustifiably portray civilian deaths from drones as unavoidable accidents, thus relieving those involved of moral responsibility. By reinforcing and reflecting these assumptions, the narrative of honest mistakes entrenches what we argue in the following sections is a morally objectionable and unjustified denial of moral and legal culpability for civilian deaths caused by drone strikes. These deaths, we argue, are not the result of exculpating honest mistakes, but instead are often the result of biases and intentions that justify the attribution of moral blame.

Both international humanitarian law (IHL) and just war theory[9] operate on the assumption that some civilian deaths in conflict are inevitable. IHL requires combatants to take all feasible steps to ensure that the direct targets of military actions are legitimate military targets and to choose options that minimise foreseeable harm to non-combatants (even at some increased risk to combatants). But military actions that meet the principles of distinction, proportionality, necessity, and precaution are not war crimes even if civilians are killed as a result. As Marko Milanovic puts it, "the overall architecture of these rules, e.g., as written in API or the ICRC Customary IHL Study, would seem to imply that if [these principles] are all respected the mistaken death of a civilian, however unfortunate, would not ipso facto violate IHL."[10]

There are, of course, important questions to be asked about how the principles of distinction, proportionality, necessity, and precaution are to be interpreted.[11] But, what is important for our analysis here is how the supposed inevitability of civilian deaths is connected to narratives that excuse the institutions and individuals who cause those deaths from blame. If it is impossible to avoid harm to civilians in a conflict, then there is little motivation to question whether any specific incident of civilian deaths could have been avoided. As Neta Crawford argues: "incidental 'collateral damage' deaths are often understood as the tragic outcome of war—they are described as natural and framed as inevitable and certainly not the result of deliberate choices by individuals."[12] But, as we discuss in more detail in Sect. 11.4, this narrative misrepresents the degree of control that the US military can and has exercised over the risks posed to civilians from US military actions. As Crawford explains, "the argument that 'civcas' [civilian casualties] were inevitable and unforeseeable is

[9] "Just war theory" refers to a historical and contemporary body of literature that discusses the conditions under which the resort to war is justified (*jus ad bellum*) and the moral constraints that apply to the conduct of war (*jus in bello*). While there are many disagreements within this tradition regarding both sets of criteria, there is broad agreement in traditional just war theory that collateral civilian deaths may be morally permissible if they are not directly intended and if they are proportionate to the importance of military goals to be achieved by the action in question. See "War" in the Stanford Encyclopedia of Philosophy (https://plato.stanford.edu/) [accessed 1 April 2023] for an overview of just war theory and its central debates.

[10] Milanovic 2020.

[11] These questions are beyond the scope of this chapter, however. See Haque (2011 and 2017) for an overview of these issues.

[12] Crawford 2013, p 40.

belied by the fact that when US rules of engagement or procedures changed, the incidence of civilian killing waxed and waned."[13] And so, she argues, "many episodes of collateral damage are foreseeable, foreseen, and preventable, albeit strictly legal."[14]

When uncritical acceptance of the view that civilian deaths are inevitable is combined with modern targeting technologies, like drones, that are described as "precise" and "humane",[15] civilian casualties caused by these technologies are even more likely to be framed as unavoidable and thus as not challenging the US military's claim to be a humane organisation dedicated to protecting civilians. As Patricia Owens argues: "Alongside the basic laws of war, which allow for 'collateral' or unintended damage, and the over-selling of precision technology, such claims [of civilian deaths as accidental] are supported by widespread assumptions that the conduct of war for the West is becoming more 'humane'."[16]

As is apparent, then, the description of civilian casualties resulting from drone strikes as unavoidable accidents—"unintentionally consequential random happenings", to use Owens's phrase[17]—has significant implications for judgments of moral and legal responsibility for those deaths. If civilian casualties are unavoidable and unintentional and the US military is committed to protecting civilians, as is claimed, then, the thinking goes, all reasonable steps must have been taken to ascertain that the targets were not civilians and/or that any collateral damage would be minimal. So, there is no basis on which to say that a strike that killed civilians should not have gone ahead. This means that while it might be appropriate for the individuals involved in such a strike to express regret about the "tragic mistake", feelings of guilt or shame that manifest an awareness of moral blameworthiness would be inappropriate.

This way of framing moral and legal responsibility for civilian deaths from drone strikes asks us to evaluate the knowledge and intentions of individuals involved in the strike. But this approach obscures the fact that a drone strike is a *collective* action resulting from the decisions and actions of many people operating in a complex and hierarchical institution, many of whom will only have specific and partial knowledge related to their role in the process. It is, therefore, likely to be true that any given individual involved in a drone strike did not know that civilians would be harmed—and so, when we adopt the framework of honest mistakes and the individualised approach to responsibility that it implies, moral responsibility disappears from the picture.

But, as we explain in more detail in the following section, a plausible account of blame and honest mistakes reveals how the choices, actions, and intentions of those involved in the US drone programme can reflect institutionally embedded as well as

[13] Ibid., p 157.

[14] Ibid., pp 40–41.

[15] Emery 2022, p 5.

[16] Owens 2005, p 596. To fully understand the narrative of honest mistakes, it must be understood as part of a long-standing and deeply embedded social and political narrative depicting the US (and the US military) as inherently more humane and more civilised than its enemies. See Esch 2010 for examples of this narrative in relation to the war on terror.

[17] Owens 2005, p 597.

individually blameworthy forms of indifference to, and disregard for, the lives and wellbeing of the victims of drones strikes.

11.3 Moral Responsibility, Blame and Honest Mistakes

11.3.1 Blame and Blameworthiness

Given the diverse uses of "responsible" and its cognates, it is worth emphasising that we are not primarily concerned with responsibility in the sense of *having a responsibility*, such as when a captain is said to be responsible for her ship and crew. Rather, we are concerned with responsibility in the sense of *being morally responsible for* one's actions and the consequences of one's actions.[18]

In our view, a person is morally responsible for their behaviour if that behaviour is attributable to them in such a way that they are praiseworthy or blameworthy for it, where this means being open to the responses and reactions typically involved in praise and blame.[19] What this usually requires is that the person's behaviour is explained by the moral quality of their will and intentions.[20]

Given the subject matter of this chapter, we will be concerned with blameworthiness rather than praiseworthiness. But when, and under what circumstances, is it fair to blame a person for their actions? What factors would excuse a person from blame when they have done something that would normally leave them open to blame? While there are circumstances that are generally agreed to be excusing conditions, such as when a person is coerced or suffers from a severe mental illness, there are many cases where there is disagreement about whether a person should be excused (or exempted) from moral blame.

Some authors argue that the various pressures involved in military training and culture (not to mention active combat) make it unreasonably difficult for military personnel to recognise the moral or legal status of various wrongful acts, such as torturing prisoners or killing civilians. Thus, supporters of this view argue, it may often be unreasonable to expect military personnel to refrain from these behaviours. If this view is correct, it may also follow that it would be unfair to hold military personnel morally or legally responsible, and to blame them, for engaging in the relevant wrongful (or illegal) conduct. For example, John Doris and Dominic Murphy argue

[18] In addition to distinguishing between *being* morally responsible and *having* a responsibility, moral responsibility should also be distinguished from mere causal responsibility. It may be that one needs to be causally responsible for an outcome in order to be morally responsible for it, but bearing such a causal relationship is not sufficient for moral responsibility: we cause a great many outcomes without being morally responsible for them.

[19] In defining moral responsibility in terms of openness to praise and blame, we follow many other accounts in the current literature. For overviews of contemporary accounts of moral responsibility and blame, see the articles on "moral responsibility" and "blame" in the *Stanford Encyclopedia of Philosophy*: https://plato.stanford.edu/ [accessed 1 April 2023].

[20] Strawson 1962 is the classic source for this influential perspective.

that military training and culture can lead military personnel to see objectionable behaviour as morally permissible and that it would therefore be unfair to hold them accountable for engaging in that behaviour:

> Our central conclusion is an unsettling one: *Perpetrators of atrocity typically occupy excusing conditions and are therefore not morally responsible for their conduct.* [...] many perpetrators manifest cognitive impairments that profoundly degrade their capacity for moral judgment, and such impairments, we shall argue, preclude the attribution of moral responsibility.[21]

We grant that there might be cases (in and out of active combat) where it would be unreasonable to expect war crimes perpetrators to recognise the wrongfulness of their behaviour and where perpetrators may sincerely believe that their actions are morally permissible. We argue, however, that this does not necessarily mean that such perpetrators are not blameworthy for their wrong and harmful actions.[22]

For example, imagine that, because of propaganda and acculturation into a particular military context and through no fault of their own, a combatant believes that it is permissible to torture prisoners of war. Perhaps this person believes that torture is necessary to achieve military and political goals that they regard as legitimate. Is this torturer morally responsible—are they blameworthy—when they intentionally and knowingly torture an enemy prisoner? In our view, the answer to this question can be found by considering whether it would be appropriate for the torture victim to blame their torturer. The appropriateness of the victim blaming the torturer will depend on the judgments and attitudes that the torturer expressed through their actions. If it is reasonable for the victim to interpret the torturer's actions as expressing morally inappropriate disregard for the victim's welfare, then moral blame seems appropriate. Note, though, that the appropriateness of the victim's blaming responses is not necessarily affected by the causal story of how the torturer *acquired* their offensive judgments and attitudes, or by the fact that the torturer believes that torture is permissible. This is because neither of the factors just mentioned necessarily affect the moral significance, for the victim, of the judgements and attitudes expressed through the torturer's actions.

Simply put, the torturer's (perhaps sincere) belief in the permissibility of torture does not change the fact that their actions express disregard for, or indeed active hostility towards, the victim's basic welfare and moral standing. It is the torturer's lack of moral regard that makes blame appropriate. And if we think that a torture victim is justified in believing that they have been treated with morally inappropriate disregard, then we should also think that it is appropriate that they respond to the person who harmed them with the moral emotions that characterise blame and communicate the offense taken at such disregard. And this means that the perpetrator is blameworthy: they are open to moral blame.

---

[21] Doris and Murphy 2007, p 26, emphasis in original; also see Doris and Murphy 2022. Doris and Murphy offer a clear application of this perspective to war crimes, but other philosophers have constructed related arguments that call into question the blameworthiness of individuals who, because of the environments in which they were raised, have difficulty recognising the wrongfulness of, for example, racism and so cannot reasonably be expected to refrain from racist behaviour; see, for example, Benson 2001, Levy 2003, and Wolf 1987.

[22] See Talbert and Wolfendale 2019, Chapter 5, "Blaming Perpetrators".

Of course, not all harmful behaviour is blameworthy. So far, we have argued that it is typically appropriate to blame a person when their actions express the kind of moral disregard that would make the responses involved in moral blame fitting. But there are cases where a person's harmful behaviour does not necessarily express such disregard and, in those cases, blame would be inappropriate. So, for example, the fact that *A* accidentally harms *B* does not, by itself, prove that *A* is not appropriately concerned with *B*'s welfare and moral standing. But it does not follow from this that *all* accidental harms are therefore not blameworthy. Perhaps a person does not realise that their action will harm another, but their failure to realise this may stem from a criticisable lack of concern about the impact of their actions on other people—an idea captured in the concept of negligence. We might think that if a person who unwittingly causes harm had been appropriately concerned with others' welfare, then they would have been aware of the potential consequences of their actions. Moral blame may thus be an appropriate response to unwitting and unintended harms of this sort.

The cases most interesting to us are those in which harm to civilians (or the extent of this harm) was unanticipated—these are the cases most often described as honest or tragic mistakes, as we explored in Sect. 11.2. This way of framing moral and legal responsibility for civilian deaths from drone strikes individualises responsibility and focuses on the intentions and knowledge available to individual actors. In our account of blameworthiness, however, the fact that individuals involved in a drone strike may not intend to hit civilians, or may not know that civilians are at risk, does not settle the matter of blameworthiness. When civilians are unwittingly harmed, we may ask, for example, whether a (morally) sufficient effort was made to determine whether the proposed targets were in fact military targets, whether civilians were threatened by a proposed strike, and whether that effort indicates an appropriate degree of concern for avoiding harm to innocents. If the level of concern for avoiding harm is morally insufficient, then blame may be appropriate even in a case where harm is unwittingly caused. In addition, we must also consider how efforts to mitigate harm (and failures to make such efforts) shape, and are shaped by, features of the military institutional and organisational structure (including, for example, targeting guidelines) that impact the knowledge and moral awareness of individuals acting within the institution (a topic explored in Sect. 11.4).

11.3.2 Blame and Collateral Damage

In this context, it is helpful to introduce material from Neta Crawford's important book *Accountability for Killing: Moral Responsibility for Collateral Damage in America's Post-9/11 Wars*. Crawford distinguishes three types of collateral damage in warfare.[23] First, there are "genuine accidents". These occur when civilians are

[23] The third form of collateral damage that Crawford discusses is what she calls "foreseen proportionality/double effect killing". Here, "the civilian deaths were foreseeable, foreseen, and judged to

harmed, but "[n]o one wanted the outcome and no one could have reasonably foreseen it."[24] Such cases are truly exculpating. Though the issue of blameworthiness may arise in the context of even genuine accidents, we set aside such cases in what follows.

Of more interest to us, and to Crawford, are cases of the second form of collateral damage that she discusses: those instances in which harm to civilians was, while not precisely intended, not entirely unforeseeable. Here, Crawford refers to "systemic collateral damage". Harm to civilians is "systemic if the [military] organization's practices and beliefs are structured so that [...] accidents predictably recur"; if there is, in other words, a "structural context" in which "collateral damage becomes a normal [and anticipatable] accident".[25] Crawford says that in such cases we can speak not just of individual responsibility for harm to civilians, but also

> of organizational responsibility in the sense that such an outcome should have been foreseen because [military operations of a given sort] frequently lead to civilian harm—due to the rules of engagement, the choice of weapons, or conditions under which such operations are approved to take place.[26]

At first glance, such cases of incidental collateral damage may not seem to involve mistakes, since the harm to civilians is foreseen (or at least foreseeable) and thus these are not cases of "mistaken identity" whereby civilians are mistaken for combatants. Crawford's point here is that background conditions (for example, the choice of weapons and rules of engagement) affect judgments regarding the likelihood and degree of collateral harm as well as judgments about the status of targets. As a result, erroneous assessments about the likelihood and severity of civilian harm are likely to occur, leading to excessive collateral harm. So, both excessive collateral damage (or incidental killings) can be the result of mistakes, as is revealed in the apologies sometimes issued by the military when such cases occur. That the military takes an apology to be warranted when military action causes unintended or unforeseen civilian deaths suggests that the military itself regards such cases as mistakes. And, as Crawford argues (and we agree), if these incidents result from attitudes and practices regarding estimates of collateral damage and target identification that increase the likelihood of such mistakes, these attitudes and practices are morally problematic.

As Crawford observes, collateral damage often results from "a morally troubling pattern of failing to correct procedures that lead to foreseeable and foreseen death or valuing military necessity and force protection [...] over civilian life."[27] What makes

---

be worth the military advantage that would result from an operation". According to the traditional doctrine of double effect, often relied upon in articulations of just war theory, "[t]hese deaths may be excused if they were an unintended consequence of a necessary military operation and if some effort was made to 'minimize' civilian casualties" (Crawford 2013, p 10). As we noted in Sect. 11.2, such deaths are also judged to be legal within IHL if they meet the criteria of distinction, proportionality, necessity, and precaution. Because such cases, important though they are, do not fall into the category of mistakes, we will not discuss them here.

[24] Crawford 2013, p 8.

[25] Ibid., p 9.

[26] Ibid.

[27] Ibid., p 29.

these trade-offs "morally troubling" is that they may indicate a lack of appropriate concern for civilian life. As Crawford notes, "how much we care [about the lives of civilians] will determine the amount of risk citizens ask soldiers to take in war to see that they [i.e., civilians] are protected",[28] so we may infer something about a military's degree of care for civilians from the policies and strategies (such as those discussed in Sect. 11.2) that it adopts.

Even more relevant for our account of blameworthiness is Crawford's suggestion that attitudes of "contempt" toward enemy civilians contribute to institutional structures that facilitate collateral damage by making "it difficult to see systemic collateral damage even as it is being produced."[29] Crawford also seems to approve of C.A.J. Coady's suggestion that "a good deal of accidental killing of enemy civilians in war exhibits a culpable lack of concern for their lives and safety."[30]

Most of the civilians killed in the US's recent drone campaigns have been, we shall assume, "innocent" in the sense that they were not legitimate targets of wartime violence. As mentioned earlier, IHL and just war theory may both excuse the incidental killing of innocent people under certain conditions (e.g., in cases of military necessity where the harm to civilians is proportionate to the value of the military goal to be achieved by the attack in question). This means that rules of engagement that allow for such incidental killings are not *necessarily* objectionable. However, sometimes the killing of innocent people may result from adhering to rules of engagement that express a lack of appropriate moral concern, or even contempt, for those killed. In such cases, both the rules of engagement and the killings themselves invite the morally offended responses involved in moral blame. And this may be true whether the deaths of innocent people were foreseen (and taken to be justified by military necessity) or not.

So, the question for our purposes is whether the US military's procedures for determining the acceptability of targets and for authorising strikes manifest a blame-grounding lack of concern at the individual and/or the collective/institutional level. Put simply, do these policies represent a perspective that *cares enough* about the lives of enemy civilians, or does it represent a morally reprehensible (and blame grounding) perspective on the matter? It is worth noting that the standard for what counts as "caring enough" should not be one that entails that *no* civilians are killed. One may care enough about not harming innocents—enough to meet a standard of moral probity—without this ensuring that no civilians are killed: genuine, excusable accidents may happen even if one cares as much as one morally ought to about avoiding them.

Thus, the notion of "caring enough" should be given more substantive content. As a starting point we shall propose a *principle of the moral equality of non-combatants*

---

[28] Ibid.

[29] Ibid., pp 345–46.

[30] Coady 2009, p 206.

(henceforth "Principle of Moral Equality") as a basis for articulating the moral framework that we argue should be used to assess the blameworthiness of civilian casualties, whether caused by mistaken identity or by mistaken projections of collateral harm. This principle states that, other morally relevant factors being equal, all non-combatants should be considered to have an equal claim to not being harmed.[31] Specifically, non-combatants in Afghanistan, Iraq, Syria, and elsewhere have as much claim to not being harmed as non-combatants in the United States, and these claims should be honoured with equal scrupulousness in both cases. While this principle does not tell us exactly how much concern the US military should devote to avoiding harming Iraqi or Afghan non-combatants, it does suggest that this level of concern should at least not be less than what US military planners would accept as appropriate if US civilians were at risk from enemy military operations. A different, and perhaps more demanding standard might suggest that US planners should show the same regard for enemy civilians as they would show for US civilians if it were the latter who would suffer the collateral consequences of US military activity. As we will argue, however, even measured against the more lenient standard described in the text, current US attitudes and policies fall far short of what is required.

In *Accountability for Killing*, Crawford suggests something similar:

> Do we care about them as much as we care about our own civilians? Usually not. But should we care about them as much? The presumption here is that those civilians in distant countries where the United States is fighting [...] are just as presumptively innocent as civilians in the United States. They deserve as much care as we would want to be taken with our own lives.[32]

So, we should ask: What degree of restraint and precision, what degree of certainty, would we demand if US civilians were in the crosshairs? Is this the degree of concern for the welfare of civilians reflected in the policies governing US operations abroad? If not, then these operations are not in conformity with the Principle of Moral Equality and are, we suggest, *prima facie* morally suspect. In particular, these operations may be taken to express the US military's lack of appropriate moral concern for those affected by its policies and actions, which provides grounds for attributing moral blameworthiness to the US military as an institution and to many individuals within it.

If current US military operations do not meet the standard of concern for non-combatants required by the Principle of Moral Equality, then blaming responses would be appropriate. But to whom, or to what, should these responses be directed? In order to better understand when and under what conditions blame would be appropriate, we must examine the conditions under which those involved in the drone programme form and act on decisions regarding the targets of drone strikes.

[31] See Chap. 10.

[32] Crawford 2013, p 29.

11.4 Are Honest Mistakes Possible in the US Drone Programme?

In the above section, we outlined the theory of moral blameworthiness that motivates our claim that unintentional or accidental civilian deaths that are caused by drone warfare may be blameworthy even when the individuals involved do not intend to harm civilians. Here, we focus specifically on the features of the drone programme, and the military institution in general, that mitigate against the likelihood that civilian deaths caused by drone strikes could meet an honest mistake standard that excuses those involved from moral blame, such as the standard outlined in the Rome Statute of the International Criminal Court,[33] to be discussed below.

In IHL and in just war theory, collateral civilian deaths are war crimes only if those deaths are disproportionate to the military advantage gained by the action in question, and/or if insufficient precaution was taken to minimise the risks to civilians.[34] As Adil Haque explains, IHL requires that

> [a]rmed forces are first to distinguish between civilian and enemy combatants; then to direct attacks only at enemy combatants and not combatants; then to plan and carry out attacks in a manner that avoids or at least minimizes harm to civilians; and finally to refrain from attacks that would cause disproportionate harm to civilians in relation to the military advantage the attacks would achieve.[35]

But, while IHL imposes a demanding standard on combatants in terms of their duties to avoid harming civilians (one that is consistent with our Principle of Moral Equality), a failure to meet this standard only meets the legal criteria of a war crime in the Rome Statute in limited circumstances. Firstly, Article 8(2)(b)(i) states that only intentional attacks against the civilian population or against civilians who are not directly taking part in hostilities constitute a war crime.[36] Thus, as Haque argues, the "Rome Statute imposes no criminal liability on combatants who recklessly or negligently fail to distinguish civilians or combatants",[37] even though such actions clearly fall far short of the positive duty to avoid civilian harm outlined in IHL. Secondly, to be guilty of the war crime of causing excessive incidental civilian death, the perpetrator must intentionally launch at attack

> in the knowledge that such attack will cause incidental loss of life or injury to civilians or damage to civilian objects or widespread, long-term and severe damage to the natural

[33] Rome Statute of the International Criminal Court, opened for signature 17 July 1998, 2187 UNTS 3 (entered into force 1 July 2002).

[34] Obligatory precautionary measures include not only taking steps to ensure (as much as possible) that there are few, if any, civilians or civilian targets in the area of the attack, but also that the means and methods of warfare used the attack are not unlawful due to imposing a high risk of indiscriminate effects.

[35] Haque 2011, p 520.

[36] Rome Statute, Article 8(2)(b)(i).

[37] Haque 2011, p 521.

environment which would be clearly excessive in relation to the concrete and direct overall military advantage anticipated.[38]

So, this means that the perpetrator must know that the attack will cause "clearly excessive" civilian harm, intend (nonetheless) that the attack go ahead, and then launch the attack.

But in practice, the difficulty of ascertaining whether a commander knew that a military attack would result in clearly excessive civilian harm (relative to the foreseen military advantage) *and* intended to carry out the attack in light of that knowledge has meant that, since the Rome Statute, few (if any) individuals have been prosecuted, let alone found guilty, for causing excessive incidental civilian death. Instead, defendants charged with this crime can plead a mistake of fact defence. As Article 32(1) of the Rome Statute states, lethal force against civilians or civilian objects resulting from an honest mistake of fact may not be culpable when the mistake of fact negates the mental element required by the crime.[39] This is essentially the view expressed by the judges in *Hostage*, when the US military tribunal acquitted Lothar Rendulic of the devastation in northern Norway on the grounds that "the conditions, as they appeared to the defendant at the time were sufficient on which he could honestly conclude that urgent military necessity warranted the decision made."[40]

While an "honest mistake" defence may initially seem reasonable, Haque argues that the Rome Statute's requirement that a defendant possesses both intent and knowledge "with respect to every material element of the relevant war crime" means that "even an *unreasonable* mistake of fact regarding the civilian status of those attacked or killed will negate the required mental states of intent or knowledge."[41] So, a combatant who does not try very hard to ascertain if the proposed targets of an attack are military targets or whether civilians will be collaterally harmed, and a combatant who does not "even pause to consider whether an attack will likely harm civilians" will both "lack the required mental state [for the war crime] and must be acquitted."[42] The upshot is that defendants who act on mistaken factual beliefs about the degree of collateral harm likely to be caused by a military action will be exonerated even if they failed to take *reasonable* steps to ascertain the facts. Similarly, a defendant who failed to be aware of the likely collateral harm caused by a military action because they were indifferent to the welfare of innocent people would also be exonerated. As Haque puts it, this effectively "eviscerates the principle of discrimination [between combatants and civilians]".[43]

[38] Rome Statute Article 8(2)(b)(iv).

[39] Rome Statute Article 32(1).

[40] US Military Tribunal V, *The Hostage Case (United States of America v Wilhelm List, et al.)*, 1948, 11 Trials of War Criminals Before the Nuernberg Military Tribunals 757, p 1297.

[41] Haque 2011, p 529, emphasis in original.

[42] Ibid., p 546.

[43] Ibid., p 521. Haque's proposal in response to this problem is the creation of a war crime of negligent killing which would criminalise actions that cause harm to non-combatants where the perpetrator (or perpetrators) "was aware or should have been aware of the factual circumstances that established the protected status [of the potential targets of the attack]" (2011, p 568), and the

In part because of the leniency with which the honest mistakes defence has been applied, Yasmin Naqvi argues that the most plausible interpretation of the Rendulic Rule involves both a subjective test (did the defendant sincerely hold the belief in question?) and an objective or "reasonable commander" test (was the defendant's belief reasonable, given the information available to them, and did they make a good faith effort to check the accuracy of that information?).[44] In order for a commander to be found guilty of the war crime of excessive incidental civilian harm, the prosecution must show that the commander's belief that their action would not cause excessive collateral harm relative to the expected military advantage of the action was either dishonest (not sincerely held) and/or unreasonable (a belief that a reasonable commander would not hold given a good faith attempt to ascertain reliable available information).[45]

This brief summary of the treatment of honest mistakes in the Rome Statute reveals the challenges facing attempts to prosecute a commander who orders a military action that causes excessive harm to civilians. Deciding whether a targeting error was based on an honest, let alone reasonable, belief requires a difficult (perhaps impossible) investigation into the subjective and objective bases of the defendant's belief in the circumstances in which they were acting. An additional problem, as we noted in Sect. 11.2, is that focusing on the bases of an *individual* combatant's beliefs distracts us from the fact that their beliefs occur in the context of, and because of, the decisions, intentions, and knowledge of many other individuals who are acting within a hierarchical institution. As Crawford argues, "systemic collateral damage is produced more at the institutional level than at the individual level."[46] Thus, focusing on individual responsibility can lead us to ignore or discount the institutional factors that shape individual decisions and the context in which they are made. In contrast, "[a]ttending to the moral agency of an organization [...] highlights how it is that certain outcomes were not inevitable or accidental, but created by the organization's beliefs, structures, procedures, and effects on individuals."[47]

---

inclusion of recklessness in the mental elements of the war crime of wilful killing (2011, p 567). Such a proposal would be consistent with the principle of the moral equality of non-combatants that we propose.

[44] See Chap. 8. Naqvi argues that the judges' reasoning in the *Hostage* case (and similar reasoning in later IHL cases involving reference to the Rendulic Rule) shows a close link between the "reasonable commander test" and the defence of "mistake of fact". See Milanovic 2020 for an alternative view, arguing that IHL requires that mistakes of fact need only be honest, but not necessarily reasonable, in order to be exculpating.

[45] The subjective and objective tests might appear to be closely related, in that the more objectively unreasonable a defendant's belief, the harder it might be to credit that the belief is sincerely held. But this is not necessarily a warranted inference—it is certainly possible that a person might sincerely hold a belief that is objectively unreasonable.

[46] Crawford 2013, p 43.

[47] Ibid., p 344. The upshot of Crawford's argument, and one that we agree with, is that "moral responsibility for [unintended collateral harms] should be shared among individuals and institutions" (ibid., p 43). However, an important concern with widening the focus of responsibility to include institutions and collective agents is that it is harder to see what blaming an institution means in practice whereas, in cases of individuals, the implications of holding a person accountable for their

Because the wider institutional context in which decisions are made is ignored, it is possible that a commander's belief in the accuracy of their information regarding projected collateral harm and expected military advantage may be both reasonable *and* honest. However, it may nonetheless be true that if they had had access to the full scope of information and decision-making procedures that shaped the context in which they acted, they would have formed a different belief. Given the circumstances in which they made their decision (including time constraints and other factors), it may *not* be reasonable to expect them to have formed different beliefs. Thus, even a commander's reasonable and honest belief in the accuracy of the information on which they acted might nonetheless lead to instances of unjustified civilian harm. Collective decisions, policies, and procedures regarding targeting can and do combine in ways that mean that "many episodes of collateral damage are foreseeable, foreseen, and preventable, albeit strictly legal."[48] Yet, when the focus of the law, the military, the media, and political leaders is solely on the individual(s) who are causally closest to instances of civilian deaths, the broader context vanishes and responsibility for these deaths disappears. This represents a serious and ongoing injustice to the many victims of drone attacks.

When we consider whether and under what conditions "honest mistakes" would be a fair description of at least some, if not all, civilian killings, we must look at how the relationships between available knowledge, intention, and individual action are constructed and constrained in a complex hierarchical institution such as the US military and in the context of the drone programme. This analysis will require that we reconsider how legal and moral responsibility is conceptualised in relation to wrongful cases of civilian harm.

11.4.1 Knowledge and Intention in the Military Institution

In the military, as in most large complex organisations, responsibility for decisions, tasks, and actions is divided amongst many individuals, all of whom possess different degrees of knowledge and intention relative to the roles they occupy. This means that when we consider what any given individual in the military institution knows, does not know, and should be expected to know, we must look at how knowledge is distributed, made available, compartmentalised, suppressed, and shaped by the nature of the military institution and the contexts of military operations.

Säde Hormio identifies several ways in which an organisation might gain, lose, or lack knowledge. An organisation might lack knowledge because of "ignorance about facts or [...] from the suppression of knowledge".[49] An organisation might recognise that it is ignorant of some facts but understand how to gain knowledge

---

actions are often reasonably clear. In our final section, we will briefly discuss what form *blaming/holding accountable the US military* might take.

[48] Crawford 2013, p 40.

[49] Hormio 2018, p 8.

of those facts ("knowable recognized unknowns"[50]); it might possess knowledge it does not realise it possesses ("unknown knowns"[51]); and it might think it possesses knowledge but be mistaken (errors arising from "inaccuracy, confusion, uncertainty or incompleteness"[52]).

Here, we focus first on how errors can occur within the US military's drone programme; afterwards, we consider how the category of "knowable recognized unknowns" applies to cases where military personnel responsible for planning and executing drone attacks fail to seek out easily accessible information that is directly relevant to the legality and morality of drone attacks. For example, personnel may fail to seek out information about the impact of drone warfare on communities living under drone surveillance, and information about problems with algorithmic targeting. As will become apparent, both errors and knowable recognised unknowns have implications for the proper assessment of moral and legal responsibility for unintended civilian deaths.

11.4.2 Errors and the Suppression of Knowledge

What kind of knowledge would personnel involved in carrying out a drone strike be likely to possess about the target of the strike? If drone operators engage in long-term surveillance of a potential target, they may have intimate access into the daily lives of those they surveil.[53] However, this does not mean that drone pilots are in the best position to know whether the people they surveil are legitimate targets. Because of the broad definition of legitimate targets used by the US military in planning and executing drone attacks,[54] a person or object who appears to be a non-combatant on surveillance footage (in their appearance, dress, demeanour, and behaviour) may nonetheless be selected as a target by the algorithms and targeting policies used by

---

[50] Ibid., p 10.

[51] Ibid. What Hormio has in mind here is institutionally shared knowledge that is often "embedded in routines and collective practices", and that may not become apparent until, for example, a person retires (ibid.). See Hormio 2018.

[52] Ibid.

[53] Coeckelbergh 2013, p 95.

[54] As Emily Rosen argues (Rosen 2021), citing the 2016 US Department of Defense Laws of War Manual:

> the U.S. military uses far broader criteria to determine which individuals are "formally or functionally" part of a non-State armed group, an approach that allows individuals who perform a wide range of non-military functions for the group to be targeted continuously. In the U.S. view, evidence of formal membership in an armed group may include "accessing facilities, such as safehouses, training camps, or bases used by the group," "traveling along specific clandestine routes used by the group," or "traveling with members of the group in remote locations or while the group conducts operations".

military officials in charge of planning drone strikes. This seems to have been the case in the 29 August 2021 Kabul bombing. The Pentagon investigation into the bombing attributed the mistake to an incorrect "interpretational assessment" of the footage, which tracked a white Toyota Corolla over several hours: "The drone operators saw what they expected to see, assuming that the white Toyota in their sights was the same as the one they had been tracking."[55]

The knowledge that a drone pilot possesses regarding the status of targets will come from the reports or orders they receive and not (or very rarely) from their first-hand assessments. Typically, drone pilots do not develop target-selection policies, or select targets, themselves. Like other "front line" military personnel, the drone pilot's role is to carry out their orders rather than to assess the moral status of these orders. Thus, drone pilots are unlikely to question the orders they receive. As a result, it may well be the case that, from their subjective perspective, a drone pilot honestly believes that a target they are asked to strike is a military target and/or that the attack will not cause excessive civilian harm. Their belief may also be reasonable, if the standards of the Rendulic Rule are applied, and if the pilot (or the commander ordering the strike) could not reasonably be expected to devote the time and resources necessary to verify a target identification. But the objective reasonableness of the pilot's belief (and thus whether the belief is fully exculpating) will depend on the ways in which judgments about legitimate and illegitimate targets are formed higher up the chain of command.

We have good reason to doubt that judgments about the status of the targets of drone programmes and predictions about degrees of probable collateral harm are reliably tracking morally defensible assessments of the objective's targetability and/or the impact of an attack on civilian targets. This is for several reasons, some of which relate to broader patterns of the suppression of knowledge in complex, hierarchical organisations like the military, and others which relate specifically to the tools and assumptions that are used to determine the status of targets of drone strikes.

11.4.3 Suppression and Denial of Knowledge in the Military

As Hormio notes, organisations might suppress or deny knowledge that "is too painful to acknowledge, or [...] does not fit with [the organisation's] worldview".[56] For example, knowledge of widespread sexual harassment and assault in military training institutions and bases has been covered up and minimised,[57] as have reports of war crimes such as torture and murder committed by soldiers against civilians and detainees.[58] Similarly, it is now well-documented[59] that numerous cases of civilian

[55] Borger (2021), see n. 6 above.

[56] Hormio 2018, p 16.

[57] Wood and Toppelberg 2017

[58] See, for example, IGADF 2020.

[59] Khan (2021), see n. 1 above.

killings resulting from US drone strikes were improperly investigated by the military and frequently covered up. Such practices of hiding or distorting information about wrongful civilian killings from drone strikes is an example of an organisation "introduc[ing] a condition (through denial, secrecy, or taboo) [...] which made it difficult for employees to acquire true belief about the wrongness of being involved in some particular collective action."[60] Because of these practices, drone pilots and many others involved in the drone programme are denied the information they need to form true beliefs about the impact of the drone programme on civilians, and thus about the sincerity of the US military's stated commitment to minimising risk to civilian lives.

Secondly, and of particular relevance to military operations, "organisations sometimes deprive individuals of their capacity to make good moral judgments by fragmenting available information."[61] In the military, subordinates in the chain of command are rarely, if ever, given reasons or explanations for the orders they receive. A drone pilot will typically not know why a particular person is selected as a target for a drone strike. Nor are they likely to have access to the reasons why particular targeting guidelines are used or how judgments about acceptable risk to civilians are made. Yet, such information is clearly relevant to whether or not a particular strike (and the degree of risk that strike poses to civilians) is morally justified. Such fragmentation of information need not be morally problematic in and of itself—arguably, it is necessary for the efficient functioning of large-scale, complex, hierarchical organisations. However, when fragmentation of information is combined with the denial or obfuscation of the true scale of civilian killings resulting from drone strikes, it contributes to moral distortion at the level of decision-making regarding drone attacks and makes it extremely difficult for those involved to form reasonable beliefs that a strike is morally permissible.

11.4.4 Knowable Recognised Unknowns

In addition to the problems of denial, distortion, and fragmentation of knowledge, an organisation may be blameworthy for failing to address knowable recognised unknowns that are relevant to the organisation's primary focus or *ethos*. Hormio defines an organisation's ethos as encompassing the "central questions and practical matters that are vital to the purpose of the group [...] and the answers it has collectively accepted to be its view."[62] Questions about "what should fall within the ethos of an organization" are "a normative matter" and are subject to change and negotiation depending on the organisation's focus and practices.[63] What are the knowable recognised unknowns relevant to ensuring that the US's stated commitment

[60] Hormio 2018, p 17.
[61] Ibid., p 22.
[62] Ibid., p 13.
[63] Ibid., p 14.

to minimising civilian casualties is realised in the operation of the drone programme? Such knowable recognised unknowns must include not only ascertainable facts about whether possible targets of drone strikes are combatants or non-combatants, but also facts about the broader impact of drone warfare on civilian welfare in the communities under drone surveillance, and facts about potential problems with targeting algorithms. As Crawford explains:

> Military organizations, which procure the weapons that increase the chance of indiscriminate killing, or which approve strategies or rules of engagement that can be foreseen to cause great civilian harm, and which shape the moral atmosphere and frames of reference for soldiers, are organizationally responsible for setting up the conditions for the killing of innocents or for protecting them.[64]

For example, despite the language of "precision" that accompanies drone warfare, and repeated claims that the US military is committed to preventing harm to civilians, there is little evidence that the US military has considered the broader, and extremely harmful, impact of drone surveillance on civilian lives.[65] Yet, this harm has been well-documented and publicised since at least 2012 in a report from New York University and Stanford Law Schools, which outlines the devastating psychological and physical trauma that living under drone surveillance inflicts on all those in a community, not just the intended targets.[66]

Additionally, despite extensive and compelling literature on the problems of algorithmic and confirmation bias,[67] the use of algorithms to ascertain potential targets has rarely been questioned. This holds true particularly in relation to what is known as "signature strikes" that use patterns of behaviour to predict hostile intent.[68] Indeed, confirmation bias and the issues of bias in target selection appear to have been another factor in the 29 August 2021 Kabul drone strike. In the wake of the Pentagon's investigation into the strike, Lt. Gen. Sami D. Said, Inspector General of the US Air Force, "blamed a series of assumptions, made over the course of eight hours as U.S. officials tracked a white Toyota Corolla through Kabul, for causing what he called 'confirmation bias'".[69] Yet, the killing of people based purely on biased and highly unreliable computer-predicted assumptions about the meaning of their behaviour is taken for granted to such an extent that it is rarely deemed worthy of comment. As Elke Schwartz explains, "set against a background where the instrument is characterised

---

[64] Crawford 2013, p 316.

[65] Because of the traumatic effects of living under drone surveillance, the philosopher Harry van der Linden argues that "drones are in their psychological impact indiscriminate weapons" (ibid., p 351).

[66] International Human Rights and Conflict Resolution Clinic at Stanford Law School and Global Justice Clinic at NYU Law School 2012.

[67] Bacchin and Lorusso 2019; Benjamin 2019.

[68] Wolfendale 2021, pp 14–16.

[69] Cooper and Schmidt (2021) Video showed at least one child near the site minutes before the strike in Kabul. The New York Times, https://www.nytimes.com/2021/11/03/us/politics/drone-strike-kabul-child.html [accessed 1 April 2023].

as inherently wise, the technology gives an air of dispassionate professionalism and a sense of moral certainty to the messy business of war."[70]

Regardless of the intentions and knowledge of the personnel who order and carry out US military drone strikes, it is unlikely that civilian deaths caused by these strikes, either from mistaken identity and/or excessive collateral harm, can meet the criteria of an honest mistake. This is because of the way these deaths are made possible by organisational choices and practices that distort, deny, and ignore morally relevant knowledge. Insofar as these choices stem from a lack of appropriate moral concern for civilians affected by drone strikes, the so-called "mistakes" resulting from these choices are not *honest* mistakes and so those involved are not absolved from blame. The evidence that the choices in question here *do* stem from a lack of appropriate concern comes from our proposal—expressed in the Principle of Moral Equality—that the US military should conduct itself with respect to enemy civilians with the same degree of care and concern that it would demand were US civilians the potential victims of military actions.

If the US military cared about avoiding civilian casualties to the degree that it ought to (and to the degree that it claims to), then it is plausible to suppose that it would have addressed the institutional features that create consistent failures of knowledge that make avoidable and unjustified civilian deaths likely to occur. For it certainly seems plausible that the US military, the US political leadership, and members of the US public in general, would interpret similar failures on the part of enemy forces (where such failures led to preventable US civilian casualties) as evidence of a culpable lack of respect for, or a blameworthy indifference to, the lives of US civilians.

11.5 Conclusion

In this chapter, we have considered how policies and tactics concerning the targeting of drone strikes, as well as inadequacies in how the US military collects and disseminates information related to these strikes, increases the risk of mistakenly killing (and otherwise harming) civilians in areas where US drone campaigns are conducted. Furthermore, we have argued that if these mistaken killings—and the failures that make them likely to occur—stem from a lack of appropriate regard on the part of the US military for non-US civilians, then the US military as an institution is morally blameworthy for these killings. In other words, civilian killings resulting from mistaken identity and/or from failures to predict excessive civilian harm cannot be regarded as blameless "honest mistakes". As for evidence that these mistakes, and the policies and tactics that lead to them, stem from a blame-grounding lack of appropriate regard, we have suggested (with our Principle of Moral Equality) that a morally adequate level of regard for non-US civilians would be the level of

[70] Schwarz 2018, p 88.

regard that US military and political leaders would demand be shown to US civilians by foreign militaries. Yet, the US military does not seem to show the degree of regard for non-US civilians that it would demand for US civilians. After all, the US government and military would surely not find that appropriate regard for US civilians was compatible with a foreign government leaving in place known deficiencies that predictably and regularly led to the killing of these civilians. In the rest of this concluding section, we will take stock of what the foregoing might mean for those who enlist in the US military, and we will consider the implications of our view for the legal status of actions that cause unintended civilian harm, as well as concrete steps that the military might take (and that it plans to take) to reduce the risks that its operations pose to civilians.

11.5.1 The Moral Risk of Joining the Military

As we have discussed above, the hierarchical nature of the military profession and features of the drone programme are emblematic of the kinds of fragmented and faulty knowledge structures outlined by Hormio. While there is always going to be a degree of "moral risk"[71] for someone who decides to enlist in the military, this risk is higher when it is known that the US military has routinely displayed a blameworthy lack of regard for the lives and welfare of enemy civilians, particularly if an individual is interested in military service related to the drone programme.

Considering the problems that we have discussed above, we suggest that any person who is contemplating joining the military has a moral duty to assess whether the military and the political leadership is committed to acknowledging and addressing the problems of fragmented and faulty knowledge and has demonstrated a commitment to taking responsibility for the unintentional killing of civilians. There have been promising developments in this respect, such as the publication of *Civilian Harm Mitigation and Response Action Plan* (CHMR-AP),[72] which outlines several objectives geared towards minimising civilian harm, including the establishment of

[71] "Moral risk" refers to the risk that a person's choices can lead them to be involved in, or complicit in, the commission of morally blameworthy actions. Of course, moral risk is not limited to the decision to enlist in the military—many everyday choices (such as buying clothing produced in sweatshops) can make a person (perhaps unwittingly) complicit in morally blameworthy practices. But the degree to which someone is blameworthy for such choices will depend on a complex range of factors, including the information that they had access to regarding the impact of their choices, as well as whether other choices were reasonably available to them. That said, while we cannot control or eradicate moral risk, arguably if someone is aware that a choice could have extremely morally serious consequences (such as the deaths of innocent people), then they are particularly likely to be taking a serious moral risk.

[72] Department of Defense (2022) Civilian Harm Mitigation and Response Action Plan. https://media.defense.gov/2022/Aug/25/2003064740/-1/-1/1/CIVILIAN-HARM-MITIGATION-AND-RESPONSE-ACTION-PLAN.PDF [accessed 1 April 2023].

a Civilian Protection Center of Excellence.[73] Of course, it remains to be seen how effectively these proposals will be implemented. It should also be noted that this plan does not acknowledge or refer to the importance of (as we have argued) identifying the broader negative consequences for the "civilian environment" of living under drone surveillance. In the meantime, if a person knows (or has good reason to believe) that, by joining a particular organisation, they will lack access to (and even be denied access to) morally relevant information about the actions in which they will take part, they run the risk of moral culpability for choosing to join that organisation.

11.5.2 Punishing and Preventing Unintended Civilian Harm

How could the Rome Statute be reformed to better protect civilians, and to more accurately reflect the stringent duty to minimise harm to civilians that is codified in IHL? One possibility would be to introduce a strict liability standard, under which military strikes that kill civilians unintentionally and that fail to meet standards of proportionality would automatically incur a finding of liability.[74] However, we agree that there are significant objections to such a proposal. For one thing, it might be hoped that a finding of liability would reliably track the presence of fault, and strict liability standards are at odds with this hope since they impose liability regardless of fault.

In addition to our suggestion of the adoption of a principle of the moral equality of non-combatants, a second response is to explore more carefully the ways in which the military can take responsibility for unintentional civilian deaths. This is a process that would not only require significant changes to the policies and procedures that govern targeting in the drone programme,[75] such as the changes proposed in CHMR-AP, but also significant changes in how the military institution communicates publicly about such cases and educates military personnel about the need to take all feasible steps to protect civilians from harm. In relation to how the military publicly discusses cases of civilian killings, we have already argued that approaches that minimise or

[73] A couple of additional initiatives mentioned in the CHMR-AP are noteworthy given the issues we have raised in this chapter. First are those initiatives that emphasise the importance of acquiring a "robust understanding of the civilian environment—including [...] infrastructure, essential services, and systems on which civilian life depends", which "can improve the commander's ability to distinguish non-adversarial aspects of the operational environment [...]" (ibid., p 9). Also of significant importance is the goal of "[i]ncorporat[ing] deliberate and systemic measures to mitigate the risks of target misidentification", which "includes addressing cognitive biases, such as confirmation bias" (ibid., p 15).

[74] Owens 2005, pp 603–606.

[75] Crawford outlines a series of proposals for such changes in Chapter 9 ("Accountability for Killing"). Notably, while some of her proposals are similar to those outlined in the CHMR-AP, others go beyond those proposals. For example, she urges the retirement of "weapons and practices [such as the use of landmines and cluster munitions] that are difficult to use in a discriminate way and are likely to cause foreseeable harm [to civilians]" (Crawford 2013, p 469).

erase individual responsibility, as the narrative of honest mistakes does, are morally problematic. In addition to failing to recognise the ways in which these cases arise from complex collective actions (and failures to act), these approaches fail to do justice to the victims of drone strikes by erasing moral blameworthiness from the picture. An alternative approach in such cases is for the military to publicly take responsibility for these deaths by accepting that moral blame is appropriate (without necessarily assigning that blame to a particular person) and responding with actions and words that recognise and honour the moral harm inflicted on the victims of drone strikes. Taking responsibility and accepting warranted blame for unintended killings involves more than simply acknowledging that such killings were unintended and offering compensation (a practice that, in relation to torts offenses, reflects a recognition of harm caused, but not moral culpability).[76] The US practice of paying monetary compensation[77] to family members of civilians killed in drone strikes is insufficient to reflect the moral gravity of harms caused by blameworthy practices that distort and hide relevant knowledge of attacks on civilians and that reflect a lack of regard for civilian lives. Instead, we argue that the military (and US political leaders) should publicly accept blame for such killings, and publicly offer apologies to the families and communities of the victims of these killings.

There is precedent for such forms of taking responsibility. In 2010, Vice Admiral William McRaven personally apologised to the surviving family members of a drone strike that killed five innocent people by offering two sheep to the family—an act that, according to the cultural norms of the region, signified a request for forgiveness.[78] Admirable though this example is, however, it falls far short of the substantive institutional and cultural changes and public acknowledgement of blame that is warranted by the scale of unintended civilian killings over the last decades.

The moral debt owed to the many civilians killed over the last decades warrants an institutional commitment to ensuring that military personnel of all ranks internalise and understand the significance of the prohibition against harming civilians. Military personnel must also understand their duty (encoded in IHL) to take all feasible precautions to avoid harm to civilians, even when doing so might increase the risk of harm to military personnel. One way we think this could be done is by framing military ethics education on this issue around the principle of the moral equality of non-combatants. Incorporating this principle explicitly into military ethics education at all ranks would require military personnel to imagine what they would tolerate were US citizens' lives on the line. Such an empathetic thought experiment would force the recognition that there is no justifiable moral or legal basis for treating non-US civilians with less moral regard than US civilians deserve.

---

[76] Haque 2011, p 559.

[77] See Schmitt (2021) U.S. Pledges to Pay Family of Those Killed in Botched Kabul Drone Strike. The New York Times, https://www.nytimes.com/2021/10/15/us/politics/kabul-drone-strike-victims-payment.html [accessed 1 April 2023].

[78] Schifrin and Agha (2010) U.S. Vice Admiral Apologizes for Afghan Deaths. ABC News, https://abcnews.go.com/WN/Afghanistan/special-forces-apologize-afghan-civilian-deaths-sheep/story?id=10320603 [accessed 1 April 2023].

References

Bacchin F, Lorusso L (2019) Race, again: how face recognition technology reinforces racial discrimination. Journal of Information, Communication, and Ethics in Society 17:321–335
Benjamin R (2019) Race after Technology. Polity, Cambridge
Benson P (2001) Culture and responsibility: a reply to Moody-Adams. Journal of Social Philosophy 32:610–20
Coady C (2009) Bombing and the morality of war. In: Tanaka D, Young M (eds) Bombing Civilians: A Twentieth Century History. The New Press, New York, pp 191–214
Coeckelbergh M (2013) Drones, information technology, and distance: mapping the moral epistemology of remote fighting. Ethics and Information Technology 15:87–98
Crawford N (2013) Accountability for Killing: Moral Responsibility for Collateral Damage in America's Post-9/11 Wars. Oxford University Press, Oxford
Doris J, Murphy D (2007) From My Lai to Abu Ghraib: the moral psychology of atrocity. Midwest Studies in Philosophy 31:25–55
Emery J (2022) Probabilities towards death: bugsplat, algorithmic assassinations, and ethical due care. Critical Military Studies 8:179–97
Esch J (2010) Legitimizing the "War on Terror": political myth in official-level rhetoric. Political Psychology 31:357-358
Haque A (2011) Protecting and respecting civilians: correcting the substantive and structural defects of the Rome Statute. New Criminal Law Review 14:519-575
Haque A (2017) Law and Morality at War. Oxford University Press, Oxford
Hormio S (2018) Culpable ignorance in a collective setting. Acta Philos Fennica 94:7–34
Inspector-General of the Australian Defence Force (2020) Afghanistan Injury Report ("Brereton Report"). The Inspector-General of the Australian Defence Force. Canberra, ACT
International Human Rights and Conflict Resolution Clinic at Stanford Law School and Global Justice Clinic at NYU Law School (2012) Living Under Drones: Death, Injury, and Trauma to Civilians from US Drone Practices in Pakistan. Available at https://law.stanford.edu/publications/living-under-drones-death-injury-and-trauma-to-civilians-from-us-drone-practices-in-pakistan/
Levy N (2003) Cultural membership and moral responsibility. The Monist 86:145–63
Milanovic M (2020) Mistake of fact when using lethal force in international law: part I. EJIL:Talk! Available at https://www.ejiltalk.org/mistakes-of-fact-when-using-lethal-force-in-international-law-part-i/
Murphy D, Doris J (2022) Skepticism about evil: atrocity and the limits of responsibility. In: Nelkin D, Pereboom D (eds) The Oxford Handbook of Moral Responsibility. Oxford University Press, Oxford, pp 697-726
Owens P (2005) Accidents don't just happen: The liberal politics of high-technology "humanitarian" war. Millennium: Journal of international studies 32:595–616
Rosen B (2021) Tragic mistakes: Breaking the military culture of impunity. Just Security. Available at https://www.justsecurity.org/79256/tragic-mistakes-breaking-the-military-culture-of-impunity/
Schwarz E (2018) Technology and moral vacuums in just war theorizing. Journal of International Political Theory 14:280–298
Strawson P (1962) Freedom and resentment. Proceedings of the British Academy 48:1–25
Talbert M, Wolfendale J (2019) War Crimes: Causes, Excuses, and Blame. Oxford University Press, New York
van der Linden H (2016) Arguments against drone warfare with a focus on the immorality of remote control killing and "deadly surveillance". Radical Philosophy Review 19:331-358
Wolf S (1987) Sanity and the metaphysics of responsibility. In: Schoeman F (ed) Responsibility, Character, and the Emotions: New Essays on Moral Psychology. Cambridge University Press, Cambridge, pp 46-62

Wolfendale J (2021) Technology as terrorism: police control technologies and drone warfare. In: Henschke A, Reed A, Robbins S, Miller S (eds) Counter-terrorism, ethics and technology: Advanced sciences and technologies for security applications. Springer Nature, Cham, pp 1-22
Wood E, Toppelberg N (2017) The persistence of sexual assault within the US military. Journal of Peace Research 54:620–633

Matthew Talbert Professor of Philosophy, West Virginia University, USA; Senior Researcher, Lund-Gothenburg Responsibility Project, Sweden, e-mail: matthew.talbert@mail.wvu.edu

Jessica Wolfendale Professor of Philosophy, Case Western Reserve University. Address: Clark Hall 211, 11130 Bellflower Road, Cleveland, OH 44106, USA, e-mail: jessica.wolfendale@case.edu

Part V
Conclusion

Chapter 12
Conclusion: The *Hostage* Case, Present Day Knowledge, and Future Implications

Carola Lingaas and Nobuo Hayashi

Contents

12.1 Introduction 290
12.2 Rendulic's Order to Destroy Northern Norway 291
12.3 The *Hostage* Trial Phase 292
12.4 The Rendulic Rule's Significance 296
12.5 Algorithmic Honest Errors, Empathy, and Reasonableness 298

Abstract Seventy-five years after a US tribunal in Nuremberg acquitted Lothar Rendulic of devastating and forcibly evacuating Northern Norway, the Rendulic Rule stands firmly in international law. This concluding chapter summarises the anthology's main historical, legal, and military-ethical findings. It provides an overview of the historical developments that culminated in the scorched earth tactics applied by the retreating German 20th Mountain Army under Rendulic's command. It then discusses the preparations and legal peculiarities of the trial, as well as reactions to the judgment. The chapter shows that the case against Rendulic is arguably the wrong foundation for the no second-guessing rule, since he did not consider the complete devastation of Northern Norway and the forcible evacuation of its entire civilian population militarily necessary. Although the Rendulic Rule rests on meagre legal forensics, it has acquired legal significance in primary rules of conduct in the shape of the reasonable commander test in international humanitarian law and the mistake of fact defence in international criminal law. Numerous domestic, regional, and international courts and tribunals have applied the rule that nowadays has a strong legal standing. Yet, despite rapidly evolving military and information technology, reasonableness, empathy, and (institutional) bias in combat remain challenging issues.

C. Lingaas (✉)
VID Specialized University, Oslo, Norway
e-mail: carola.lingaas@vid.no

N. Hayashi
Swedish Defence University, Stockholm, Sweden
e-mail: nobuo.hayashi@fhs.se

N. Hayashi and C. Lingaas (eds.), *Honest Errors? Combat Decision-Making 75 Years After the* Hostage *Case*, https://doi.org/10.1007/978-94-6265-611-6_12

Keywords Rendulic Rule · Lothar Rendulic · *Hostage* Case · Nuremberg trial · Telford Taylor · Northern Norway · scorched earth tactics · forcible evacuation · Josef Terboven · Alfred Jodl · honest error · reasonable commander · mistake of fact · no second-guessing rule · military necessity · empathy in war · moral equality of civilians · drone warfare

12.1 Introduction

> Villages were destroyed. Isolated habitations met a similar fate. Bridges and highway were blasted. Communication lines were destroyed. Port installations were wrecked. A complete destruction of all housing, communication, and transport facilities took place [...] The destruction was as complete as an efficient army could do it.[1]

The Rendulic Rule is an established rule of international humanitarian law (IHL). It holds that decisions and actions of military personnel should not be judged *post factum* but rather based on the military situation as encountered at the time. A commander's understanding and assessment of the military situation, as it presented itself prior to his or her decision, is the point of departure for a factual and legal analysis of the decision's rightfulness. Military necessity can thus only be judged properly from the circumstances prevailing at the time and according to the particular situation.

The Rendulic Rule is based upon the idea that, in a combat situation, there is no opportunity to second-guess. At the time when the rule emerged, armed conflicts were fought by humans who naturally make mistakes. The law that subsequently developed from this rule takes into account that honest errors can occur, which should be evaluated based on a subjective understanding of the individual concerned as the situation presented itself to him or her. Indeed, the rule prohibits second-guessing commanders' decisions in combat according to information gained *post hoc*. Although modern warfare has changed significantly since World War II, it did not obliterate human decisions. The so-called revolution in military affairs led to a tremendous increase of information communication technology (ICT) in warfare, however, the human element, empathy (or the lack thereof) and thus the risk of errors, remain present.

[1] US Military Tribunal V, The *Hostage* Case, *United States of America v Wilhelm List et al.* 19 February 1948, Judgment, p 10512, https://nuremberg.law.harvard.edu/transcripts/4-transcript-for-nmt-7-hostage-case?seq=10428&date=1948-02-19 [accessed 1 April 2023].

12.2 Rendulic's Order to Destroy Northern Norway

The Rendulic Rule originates—at least in its name—from the case of General Lothar Rendulic, Commander of the 20th Mountain Army of the German Armed Forces in Northern Norway during the second half of 1944. On 29 October 1944, Rendulic implemented orders from the German High Command that the entire Norwegian population east of the Lyngenfjord be evacuated by force "in the interest of their own security", that all homes be burned down or destroyed, and that "pity for the civilian population [be] out of place."[2] This harsh and uncompromising order followed a period during which Norway's occupation regime encouraged a voluntary evacuation, albeit based on threats, scare tactics, and retaliations. The civilian population, however, resisted with blatant reluctance. "Freiwillig gehen nur wenige Norweger mit," complained Rendulic in a statement of 24 October 1944: only a few Norwegians leave voluntarily.[3]

In Chap. 2, **Sven Holtsmark** and **Gunnar Åselius** provide a detailed historical account of the developments in the north in the last months of World War II that led to the German order of total destruction and evacuation. Following an armistice agreement between Finland and the Soviet Union in September 1944, Germany had to withdraw its forces from Finnish territory. A direct consequence of the agreement was that Finland lost its only access to the Barents Sea and that Norway became a neighbour with the Soviet Union, sharing a border of nearly 200 km. Unknown to many, the withdrawal of German troops from Finland was accompanied with an evacuation of the civilian population and a scorched earth policy resembling the one effectuated in Norway a few months later.[4]

Based on Russian original archival sources, **Sven Holtsmark** in Chap. 3 discusses how, with Finland out of the conflict, the German forces' northern flank was vulnerable to attacks from the Red Army's Karelian Front under the command of General Kirill A. Meretskov. Rendulic and his superiors were fearful, among other things, of an imminent Soviet invasion from the east. Therefore, Rendulic was ordered to withdraw his two southern corps to fortified positions behind the Lyngen Line. Later, during operation *Nordlicht*, Rendulic received orders that the entire 20th Mountain Army was to follow suit. These developments were unbeknown to Stalin and his leaders, including Meretskov. Anticipating German strongholds, the Soviet Union launched an offensive and moved into the abandoned Norwegian town of Kirkenes. Soviet detachments stopped and took up defensive positions at the Tana River. Until the last weeks of the war in Europe in April 1945, the Soviet military leadership was constantly elaborating plans to counteract a possible German counterattack.[5]

At the end of October 1944, events superseded one another: on 25 October, the Red Army took control of Kirkenes. On 28 October, Adolf Hitler issued an order to evacuate and destroy the Northern Norwegian province of Finnmark. And on

---

[2] Chapter 2.

[3] Chapter 4.

[4] Chapter 2.

[5] Chapter 3. See also Chap. 4, in which *Nordlicht* is discussed.

29 October, Rendulic issued his own order to implement the *Führer*'s order. In their chapter on the actors and motives of the devastation and forcible evacuation (Chap. 4), **Stian Bones** and **Gunnar Hatlehol** reveal that Hitler's order was the direct result of an appeal from Josef Terboven, *Reichskommissar für die besetzten Norwegischen Gebiete* (German Reich Commissioner for Occupied Norway), to Martin Bormann. Bormann was the leader of the German Nazi Party (NSDAP) secretariat and effectively Hitler's private secretary. Thus, in effect, the appeal from Terboven to Hitler, via Bormann, bypassed the military chain of command. In other words, the order to completely destroy Northern Norway was the result of an intervention on the political rather than military level. Neither the *Wehrmachtsbefehlhaber Norwegen*, Nikolaus von Falkenhorst, nor Rendulic himself advocated the total destruction and the forced evacuation of all civilians. Quite on the contrary, until Hitler's crucial order was issued, they and other German field commanders questioned the necessity of such an intervention. When von Falkenhorst was interrogated after the war, he even claimed that the evacuation and destruction were "*sinnlos*"—meaningless. Rendulic's own war diary also discloses that he was personally strongly opposed to the "*totale Vernichtung*", the complete destruction. Yet, once the order was issued, it was carried out with effectiveness and ruthlessness.[6] When the German *Wehrmacht* left the Norwegian town of Hammerfest on 10 February 1945, the cemetery chapel was the only building left standing.

12.3 The *Hostage* Trial Phase

After the war, in June 1947, Rendulic together with eleven other German defendants faced trial for war crimes before a US military tribunal at Nuremberg in the so-called *Hostage* case.[7] The indictment against Rendulic was filed on 10 May 1947, almost exactly two years after the German troops surrendered and withdrew from Norway. It alleged that Rendulic's order "was effectively and ruthlessly carried out. For no compelling military reasons, and in literal execution of instructions to show no sympathy to the civilian population, the evacuated residents were made to witness the burning of their homes and possessions."[8] Surprisingly, the indictment did not include Rendulic's decisions to practice a scorched earth policy in Northern Finland nor the fact that the 20th Mountain Army forcibly evacuated about 100,000 inhabitants of the area.[9]

[6] Chapter 4.

[7] *United States of America v Wilhelm List et al.*, Indictment, filed 10 May 1947, reprinted at Office of Military Government for Germany (US) (1947), Trial 7—*Hostage* Case, p 9, https://digitalcommons.law.uga.edu/cgi/viewcontent.cgi?article=1000&context=nmt7 [accessed 1 April 2023].

[8] Ibid.

[9] Chapter 2.

In her detailed examination of *Hostage*, **Emily Crawford** in Chap. 6 highlights many legal peculiarities of the case.[10] Among other things, she describes the prosecution's failure to litigate more effectively the weaknesses in Rendulic's justification of military necessity, as well as obvious gaps in the reasoning of the tribunal. *Hostage* discussed in great detail and adjudicated the German practices foremost in Greece and Yugoslavia. The indictment describes how the civilian populations were terrorised, deported to slave labour, and how cities, towns and villages were destroyed without any military necessity. The Finnmark devastation charge against Rendulic stood out from the other charges in lacking details regarding the criminal allegations. Moreover, it dealt with the scorched earth tactics in Northern Norway, thus a distinctly different arena of war than Southeastern Europe. Nevertheless, the common denominator was the allegations of criminal acts of devastation not justified by military necessity.[11]

In his defence, Rendulic claimed that the orders to devastate Northern Norway were a military necessity and the only way to hinder the presumably advancing Soviet troops, to prevent a disorderly retreat of the German army, and to protect the Norwegian civilians from Bolshevism. At trial, Rendulic asserted that when the orders were issued, the German troops were convinced that they were facing a twofold threat: an Allied invasion from the seaside that would have strengthened Norwegian resistance—and the risk of a Soviet land invasion from across the Tana River. In order to discourage Soviet troops from following the retreating German troops, it was in the view of the German leadership militarily necessary to burn down civilian dwellings, storages and other buildings, in addition to military installations. Without shelter, Soviet troops would not survive in Northern Norway's harsh winter conditions, so the German logic went. The defence argument was, however, not focused on the delay of a Soviet advance alone. Rather, Rendulic himself repeatedly stated that the destruction of Northern Norway was for the protection of its civilian population, thus a welfare and relief measure. The Germans would save the Norwegians from the Soviets and, in the words of Rendulic, "is [it] wrong if one tries to save people from Bolshevism?"[12]

The tribunal rendered its judgment on 19 February 1948. Although Rendulic was found guilty of crimes perpetrated in Southern Europe and sentenced to 20 years imprisonment, he was acquitted of ordering and implementing scorched earth tactics in Northern Norway, viz., the destruction of the Finnmark region, on grounds of military necessity. The acquittal came as a complete surprise to much of the Norwegian population who expected a conviction, especially since Rendulic's superior, *Generaloberst* Alfred Jodl, was convicted of unlawful devastation and evacuation before the International Military Tribunal (IMT). Based on the exact same facts as Rendulic, Jodl was sentenced to death by hanging.[13] Both Nuremberg-based tribunals operated

[10] Chapter 6.

[11] Chapter 6.

[12] Chapter 6. See also Chap. 4 on the perceived threat of the Bolsheviks crossing the Norwegian border.

[13] Chapters 5, 6 and 8.

under a broad mandate of just and prompt trials and punishment of the major war criminals of the European Axis.[14] They referred to the same facts, laws, and customs of war, yet differed significantly in their legal reasoning.

Despite the prosecution's assertation that the devastation of Finnmark under the command of Rendulic was "wholly unjustified from a military standpoint,"[15] the judges concluded differently: Rendulic had ordered the devastation based on an honest error of the factual situation on the ground. They considered it plausible that, based on German military intelligence available at the time, Rendulic feared a two-pronged threat: an imminent Soviet attack into Norway to pursue the retreating German troops and Allied landings. With these two—perceived—threats, Rendulic acted in good faith, although in hindsight his decision was faulty.[16]

Holtsmark's historical research for this anthology concludes that, when, on 29 October 1944, Rendulic ordered the forcible evacuation of the civilian population and the destruction of all shelter and means of existence, he lacked reliable information about Soviet or Western Allied plans. Indeed, after the end of the Petsamo-Kirkenes operation in early November 1944, the Soviet leadership never considered or planned an offensive into Norway's interior. Moreover, at this stage of the war, the Western Allies viewed Norway as a marginal theatre, and large-scale landing operations were not an option. The Norwegian exile government's pleas to halt the German destruction of Northern Norway went largely unheeded.[17]

These developments, however, were unbeknown to the German military and political leadership—and to Rendulic. Their assumption was that Soviet and Western Allied moves into Northern Norway were possible and remained their framework until the end of the war. The Germans were also concerned that such Allied moves would enable the Norwegian government-in-exile to gain a foothold on Norwegian soil and strengthen the resistance movement. If, during the German withdrawal, some parts of the population were left behind rather than evacuated, they would inevitably cooperate with that government. Such development would have sent a strong signal that Vidkun Quisling's National Socialist government was losing its grip and at risk of collapsing. These threats that the Germans and Rendulic perceived, however, were not grounded in the Allies' actual military plans. There was—objectively—no military reason to forcefully evacuate the entire civilian population from Northern Norway or to burn to the ground anything of presumed military importance.[18] At trial, however, subjective reasons were foregrounded: the judges concluded that Rendulic believed he was acting in military necessity, which retrospectively turned out to be an honest error. The Rendulic Rule was born.

---

[14] Charter of the International Military Tribunal, enacted 8 August 1945, London (entered into force 8 August 1945), Article 1.

[15] US Military Tribunal V, Evidentiary Document No. NOKW-086, Order for the Evacuation of North Norway, 22 October 1944 (official translation, Office of the Chief of Counsel for War Crimes), https://nbg-02.lil.tools/transcripts/4-transcript-for-nmt-7-hostage-case?seq=92, p 95 [accessed 1 April 2023].

[16] Chapters 6, 7 and 8.

[17] Chapter 3.

[18] Chapters 3 and 4.

When, during his trial in Nuremberg, Rendulic emphasised his fear of large-scale Soviet and Western Allied attacks on German positions in Northern Norway at the time, he spoke the truth. In so far as the judges based their verdict on Rendulic's threat perceptions of Allied plans and options when the evacuation and destruction was ordered and carried out, they reached the right conclusion.[19] However, there is strong evidence for the claim that, at the time, Rendulic did not consider Northern Norway's total destruction and the forcible evacuation of its entire population a military necessity. Indeed, he and other military commanders argued against such solutions, not for humanitarian, but for strictly military, reasons: they would be a burden to the retreating 20th Mountain Army.[20] Hence, when at trial Rendulic fully endorsed these measures as an absolute military necessity, it may have been contrary to his perception of what constituted "military necessity" at the time of the actual events. The drastic actions taken in Finnmark were therefore not militarily justified and, most importantly for this anthology, Rendulic did not act in honest error or good faith. Thus, the Rendulic Rule originated from a one-sided weighting of (legal) arguments presented in court.

The trial against Rendulic lasted around nine months, and its transcripts cover more than 10,500 pages. The tribunal received over 1,700 exhibits from the litigants. The events in Norway were largely uncontested and undisputed at trial.[21] However, the historical analysis by **Stian Bones** and **Gunnar Hatlehol** in Chap. 5 reveals that the tribunal did not consider all available information, especially the incriminating parts. In gathering evidence, Telford Taylor, Chief of Counsel for the US prosecution, was dependent on cooperation with Norwegian authorities and therefore approached the Norwegian envoy to the United Nations War Crimes Commission. The envoy was based in London and collaborated with Taylor, who was "anxious to secure whatever evidence you might have […], [p]articularly […] the activities of Generaloberst Rendulic in Finnmark."[22] Unfortunately, this cooperation was not communicated to the Norwegian Director of Public Prosecutions in Oslo, who after the war initiated an investigation against Rendulic too. Confusion increased when the authorities in Oslo requested Rendulic's extradition to Norway, unaware that Taylor had already launched an investigation in Nuremberg.[23]

When the misunderstanding was clarified, Ivar Follestad, Justice of the Norwegian Supreme Court, sent 92 documents, each containing several hundreds of pages, to Taylor's office. Only a few were translated to English. The case against Rendulic was mainly built on one document that the Norwegian authorities in London had sent to Nuremberg. Follestad was unaware of this source. Moreover, the Director of Public Prosecutions decided against sending eyewitnesses to Nuremberg, which weakened the charges of forced evacuations. Another failure was the omission of the US prosecutors to submit to the tribunal Rendulic's interrogation report of 6 March 1947,

[19] Chapter 3.

[20] Chapter 4.

[21] Chapter 7.

[22] Chapter 5, Sect. 5.3.

[23] Chapter 5.

where he admitted that the destructions of North Norway did not appear necessary and that it could in part have been avoided.[24]

The judges were thus set to deciding the case against Rendulic on fragmented and incomplete data. Had they had knowledge of the content of all transmitted documents, the trial's outcome would likely have been different.[25] Another contentious matter was the judges' civilian legal background and their lack of competence in international or military law. This contributed to the legal matters of the case against Rendulic being seen under secondary rules relating to its enforcement and implementation rather than the law of war proper.[26]

12.4 The Rendulic Rule's Significance

One key point of contention during the trial was the definition of military necessity and the degree to which it was to be informed by a commander's own assessment. This matter is what ultimately gave rise to the Rendulic Rule in modern IHL—and to interconnected legal concepts such as the reasonable commander test and the mistake of fact defence in international criminal law (ICL).

Hostage is arguably the wrong case to demonstrate the no second-guessing rule, let alone the creation of a principle of international law. Nevertheless, in his examination of the genesis and significance of the Rendulic Rule (Chap. 7), **Sean Watts** concludes that it "has aged well and now constitutes an established, perhaps even fundamental facet of the law of war."[27] What started out as a legal peculiarity before a military tribunal with three US civilian jurists with no training or experience in military or international law, gradually matured beyond a mere secondary rule into the realm of primary rules of the law of war, where it features prominently. It is furthermore a central aspect of the law of war implementation by states and commanders. Due to its implications for military decisions in the battlefield, the Rendulic Rule is, in Watts' view, also "a sort of legal marketing tool, essential to securing military confidence and faith in the law of war."[28] Since military commanders are required to take reasonable decisions based on the circumstances at the time, they need not be concerned about a strict liability that may subsequently render their decisions objectively unjustified.[29]

Although the Rendulic Rule rests on "meager legal forensics",[30] its current legal significance should not be underestimated. It is now reflected in primary rules of conduct in IHL treaties and extends to liability theories of ICL that equally feature

[24] Chapter 5.
[25] Chapter 5.
[26] Chapter 7.
[27] Chapter 7.
[28] Chapter 7.
[29] Chapters 7 and 8.
[30] Chapter 7.

Rendulic Rule-like aspects. As **Yasmin Naqvi** shows in Chap. 8, treaties addressing command or superior responsibility impute responsibility to commanders for crimes committed by their subordinates. For example, Article 86(2) of Additional Protocol I to the Geneva Conventions reads:

> The fact that breach of the Convention [...] was committed by a subordinate does not absolve his superiors from [...] responsibility, [...] if they knew, or had information which should have enable them to conclude in the circumstances at the time, that he was committing or was going to commit such a breach [...].[31]

Here, the Rendulic Rule is contained implicitly by reference to the information available to the commanders as it appeared to them in the circumstances. Hence, the rule of no second-guessing that originated in the Rendulic Rule is carried on into modern-day treaties. The same is valid for defences available to accused individuals, including mistake of fact. The Rome Statute of the International Criminal Court (ICC)[32] in Article 32 provides that a "mistake of fact shall be a ground for excluding criminal responsibility only if it negates the mental element required of the crime." While the Rendulic Rule is not explicit, it signifies that a mistake of fact based on honest errors is a valid defence before the ICC.[33]

In her comparative legal analysis, Naqvi connects the dots from *Hostage* to the Rome Statute and beyond. Drawing upon domestic, regional, and international jurisprudence in civil and common law jurisdictions in both civil and criminal cases, including *Hans* in Norway, *Pistorius* in South Africa, *Galić* before the International Criminal Tribunal for the Former Yugoslavia, and *McCann v UK* before the European Court of Human Rights, she shows that *Hostage* essentially applied to the issue of military necessity what is today known as the "reasonable commander test". This is a tool used to assess whether the standards set out in IHL requiring the exercise of judgment by a commander in a specific situation were met. The reasonable commander test is commonly applied to assess decisions on proportionality, which dictates limits on the legality of an attack.[34]

Discussing the 1951 and 1954 Draft Codes of Offences against the Peace and Security of Mankind by the International Law Commission, the drafting history of the Rome Statute, and legal scholarship, Naqvi meticulously analyses the development of mistake of fact. She concludes that in contemporary cases where the reasonable commander test is applicable, mistake of fact will only provide a defence where the mistake is both honest and reasonable, thus involving both objective (reasonableness) and subjective (honesty) considerations. The often advocated purely subjective approach is, in Naqvi's view, dangerous because it frustrates the goal of fostering compliance with IHL. If mistakes that are honest but unreasonable due to incomplete

---

[31] Protocol Additional to the Geneva Conventions of 12 August 1949, and relating to the Protection of Victims of International Armed Conflicts (Protocol I), opened for signature 8 June 1977, 1125 UNTS 3 (entered into force 7 December 1978), Article 86(2).

[32] Rome Statute of the International Criminal Court, opened for signature 17 July 1998, 2187 UNTS 3 (entered into force 1 July 2002).

[33] Chapter 8.

[34] Chapter 8.

intelligence or confirmation bias exculpate perpetrators of criminal liability, they will lead to more civilian casualties and damage.[35]

12.5 Algorithmic Honest Errors, Empathy, and Reasonableness

Chapter 9 by **Tae Hoon Kim** shows that, even in an age of information overflow with ICT and advanced command, control, communications, computers and intelligence processing (C4I) systems, legal questions remain by and large the same as during WWII. More specifically, the information available when a commander makes a military decision does not provide sufficient clarity for the objective side of the reasonable commander test. The test depends on the subjective, human element in the commander's decision-making process. This aspect raises questions about how honest errors are or should be dealt with when artificial intelligence (AI) is used in the battlefield. In recent and current armed conflicts, conventional weapons systems have increasingly been equipped with AI, and AI is evolving to become the dominant feature of warfare, on the battlefield as well as in cyberspace. As such, how errors are dealt with in a situation that is—at least to a certain extent—decided based on algorithms, is a highly relevant matter. In discussing the very timely case of Russia's invasion of Ukraine and comparing it to the earlier cases of US invasions of Afghanistan and Iraq, Kim raises complex issues that are as relevant today as they were for Rendulic in 1944.[36]

The *Hostage* tribunal asked whether Rendulic "acted within the limits of honest judgment." Although the term did not specifically appear in its judgment, *Hostage* is frequently identified as one of the first cases where the reasonable commander test involving the understanding and construction of a fictional figure was applied. In his chapter (Chap. 10), **Valentin Jeutner** construes the reasonable military commander test as a legal perspective-taking devise that focuses on the legal evaluation of empathy in decisions. Building on the *Hostage* case, Jeutner compares how rational enlightenment thinkers on the one hand and sentimental enlightenment thinkers on the other sought to identify moral principles.[37]

He argues that moral requirements in the battlefield, among other things, are judged with reference not to independent abstract standards but rather to concrete sentiments that an impartial spectator would deem appropriate for another individual and for society to feel in a given situation. The impartial spectator thus enables the evaluation of a situation from an imaginary external point of view, which in turn requires imagination and empathy. When imagination and empathy are used in this manner, the impartial spectator's perspective can be invoked *ex post* to judge any

[35] Chapters 8, 10 and 11.

[36] Chapter 9.

[37] Chapter 10.

given act or circumstance that occurred in the past, for example in the assessment of a defendant's conduct in court.

But who is a "reasonable commander"? Jeutner distinguishes between a reasonable commander as a military avatar of its domestic counterpart, viz., a civilian character in uniform, and a reasonable commander as one who subscribes to the logic of waging war and possesses military training. The applicable standard would obviously differ significantly if reasonableness were linked to civilians who should evaluate a (complex) military situation.

In *Hostage*, the tribunal analysed reasonableness based on the fictional construct of a military commander with specialised knowledge, military training and competence, including a mission to take military decisions and issue orders. This standard inevitably leads to questions about how conduct in times of war should be evaluated. Related issues also arise as to whether a soldier's preparedness to kill becomes an obstacle to empathic behaviour—and, accordingly, an obstacle to the reasonable commander test. Moreover, the more power people have, the less empathy they have. Translated to military organisations, this would mean that the higher rank, the less ability to empathise. These concerns become ever more exigent in modern militaries which seek to expand the physical and psychological distances between military commanders and their targets—with the help of long-range weapons, drones, and AI-controlled weapon systems, for instance. Indeed, de-empathetic modes of fighting are progressively more promoted. If empathy is removed, then the currently valid reasonable commander test may become ill-suited.

Key aspects of these abstract and legal-philosophical discussions on empathy are taken further in Chap. 11 by **Matthew Talbert** and **Jessica Wolfendale** through a case study on the institutional and organisational relevance of honesty and honest mistakes. The two authors examine the United States and its practice of warfare, especially with high-tech combat drones in conflicts such as Afghanistan and Iraq. The commonly applied narrative of "tragic mistakes"—by which US officials try to explain the inevitability of civilian deaths in situations of combat—serves as a point of departure in Talbert and Wolfendale's examination of moral responsibility and blameworthiness. They hold narratives like these, and their uncritical acceptance, as knowledge-distorting practices and injustices, since they downplay or outright justify the very serious consequences warfare entails for innocent non-combatants. Narratives of "humane" warfare and "collateral damage" have become ever more present in modern combat with precision technology like drones.[38]

In applying a philosophical perspective on modern-day warfare and its institutional context, Talbert and Wolfendale consider the moral standing of non-combatants. More specifically, the two authors propose incorporating a principle of moral equality of non-combatants into any military assessment where risks to civilians are present. They arrive at this proposition after a careful examination of complex matters of moral responsibility, blameworthiness, innocence, and caring enough. The authors unpack the purported moral superiority of the US military as well as its dubious claim that it is committed to protecting lives and, hence, civilians'

[38] Chapter 11.

deaths are simply very unfortunate events for which nobody is to blame, let alone to be held responsible or even prosecuted. The chapter construes the United States as morally objectionable, suspicious, and dishonest because the honesty of the decisions becomes tainted by a lack of morality. In their conclusion, Talbert and Wolfendale advocate more empathy—and honesty—among US commanders and drone operators. In scrupulously applying the principle of moral equality of non-combatants, all non-combatants would have an equal claim to not being harmed, in Afghanistan or Iraq as well as anywhere else in the world.[39]

The ground-breaking research in this anthology sheds doubt on Rendulic's role and actual knowledge. It concludes that it is troublesome to rely on his case held before the US tribunal in Nuremberg in 1948 and suggests revisiting the Rendulic Rule and its legacy. More specifically, the *Rendulic* case is arguably the wrong case to demonstrate the no second-guessing rule of international law.

Carola Lingaas Associate Professor of Law, VID Specialized University. Address: PO Box 184 Vinderen, 0319 Oslo, Norway, e-mail: carola.lingaas@vid.no

Nobuo Hayashi Associate Senior Lecturer, Swedish Defence University; Visiting Professor, University for Peace, UN Interregional Crime and Justice Research Institute. Address: Drottning Kristinas väg 37, 114 28, Stockholm, Sweden, e-mail: nobuo.hayashi@fhs.se

[39] Chapter 11.

Annex

List of Historical Names

Jakob Bjertnæs	Lawyer and investigator, Office of Chief of Police in Finnmark. Bjertnæs' report helped clarify the role played by Terboven's *Reichskommissariat* and Quisling's Norwegian Nazi government in the destruction of Northern Norway.
Martin Bormann	Hitler's deputy, leader of the secretariat of the German Nazi Party (*Nationalsozialistische Deutsche Arbeiterpartei*, NSDAP) headquarters. Bormann received Terboven's appeal for total destruction and forcible evacuation. Bormann transmitted the matter to Alfred Jodl.
George J. Burke	Member, Bar of the State of Michigan. Member of US Military Tribunal V. Together with Carter and Wennerstrum, Burke judged *Hostage*.
Asbjørn Bryhn	Inspector, Norwegian Police. Bryhn went to the American Zone in Germany to locate Rendulic and secure his extradition to Norway. Rendulic admitted to Bryhn that he had acted under orders, that Northern Norway's destruction did not appear necessary, and that it was something that could in part have been avoided.
Edward F. Carter	Judge, Supreme Court of the State of Nebraska. Member of US Military Tribunal V. Together with Burke and Wennerstrum, Carter judged *Hostage*.
Lucius D. Clay	General, US Army. Military governor of the US Zone, Germany. Clay declined to overturn Rendulic's acquittal.
Arne Dagfin Dahl	Major General, Norwegian Army. Witness for the prosecution in *Hostage*. Dahl testified how he found Finnmark's devastation excessive and implemented for revenge rather than for military necessity.

N. Hayashi and C. Lingaas (eds.), *Honest Errors? Combat Decision-Making 75 Years After the* Hostage *Case*, https://doi.org/10.1007/978-94-6265-611-6

Eduard Dietl	Lieutenant General and later General (*General der Gebirgstruppe*), German Army. Commander of the 20th Mountain Army until his death in June 1944. Rendulic succeeded Dietl in that position.
Curt Ebeling	Lieutenant General, German Army. Commander of the 210th Infantry Division. As early as 1943, Ebeling advocated the evacuation of women, children and the elderly from Finnmark. Ebeling supported forced evacuations in August 1944 but later opposed the idea on account of poor preparation and other military priorities.
Nikolaus von Falkenhorst	Colonel General, German Army. *Wehrmacht* Commander Norway (*Wehrmachtbefehlshaber Norwegen*) and Commander of Army Command Norway (*AOK Norwegen*). Unlike Rendulic's staff, von Falkenhorst's staff considered Soviet or British-led operations against Northern Norway unlikely.
Theodore F. Fenstermacher	Chief Prosecutor, US Military Tribunal V. Together with Taylor, Fenstermacher led the prosecution's case in *Hostage*.
Ivar Follestad	Justice, Supreme Court of Norway. Follestad sent voluminous evidence to Taylor, assisted in the preparation of the US prosecution's case against Rendulic and reported on its progress to Oslo.
Stefan Fritsch	Defence Counsel for Rendulic in *Hostage*.
Oscar Christian Gundersen	Minister of Justice, Norway. Gundersen stated before the Norwegian National Assembly that Rendulic had been acquitted on grounds of superior orders and that his acquittal might be appealed to the US Supreme Court or overturned by Clay.
Ragnar Hansen	Leader of the evacuation commission in Tromsø. Hansen documented how, from around 20 November 1944, the Germans knew that the Red Army was not in pursuit.
Jens Christian Hauge	Minister of Defence, Norway. Hauge concluded that, given its involvement in *Hostage* and hence tacit acceptance of the indictment against Rendulic, Norway would have to regard his acquittal as final.
Heinrich Himmler	*SS-Reichsführer*. Himmler cooperated with Terboven in Norway to expand control over the *Wehrmacht*. At Terboven's urging, Himmler declared Norway a "partisan war zone" leaving the SS responsible for fighting organised guerrilla forces.

Gard Holtskog — President of the Police Force, Finnmark. In October 1943, Holtskog began preparing Kirkenes' voluntary evacuation but was held back by the occupation authorities.

Hermann Hölter — Major General, German Army. Chief of Staff to Rendulic. Witness for Rendulic's defence in *Hostage*. In his testimony, Hölter described the overwhelming threat of highly skilled Finnish and Soviet troops, considered Finnmark's devastation militarily necessary, and argued that military necessity could only be judged from the circumstances prevailing at the time.

Oskar von Jagwitz — Associate Defence Counsel for Rendulic in *Hostage*.

Alfred Jodl — Colonel General, German Army. Chief of the Operations Staff of the German Armed Forces High Command (*OKW*). Ferdinand Jodl's elder brother. Alfred Jodl was tried before the International Military Tribunal, convicted and executed *inter alia* for devastating Northern Norway and forcibly evacuating its inhabitants.

Ferdinand Jodl — General (*General der Gebirgstruppe*), German Army. Commander of the XIX Mountain Corps. Alfred Jodl's younger brother. Witness for the prosecution in *Hostage*. Ferdinand Jodl testified that Finnmark's devastation would have been necessary but only if the Soviet invasion had clearly been imminent—which, in his opinion, it was not.

Hans Jordan — Major, German Army. Head of a subdivision of the *OKW* Operations Staff. Jordan's unit received Terboven's scorched earth proposal from Bormann and recommended its implementation on the ground that destroying the evacuated areas would prevent the Norwegian government-in-exile from establishing itself there and gaining access to Norwegian troops from Sweden.

Wilhelm Keitel — Field Marshall, German Army. Commander of the *OKW*. Keitel rejected Himmler's suggestion that Rediess replace von Falkenhorst and insisted that Rendulic do so instead.

Johannes Kummeneje — City engineer, Hammerfest. Kummeneje reported on the destruction of Hammerfest by retreating German forces.

Jonas Lie — Minister of police in Quisling's collaborationist government and *styresmann* of Finnmark. On 11 October 1944, together with Lippestad, Lie met with German commanders, including Ebeling and

	Ferdinand Jodl, in Kirkenes to discuss evacuations. With Terboven's support, Lie initiated an evacuation campaign built on threats, scare tactics and retaliations.
Johan Lippestad	Lie's deputy. On 11 October 1944, together with Lie, Lippestad met with German commanders, including Ebeling and Ferdinand Jodl, in Kirkenes to discuss evacuations.
Kirill A. Meretskov	General, Red Army, and later Marshall of the Soviet Union. Commander of the Karelian Front. Meretskov advocated an offensive against Rendulic's XVIII and XXXVI Corps into Finnish territories. Stalin rejected Meretskov's suggestions.
Willi Moser	General, German Army. Commander of the LXXI Corps. Together with Neumann, Moser encouraged voluntary evacuations but opposed Northern Norway's total destruction and forcible evacuation.
Hans-Hendrik Neumann	*SS-Obersturmbannführer*. Commander of the *Einsatzstab Norwegen*. From October 1944, Neumann acted as Terboven's liaison with Rendulic to coordinate voluntary evacuations. Contemporaneous sources indicate that Neumann was opposed to Northern Norway's total destruction and forcible evacuations.
Finn Palmstrøm	Magistrate in Tana. Palmstrøm collected witness statements detailing the ordinary people's experience of devastation and forced evacuation in Northern Norway.
Frederik Prytz	Minister of finance in Quisling's collaborationist government. In September 1944, having realised that an Allied occupation of Northern Norway would trigger his government's collapse, Prytz sought unsuccessfully to have Hitler formally establish peace with Norway.
Vidkun Quisling	Founder and *Fører* (leader, as in German *Führer*) of the Norwegian *Nasjonal samling* (National Unity, NS). On 1 February 1942, Quisling became head of Norway's collaborationist government subordinated to the *Reichskommissariat* and remained in this position until the end of World War II. After the war, Quisling was tried, sentenced to death and executed in Norway.
Walter Rapp	Associate Counsel for the Prosecution, US Military Tribunal V. Rapp cross-examined Rendulic in *Hostage*.

Wilhelm Rediess	*SS-Obergruppenführer*. Supreme Commander of all SS and police departments in Norway. Together with Himmler and Terboven, Rediess attempted unsuccessfully to develop security forces in Norway that was less dependent on the German military.
Lothar Rendulic	Colonel General, German Army. Commander of the 20th Mountain Army, and later Armed Forces Commander North (*Wehrmachtbefehlshaber Nord*). On 29 October 1944, having received the so-called "*Führer*'s Order" the previous day, Rendulic ordered his subordinate units to devastate Northern Norway and forcibly evacuate its inhabitants. Rendulic was acquitted of war crimes charges for these acts when US Military Tribunal V in Nuremberg agreed that he honestly, albeit erroneously in hindsight, believed that military necessity justified his decisions.
Trygve Schance	Police sergeant-major serving in Vardø. Witness for the prosecution in *Hostage*. In his testimony, Schance described collecting information about Finnmark's devastation from returning residents.
Vladimir I. Shcherbakov	Lieutenant General, Red Army. Commander of the 14th Army. On 7 October 1944, Shcherbakov launched an offensive against Ferdinand Jodl's XIX Mountain Corps. Elements of Shcherbakov's forces advanced through Kirkenes and took up defensive positions at Tana, where they engaged German forces for the last time, in early November.
Albert Speer	Minister of Armaments and War Production, Germany. In late September 1944, Speer reported to Hitler that Germany had accumulated supplies of nickel large enough to make deliveries from Petsamo in Northern Finland redundant. This triggered the entire 20th Mountain Army's withdrawal through Northern Norway.
Telford Taylor	Brigadier General, US Army. Head of the Subsequent Proceedings Division, US Office of Chief Counsel, Nuremberg, and Chief of Counsel for the Prosecution, US Military Tribunal V. Taylor led the prosecution's case in *Hostage*.
Josef Terboven	Reich Commissioner for Occupied Norwegian Territories (*Reichskommissar für die besetzten Norwegischen Gebiete*). Though initially disinclined, in October 1944 Terboven sought and obtained Hitler's approval for the total destruction of Northern Norway and the forcible

	evacuation of all of its inhabitants. Terboven committed suicide on 8 May 1945.
Emil Vogel	General, German Army. Commander of the XXXVI Mountain Corps. Witness for Rendulic's defence in *Hostage*. In his testimony, Vogel described the overwhelming threat of highly skilled Finnish and Soviet troops and considered Finnmark's devastation militarily necessary.
Charles F. Wennerstrum	Justice, Supreme Court of the State of Iowa. Presiding Member of US Military Tribunal V. Together with Burke and Carter, Wennerstrum judged *Hostage*.
Harald Wrede Holm	Lieutenant Colonel, Norwegian Army. Wrede Holm prepared a detailed study of the German withdrawal in 1944, including the assessment of responsibility for the destruction of Finnmark and Northern Troms, for Norway's Military Prosecution Authority.